Without the Banya We Would Perish

Without the Banya We Would Perish

A History of the Russian Bathhouse

ETHAN POLLOCK

OXFORD
UNIVERSITY PRESS

OXFORD
UNIVERSITY PRESS

Oxford University Press is a department of the University of Oxford. It furthers
the University's objective of excellence in research, scholarship, and education
by publishing worldwide. Oxford is a registered trade mark of Oxford University
Press in the UK and certain other countries.

Published in the United States of America by Oxford University Press
198 Madison Avenue, New York, NY 10016, United States of America.

© Oxford University Press 2019

Library of Congress Cataloging-in-Publication Data
Names: Pollock, Ethan, 1969– author.
Title: Without the banya we would perish : a history of the
Russian bathhouse / Ethan Pollock.
Description: New York, NY : Oxford University Press, [2019] |
Includes bibliographical references and index.
Identifiers: LCCN 2018054953 (print) | LCCN 2019002992 (ebook) |
ISBN 9780199908974 (updf) | ISBN 9780199911950 (epub) |
ISBN 9780195395488 (hardcover : alk. paper)
Subjects: LCSH: Bathing customs—Russia—History. | Bathing customs—Soviet
Union—History. | Bathing customs—Russia (Federation) —History. |
Bathhouses—Russia—History. | Bathhouses—Soviet Union—History. |
Bathhouses—Russia (Federation) —History. | Baths, Russian.
Classification: LCC GT2846.R8 (ebook) | LCC GT2846.R8 P65 2019 (print) |
DDC 391.6/4—dc23
LC record available at https://lccn.loc.gov/2018054953

1 3 5 7 9 8 6 4 2

Printed by Sheridan Books, Inc., United States of America

to Amy, Zachary, and Nadia

Contents

To do:
by 01/20 — FIRST DRAFT OF STORY

Prologue

MOSCOW, RUSSIA, DECEMBER 1991. We lie naked on a wooden bench, close our eyes, and let the intense heat envelop us. The thermostat reads over 95° Celsius (over 200° Fahrenheit). We sweat, releasing toxins from deep within our bodies. When it becomes unbearable, one by one we file out of the small room and cool off by jumping in an icy pool. Then we go back into the steam room and are sweating again within moments. We wave birch switches—*veniki*—and whack them down on ourselves and on each other's backs. Some suggest they are medicinal; others claim they bring more heat down upon us. I'm not sure, but use them just the same. Afterward, wrapped in linens, I feel as if I have new skin. I've been to the Russian bathhouse (banya) before, but usually with some trepidation. Now I'm beginning to give in to it and reap the benefits.

I ask Sergei if communal bathing is a Soviet tradition. It is, in a way, he says. Will it survive the political and economic turmoil that is raging beyond these walls? I ask. He smiles. He says its roots go much deeper into the Russian past than the Revolution. Volodia sits down next to us. He chimes in, suggesting that a person in a banya today might experience something akin to what a person experienced in a banya one hundred, or two hundred, or even one thousand years ago. Nothing here is new. The banya is eternal.

It's an illusion, though. No corporeal experience, no matter how stable and no matter how closely connected to the fundamental elements of fire and ice, is impervious to time. I know that the banya, just like Russia, must have a history.

Throughout the 1990s, friends and colleagues took me to municipal and private banyas in Moscow, St. Petersburg, and dozens of other cities and villages across the former USSR. I went with scholars, athletes, businessmen, doctors, journalists, and students. I went with respectable public figures and shady characters. I usually went with men. Occasionally the banyas were co-ed. In either case, the fleshy reality of all different shapes of human nakedness struck me as refreshingly open and shameless. The banya exposed me to bodies in a way that nothing else ever had.

On countless trips to dachas, my hosts would heat up the banya and invite me in. Sometimes I helped by sawing and chopping wood, tying together birch branches to make *veniki*, cleaning the benches and changing areas, stoking the fire, and loading vats with water. I learned to wield the *veniki*, to develop my own sense of the right amount of heat and humidity, to relish the beer or vodka (or occasionally hot tea) that followed the banya. The banya provided respite from the rapid changes we were encountering as the Soviet Union collapsed and a new Russia emerged. And it gave us a bolt of energy to head back out to our jobs and homes. It was fundamentally a communal activity.

My fascination with the banya was initially not part of my work in Russia. In the early 1990s I taught American history in Moscow. By the mid to late 1990s I was back in Moscow researching and writing a dissertation. The banya was a place to escape, relax, and bond with friends—the opposite of work. After I wrote a book on Stalin and science, got a job teaching Russian history in the United States, and started a family, I thought about what to do next. Sometimes I'd think about it while in the banya. I found myself less interested in questions of state power and more interested in the features of everyday life, such as the banya, that had drawn me to Russia in the first place.

The changes—even ruptures—in Russian politics I experienced in the 1990s and early 2000s left me searching for something solid and consistent about the people and history I had grown to love. No matter who was leading the country or in what direction, the banya seemed to bring out aspects of Russia that I held most dear—the close social bonds that sustain meaning, the ability and desire to reflect for a moment on the challenges of modern life, and a strong tradition that had the power to unite disparate parts of the population. I realized that I wanted to write about the banya.

Without the Banya We Would Perish

Introduction

WHENEVER AND WHEREVER there have been Russians, there have been banyas. Banyas have thrived in the countryside and in the city. They have catered to men and women, tsars and peasants, Eastern Orthodox Christians and atheists, nationalists and socialists, business owners and factory workers, guards and prisoners. They existed before the first east Slavic state formed, survived the Mongol invasion, persisted as Moscow rose at the center of the Russian lands, flourished after Peter the Great led a process of Westernization, and gained renewed importance in Soviet Russia. Russians brought banyas with them on expeditions to the Arctic and to Antarctica, into exile in Siberia, and in their emigration to America. They built them on railroad cars, whaling ships, and submarines. Today they remain prevalent in Russia and in Russian communities across the globe. Indeed, it would be difficult to find a cultural institution that has been so consistently present across space and time and so consistently popular across social and cultural divides.[1]

The banya is a specific variation on the steam bath. An oven packed with burning logs heats a pile of rocks. When the rocks are red-hot, the fire is tamped down and water is tossed on them, producing billowing steam that raises the temperature. Bathers perspire, whisk each other with switches (*veniki*) made from young birch or other trees, cool off in a pool or pond or by rolling in the snow, and then repeat the process. Prescriptions vary for the right humidity or temperature or what bathers should do before, during, or afterward. The context varies even more. Rural banyas are usually wooden huts consisting of a steam room and a small antechamber for undressing before and relaxing after steaming. Friends, neighbors, and family often bathe together. Some rural banyas are "black banyas"—meaning that they do not have chimneys. In those, a thick cloud of smoke builds up inside the banya during the initial heating process. Although the air is cleared before the bath begins, the walls and bathers often end up covered with soot. In contrast, urban, commercial banyas can be as large as a city block, with modern ventilation systems, waterworks, washrooms, changing rooms, and separate spaces for men, women, and private parties. They sometimes also have massage parlors, pools, billiard rooms, cafes, and hair salons. But the *parilka*—the wooden steam room—is the key common characteristic that makes these various types of rural and urban buildings all recognizable as banyas.

The banya has many cousins, from the ancient Greek baths and Roman *balneae* to the Finnish sauna, the Japanese *sento* and *onsen*, the Turkish *hammam*, and the Native American sweat lodge, to name just a few. Every society or civilization has prescribed ways of achieving personal cleanliness of the body, spirit, and mind. Some suggest taking showers. Others suggest warm water baths. Some ablutions are prophylactic, protecting bathers from unseen threats; others offer a cure for specific ailments or a means of counteracting the dangers associated with certain behaviors. Physical cleanliness often implies moral uprightness. Communal nudity can nurture honesty and emotional intimacy; it can also portend licentiousness and vulnerability.[2]

FIGURE I.1 A modern iteration of the traditional rural "black" or chimney-less banya, Novgorod Oblast, 2004. ©Joachim Radtke.

FIGURE I.2 A banya in the center of Moscow built during Stalin's rule, 1935. Courtesy of RGAKFD.

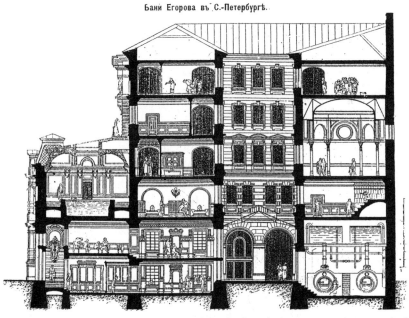

Бани Егорова въ С.-Петербургѣ.

FIGURE I.3 The Egorov banya in St. Petersburg, built in the late nineteenth century, had five floors with sections for men and women and rooms designated for snacking, cutting hair, reading, swimming, and, of course, steaming. *Stroitel'*, no. 1 (Jan. 1896), 53–54.

Modern sensibilities have emphasized the danger of germs and the benefits of ridding the body of them. The idea that the banya removes dirt and contagions and promotes physical health is deep seated. One peasant idiom declared that "the banya will drive off any illness." It was not until the end of the eighteenth century, however, that hygiene became the focus of the Imperial Russian state. A medical advisor to Catherine the Great declared that going to a banya was often more healthful than going to a doctor and could "replace two-thirds of the medicines prescribed by medical science."[3] The idea that cleaning bodies could help control diseases—especially epidemics spread by lice, ticks, and fleas—gained strength over the late nineteenth century and into the twentieth. After the Bolsheviks took power in 1917, Vladimir Lenin famously declared, "either socialism will defeat the louse or the louse will defeat socialism."[4] As tools in that struggle, banyas became a matter of national security and the Soviet state supported them accordingly.

Concerns with material, bodily needs do not encapsulate the range of meanings associated with the banya either before or during Soviet rule. Russians went to the banya long before they understood it in modern medical terms or the state prioritized public health. They continued to go even when the growth of indoor plumbing made it easier to meet hygienic goals at home. Russians understood that, unlike a shower or a bath, going to the banya could rejuvenate and transform a person in spiritual as well as physical ways. This was reflected in popular idioms as well: "After the banya, it is as if you've been born again" and "the banya washes away all sins." Especially during times of uncertainty—such as during the last years of the Russian Empire and the years before and after the collapse of the Soviet Union—interest in the banya as a place of authenticity, contemplation, and rebirth took on greater significance. The banya renews the mind and soul, not just the body.

The banya is also communal. In rural settings and in cities, friends and family bathe together, passing along rituals and techniques and acting out what is permissible and what is forbidden. Prohibitions against going to the banya alone and at certain times reinforce the idea that it is filled with potential danger. It is a rite by which the young and marginalized become part of the community. One philosopher wrote in the late nineteenth century, "If you would like to make friends with someone, but are wavering, ask him if he loves the banya." He continued, "If [he says] 'yes,' then you can confidently stretch out a hand to him and welcome him into your family."[5] At around the same time a doctor added, "Our banyas are of the people to the extent that [one's attitude toward them] often determines one's love for the fatherland."[6] Celebration of the social—even nationalistic—banya served as a counterpoint to those who attempted to represent the banya in universal, medical terms. Rather than seeing the banya as the ideal way for everyone to wash, many understood that the significance of the banya rested with its power to draw Russians together and to help them distinguish friend from foe.

As a communal endeavor, the banya shares some characteristics with other social settings such as coffeehouses, pubs, gyms, barbershops, or hair salons. These places, outside home and work, are often associated with some combination of open accessibility, a welcoming and comfortable atmosphere, the mixing of new friends and old, the creation of neutrality, social leveling by which positions of authority or subordination on the outside do not necessarily equate to similar positions on the inside, an emphasis on conversation, and the sense of a home away from home.[7] Commentators have consistently described the banya in similar terms. The banya's association with transparency and intimacy (heightened by physical nudity) also suggests it fits within this general category. Not all banyas at all times, as the following history will show, nurtured all of these traits. Still, thinking of banyas in these terms might help those who know little about the Russian bathhouse to begin to understand its importance as a place of human communion.

In some significant respects, however, the banya is not like other social places. Concepts of public and private that originated in Western European society and are crucial to understanding coffeehouses and the like do not easily map onto the Russian experience. The banya was in some ways public (in the sense that it was often supported by the state and collective) and in some ways private (in the sense that it was intimate and set apart). Further, the banyas served at least some of these social functions long before the emergence of the modern world and the capitalist economic relations that scholars cite as essential prerequisites for the emergence of this sort of communal gathering. The banya survived in autocratic Russia and in the socialist USSR.[8] The history of the banya suggests that the drive to create public places for meaningful social contact is not strictly tied to a Western European or modern timeline.[9] Finally, the communal nature of the banya captures only part of its significance. Going to the banya is a bodily and soulful experience and not just a social one. The physicality of the banya and the sense of spiritual transformation are equal pillars of its appeal. To go to the banya just to talk and socialize as one might in a café or a pub, without undressing, sweating from exposure to extreme heat, and washing, would be to miss the point altogether.

In the banya, each of its essential functions—cleaning, purifying, and establishing community—is fraught with potential risks. The banya removes dirt, but it also potentially exposes bathers to bodily fluids and filth that can spread disease. The banya restores purity, but it is also a place where sinful and defiling acts might be undertaken with abandon. As a social practice, it serves to delineate the range of acceptable behaviors and identify those who belong. The banya also exposes transgressions and conjures the threat of those who do not fit in or abide by the rules. By trying to bring order to the world, the banya makes disorder apparent. It is about health, birth, rebirth, renewal, salvation, and the affirmation of community. At the same time, it exposes people to effluvia, parasites, soot, dampness, social mixing, fornication, fire, and corruption. The banya promises purity even as it introduces the potential for danger. Without the banya, Russians would perish (as yet another idiom declares) because without it they would lose their bearings, their sense of the sacred and profane, body and soul, their knowledge of what is permissible and what is proscribed.

Inasmuch as the banya is a relatively consistent physical setting for so-cial relations, it serves as a prism through which to filter Russian history. As defining features of Russia's past shine through the banya, they appear both recognizable and refracted in new ways. Studying the banya across time illuminates from unfamiliar angles the contours of Russian identity, the na-ture of Russia's complex relationship with the rest of Europe, the potential and limits of a powerful state overseeing a vast polity, the difference between expert and vernacular knowledge, and the struggle to come to terms with modernizing forces. Changing understandings of sociability and sexuality, gender and class, empire and religion, business and leisure appear in the banya as well, but not always in predictable ways or as sharply as they might when viewed through a different prism.

The banya was not just a physical space where things happened. It was also an idea, whose value rested in the emotions assigned to it. Physically, the banya has been stable and persistent. As a social construct, the banya has been malleable across time and space and for different genders, ethnicities, and classes.

Medieval chronicles depicted the banya as an emblem of identity (for better and for worse) and as a liminal place encompassing spirituality and blasphemy, godly powers, and earthly desires. Foreigner diplomats, doctors, travelers, and journalists, ranging from Herodotus to Hedrick Smith, have noted the bathing habits of the people of the region, often linking them to broader conclusions about their character. The banya appears in the novels of Fyodor Dostoevsky as a site of danger and violence and in the short stories of the doctor-turned-playwright Anton Chekhov as an innocuous social space, where conversation was more important than health. Some writers, such as

Mikhail Zoshchenko, used humor to draw attention to the poor conditions in the banyas, while others left clues about the sexual encounters they arranged there. Diaries and memoirs describe the banya during the Russian Revolution, during the Siege of Leningrad, and in Soviet labor camps. Anonymous and well-known artists used the banya as a symbol of Russianness and patriotism, of Sovietness and humor, of virtue, vice, and sex. Grigory Rasputin took aristocratic women and prostitutes to the banya to test their spiritual purity—or to have sex with them. Catherine the Great, Joseph Stalin, Boris Yeltsin, and Vladimir Putin saw it as a crucial tool for the public to fend off diseases and as a social activity that they personally enjoyed.

The banya is at the center of a web of evolving meanings, with certain strands and connections strengthening or atrophying or even breaking over time. People in various generations made and remade the banya's significance. The effort by some to enforce a particular understanding of the banya and to deem alternative understandings inauthentic only raised the moral stakes. The material banya appeared as a neutral, egalitarian place where anyone could go to wash. The idea of the banya, however, had the power to renew sprits, create community, and suggest how to find meaning in the world.

Despite its centrality to Russian life, the banya's past is not easy to recover. Relevant information can be found in a variety of sources, but no single archive or approach exists. Books and articles that address the banya directly have ranged from medical reports about their importance for health, to technical descriptions of how to properly build them, to popular accounts of particular banyas, to pornography that happens to take place in them. Self-proclaimed banya enthusiasts have researched and written dozens of books, often in a hagiographic key.[10] Foreign journalists have written many articles describing their own experiences in the banya.[11] Occasionally, scholars cite the banya as evidence of Russia's "moral masochism."[12] More often, scholars have tackled crucial aspects of the banya without attempting to draw it all together.[13] Mostly, though, the banya has been taken for granted. It is usually as inconspicuous as it is ubiquitous.

Vladimir Giliarovsky, a chronicler of Russian life in the late imperial period, pointed out that the banya was so self-evident that nobody felt a need to write about it: "No literature addressed the banya. . . . At that time it was all in front of everybody's eyes and nobody was interested in writing about something that everyone already knew."[14] Giliarovsky was right to a certain extent. Governments kept track of banyas either as sources of revenue, sites of public health, or dens of depravity. Peasants usually attested to their importance when ethnographers asked. But very few people explicitly recorded the rituals of bathing per se. As in all areas of the history of everyday life, there are gaps and inconsistencies in what has been preserved. Like the soot in the banya, there are places where the evidence is deep and other areas where it has been completely washed away. There are at least some accounts from every era of Russian history and from all regions of the polity, although information tends to be thinner further back in time and farther away from European Russia. Some questions about the banya cannot be definitively answered using the extant records. The Russian bathing tradition clearly evolved in relation to the bathing habits of various other ethnic groups in Eurasia, but exactly how is hard to say. Particularities about men and women having sex in the banyas are often only obliquely referenced; details about men having sex with men or women having sex with women are even more difficult to discern, although the basic fact of same-sex sexual acts in the banya is evident. Far more men than women have left accounts about their experiences of the banya, meaning that male perspectives are often depicted as universal, though they clearly were not. Unavoidable gaps in the sources mean that this book cannot be comprehensive.

Nonetheless, much of the banya culture that Giliarovsky feared had disappeared can yet be discerned through careful readings of written sources and images. The banya appears in paintings, posters, and films, law codes, diaries, and memoirs, popular and professional health journals, municipal regulations, ethnographies, architectural plans, political cartoons, and religious texts. This book uses over a thousand of these sources to move the banya from the edges of Russian history to the center.

Bathing is universal, and communal bathing is common in cultures across the globe.[15] But not every culture assigns great value to their ablutions; nor have all bathing customs remained the same over time. The banya, though, persisted in Russia despite radical changes in ideas about what constitutes bodily cleanliness and despite remarkable social ruptures. The more Russian politics and culture changed, the more the banya accrued value as something that was ancient and consistent. In a country where the state and religion (and ideology) usually loomed large, the banya lay beyond the control of secular or ecclesiastical authorities. The banya's relative stability in form meant that it appeared timeless, especially during political, economic, and social upheavals. The banya's relative malleability in meaning allowed people of all walks of life, in all epochs, to assign it physical, spiritual, and communal power.

This is the first book in any language to tell a detailed history of the banya over the long arc of Russian history. The following ten chapters proceed chronologically. Chapters 1 and 2 take the story from the earliest written records of the banya to the end of Catherine the Great's reign in the eighteenth century, when doctors began to assert that the banya's primary function was related to health and hygiene. Chapters 3, 4, and 5 cover the period from the early nineteenth century to the end of the Romanov dynasty in 1917, when the recognition of the banya's potential for improving public health developed unevenly alongside a newfound appreciation of its importance to national identity and its popularity as a place for social mixing, relaxation, violence, and sexual license. Four chapters cover the Soviet period. Government officials struggled to find ways for the banya to meet its utilitarian potential, while others saw the banya less as a place to get clean than as a symbol of purity and as a space for meaningful social interaction and contemplation of identity and fate. The final, concluding chapter, on post-Soviet Russia, shows how various and contradictory aspects of the banya's history and meaning continue to be nurtured, uncovered, and rediscovered. Each chapter weaves together cleanliness (and filth), purity (and defilement), and social cohesion (and transgression). While each of these elements has ebbed and flowed over time and place, to one extent or another some things have been constant in Russian history: the impulse to use extreme heat to clean the body, to think of bathing as something profound and not just physical, to respect the power of tradition and age-old customs, and to bathe with others, not alone. It would be too much to claim that Russia's history is the banya's history writ large or that the banya's history is Russia's history in a microcosm. But there is no doubt that the two are inextricable.

I

Older Even Than the Tsar

ancient greed

BEFORE THERE WAS Russia, there were banyas and before there were banyas, there were other kinds of bathhouses. Circa 440 BCE Herodotus, the Hellenic "father of history," commented in his *Histories* on the people living north of the Black Sea in an area that would later become part of the Russian Empire:

> The Scythians take the seeds of this cannabis, creep beneath the wool covering the stakes, and throw the seeds onto the blazing-hot stones within. When the seeds hit the stones, they produce smoke and give off a vapor such as no steam bath in Hellas could surpass. The Scythians howl, awed and elated by the vapor. This takes the place of a bath for them, since they do not use any water at all to wash their bodies.... The Scythians are another people who avoid foreign customs at all costs.[1]

Herodotus may have been more interested in affirming the righteousness of his own, Hellenic cultural practices than he was in understanding the Scynthians, but his description of their bathing customs appears accurate. In the twentieth century archeologists located, among other things, a "vessel filled with stones...with a small quantity of hemp seeds" and determined that they had uncovered "the full set of articles for carrying out the purification ritual, about which Herodotus wrote in such detail."[2]

In the first half of the tenth century, Ibn Rusta, a Persian scientist and traveler, also visited the region and noted the people's bathing habits. Rusta pointed out that "because of the cold" people there lived in dugouts in which "they heat a fire and spread stones on the fire. When the stones are red hot to the highest degree, they toss on water from which steam spreads to the point where people take off their clothes."[3] Both Herodotus and Ibn Rusta saw bathing habits as a powerful indicator of difference that defined the people of the steppe.

At the time Ibn Rusta was writing, Kievan princes were in the process of uniting the east Slavic tribes of the region under their rule. Kievan Rus'—as their polity came to be known—was centered at a crossroads, along the trade routes that brought together people from different medieval cultures. The early banya emerged there from a mixture of various customs and rituals. To the south, Byzantium had inherited the rich bathing tradition of the Greeks and Romans, with large urban bathhouses serving social and hygienic functions. Some of that tradition had also been integrated into the Muslim world, where bathing in the *hammam* was central to both religious rites and urban social life.[4] Jews, who lived among the eastern Slavs, went to the *mikvah* to purify themselves. To the north of Rus', Finns sometimes took steam baths in small wooden huts.[5] The various Khazar tribes that controlled much of the Eurasian steppe and the trade routes to the Far East also had their own bathing habits, although little is known about their precise nature.[6] These broad traditions no doubt gave way to more specific variations, but neither Rus' nor the banya emerged out of nowhere.

In the steppe, Byzantium, and Scandinavia, and among Jews, Christians, and Muslims, bathing was associated with virtue and vice, holiness and indecency, cleanliness and defilement. The people of Rus' created their own bathing customs by adapting the practices and taboos with which they came into contact. Baths served as a meeting point and as a place where markers of individual differences could be both manifest and overcome. In the process, the banya became a defining feature of Rus' culture. Like the *hammam* and *mikvah*, it was integrated into religious doctrine and key rites and rituals. As in Byzantium, the banya could take the form of large, urban institutions that marked a city or community as respectable. And like the sweat lodges of the Finns and others to the north, the banya remained associated with sorcery, magic, and other unworldly powers. Just as the Russian state emerged over a five-hundred-year period (circa 1000 to circa 1500) as an amalgamation of peoples from various principalities and ethnic groups, the banya was an admixture of various bathing traditions. Undertaking the right practices in the right manner in the banya clarified the relationship between the sacred and the profane and in turn helped identify those who belonged in the community. By the same token, failure to adhere to the rituals brought the risk of unhealthy mixing and violations of the social contract. The banya itself was like a crossroads, leading sometimes to righteousness and sometimes to damnation.

Brief references to bathing in Herodotus and Ibn Rusta aside, the story of the Russian banya usually begins with the first native written sources about early Kievan Rus'—the medieval state to which Russia traces its origins. *The Primary Chronicle*, a founding set of documents of Russian history from the twelfth century, mentioned bathing in a number of places, providing support for the claim that the banya was always inseparable from the very idea of Russia and Russians.

The most cited banya passage in the *Chronicle* concerns the Apostle Andrew, whose supposed visit to the Slavic lands helped to legitimize the Christian roots of the Kievan state. The story is crucial to East Slavic identity: Andrew later became the Patron Saint of both Ukraine and Russia. The *Chronicle*'s depiction of Andrew's trip focused considerable attention on the banya, which was strikingly different from the bathhouses he had experienced in the Roman world.

> He [the Apostle Andrew] reached the Slavs at the point where Novgorod is now situated. He saw these people existing according to their customs and on observing how they bathed and scrubbed themselves, he wondered at them. He went thence among the Varangians and came to Rome where he recounted what he had learned and observed, "Wondrous to relate," said he, "I saw the land of the Slavs, and while I was among them, I noticed their wooden bathhouses. They warm them to extreme heat, they undress, and after anointing themselves with an acid liquid they take young branches and lash their bodies. They actually lash themselves so violently that they barely escape alive. Then they drench themselves with cold water, and thus are revived. They think nothing of doing this every day, and though tormented by none, they actually inflict such voluntary torture upon themselves. Indeed, they make of the act not a mere washing but a veritable torment."[7]

The writers of *The Primary Chronicle* were most likely Kievan monks. In calling attention to the banya and associating it with Andrew, perhaps they hoped to highlight a point of pride among the region's people. If so, it is odd that they emphasized that Andrew found the Slavs' bathing habits reminiscent of "torture" and "torment." So why include the passage at all?

When the *Chronicle* was written, Kiev was only the first among many rival principalities, all of which sought to assert their supremacy over the Slavic lands. The authors, who presumably were attempting to emphasize the importance of Kiev, may have been derisively highlighting the pagan and barbaric customs of their competitors from the northern city of Novgorod, who appeared to bathe in huts like Norsemen, not in large civic buildings like the civilized Romans of Andrew's time or their Byzantine contemporaries. To make the contrast explicit, the *Chronicle* related that when Andrew visited the land where the future city of Kiev would be built, his concern was with consecration and not local bathing habits. Andrew apparently said, "See ye these hills? So shall the favor of God shine upon them that on this spot a great city shall arise, and God shall erect many churches therein." He then blessed the hills, planted a cross on them, and prayed to God.[8] The two passages were juxtaposed in the *Chronicle*, furthering the impression that the people of Novgorod were less worthy of a blessing than those who lived around what would become Kiev. Kiev, the authors seem to say, was a city of churches. Novgorod was a city of banyas.

Something akin to the banya existed in eleventh-century Rus', but it hardly seemed a point of pride to the Kievan chroniclers. Instead they portrayed it as an unfortunate practice associated with a time that preceded Christianity. Based on this section of the *Chronicle* one modern historian concluded that the denizens of Kiev saw the bathhouse customs of Northern Rus' as "alien and ludicrous" and that the *Chronicle*'s reference to banyas was "one of the oldest Russian ethnographic jokes."[9] Just because "the *venik* in the banya is older even than the tsar," as one idiom states, does not mean that the banya was a point of unambiguous pride.[10]

Others, though, have turned to the same passage in the *Chronicle* to highlight the significance of the banya for an authentic Russian identity that was all the more important because outsiders like Andrew could not comprehend it. In this reading, Christianity was the new, foreign element and the banya was part of a deeper, truer Russian history. As one scholar wrote:

All of Old Russia, in the Apostle Andrew's imagination, is seen as two main institutions: the churches that would soon blanket the land, and the bathhouses that had always existed. These are indeed two cultures: the Church above, and the folk culture and way of life below. Holiness above, humor below. It seems that this small text in the chronicle, this paragraph, captures all of Rus' and its defining characteristics—the soul and flesh of Rus', the fantastic character of the people, which promises even greater surprise in the future.[11]

This suggests that in Russian culture Christianity was imposed from above and from abroad and that the banya existed in parallel to the Christian world. In this reading the banya was an alternative place of worship, a remnant of a pagan, pre-Christian age.[12] When the rest of the population went to church, sorcerers went to bathhouses to perform magic, such as casting spells. It followed that anyone who did not bathe at the usual time was "suspected of being a *koldun* [sorcerer]."[13]

Another passage in the *Chronicle* supports the idea that the banya was a symbol of non-Christian beliefs. In it a Boyar named Yan traveled to the town of Beloozero to collect tribute for his Kievan Prince. Sorcerers there had wreaked havoc in the region, complicating the fulfillment of his duties. When the sorcerers had been captured, Yan entered into a discussion with them about the origin of man. Yan affirmed his faith in the Biblical story of Adam and Eve. The sorcerers countered that man was made when "God washed himself in the banya, and after sweating, dried himself with straw and threw it out of heaven upon the earth. Then Satan quarreled with God as to which of them should create man out of it. And the devil made man, and God set a soul in him. As a result, whenever a man dies, his body goes to the earth and his soul to God."[14] The banya was present at the creation. Orthodoxy was not. Or at least that is what some medieval sorcerers evidently claimed.

This evidence notwithstanding, juxtaposing the banya and Orthodox religion obscures the extent to which the Church and the banya were culturally intermingled. Christianity did not run directly counter to a "folk culture" and a "way of life below" symbolized by going to the banya.[15] Its teachings deeply penetrated Slavic culture and subsumed and integrated pre-existing beliefs into a coherent whole. Other passages in *The Primary Chronicle* treated the banya as patriotic and in no way problematic for Christians. In the middle of the tenth century, the *Chronicle* reported, Derevlians—an East Slavic tribe—murdered Igor, the prince of Kiev, while he was collecting tribute. The Derevlians then went to Kiev to attempt to convince Igor's widow, Olga, to marry their prince. Instead, she undertook a series of steps to avenge her husband's death. In one case, she insisted that the people of Kiev would only let her marry the Derevlian prince if she was approached honorably. When the Derevlians sent a group of their "best men" to Kiev, she "commanded that a banya be made ready, and invited them to appear before her after they had bathed," a request that may have been in keeping with Kievan marriage rituals of the time. The banya was then heated and when the Derevelian men entered it, Olga's men "closed up the banya behind them, and she gave orders to set it on fire from the doors, so that the Derevlians were all burned to death."[16] Olga, regarded as a saint for her efforts to spread Christianity, used the banya to help save Rus'. Again the banya found itself at the center of one of the founding tales of the Kievan state. The chroniclers did not seem to have any trouble reconciling this gory incident with the actions of a venerated Christian.

The banya and Christianity reinforced each other in another passage of the *Chronicle* as well. In 1090, Ephraim, the Metropolitan of the church, consecrated the Church of St. Michael in the town of Pereyaslavl' as well as other churches in the region. At the same time, the *Chronicle* reported, "he also constructed a stone banya such as had never heretofore existed in Rus'."[17] This brief mention of the banya is particularly important since it was unambiguously associated with a pious man and other acts that established the Orthodox Church's presence in the region.

Descriptions of the banya in *The Primary Chronicle* highlighted another tension that would continue to define the institution for centuries. The chroniclers described two types of banyas. There were great civic buildings whose roots might be traced back to the ancient world and that arrived in Rus' via Byzantium, Islam, and Christianity. This was the banya of Metropolitan Ephraim and perhaps of Olga. The other banya was associated with local customs and rituals—the banyas of sorcerers and pre-Christians in Novgorod. That the two sometimes converged and sometimes remained distinct was already suggested in the earliest written materials on Rus'.

FIGURE 1.1 Olga burning the Derevlians in the banya in 945 AD, as depicted in the Radzivill Chronicle, fifteenth-century copy of a thirteenth-century original. Courtesy of HathiTrust.

The disintegration of the Kievan state into competing principalities in the thirteenth century and the occupation of Slavic lands by the Mongols through the fourteenth century and into the fifteenth century left few sources, and references to the banya are not readily discernable. It is clear, however, from subsequent materials that the understanding of the banya as a space of both good and evil remained powerful. The Mongols were more concerned with collecting tribute and maintaining control than with reforming native habits or world views. Indeed, Orthodox Christianity, if anything, became more firmly established, subsuming and synthesizing vernacular practices.[18] The Mongols had their own communal and private baths, but do not seem to have imposed them on their Slavic subjects.[19] It makes sense, then, that the banya survived Mongol occupation. Small, localized, private banyas may have even thrived, given that the center of political and economic power in the region shifted from Kiev to the wooded areas of northern Russia, where domestic banyas had been more prevalent anyway. But this conclusion is speculative, based on the existence of banyas both before the arrival of Mongols and after their departure. By the sixteenth century Muscovite Princes had reunified much of Rus', tracing their political and cultural authority to the earlier Kievan state by way of the Riurik princely line. In the process, the banya emerged as an even stronger marker of ethnic identity.

—•—

Going to the banya was a normal part of everyday life in Muscovite Russia. The rich and poor, urbanites and peasants, men and women gathered in banyas. Domestic banyas—maintained for the use of family and neighbors— were common in peasant villages, on noble estates, and even in some urban areas. Larger, commercial banyas existed in towns large and small throughout Muscovy. Generally, though not always, men bathed with men and women bathed with women. In large, urban bathhouses—which were usually open to the public and run as commercial enterprises—the sexes were supposed to take turns, sometimes depending on the time of day, sometimes depending on the day of the week. Low entrance fees made the commercial banyas affordable to both common urban dwellers and those traveling through a town. Banyas were often at the center of urban social life. Visitors went with their companions, where they could drink and fraternize with others. Banya operators often procured from the state the exclusive rights to the sale of *kvas* (a drink made of fermented brown bread) and *suslo* (a distilled mash for making beer). In a number of circumstances, the banya operators also had the legal authority to oversee games of chance in their area.[20] In addition to offering drinking and gambling, banyas provided a way station for "outsiders and wanderers without letters of guarantee and without papers" who lived in the commercial banyas and "undertook thievery." By changing their names and identities, these people evidently evaded the authorities.[21]

The banya remained an important institution in Muscovy because of the rites and rituals that were supposed to take place there. Saturday, the traditional Sabbath, was set aside as the "bath day" (*bannyi den'*), presumably so people would be clean before church on Sunday. Women, from simple peasants to the tsarina, gave birth in bathhouses, accompanied by midwives and other attendants.[22] The tsar was supposed to first meet his newborn children in the bathhouse as well.[23] Banyas also played a central role in marriage ceremonies. The *Domostroi*, a mid-sixteenth century text that described an idealized set of rules for Russian households, noted that on the second day of a multiday marriage ritual, bathhouse workers prepared the banya and the bride's family provided the groom with bathing implements. When the groom awoke after the first night of the wedding, he headed to the banya while his bride remained in bed. There, he and his servants bathed and drank alcohol. Then the groom returned to his rooms and went back to sleep.[24] The idea that the banya cleansed a person after sexual intercourse may have played a part in this ritual. The groom was also supposed to return to the banya on the third day, presumably because the newlyweds were expected to have sex again.[25] These rules did not just apply to the common people or lower nobility. The tsar also integrated the bath into marriage rituals. At the time of the marriage the tsar visited the bath and, after he left, the tsarina did so as well, along with her mother and close female companions.[26]

Birth and marriage rituals aside, Russians in the countryside in the early modern period saw the banya as potentially dangerous. It was an "unclean place"—where evil spirits, witches, and the dead gathered and where various divination ceremonies took place. It was especially dangerous to go there alone or at midnight.[27] The bathhouse, like other dwellings, had a fairy-like owner — the *bannik*—who possessed magical, usually malicious, powers. According to custom, every third or fourth turn in the steam room belonged to the *bannik*, who sometimes bathed with other spirits. To appease him (in some accounts the goblin was a female, but in most it was a male) and to avoid evil spirits, bathers would make offerings and utter incantations. The *bannik* might bestow either good luck or bad. For instance, if young women approached the banya and exposed their naked backsides to it, a soft touch from the *bannik* signaled good fortune, a swat might be accompanied by a deforming spell.

One's fate could be revealed—or even determined—in the banya. The *bannik* was occasionally seen—usually taking on the form of someone from the community who was said to be elsewhere at the time of the encounter. The sense of danger was compounded by the fact that people customarily took off their crosses on entering the banya and thus gave up one of their main protections against evil spirits. Likewise, icons could not be taken into the banya.[28] Other bits and pieces of folk belief suggest that the bathhouse was a charged space. Bathers used mirrors in the banya to conjure an image of a future spouse. Locking a black cat in a banya was part of a spell that could bring fortune. The place where a banya had burned down was considered dangerous. Objects from the banya were associated with magic and uncleanliness, and thus were not supposed to be removed from the banya.[29]

The *Domostroi*, the guide for households, highlighted the hazards posed by the banya. In a section on illness and healing it warned against going to sorcerers or herbalists, or other practitioners of magic. It also stated "no Christian may have contact with Jews. If a cleric is found . . . mixing with Jews at a bathhouse . . .he shall be defrocked." The penalty for the layman was excommunication for nineteen years.[30] The early modern banya was a liminal space, between life and death, mixed-sex coupling and same-sex bonding, official ablutions and magic. It was a space where certain acts promised power or good fortune, but with the recognition that if they were performed at the wrong time or with the wrong person, they could be harmful or even fatal.

During the political upheaval of the Time of Troubles—a fifteen-year crisis between the end of the Rurik dynasty in 1598 and the establishment of the Romanov dynasty in 1613—critics took it as a sign of sorcery that a pretender to the throne (the so-called False Dmitrii) went to the banya with his wife at precisely the time he was supposed to be at church with the princes and boyars. Paradoxically, other sources were suspicious of Dmitrii for not going to the bathhouse as part of his wedding ceremony.[31] Dmitrii, likely a foreigner, failed to negotiate successfully the banya's dual association with cleanliness and defilement, its importance as a sacred place and as a place of sacrilege.

The association of the banya with magic, spells, and danger continued through the end of the century. In the late seventeenth century Prince Vasily Golytsin was accused of having kept "a *koldun* [sorcerer] in his bathhouse to make magic love spells to attract the Regent Sofiia," whom he supported in her contest with her brother Peter for the throne.[32] These examples may at first appear to support the idea of the banya harboring identities that existed independently of or ran parallel to Christianity. However, Orthodox

FIGURE 1.2 This seventeenth-century miniature depicts the basics of the banya: a changing room, a hot oven that produces heat and steam, and a bench on which a young man whisks an older man with a *venik*.

teachings integrated the banya as something that could both defile people and purify bathers. The dangers of the banya were widely accepted in Orthodoxy. Its association with evil can be traced to an ecclesiastical history that was often imported with Church teachings into Russian Orthodoxy. Because public baths were associated with vice, promiscuity, and prostitution, Church authorities elsewhere in the medieval period sought to regulate activities within them. As early as the sixth century, according to one scholar, Justinian "laid down strict penalties for misbehavior at the bathhouse, and condemnations of mixed bathing as an occasion of sin appear often in the

records of councils and synods, and in patristic and later Christian literature."[33] By the sixteenth century public bathhouses had been closed down
entirely in many Western European countries, because of their association
with illicit sex and the spread of sickness.[34] This ecclesiastical literature was
known to Orthodox Church leaders and may have influenced their law
codes. Yet adopting those prohibitions entirely was difficult if not impossible. In Russia, banyas remained open and legal. Indeed, they seemed to
have thrived in this period.

Some Orthodox writings portrayed the banya as rife with sinful
temptations. Pre-Christian Slavs undertook mixed-sex bathing, which along
with ritual sex, was part of a fertility celebration that corresponded with
the summer solstice.[35] The established religion struck back. The *Komchaia
Efremovskaia*, a twelfth-century code of canon law, prohibited mixed-sex
bathing, but not bathing altogether.[36] The Moscow Church Council of
1551 listed mixed-sex bathing among the sins of both laypeople and ecclesiastical figures. The council reviewed a situation in which "in the city of
Pskov, men and women, and also monks and nuns, are bathing together in
the same bathhouse without shame. This should be prohibited, so that they
cease from this impropriety." The response from the council was clear: "In
accordance with sacred canons, it is not fitting for men and women to bathe
together in the same bathhouse. Likewise it is prohibited and forbidden for
monks and nuns to enter a [public] bathhouse, and if they do enter, they
will be under the interdiction of sacred canons."[37] For laypeople mixed-sex
bathing was prohibited. For the monks and nuns, even entering a public
bathhouse was forbidden, but they could—and even should—use banyas in
their monasteries.

Certain types of mixed-sex bathing among laypeople were more sinful than
others. If a married woman attended a public bath when men were bathing she
was presumed to be unfaithful to her husband, giving him legitimate grounds
for divorce.[38] Unmarried women, however, were not mentioned. Historian
Eve Levin has pointed out that other penitential codes "imposed penance on
those who engaged in mixed-sex bathing, but only when an illegitimate child
was conceived."[39] The concern seems to have been with sex, rather than simply
the opportunity for men and women to see one another naked.

The church did not move to shut down banyas altogether. Going to the
banya was not just allowed in Russian Orthodoxy of the Muscovite period,
but was essential for ritualized cleaning. The banya was tightly integrated
into Church rituals—so long as men and women avoided bathing together.
According to various religious doctrines, going to the banya after sex—even

sanctioned marital sex—was required before either a man or a woman could kiss relics, enter the church, or visit a holy man. Some clerics determined that sex made people ritually impure and required baths to be taken by both husbands and wives after all marital relations. Failure to bathe after sex left people susceptible to evil spirits and demons. Men who had masturbated or experienced nocturnal emissions were deemed to have been visited by the Devil and could not "enter the church, kiss the cross or icons, or receive the Virgin's bread until he had bathed."[40] Parish priests who experienced nocturnal emissions, likewise, were usually not allowed to perform the sacraments that day. But if there was not another priest in the community to perform these essential duties, the priest was permitted to serve after he bathed. Baths were also used to purify women after childbirth. In normal circumstances a new mother had to wait forty days before participating in ecclesiastical rites. The only exception was if she was dying, in which case she could bathe before receiving the rites.[41] While most sources from this period emphasize the banya as a means of obtaining spiritual health, the implication was that physical health was closely connected. During a period of "pestilence," the pious woman Iuliania Osor'ina ventured out among the sick and evidently healed them by bathing them in the banya.[42]

Various sources noted the importance of the banya in various strata of Russian culture, from peasants to the nobility, from the countryside to cities. Even prisoners were expected to go to the banya.[43] The banya's long-standing importance was accepted and integrated into Orthodox church teachings. The deep body of ecclesiastical writing on bathing made that process straightforward, even after bathhouses had fallen out of favor in many other regions of Christendom. The first references to the banya in *The Primary Chronicle* may have been included as an "ethnographic joke" to mark the pagans of Novgorod as different from the religiously blessed of Kiev, but by the Muscovite period a half a millennium later the banya was fully integrated into both everyday practices and beliefs and official church doctrine. The banya had successfully navigated the conversion of Rus' to Christianity.

Western Europeans took a very different approach to bathhouses. While banyas survived and even thrived in Muscovy, bathhouses were dying out in other parts of Europe. To European travelers, this made the banya appear strange—indicative of Russia's cultural oddness more generally. But it also made the banya distinctive, a custom associated with the earliest periods of

Russian history and therefore a practice that united the community through a shared tradition. The fact that Russians continued to go to the banya in the Muscovite period made them different from their Western European counterparts. In the sixteenth century the Catholic Church had moved to shut down bathhouses. By the seventeenth century doctors throughout much of Western Europe considered washing with water to be dangerous and unhealthy. By penetrating the skin, water could easily destroy the delicate balance of humors, in turn wreaking havoc on internal organs and the blood. While bathing was occasionally prescribed to realign the body's fluids, it was also considered a desperate and potentially life-threatening measure.

The consensus around this was so strong that even those who extolled the benefits of bathing did so with a keen sense of the risks involved. For instance, Francis Bacon, the seventeenth-century English philosopher, concluded that it was acceptable, under specific conditions, to take regular baths. But caution led him to develop an intricate way to allow water to moisturize the skin without penetrating the body. First, the water itself had to be "composed of materials whose substances are similar to those of the flesh and the body."[44] Then, as part of his own ablutions, he followed a day-long process in which his body was sealed by oils before being exposed to bath water. On exiting the bath he wrapped himself in waxed linens that had been soaked in various herbs designed to close the pores. He kept the linens on for twenty-four hours before he considered it safe for them to be removed.[45] These were the lengths that advocates of bathing went. The vast majority rarely bathed at all.

From the fifteenth century to the beginning of the eighteenth century, Europe—or at least Western Europe—went through a period that the French historian Georges Vigarello has referred to as three hundred years without a bath. Changing linens, rather than bathing, became the preferred method for maintaining personal hygiene.[46] In seventeenth-century France architects did not include baths in their plans for residences. They were simply not necessary, because of the "use of linen, which today serves to keep the body clean, more conveniently than could the steam-baths and baths of the ancients."[47] On those occasions when water was used—almost always on the face and hands only—cold water, which did not threaten to open the pores and expose the body to pestilence, was the norm. Public bathhouses, once popular in medieval Western Europe, fell out of favor. Indeed, "the baths" or "bagnios" had become synonymous with brothels and associated with the plague. Bathhouses were out of date and their disappearance was taken as a sign of cultural advancement. Whereas Herodotus and Ibn Rusta were struck by bathing habits they did not recognize as normal, early modern Europeans were shocked by the prevalence of any sort of bathhouse at all.

It is no surprise that Western Europeans visiting Muscovy found the banya at best strange and risky and at worst indicative of barbarism and licentiousness. In 1588 Giles Fletcher, an ambassador from Queen Elizabeth to Tsar Fyodor, suggested that the Russians went to the banyas to help prevent diseases that otherwise would have resulted from their tendency to drink. But Fletcher clearly saw this "cure" as bizarre. Russians, he reported, "come out of their bath stoves all on a froth and fuming as hot almost as a pig at a spit, and presently leap in to the river stark naked or pour cold water all over their bodies, and that in the coldest of all the wintertime."[48] The hot baths and the cold climate presented a dangerous combination; the nudity suggested just how outlandish the process was.

Perhaps the most often cited description of the banya prior to the eighteenth century came from Adam Olearius, a scholar who had traveled to Russia in the 1630s and wrote a highly influential narrative of his time there. Olearius first mentioned the banya in the context of the Muscovites' "lusts of the flesh and fornication" and their addiction to the "vile depravity we call sodomy."[49] The banya—and the incidences of naked men and women coming out of the baths together to cool off—presented Olearius with examples of the ways Russians "divested themselves of every trace of shame and restraint." When he detailed the theme of the bath in his book, Olearius again remarked on the open nudity and the degree to which the sexes mingled and were visible to one another even on those occasions when the bathhouses were partitioned "so that men and women could sit separately."[50] After bragging that he was able to observe the baths in Astrakhan by going into them "incognito," Olearius emphasized that naked women in the midst of their cold plunge were "not dismayed or indignant" about the appearance of men among them. He quoted a verse that he had heard among foreigners in Russia that suggested that "To bathe in common, bodies bare," was as indicative of Muscovite "life and character" as "churches, ikons, crosses, bells; painted whores and garlic smells." The banya defined Muscovy for European visitors.[51]

Olearius was willing to credit the banya—at least for those exposed to it from an early age—for giving the Russians "toughness, strength, and endurance" and for enabling them to bear "extremes of hot and cold." Still, he contrasted the crude Russian baths with "honorable and clean" baths run by the Germans in Moscow. In those baths, Olearius was less offended by the fact that each male bather was assigned a "woman or girl" to attend to him. Instead, such "honorable hospitality and cleanliness" only further clarified the "arrogant, self-interested, and dirty Russians, among whom everything is done in a slovenly and swinish fashion."[52] Olearius's conclusion that the banya was indicative of both Russian openness to sexual promiscuity and its uncivilized nature was common among Western observers. Indeed, including a description of the banya became a cliché in foreigners' accounts of Russia at the time.[53]

When the emphasis on immorality and animalism was counterbalanced by a concession that perhaps something distinctive about Russians made bathing for them healthy, the point was still to associate Russians with banyas and banyas with Russians. The Earl of Carlisle, for example, came away with a positive impression of the banyas when he traveled to Muscovy on behalf of Charles II. He praised the ubiquity of the banyas and noted that people used them "in imitation of the ancients" as a "universal remedy" that gave the Muscovites a "great advantage above other nations." He noted that the bathhouses helped Muscovites keep "their bodies clean" and provided for the "conservation of their health."[54] Jacques Margeret, a French visitor to Muscovy in the seventeenth century, also noted that Russians treated "all sorts of maladies" by going "immediately to the hothouse which is so hot as to be almost unbearable, and [they] remain there until they have sweated an hour or two."[55] Foreign observers could see going to the banya as healthy for Russians but not something that they advocated for their readers.

Even medical experts emphasized sexual promiscuity and Russian peculiarity over general health effects. Doctor Jodocus Crull, a fellow of the Royal Society and member of the College of Physicians in London, traveled to Muscovy in the late seventeenth century. He described in detail the bathhouses he saw there, noting that they were "the universal remedies of the Muscovites, not only for cleaning their bodies but also for the preservation of their health." The banyas contributed to their "healthy constitutions," their long lives, and the fact that they were "seldom troubled with any distempers." "They live," he noted, "for the most part without physicians and many of them without diseases."[56] Yet he did not suggest that bathing was generally advisable, nor did he explore which diseases and dispositions were best treated by a process that appeared to put extreme stress on the body.

Most Western European observers failed to accept that the benefits of the banya might extend beyond Russians. They simply assumed that it was peculiarly Russian and were too constrained by their own sexual mores to see past that. The physician in Crull saw health benefits in the banya, but the moralist in him saw danger. He noted, "When they find the heat too intense, both men and women will run out of the stoves stark naked" into cold water. Inside the banya where sexes were supposed to be separated, men and women were able to gaze at one another's nakedness. The "great number of public bathing places every where [in Muscovy]," Crull explained, were often "carelessly built" so that it was easy to look from the men's sections into the women's sections of the bath. The locals, he observed, thought that this was of "no great consequence, though either sex has nothing else to hide their privy parts but a handful of herbs moistened in water, which a great many don't think it worth their while to make use of, being not very shy to be seen by men." He added, "when they go out to cool themselves in cold water, both sexes commonly [go] out and in at one and the same door to their [respective] bathing rooms."[57] Any health benefits of the banya, the trained physician implied, were undermined by the Russians' peculiar sexual practices.

Even into the early 1700s—when bathing was beginning to find more adherents in Western Europe—sex trumped health when it came to travelers' assessments of the banya. Friedrich Weber, a Hanoverian diplomat who represented England to Peter the Great's court in the 1710s, acknowledged that Russians made use of the bath as a "universal medicine against any indispositions." Yet his account of the banya's medicinal qualities was overshadowed by a more detailed description of sexual comingling. When Weber described the "bagnios," he too emphasized impropriety. Children would evidently holler when the baths were heated, at which point, "those who have a mind to bathe, undress under the open sky and run into the bagnio." He was "astonished" to see "not only the men, but also the women unmarried as well as married . . . running about . . . stark naked without any sort of shame or decency."[58] Account after account clarified that the banya was an institution peculiar to Muscovite Russia.

The Muscovite state was less concerned with shutting down banyas or regulating behavior in them that it was in figuring out how to tax them. In the early seventeenth century, town records, such as those kept in Yaroslavl, counted bathhouses as among the most important municipal buildings.[59] Given their ubiquity and popularity, it only makes sense that banyas would emerge as a steady source of revenue for a state that perpetually needed to refill its coffers. By the seventeenth century the central administrative state had developed a wide array of taxes it could impose on banyas. The *Ulozhenie* of 1649—the first major systematization of Muscovite law since the middle of the previous century—addressed banyas and taxation explicitly. The law clarified that the tsar used commercial banyas as tax farms (*otkup*). Merchants paid the sovereign for the exclusive right to run a banya in a particular town or region. When the agreed upon period of time—usually between one and five years—was up, the cost of rent would automatically rise. If the renter did not wish to continue with the deal, the state could enter into agreement with another merchant.[60] This arrangement had its advantages for the state. The sovereign remained in control—and could change contracts—but did not need to rely on a weak bureaucracy to operate banyas in towns and cities across a vast empire. If a banya was unprofitable or failed for any other reason, the tax collectors could still collect its *otkup* or turn over the monopoly to another party. This created a fairly consistent revenue flow, while leaving the details of economic viability to others. Banya operators, for their part, could then seek to make a profit by charging more for access to the banyas than they owed the sovereign in rent.

Political instability and economic disruption during the Time of Troubles at the beginning of the seventeenth century drained the treasury considerably. The newly established Romanov family used the *otkup* system as a way to raise revenues and stabilize the budget. They farmed out monopolies for the use of state land for hunting and fishing, for the use of mills and forests, and for the right to undertake industry, crafts, or trade. Those who sought the banya monopoly in a given region often did so in coordination with other forms of tax farming. It was common for the state to farm out banyas to groups of two or more people and also to cluster monopolies of various services and industries in a region. Renters may have seen running a banya as burdensome—they needed people to transport water, man the fires, collect wood for the stove, and repair and maintain the ovens. But paying the tax was worthwhile, especially if it allowed them also to control other sectors of the local economy.[61]

Banya tax farmers paid the state regularly. The details of the rent were worked out at the local level, taking into account local economic conditions. The cost of renting out the banya for a year ranged from 17 rubles in some places to 50 rubles in others. But if other monopolies were added (such as the right to sell spirits or to organize games of chance), then the cost could easily balloon to hundreds of rubles per year. Indeed, over the course of the first half of the seventeenth century, prices appear to have gone up considerably.[62]

Tax farming was not the only means the state had of extracting money from banyas. Tax collectors also charged a "seal tax" (*poshlina*)—basically requiring each commercial banya to be licensed to operate. Merchants who had already paid for multiyear deals to operate banyas as tax farms were only required to pay the seal tax once.[63] But the annual burden of the seal tax on

operators of smaller banyas could be significant.[64] The two tax methods together created a steady flow of income for the state.[65]

The importance of banya taxes was not lost on the tsar's administrators.
In the 1680s, a legal code clarified and emphasized that the collection of fees
to run commercial banyas was the exclusive domain of the Grand Prince.[66]
Even this did not exhaust the state's tools for extracting revenue. In addition
to tax farming and the seal tax, the banya could be taxed in three other ways.
Bannyi sbor was a tax on private banyas; *bannye den'gi* were taxes leveled on
the profession of running a banya; and *obrok* or quitrent were paid by individual merchants to the sovereign for the right to operate a banya, although
without the monopoly that came from tax farming.[67]

The laws distinguished between commercial (*torgovye*) banyas and domestic (*domovye*) banyas and administered and taxed them accordingly.
Some people with domestic banyas charged predominantly poor travelers and
visitors a small fee to bathe, thus bypassing the taxes that they would have had
to pay had they been running an official commercial banya. Both the state
and those licensed to run commercial banyas had a vested interest in shutting down the domestic banyas that were acting surreptitiously as commercial
banyas.[68] Taken together, the tax laws suggest that the Muscovite state treated
banyas first and foremost as a source of revenue to be exploited, not as a source
of magic, sin, or ablution to be regulated. Unlike Western commentators, the
Muscovite state did not seem concerned with sex or licentiousness. Nor did
it understand the banya in terms of health. In Muscovy, regulation began and
ended with taxation.

Effort to rationalize tax collection preceded Peter the Great's reforms. But
during his reign the process became more systematic, closing loopholes that
had allowed some proprietors to avoid taxes. At the beginning of the eighteenth century Peter led a massive drive to Europeanize Russia, with the main
incentive of modernizing Russia's military and administrative structures.
Taxes were necessary to pay for the effort.[69] Many markers of Russianness—
from the style of the Muscovite court to the customary beards and dress of
the elites—were forcefully uprooted and replaced. But the banya remained.

Peter neither reformed the banya nor recognized it as an institution that
could aid the state by keeping the population healthy. Instead, he oversaw
the intensification of tax collection from their operators. In 1704, a law
directed that levees from both commercial and domestic banyas be sent to the
Inzherskii Chancellery, which was run by Alexander Menshikov, Peter's right-
hand man and a prime administrator of his reforms. The law stated explicitly
for the first time that urban banyas, banyas on gentry and noble estates, and

even monastery banyas all had to pay quitrent, whether they were officially commercial or not.[70] In towns with over five hundred people, banyas were to be built by merchants who would also pay quitrent on a fixed schedule. In some cases, a town's administrator could build banyas, but these too had to be registered with a tax collector. People in towns and monastic settlements who insisted on keeping their banyas without paying the requisite levees would have their banyas destroyed and be forced to pay a penalty. The money, naturally, would be sent to the central administration.[71]

The scope of Peter's administrative effort to increase tax revenues from the banyas was astounding. The law specified that all commercial banyas were required to record and register their profits, allowing the state to set rates to its advantage. If a banya changed hands, additional fees applied. If there were disagreements or petitions among those who rented out the banyas, the disputes would be heard by Menshikov's office. In towns and regions where there were no banyas, they were to be built and rented out. And where they did exist, the central authorities ensured that Peter received the taxes.[72] Weber, the diplomat who represented Britain in Peter's court, astutely observed midway through Peter's reign that because "the Russians in general both Men and Women" bathed twice a week all year round, the taxes on the banyas brought "a considerably Revenue into the Czar's coffers."[73]

The tax burdens could not be so onerous, however, that they dissuaded merchants from running commercial banyas or encouraged them to hide their commercial endeavors from the tax collector. From the point of view of the state, the more banyas that paid quitrent and licensing taxes the better. At the same time, banya operators wanted some assurances that they could profit from their efforts. Recognizing this, Peter promulgated laws designed to aid commercial banyas in certain circumstances: new banyas had to be built far enough away from existing ones so as not to interfere with profits; if existing owners could pool resources to form a banya monopoly, they could limit their tax liability.[74]

When commercial banyas had broken down or had ceased to operate, tremendous investments were required to get them back up and running. In those cases, to encourage merchants to take on the risk and expense, the state struck deals. In one case, which occurred after Peter's death, a merchant agreed to build and then run a banya if he could pay a discounted quitrent and also receive a license to run a tavern. In order to make the investment even more attractive, the state granted the merchant a five-year reprieve from his taxes, unless he had earned back his initial expenses.[75] These laws were designed to encourage investment in banyas while ensuring that taxes eventually made their way into the treasury.

The losers in this process were those who had been charging customers to bathe in their private, domestic banyas. Although officially forbidden from charging money for access, domestic banyas clearly competed with the commercial bathhouses, despite generally serving poorer patrons. Here too the law favored commercial banyas by shutting down domestic banyas except for the owners' personal use. In 1719 a fine was imposed on those who heated their domestic baths on any day except Saturdays. Licensed banyas could operate throughout the week. The law authorized St. Petersburg police to issue a fine for the first offense, to double it for the second offense, and triple it for the third offense. The penalty for the fourth offense was to be "beaten with a baton mercilessly" so that those breaking the rule would "subordinate themselves" and "understand that they should not heat their banyas except on Saturdays."[76] Another law simply forbade people of lower classes from building domestic banyas in St. Petersburg. Later laws specified which materials could be used in building a banya and required operators to take measures to prevent fires. Domestic banyas could not be heated during hot or dry times.[77] These laws suggested more traditional police powers—regulation in the name of the general well-being of a city or community. While fear of fires may have been the central motivation behind some of these laws, they might just as easily have been a way to tighten controls on the domestic banyas that charged money. This had been the explicit goal of similar local rulings in the first half of the seventeenth century, where on at least two occasions the prohibition against heating domestic banyas in warm weather was about both preventing fire and increasing revenues to the official commercial banyas.[78]

Peter the Great transformed much of Russia's foreign policy, military affairs, and intellectual and cultural life to align with the rest of Europe. It is not hard to imagine a scenario in which he would have outlawed the commercial banya in keeping with contemporary European trends. In the early eighteenth century, true Westernization would have meant forgoing bathing altogether. Yet the banya was not among the Russian traditions that Peter either ridiculed or attempted to modernize. When he built his self-consciously rational and European capital on the Neva, banyas were there and they looked more or less like those that had existed in Russian cities for centuries.[79] What was new was the state's effort to systematically tax them. Peter modernized existing taxes to maximize revenues, charging quitrent on all banyas, licensing fees, and professional fees for all commercial banyas. When it appeared that domestic banyas were operating as de facto commercial banyas, laws attempted to clamp down on them. The banya may have been beloved by the people, but from the point of view of the crown, it was primarily a revenue generator. Peter's impact came in strengthening and enforcing the existing system.

———•◆•———

The persistence of commercial banyas long after they had been outlawed elsewhere in Europe contributed to a sense that Russia and Russians were uncivilized. Perhaps the most popular foreign account of Peter's reign, Foy De La Neuville's *Curious and New Account of Muscovy in the Year 1689*, summed up this perspective: "To tell the truth, the Muscovites are barbarians. They are suspicious and mistrustful, cruel, sodomites, gluttons, misers, beggars and cowards, and all are slaves except for the members of three foreign families . . . . They are very dirty, although they bathe very often in places made for the purpose which are heated by ovens to such an extent that in the whole world there is only themselves who can bear it. Men and women are mixed in these places."[80] For those predisposed to see Muscovy as backward and debauched, the banya served as a prime piece of evidence.

Within Russia, the policies of Peter the Great, which famously caused a rupture between the *narod* (or people) and the increasingly Europeanized aristocracy, did not inexorably alter the banya. To be sure, Peter figured out ways to tax them more efficiently. Distinctions between how different strata of society used the banya also became more visible. Communal banyas in cities faced different rules and regulations than private banyas or those on noble or church estates. Unlicensed, domestic banyas also ran as small businesses, catering to the poor and hoping to remain either unseen by the state or at least deemed insignificant enough as a source of revenue to be ignored. But in all these iterations, the Russian banya, "the soul and flesh of Rus," remained relatively stable. Large, communal urban banyas had existed since Kievan Rus', if not earlier. Small sweat lodges had been in the region at least as long. Magic, marriage rituals, gambling, drinking, and sex did not necessarily conflict with the state's focus on tax revenue. The banya was a space where naked men and women gathered "without shame," sorcerers twisted fates, and bathers inflicted a "voluntary torture upon themselves." It also helped wipe clean impurities so that the faithful could return to church and kiss the cross.

Depending who was writing and when, the banya was akin to bathing customs elsewhere or a sui generis marker of Russianness; it was a place where bathers could be purified and a place where they could be defiled; and it was the object of state policy partly as a private space (separated out from other ac-tivities and, at times, owned and operated by individuals) and partly as public space (social, commercial, and licensed by the state). It challenged the very categories that emerged to define modern "civilization." These contradictions have their roots in the earliest stories told about the banya and about the territory that would become Russia. And they survived intact as markers of a Russian ethnic identity from the emergence of Rus' in the tenth century through Peter the Great's efforts to modernize Russia in the early eighteenth century.

2

The Great Healer

EVEN AFTER PETER THE GREAT radically transformed Muscovy into a more European empire, the banya remained a peculiarly Russian institution. As the process of Westernization intensified, two trends affected how people understood the banya. First, some Western Europeans began to recognize the potential health benefits of bathing in general. Baths and bathhouses, which European elites treated skeptically at best in the seventeenth century, gradually became the topic of medical curiosity and even advocacy.[1] This invited a reconsideration of the banya, as the positive effects of steaming *à la Russe* could be measured against other sorts of bathhouses. Second, the Russian state's relationship to "civilized Europe" became a topic of great debate among Enlightenment thinkers, particularly in France.[2] For those who saw Russia as helplessly barbaric, the banya continued to serve as a convenient and ubiquitous symbol of Russian difference. But for those who hoped to show that Russia was civilized, the evolution of medical opinions about bathing made it possible to reascribe the banya as a healthy, even progressive, institution. Some—probably most—elite observers in Europe were still put off by behavior in and around the banya that they deemed sexually deviant. But by the end of the century, such moral judgments had to contend with positive interpretations presented in the learned language of medical experts that claimed that the banya was first and foremost an institution that could promote personal and public health.

The eighteenth-century banya was about sex, tradition, and medicine. It was also about international politics and the ability of the Russian state to thrive militarily and economically. Empress Catherine the Great, who came to power in 1762 and ruled until 1796, directly engaged with contemporary European debates about the banya. Born in Prussia, she married into the Russian royal family and, after arriving in St. Petersburg, made a point of fitting into her adopted land.[3] In addition to mastering the Russian language, she took a personal liking to the banya, which she defended against those foreigners who saw it as a sign of Russia's backwardness.

In keeping with the latest trends in Western European medicine, Catherine promoted going to the banya as integral to the empire's health and therefore its economy and power. The banya fit squarely within her plans for improving Russia. Keenly aware of the health challenges the empire faced, she focused her attention on high infant mortality, dangerous rates of infectious diseases, the small number of medical doctors in the empire, the poor distribution of apothecaries and hospitals, and the compromised health of soldiers in the military. These issues threatened the population's size and vitality, which Catherine recognized would limit productivity and the ability to conduct war.[4] In one form or another, the banya could help address each of these health concerns.

By the end of Catherine's reign, many aspects of Russian culture were associated with either traditional Russia or with civilized, Europeanized governance. Remarkably, perhaps uniquely, the banya managed to be associated with both. Russia's ambiguous status was reflected in Western European attitudes toward the banya. Two men of science, Jean-Baptiste Chappe D'Auteroche and António Ribiero Sanches, represented the competing strands. Chappe and Sanches were both members of the Royal Academy of Sciences in Paris; both were active participants in the transnational exchange of ideas that dominated intellectual life in the period; both spent time in Russia; and both commanded Catherine's close attention. Finally, both could agree that the banya was essential to the nature of eighteenth-century Russia.

Their commonalities aside, Chappe and Sanches took opposing positions on the banya. In 1768 Chappe, a French astronomer and priest, published a description of the banyas that fit neatly with the disparaging tone adopted by European travelers of previous centuries. His three-volume "account of the manners and customs of the Russians" dismissed the banya as absurd and even dangerous. Catherine directly rebutted Chappe in a pamphlet of her own. In contrast, Sanches was a medical doctor attuned to new opinions about bathing emerging at the time in Western Europe. Beginning in the 1760s Sanches avoided the scintillating details of mixed-sex bathing in favor of a learned, medical argument for the health benefits of the banya. In 1779, the publication of his book *Treatise on the Russian Steam Baths* introduced a new level of serious study of the Russian tradition and placed it at the center of ongoing debates in the West about the benefits of bathing more generally.[5] Catherine cited Sanches in an attempt to further systematize the use of the banya in Russia. She saw the banya, at least in principle, less as a means to increase state revenues than as an institution that could keep the population, and in turn the state, healthy. To Chappe the banya and Russia were barbarous and crude; to Sanches they were progressive and vital.

Chappe D'Auteroche was drawn to Russia by its latitude and longitude, not by its culture or history. In 1761, as a thirty-nine-year-old, he traveled to the town of Tobol'sk in Siberia to observe the transit of Venus between the sun and the earth. Astronomers at the time understood that such transits were very rare but predictable celestial events. Two occur within an eight-year period and then not again for over a century. Learned men seized the opportunity to contribute to celestial knowledge and funded a series of expeditions to all corners of the globe for the purpose.[6] The observation would take a matter of hours, but to be in the right place at the right time, Chappe spent fifteen months in Russia. This afforded him plenty of time to turn from celestial concerns to more earthly matters. When he did, he came across the banya.

To Chappe, geography, astronomy, and health were intertwined. He held, as did many in his age, that terrain and climate determined national character and even distinctive regional body types and human physical attributes. The banya was not just an odd custom to Chappe; it was further evidence to support his generally negative view of Russian character and health. The banya seemed to confirm his sense of the peculiarities of Russian bodies and the prevalence of sexual promiscuity in that part of the world.[7]

The company he kept in Paris further prejudiced him against Russia. Among French diplomats of the eighteenth century, there were two schools of thought when it came to Russia. One—influenced by Voltaire and the Encyclopedists—understood Russia as being on the road to enlightenment. It was at the far edges of "civilization" to be sure, but it was still fundamentally a European—and civilized—country.[8] The other camp, in which Chappe belonged, continued to see Russia as oriental and not European, despotic and not ruled by law. For them, efforts at Westernization undertaken by Peter and his successors had done nothing to change these facts. Chappe's trip was primarily about the transit of Venus, but he could not help but look for evidence that supported the anti-Russian views he shared with some French diplomats.[9]

After an arduous trip across Europe by carriage and then across Russia by sled, Chappe arrived in Tobol'sk in the spring of 1761. He first observed a lunar eclipse, which allowed him to calculate his exact longitude. Then he observed the transit of Venus. He reported his findings from St. Petersburg, where he was in residence at the Academy of Sciences.

Five years after returning to France, he published *Voyage en Sibérie*, which was accompanied by illustrations by Jean-Baptist Le Prince. While the book was nominally about Chappe's time in Russia in the early 1760s during the reign of Elizabeth, its publication in 1768 turned it into a major touchstone of Enlightenment debates in France and beyond about Catherine the Great's Russia. Within a year it had been reprinted in Amsterdam. Within three years it had been translated and published in English, Dutch, and German.

Given that his primary interest was observing the sky, it was perhaps understandable that Chappe found his day-do-day interactions with Russians tedious and challenging. Chappe described his first trip to a banya in the town of Solikamsk. He expressed surprise at what he thought was smoke coming out of the bathing room. He was reluctant to expose his body to the heat and to submit to the sweating that would follow. Only after his servant suggested that he would insult his host if he were to turn down the bath—which had taken hours to prepare—did Chappe agree. He wrote, "[I] found myself in a small square room, so much heated by a stove that I was instantly in profuse sweat." Looking for more air, but not realizing that the heat increased toward the ceiling of the room, he scrambled to the highest level of the tiered benches. "I could scarcely bear the pain I felt in the soles of my feet, and I could not have stayed here, if they had not thrown some cold water upon the spot, which evaporated almost instantaneously." The heat from the steam, however, "seized [his] head" and made him ill. He managed to fall to the lower level and "ordered" that the door and window be opened. He then recovered by sitting in cold water and asking his servant to throw more water on him as he sat quietly, afraid to move. Unable even to dress himself—he was too wet and too cold—he threw on his coat and ran to his carriage with his clothes in his hands and went home to bed immediately. His disappointed servant informed him that he had not really stayed long enough to benefit from the banya.[10]

This first experience of the baths did not deter Chappe from trying them again in Tobol'sk. There he hoped that the banya could aid his health, which he determined had been adversely affected by the Russian climate. Again the heat was too much for him to bear. He noted that he did not like the "violent" rub-down with the twigs and "got out of the baths as soon as I could." He reported that the Russians, in contrast, bathed for over two hours and repeated the process several times.

Chappe's initial efforts did not curb his curiosity about the banya, in part because the custom seemed to provide obvious and entertaining proof of the degree to which Russia remained far from civilized. Chappe pointed out that banyas were in use "all over Russia" and that "every inhabitant of this vast tract of land, from the sovereign to the meanest subject, bathes twice a week, and in the same manner."[11] The reference to the sovereign was no accident. The implication was that no matter how civilized and aristocratic the Russian tsars appeared to be, they still engaged in customs that revealed their more barbarous roots. Readers at the time would have read this as a condemnation of Catherine, since to a French audience habitual bathing signaled a high degree of boorishness.

Chappe's disdain was not reserved for the heat or the habit of bathing. He also targeted the mixing of the sexes. He reported that those who could afford them had domestic banyas where whole families bathed together. In the commercial banyas, sections for men and women officially existed, but in fact the sexes mingled freely. In poorer towns, "the two sexes are oftentimes all together in the same bath." Chappe added that even when the sexes bathed separately men would come to the door of the banyas naked and would chat with women who would bring them drinks and provisions. Chappe repeated the claim that the banya was a place of promiscuity and sexual openness.[12]

Chappe found evidence that the Russian elite was just as uncivilized as the common folk. His descriptions of domestic banyas in luxurious homes were replete with scandalous detail. He emphasized both the exotic setting and the acts of violent thrashing that took place among the Russian aristocrats. The buildings, he admitted, were well designed. What people did in them, however, he considered base and debauched. People entered with pails of water and a "bundle of twigs." The bather started on the lower rungs where the heat was not as great. After sweating, a servant would douse the bather with cold water. He then proceeded farther up the "amphitheater" and repeated the process, going higher and higher and remaining in the steam room for about half an hour. Another man "throws now and then some water on the red hot stones: volleys of steam immediately rush out of the stove with a noise." The steam rose to the ceiling and came back down in a hot cloud. It softened the twigs, which, when swung, powerfully pushed the hot air into the open pores. If the public baths were licentious, the private ones were both violent and sexually charged: a bather would lay down while someone "whips him with the twigs, expecting he will return the good office: but in many baths women are employed for this purpose."[13] Hot, violent, and open to both sexes, the banya represented an affront to Chappe's sense of proper behavior.

Chappe conceded that there could be some medical benefits to bathing for the inhabitants of Russia. His ideas about climate meant that what was good for Russian bodies accustomed to very cold temperatures might be harmful to Europeans. He reasoned that because Russians were in their houses and sweated little all winter, they were full of humeral imbalances. "These baths seem therefore to be absolutely necessary for them, as they might be liable to a great number of diseases if they did not use them." He added that they produce "Great fermentation in the blood and humors, and bring on plentiful discharges by perspiration. The extreme cold drives the humors back from the skin and restores the equilibrium again."[14]

Chappe's humeral ideas allowed him to imagine an instance when the banya could be valuable to non-Russians, albeit not as a prophylactic practice but as a means of regaining health. He concluded that banyas might be useful in Europe, but only for the treatment of "rheumatic complaints." He based this deduction on the observation that "distempers of this kind are hardly known in Russia and many foreigners have been radically cured of them by the use of these baths." In sum, Chappe's approach to the banya combined ridicule, disbelief, and disparaging comments with some praise for its health benefits, especially for Russians.

Chappe's impact was far more profound than foreigners who had written about the banya before him. His book was considered the definitive eighteenth-century account of the habits and mores of the Russian people. His standing as a renowned scientist made his opinions authoritative. He backed up his descriptions with medical theories that both explained the banya in Russia and clarified its peculiar value in light of Russia's climate and diet. This all fit within a broader disdain for Russia and Russians that defined the intellectual and diplomatic faction he represented.

Perhaps the most important reason for the broad impact of Chappe's account was its inclusion of elaborate prints by Le Prince, whose rendering of the banya was particularly risqué. Le Prince depicted men, women, and children bathing together with no apparent effort to conceal their nudity. The poses may have brought to mind classical, idealized bodies—muscle-bound men, round women, and cherub-like children. But their actions suggest that the potentially wholesome, healthy scene has been corrupted beyond reason. Naked men and women lounge together, scrubbing one another, sitting in tubs, holding birch branches, and pouring water in ways that appear designed to shock the French sense of propriety. On the highest shelf of the steam-filled room, a woman beats a man with birch switches. Elsewhere, a woman leans back with her legs spread while a man appears to be massaging her back.

While people's genitalia are discretely covered in the print, French readers no doubt could imagine that such propriety was not possible in the actual banyas of Russia. Le Prince's image made visible and visceral the crudeness of the banya that Chappe had described in words.

Catherine was not pleased with the book's anti-Russian agenda. She was particularly upset because Chappe's trip had been sponsored by the St. Petersburg Academy, which saw itself as actively contributing to the

FIGURE 2.1 Jean Baptiste Le Prince's Rendering of the Russian Banya, published in Chappe D'Auteroche's *Voyage en Sibérie*. This book in general and this image in particular incensed Catherine the Great and inspired her to write her "Antidote" as a rebuttal. Courtesy of Rosenbach Museum, Philadelphia.

enlightened project of tracking the Transit of Venus. That Chappe reported on things like the banya instead—and in a negative way—was an obvious affront.

In 1770 the empress published an anonymous rebuttal that was intended to set Chappe and his readers straight on a number of matters. The tone of Catherine's "Antidote or Refutation of a Bad Book Beautifully Printed, Entitled, Voyage to Siberia" was derisive and dismissive, pointing out the extent to which Chappe reached broad conclusions about all of Russia from his limited experience. His so-called observations, she said, often came from within his fur-lined sled. She mocked him for mistaking the banya's steam for smoke, for being scared of the banya, and for not realizing that he was supposed to sweat. Catherine found Chappes's use of the banya to inspire "horror" even worse than his obvious ignorance.[15]

Catherine was particularly appalled by Le Prince's "scandalous print." "And here, good reader," the Empress wrote, "you will find a most indecent print which the Abbe intends to be supposed to describe a Russian banya, but which in reality far more resembles a bacchanal." She pointed out that in fact men and women alternated their times in the bathhouse or went to separate sections that were partitioned off from one another. She was irked by Chappe's use of the word "promiscuous" to describe the naked bathing and rolling in the snow that often accompanied the bath. The insistence on the two sexes bathing together "is really enough to make me furiously angry," she wrote, adding: "Never were calumny and scandal carried to such an impudent height." She also found his description of the birch whisks in the banya misleading. Where Chappe claimed people "whipped" one another, Catherine retorted that the custom was to draw heat down on the bathers. If Chappe had been whipped, she mused, it was because he deserved to be whipped. She concluded that Chappe was ignorant of Russia and was "trafficking in lies."[16]

Catherine was not entirely straightforward herself. Smoke, not steam, sometimes filled rural banyas during the heating process. The mixed-sex bathing that Chappe highlighted remained common enough to prompt legal action. In 1743, a law had been enacted banning men and women from going to the banya together. In 1860, right before Chappe traveled to Russia, the Senate conceded in a law that "in the commercial banyas of St. Petersburg men and women steam in one room, which is entirely repugnant." It called on the police to strongly enforce the law "forbidding men and women from going together to the commercial banya" and called for "fines without any mercy."[17] The problem did not go away. In 1782, yet another law required commercial banyas to have separate sections for men and women, to be clearly marked by sex, and to have workers be of the same sex as the patrons.[18] Catherine claimed in her "Antidote" that the banya was not as sexually open as Chappe had described, but the legal code suggests otherwise. Catherine also seems to have enjoyed going to the banya herself, since she had one built at the Tsarskoe Selo estate. She even liaised with her lover Grigory Potemkin in the banya, suggesting that at least in the privacy of the Russian court the banya was a mixed-sex affair.[19]

Vitriol and disingenuousness aside, Catherine's defense of the banya in the "Antidote" shared Chappe's assumption that bathing less was a measure of civility. Chappe claimed that banyas were ubiquitous in Russia; Catherine retorted that "there are numbers of Russians who never bathe at all, and greater numbers who use them two or three times a year." She was referring here to Russians of the better sorts. Only "trades-people and workmen" went weekly, she claimed. This was a far cry, she pointed out, from Chappe's claim that everyone from the "sovereign down to the meanest subject" bathed twice a week.

This exchange on the baths highlights the degree to which Chappe was using the banya to make Russia appear exotic and uncivilized. His sensational-istic description reinforced the notion that Russians could not be considered part of Enlightened Europe. Russia's customs proved its backwardness. Catherine's retort argued that banyas were not as commonly used as Chappe had claimed and they were not morally repugnant.

Catherine's "Antidote" did not directly rebut Chappe's claims that banyas were unhealthy, although she clearly believed that they were not. She might have avoided the question of health because she sensed that she was unlikely to sway her readers. Only those on the cutting edge of medical thinking in Europe at the time recommended regular bathing. If Catherine had written about the physical benefits of the banya in detail, she would have lost rhetor-ical points in her attempt to defend Russia; it was best to downplay the signif-icance of the banya altogether, not to laud its virtues.

Though she eschewed the issue in her "Antidote," Catherine was well aware of the health benefits of the banya, thanks to her contact with another for-eign Enlightenment thinker—António Ribeiro Sanches. Sanches, unlike Chappe, was familiar with the latest Western medical theories about bathing. He understood, in a way that Chappe did not, that some doctors in Western Europe had begun to value prophylactic and habitual bathing, not just for the treatment of certain ailments.[20] During the 1720s Sanches studied medicine in Portugal, England, France, and at Leiden University in the Netherlands, where he worked with Herman Boerhaave, the era's preeminent medical teacher.[21] There Sanches likely came across innovative treatments for syphilis (he would later write the entry on the topic in Denis Diderot's *Encyclopédie*) and criticisms of bloodletting (which he later discovered was common in banyas).[22] On matters of the body, Chappe was a dilettante, Sanches an expert.

Over the next three decades Sanches gained experience that allowed him to propagandize about the banya's medical value and made Catherine inclined to listen to him. In 1730, when the Empress, Anna Ivanovna, sent Boerhaave a request for doctors to serve in Russia, he tapped Sanches. In 1731 Sanches was appointed chief medical doctor of the city of Moscow. He soon was called to practice in St. Petersburg and in 1735 he became the First Doctor of the Imperial Army, a position he held for six years. On campaigns with the army, first in Poland, and then on the southern steppe, he learned of the extensive use of the banya in the Russian military. He also noted the ubiquity of the banya among Russian peasants and in Russian towns.

Sanches returned to St. Petersburg as a doctor of the Russian court and as State Counselor. He treated Anna Ivanovna at the end of her life; his diagnosis of her nephrolithiasis, while too late to allow for treatment, affirmed his medical prowess to his colleagues and to the court. After Anna's death, he successfully treated the Duke of Holstein and attended to Princess Sophie Anhalt-Zerbst—the future Catherine the Great. In 1744, soon after her arrival in Russia, the fourteen-year-old princess fell gravely ill. As Catherine recalled in her memoir, she had hung in the balance "between life and death for twenty-seven days." "Finally," Catherine explained, "the abscess that I had on my right side burst under the care of the Portuguese doctor Sanchez [*sic*]; I vomited it up and thereafter recovered."[23] Sanches had earned Catherine's admiration and trust.

Despite this good deed, Sanches soon found himself on the wrong side of court politics under Anna's successor, the new Tsarina, Empress Elizabeth, and he left for Paris in 1747.[24] He kept in close—but covert—contact with Russian elites in Paris who were biding their time for a change in the imperial court. When Elizabeth died in 1762, Catherine's husband Peter ascended to the throne. He was emperor for only six months before Catherine orchestrated a coup that allowed her to assume power. For Sanches, this meant an opportunity for redemption. Within a few months Catherine issued him an annuity of 1,000 rubles "because he saved my life, with the aid of God."[25]

Soon thereafter Sanches wrote to Catherine about the banya. His main point was to emphasize its value to the health of the Russian people. His ideas quickly made their way into the law books. In 1766, Catherine cited a letter from Sanches that had emphasized to her: "It is extremely necessary to bring banyas to greater use, as the safest protection against many illnesses and as a means for the strengthening of the human body." Sanches had pointed out "because of superstition in Europe, the banyas [there] were destroyed," which revealed that "the misjudging zealots would rather their people be exhausted and weakened than healthy and strong." He also pointed out that Russian soldiers understood the benefits of the banya. Catherine agreed. The Empress noted that "using them [the banyas] in the ways that Mr. Sanches describes, was the best and unequalled means of preserving the health, strength, and firmness" of the people. She declared this was known to the wisest people, despite the fact that "a united superstition destroyed banyas in Europe," and "that the destruction led to the appearance of diseases, which began in Italy and then in France around 1480."[26]

The Empress turned to Sanches again in sanctioning a new law on the proper use of the banyas. The court's interest in the banya, as reflected in the laws, had shifted from revenue to health. Sanches had written to her: "God Grant that physicians and doctors in Russia recognize the use all the people can get out of the banya." He called on "the laws of Russian towns, villages, and hamlets" to guarantee that banyas be run not for profit, but in accordance with the needs of the population and under proper supervision by the state. The law sought to reform the use of the banya to maximize positive health outcomes. It conceded that customs often led people to bathe in ways that might have been detrimental to their health—some went when the banya was too hot, some climbed too quickly to the hottest levels, some rubbed themselves with dangerous spirits and herbs, and some drank stale, ice-cold water to quench their thirst. People occasionally died from the misuse of the banya. The law emphasized, "Against such nightmarish abuse, one needs to be fully warned." Sanches, as a medical expert, prescribed going once a week, for two hours, not after meals, and only when the cold water that was tossed on the hot stones had a chance to become "pleasant." Visitors were supposed to avoid wine or vodka or cold drinks, were to exit into a warm dressing room to lie on a couch to recover, and children especially were supposed to avoid the top benches. This codified advice was based almost exclusively on the expertise of a foreign doctor—not on the vernacular practices of Russians themselves.[27]

In 1766 Sanches clearly wielded influence with Catherine, although he apparently did so only in private letters. Then, in 1770, came the publication of

Chappe's scathing description of Russia and Le Prince's salacious print of the banya. Given Sanches's interest in Russia and the fact that he traveled in some of the same circles as Chappe, he likely read Chappe's *Voyage to Siberia*. In 1771, he sent more information about the banya to one of Catherine's closest advisors, Ivan Betskoi. By 1777, Sanches was ready to publicize his views. He made a presentation on the topic to the Royal Society of Medicine in Leiden. Then he published in Paris his *Traite sur les bains de vapeur de Russie*. It was quickly translated into German and Russian. The imperial press "for the use of Society" published it in St. Petersburg in 1779 and then in Moscow in 1791.[28]

In the book's introduction, Sanches expressed the hope that he could convince his readers of the "benefits of the banya." Aware of the broader debates about Russia's standing as an enlightened nation he saw his book as an opportunity to defend the reputation of the empire he had long served.[29] In private letters Sanches had brought the medical value of the banya to Catherine's attention. Now, with the publication of his book, he hoped to bring the word to his fellow medical experts throughout Europe. For the first time, an esteemed medical doctor made a sustained argument for the health benefits of the Russian banya.

Sanches set out to establish convincingly and in great detail that the Russian banya helped prevent and cure a wide range of diseases. First, he had to show that the banya had significant advantages over other forms of bathing that were gaining popularity in Western Europe at the time. He started by reviewing the history of "civilized" bathing dating back to the Greeks and the Romans. Those ancient civilizations understood that bathing was a necessary exercise for the maintenance of physical and mental health. The "barbarians" of Europe had failed to learn this lesson and bathing became a lost art during the Middle Ages in Western Europe. In contemporary Western Europe, he argued, bathing was too often treated as a luxury or indulgence. And, he added, even when people bathed for reasons related to health, they often did so in ways that were unlikely to achieve the desired results.[30]

Many of the practices gaining popularity in Europe, Sanches claimed, were too disorderly to offer any health benefits. The bathtub—where people submerged themselves in water—exposed a person's head to air that was a different temperature than water surrounding the rest of the body. This was bad for the lungs and created headaches, colds, and other health problems. In Germany and Italy, bathhouse attendants bled patients too often. The inconsistent temperature of the steam also led to illness. The Turkish baths gaining popularity in London were no better. The steam was often not refreshed, too many people breathed the same air, and the water that gathered and grew stagnant on the walls and the ground presented acute dangers to those who were exposed to it. All these bathing techniques threatened to weaken the body.

"The Russian banya alone," he insisted, was in a position to bring good health to people. Borrowing the best elements from ancient Greek and Roman baths, it created a room where the temperature, freshness of the steam, and the quality of the air, water, and fire could all be controlled. For people who felt strong and healthy, Sanches readily endorsed the full regimen: sweating, rubbing down with soap, steaming with a birch switch, and then washing down with warm or cold water. "From this," he explained, "the whole body will feel easy, fresh and the soul will also lighten. The banya is the great healer."[31]

For those who were sick or weak, it was even more important. He claimed that "bouts from strong exertion, from sudden changes in the air, from confusion and head colds, from many foods, from extravagant drink, and from other excesses of life, that lead to weakening and languor of the body and other things" could all be remedied in the banya. At another point, he added, "The banya is the best medicine for feelings of exhaustion, headaches, heavy eyes from movement or intense military activity, or hunting or agricultural work or from fishing or from factory work, for internal pain caused by falling off a horse, and other things." That was not all. "Great pain from the head, internal heat, or pain in the spine that does not allow you to lie down, pain in the stomach, dry tongue, jaundice, paleness or flushed face or red eyes or a change in voice, or chronic fever" could also be treated in the banya. He insisted that the banya could help with measles and "other kinds of ailments associated with strong internal heat, pain, and thirst and trouble breathing." And it could help remedy "vomiting, digestive ailments such as those that came from eating bad food, gas, sourness of the mouth and foul breath, and diarrhea." Symptoms associated with scurvy and smallpox, as well as cramps in the side, inflammation of the eyes, colds that were accompanied by fits or spasms or seizures, croup, and various blood ailments, could all be eased by the banya. He even recommended going to the banya after being bitten by "a dog or horse or cat or wolf" because sustained and intensive heat and sweating staved off rabies.[32]

Then there was the efficacy of the banya to treat venereal disease, an ailment on which Sanches was an expert and about which Catherine had expressed concern. He argued that when venereal diseases were advanced and difficult to treat, the banya helped with both pain and inflammation. Sanches had already posited that venereal diseases could be passed on from a mother to a newborn. He estimated that this fact helped explain why three out of ten children in large cities in Russia died in childbirth or soon thereafter. A well-timed visit to the banya within five or six days of childbirth could lower this death rate.[33]

When done properly, Sanches emphasized, even the mother of a newborn could benefit from the banya. During pregnancy and especially after child-birth, he explained, a woman's body was more open and exposed to air and water. This led to feelings of pain and light fevers, which the banya could help temper. And if breast-feeding did not proceed easily, the banya could also help with the flow of breast milk. Peasant women often went to the banya after giving birth; he urged well-to-do women—in Russia and beyond—to do the same.[34]

Despite the range of applications, Sanches emphasized that the banya was not a cure-all. For instance, he did not recommend that people who suffered from ailing nose, ears, face, hands, or fingers go to the banya. "Consumption, gout, paralysis and similar ailments" could not be helped by a trip to the banya either. And in some cases it was extremely dangerous to use soap or cold water. He warned that if the heat of the banya caused a bloody nose or blood in the urinary canal, then one should leave quickly, lie in a cold place, and then drink water with a bit of vinegar. He warned against entering the banya soon after eating, because the steam and heat stopped the digestive process. For that reason, the banya could not help with constipation. He also conceded that he was uncertain whether the banya could help treat various forms of cancer because he had not "experienced the success of using the banya for these ailments." Yet at least in this case he was willing to speculate that the banya might, with further study, prove beneficial.[35]

Sanches believed that the banya was dangerous if used improperly. He warned that some of the banya rituals of Russian peasants and laboring classes posed serious health risks. Unlike Westerners or elite Russians, the Russian lower classes did not need to be convinced to go to the banya. They went ha-bitually, but needed to learn how to use the banya correctly, Sanches thought. To replace what he saw as haphazard customs, he attempted to systematize treatments for specific diseases and ailments. Some diseases required the use of birch whisks; others did not. Some patients would benefit from a roll in the snow after a steam; others needed to sit in a warm bed. Some situations called for a single, long steam; others demanded a series of shorter visits. Some ailments were best treated by the first steam off the heated rocks; others were best treated when the room had cooled considerably. Sometimes drinking *kvas* or rubbing down with soap in the banya was recommended; other times these activities could cause great harm. Sanches's message was clear: making a habit of going to the banya was not enough; one had to know how to go to the banya. The implications were no less apparent: to transform the banya from a popular custom into a medical treatment, doctors were of paramount importance.[36]

Improper banya use among women, Sanches feared, could delay their menstrual periods and adversely affect fertility. Loss of blood from menstruation increased the potential dangers of any bloodletting that was undertaken in the banya. Pregnant women were especially vulnerable to having their digestion disrupted. The dangers were compounded after childbirth. "Among all the harmful uses of the banya," he wrote, "I must emphasize the habit, common throughout Russia, of mothers going into a hot banya with their newborn child within a few hours of giving birth." This harmful habit, which had "roots in the ancient customs of the people," would be hard to break. It endangered the mother because she ran the risk, at a particularly vulnerable moment, of entering into the heated room before the steam had been evenly distributed.[37]

The risks were even greater for newborns, who had yet to develop the capacity to fully circulate air through the lungs. The hot and humid air of the banya could disrupt the development of normal breathing in the crucial hours after birth. Further, babies' digestive systems were delicate. Going to the banya could delay the passing of the meconium, which the body needed to expunge in the first few days after birth. Going to the banya, he concluded, could be fatal for the "innocent child." He added, "The primary cause of death of the young in the first year of life is that they are taken to the banya during a particularly dangerous time." The proper use of the banya could help address the problem of infant mortality in the Russian empire.[38]

Sanches's systematic review of the treatment of various diseases relied both on his knowledge of the banya and on his expertise in Western medicine. The point was to convince doctors that using a Russian bathhouse had tremendous prophylactic and therapeutic potential. As Sanches noted, many ailments could be more successfully treated in a banya than by medicine. Catherine's concern with the lack of apothecaries in the empire appears to have been on his mind. "The Russian banya," he confidently declared, "can replace two-thirds of the medicines prescribed by medical science and the majority of apothecary works." Training more pharmacists would be difficult; building more banyas was fairly straightforward.[39]

Having established the potential benefits of the banya, the dangers of its misuse, and the importance of medical oversight of the process, Sanches turned his attention to what he saw as the role of the Russian state in public health. He recommended regulation and more administrative control over the empire's banyas. He pointed out that commercial banyas were in the hands of renters who ran them for their own profit and not for the benefit of the people. They were not concerned with creating conditions that were optimal for health. The police, in contrast, could regulate banyas, ensuring that people waited to enter the steam room until after it was properly prepared and that bleeding only took place with the oversight of a doctor.[40]

Sanches was on the cutting edge of a progressive vision of governance in which the maintenance of people's health was a national concern and responsibility. He called on the state to build more banyas or, at the very least, create advantageous terms for businessmen who might. Architects trained in the medical uses of the banya could design them and oversee their construction. Sanches provided details about what material to use, how to build canals to supply clean water and remove refuse, and the proper size of the oven and each room in the banya. The priority was maintaining and strengthening health, not increasing income for the banya owners or revenue for the state.

Since businessmen were bound to prioritize profits over health, Sanches proposed the introduction of banyas designed specifically for medical use. "The government," he insisted, "should find within its abilities to build banyas for the treatment of illnesses . . . . These should be built and maintained by the police." Commercial banyas were sufficient for most people, so long as attention was paid to when and how the banya was used. But certain ailments required going to a banya more than once a day or for many hours at a time. This meant that the heat in the banya had to be maintained. Commercial banyas could not always do this—the steam room was periodically cooled down to allow the humid air to dissipate. The "medical banyas" would have parallel steam rooms, so that when one *parilka* was cooling down, another could be heated. Only this would create the conditions for patients who needed extensive or complicated treatments.[41]

Sanches's vision of state intervention, administration, and regulation went even further. He called on the police, as an administrative arm of the state, to take over responsibility for the private banyas run by individuals on their own land. The police, Sanches suggested, could oversee how they were built, devise rules for proper conduct within them, and regulate their operations. "The leaders of the state economy," he wrote, needed to prioritize "the maintenance and strengthening of the body." A well-regulated banya would be a boon for the state.[42]

In keeping with modern governance practices, Sanches connected the health of individuals with the health of the state more generally. The economy and the military relied on healthy subjects. "Without food and health a people can not grow. And without growth there will be no agriculture, trade, and defense of the fatherland." Sanches pointed out that it was generally accepted that the police and government needed to make rules for the use of water and canals. Given the role of the banya in maintaining health, it should be governed by rules as well.[43]

Sanches ended his book by stating that he had once been told that when Peter the Great was forging the modern Russian military, he had been asked whether there was a need to train medical doctors. Peter evidently responded, "Not for Russia. The banya alone is enough." Sanches, the former military doctor, agreed that "it would be hard to find medical doctors that can do as much for the health of the people as can the proper use of the banya." That was the message he hoped to spread not just in Russia but at the top European medical universities.[44]

———•—•———

Sanches had a profound long-term impact on the way Europeans and Russians conceived of the banya. He was the first medical expert to articulate the importance of the banya for health and hygiene in a scholarly book and to defend banya procedures using scholarly language. Sanches was much more specific than any of his predecessors about how the banya contributed to health. He gave very detailed instructions about what diseases the banya could treat and how the proper treatments were supposed to be administered. The fact that he had Catherine the Great's ear and support only increased the importance of his writing. Prior to Sanches the banya was primarily a space for respite, spiritual ablution, and magic. For the state it contributed to the tax base. Inasmuch as it was associated with physical health, it was as a folk or vernacular practice, not something based in the medicine of doctors and scholars. Sanches changed that decisively.

He also connected the banya to broader issues of public health, noting that keeping individual citizens healthy was essential to the overall military and economic might of the state. Without a healthy populace, the ability to undertake military campaigns, conduct trade, and increase production would all be compromised. In a modern state, the banya was a crucial public good, not merely a direct source of revenue. It followed that the police would regulate and control banyas to ensure that the priorities of the state were being met.

Perhaps most importantly, Sanches was exceptionally well placed to make the case for the banya both in learned circles in Western Europe and in political circles in Russia. His stature as a well-known and well-respected doctor in Paris provided Catherine the Great with a powerful tool to rebut Chappe's disparagement of the banya and of Russian customs more generally. Sanches offered a resounding challenge to the centuries-long trend of denigrating the banya as a striking example of Russian backwardness and barbarism. Rather than confronting Chappe directly, Sanches presented a new way of viewing the banya. His timing, writing during the second half of the eighteenth century, meant that he found at least a partially sympathetic audience among progressive doctors in Europe. As medical and then popular attitudes toward bathing changed in the West, blanket denunciations began to be tempered by an appreciation for the banya as a potential tool for personal and public health.

It was one thing to prescribe how to build, maintain, regulate, and use the banya. It was quite another to ensure that the people of the empire—or the government—followed those prescriptions. Sanches's immediate impact in Russia was not broad, despite Catherine's favorable attention. The state hardly had the infrastructure or will to apply his vision. Foreigners continued to produce Chappe-like descriptions of the banya, replete with incredulity about the procedures and astonishment about open nudity. When Giacomo Casanova, the Venetian adventurer and author, bought a young peasant girl as a sex slave he was told that his only obligation was to let her "go to the bath every Saturday so that she can go to the church on Sunday." He also marveled at the chance to go with her to the banya with the "company of thirty or forty other people, both men and women and all stark naked."[45] Sanches may have won over some doctors, but popular understanding of the banya still belonged to those who thought of it as an age-old custom that was both sanctioned and titillating.

In the eighteenth century many Russian elites, influenced by their Western peers, distanced themselves from the banya as a respectable activity to undertake. For many of them the banya still meant nudity, sex, danger, and an embarrassing ancient habit, not the preservation of hygiene and the prevention of disease. But Sanches's work repositioned it as an essential tool for a modern state. Over time, as Russian doctors began to reassess what they saw as the predominantly peasant and working-class custom of going to the banya, they turned to Sanches as a key source. When they did, his book became a lodestar for understanding this sorely neglected institution of hygiene for rich and poor alike. For the majority, at least for the time being, the banya remained a marker of Russia's uncivilized tradition. For a few, the banya was on its way to becoming modern.

3

Soot, Dirt, and Human Flesh Packed Together

IN THE NINETEENTH CENTURY medical endorsements of prophylactic bathing became common in much of Europe. Outside of Russia, support for public bathhouses aligned with the further development of practical science and the use of government regulation and policing to strengthen society and the state. One might assume that Russian doctors and government officials would follow Catherine the Great's lead and the European trend and begin defending banyas in the name of public health as well. They did not. In Russia at this time the path to the acceptance of the health benefits of steam bathing and, in turn, the imperial state's advocacy of the banya as a public good was neither straightforward nor inevitable. Support for prophylactic bathing dispersed more slowly and unevenly than it did outside the country. Skeptics remained dominant among experts until the 1860s and 1870s. Even in the 1880s, some Russian doctors fretted that going to the banya was harmful to bathers.[1]

This lack of enthusiasm for the medicinal banya in Russia partly had to do with the well-established bathhouse culture that served entrenched commercial interests. Banya owners and workers (*banshchiki*) were motivated by profit. They were neither agents of the state nor or of the medical community. Indeed, they often undermined any rules and regulations that authorities tried to impose on them. Bathers, for their part, had their own ideas about how to properly go to the banya and were loath to listen to doctors' orders or to follow the state's regulations. There were technical obstacles as well. Existing banyas could not easily be remade into institutions of public health. Western European bathhouses were built from the bottom up with state-of-the art technology for filtering bath water and ventilating air. Government officials oversaw them. In contrast, in Russia existing banyas could not be retrofitted easily or inexpensively to meet new hygienic standards and the state lacked the bureaucratic infrastructure to closely regulate behavior.

Another reason banyas could not smoothly fit into the emerging role bathhouses occupied in Western Europe was the long-standing and persistent association of banyas with an unreformed Russia—and thus the common people (*narod*). In Europe the challenge became how to get the lower classes to go to bathhouses; in Russia the challenge was to convince educated doctors and municipal bureaucrats that the lower-class habit of going to the banya had some health benefits after all. In Western Europe public bathhouses were new and could be seen as exemplars of modern governance and hygiene. In Russia banyas had always existed—any new role had to be superimposed onto an existing set of assumptions and practices.

While the banya's medical utility remained a matter of debate, banyas continued to develop in Russia as sites of profit and sociability. Innovative banya operators recognized that they could draw in wealthier clients and make more money if they offered a range of services at a range of prices. The number of banyas grew in Russian cities because they were profitable, popular, and social, not because they were healthy or state-supported.

At the same time, an emerging form of cultural patriotism rooted in an image of the *narod* made it possible to see the banya as an emblem of the Russian nation. The banya's association with the peasantry made it hard for doctors to see its value. That same association, however, heightened the sense that the banya remained untainted by Westernization and therefore able to nurture the true Russian spirit. Centuries of aspersions about the banya could be recast as attributes. The "torture" and "beatings" that foreigners complained about became points of pride. The banya, like the *narod*, represented a resilient Russian authenticity that resisted Europeanization. To the deepest thinkers, this was no simple patriotism. The banya, like Russia, was full of contradictions. Later in the century, novelist Fyodor Dostoevsky was drawn to the ambiguity of the banya—as clean and dirty, as pure and corrupt, and as a potential gateway to both hell and salvation. The Russian predicament was the human predicament; the human predicament could be summed up by the banya.

Sanches's vision of a vast network of banyas designed to benefit health and overseen by a well-ordered state did not gain traction for much of the nineteenth century, at least not in Russia. Adolf Pliushar's *Encyclopedic Dictionary*, an authoritative publication that reflected the leading edge of Russian knowledge in the 1830s, makes this clear.[2] Bathing in general was worthy of considerable attention: three long entries on various aspects of the topic took up eight double-columned pages in the encyclopedia. But the sub-section on the "Russian steam bath" received only a half a page. The entries were cautious about the utility of bathing. Cold tubs slowed and weakened the pulse, making breathing hard, and shocked and chilled the whole body; warm tubs, when excessively used, weakened the body and had destructive effects; and hot water baths were even more dangerous and could only be used with extreme caution. Mineral baths, sea baths, mud baths, and sun or air baths each promised both specific potential health benefits and costs. "Animal baths" (when "a sick person surrounds his body with the insides of a freshly killed animal") and "electrical baths" (when "a person lies on a bed or sits on a stool, with a glass peduncle and then is connected by wires to an electrical machine") had limited applications. No bath of any kind was recommended for use without caution and reservations.[3]

The "Russian steam bath" or banya too was considered a viable, if risky, treatment for particular ailments. But it was neither given a privileged place in the encyclopedia's treatment of bathing nor was it considered necessary or recommended. Its main feature was extreme heat. The encyclopedia noted that the temperature in the banya, in contrast with other baths, reached as high as 60 Reaumur (or the boiling point of water). "Those who sought out heat," it explained, knew that these temperatures were best endured "when the head [of the bather] is covered with a damp bucket or a wet towel." No matter the precautions, the banya could have powerful effects (both positive and negative) "not just for the skin but for the whole body." The entry lamented that medical research on the effect of the banya was not well developed and speculated about its potential as a treatment for consumption—but little else.[4] This was a far cry from the ringing endorsement Sanches had put forth over six decades earlier.

The encyclopedia's history of baths—from the ancient world through Byzantium to the present—ignored the banya. Instead, large and luxurious public baths in Turkish cities represented the logical culmination of a millennium-long history, in part because "Ablutions are one of the first dogmas of faith for all Muslim people." It made no similar claim about the Russian people. The encyclopedia made clear that circa 1835, the banya merited little attention in doctors' understanding of bathing. There were plenty of urban banyas in Russia at the time and even more of them in rural areas, but the experts did not see them as basic necessities or as particularly advantageous ways of getting clean.[5]

Those educated Russians who were not experts on the topic of bathing were even less likely to see any practical use of going to the banya. The Europeanization of the gentry over the course of the previous century had contributed to elite disdain for the lower classes and their habits. The banyas may have been "indispensable to the common people," as one pro-bathing observer put it, but those in better circumstances had begun to follow their Western European peers' habit of either avoiding bathing altogether or privatizing their ablutions. The Russian upper classes eschewed the seemingly extreme and physically dangerous banya in keeping with what the same observer regretted was a "soft and effeminate age" in the rest of Europe.[6] This parting of the ways of the elite and the peasantry in Russia occurred in attitudes toward bathing, as in other cultural realms.[7]

Derogatory opinions about bathing brought the Russian elite closer to their European peers. Many learned people in Western Europe in the first half of the nineteenth century did not accept the new medical ideas that prescribed a daily bath. Instead, they saw bathing as a persistent remnant of an old and outdated lower-class custom. That the poor did not bathe in much of Europe was often taken as a sign of progress, not backwardness. Only the "lowly Russians," one foreigner observed in the 1830s, continued "to boil their skins in steam and perspiration" because they did not "enjoy the blessing of clean linen." According to this view, only by "giving up the practice of bathing altogether" had the Europeanized elite in Russia progressed as far as the lower classes elsewhere. The fact that the Russian lower classes still bathed indicated that they remained backward and uncivilized.[8] Writing in the late 1830s, the Marquis de Custine—a French aristocrat and travel writer who made his name by deriding Russia's veneer of European respectability—was disgusted by the public banyas of the empire: "The warm humidity there is so favorable to insect life, the clothes laid down in them are nurseries of many vermin, that the visitor rarely departs without carrying with him some irrefragable proof of the sordid negligence of the lower orders."[9] Custine's views clearly echoed Chappe's.

By mid-century, a small minority of Russia's elite may have frequented luxurious sections of public banyas in the major cities or made going to a banya on their estates an eccentric ritual, but most upper-class Russians were not familiar with the procedure or dismissed it as a habit peculiar to the peasants and manual laborers. They saw urban bathhouses in particular as vulgar commercial enterprises. The combination of the banya's association with the peasantry in the countryside and debauchery in the cities made many Russian elite dismiss out of hand the notion that habitual bathing could be healthy.

Even Russian doctors explored the medical applications of the banya from a position of deep skepticism. An 1835 article in the leading medical journal *Friend of Health (Drug zdraviia)* blamed the "peasant custom" of going to the banya for high infant mortality and even high death rates among older children of the Russian "simple people." Doctors were "completely confident" that the banya brought more harm than good. Thankfully, the "educated classes" had adopted the less harmful—though still dangerous, in their estimation—habit of bathing their children in warm baths.[10] An article in the same journal on the "use of medicines to treat ailments of the extremities" conceded that the banya could be beneficial for some respiratory ailments, but lamented that many "craftsmen and peasants" caused themselves great harm by going to the banya each week and sometimes even two or three times a day when they were sick. Their "ignorance" was even more harmful to their children, who often accompanied them. Yet doctors felt helpless in confronting the problems caused by the banya. They assumed that the lower classes would not listen to doctors' warnings. "Who from this group of people is going to admit that the banya is the primary cause of illnesses?" the article asked rhetorically. Efforts to convince the peasants to give up the banya were futile and some doctors feared that the custom was spreading.[11]

Doctors' tendency to see the banya negatively was only slightly tempered by stories of its potential value in treating dangerous medical conditions. Insights into the banya often came from outside the medical mainstream. Its use contrasted sharply with conventional, professional wisdom. Updates from the empire's periphery introduced the possibility of using the banya in extreme situations when professionally prescribed treatments proved ineffective. In Warsaw, for example, doctors were powerless in treating a child with lockjaw caused by tetanus. The patient's desperate father, having heard on the street that the banya might help, took the boy to the steam room. Miraculously, a medical journal reported, after fifteen minutes the boy's jaw loosened and in thirty minutes he was able to eat.[12] In Georgia, the banya evidently cured the symptoms caused by a rabid animal's bite.[13] In each case, going to the banya was a method of last resort after other treatments proved ineffective.

Even a lone article explicitly praising the banya clarified the extent to which it remained a novel and distrusted tool in most modern doctors' arsenals. Peter Leikhfeld, a medical surgeon and former senior physician of the Petropavlovsk Hospital, was enthusiastic about the curative powers of the steam bath, but with little impact. He argued that despite the primitive conditions in which they lived and toiled, the "Russian peasants" were healthy, strong, and able to withstand changes of temperature in part because of their use of the banya.[14] Conceding that this was primarily a peasant custom in Russia, he lamented that the elite did not habitually bathe and therefore were unable to take advantage of its medical benefits. Unfortunately, to his mind, Russian doctors were ill informed about the banya. He had a point—Russian medical journals greeted his isolated plea for the banya with silence. From 1841 to 1870 only a single article in *Friend of Health* even mentioned steam bathing and that was a translation of a French article on the Turkish bath.[15] In order to appreciate the potential value of the banya Russia doctors needed to see past its association with the lower sorts and temper their skepticism about bathing more generally. Writing in the *Moscow Medical Journal* in 1856, the doctor P. I. Strakhov—speaking for the minority—chastised his colleagues for ignoring the banya. Scorn for the peasantry, in his estimation, had hindered their ability to learn from this useful "folk wisdom." "There are many treatments and medicines in Russia," he wrote, "that appear crass and incomprehensible, but all of them are worthy of judicious attention of doctors and careful research and not disdain simply because they are used by the common people. This is exactly the situation with the Russian people's steam bath." Doctors' ridicule meant that they had been blind to the importance of banyas.[16]

While Strakhov's Russian colleagues dismissed the banya, Western doctors were taking the lead in studying the topic in earnest. Despite the disdain for bathing coming from the Marquis de Custine and his ilk, some foreign medical experts began to extol the public health benefits of the banya. One German traveler to St. Petersburg in the early 1830s informed his Western readers that "love of cleanliness implied by this universal custom must be admitted to be extremely creditable to this northern people." He added, "There is no refreshment more acceptable to the senses or more salutary than is that of the bath; it is wholesome, bracing, and purifying." He turned the class assumptions of most European elites on their head: he pointed out how odd it was that his peers in the German aristocracy considered a steam bath a rare luxury while the "lowly Russian peasant" treated going to the banya like it was an essential element of basic hygiene.[17] A French doctor explored the topic in a book titled *Characteristics of Hygiene and Medicine of the Russian*

taking place in teeming cities meant that the health of any particu.
ment of the population was of concern to the whole. Municipal govern
responded to the urban stench by building waterworks and sewage system.
by regulating slaughterhouses. They responded to the stench of individuais by
building bathhouses. For hundreds of years Europeans had associated urban
bathhouses with disease and promiscuity and they had all but disappeared
from most major cities. But with changing notions of health, bathing became
a tool for modern hygiene and bathhouses became a new marker of sound
municipal government.[28] Given the longer history of European ridicule of the
banya, it was ironic that European doctors took the lead in recognizing its
potential importance.

The irony was not lost on Russian doctors, who were forced to concede
that the banya—a quintessentially Russian institution—had been studied
and appreciated more by their European colleagues than by themselves. As
late as 1881, an article in the leading Russian medical journal noted that "it is
shameful to say" that scientific work on the banya had been undertaken "not
here [in Russia] but abroad and mostly in Germany." The author added, "Only
in the last 3–4 years has attention been paid to the question here."[29] In 1883
V. V. Godlevskii wrote in his medical dissertation "On Material for the Study
of the Russian Banya" that foreigners, not Russians, had been the driving force
behind the study of bathhouses, even in Russia.[30] It was not uncommon for
Russian doctors to need to catch up with their Western European colleagues.
The "shame" came from having to do so when exploring a topic that in practice had long been thought of—and usually ridiculed—as a Russian mainstay.

———•—•———

Banyas developed in Russia over the course of the first half of the nineteenth
century, just not in ways that Sanches or Catherine the Great had envisioned.
Banya operators, not doctors or the state, came up with the innovations.
Until 1800 urban banyas generally resembled larger versions of their rural
counterparts. They usually had one large steam room but little else. Clients
often washed off with soap and buckets of water in the courtyard or along a
riverbank. Steam was the key thing. Special medical banyas, usually associated
with foreigners, had existed in hospitals for the treatment of extreme medical
conditions. But few among the elite believed that a weekly bath was part of a
healthy prophylactic regimen. The state, at that point, was mostly concerned
with revenue, safety, and propriety. Some laws insisted that men and women
bathe separately and be out of eyesight of one another. Other laws attempted

to protect neighborhoods surrounding banyas from smoke or the constant threat of fires. Placing banyas in close proximity to rivers had less to do with ensuring clean water for patrons than with fire prevention.[31]

The main structural innovation in urban banyas of the nineteenth century—a tiered pricing and amenities system—was motivated by a drive for profits, not a concern for the well-being of bathers. The most common patrons (of both sexes) were the so-called simple people—the urban poor who, unlike the elite, never became sufficiently "enlightened" to forego bathing as a basic necessity. But from the point of view of those in the banya business, the simple people's potential as a source of revenue was limited. Banya owners and operators needed income in order to pay for a license from the state to run the banyas. They sought to make more money than they were obliged to pay. Increasing ticket prices was rarely feasible. The poor insisted on going to the banya, but could not afford to pay much more than a few kopeks. The rich could forego the banya and often did. Operators could potentially increase revenue by overselling tickets, which resulted in overcrowding. The more crowded the banyas became, the less likely they were to attract a wealthier clientele. Another option for the operators was to minimize the amount of money they spent on heat, water, buckets, soap, and basic upkeep. This combination of cost cutting and overcrowding meant that the conditions for the average bather deteriorated. Even before doctors had become advocates of bathing, they began to recognize that the drive for profits led to conditions in urban banyas that threatened the well-being of the patrons.

At the beginning of the nineteenth century, owners hit upon the idea of providing access to special rooms and extra services at higher prices. This required an initial investment in new buildings or at the very least significant remodeling of older baths. A new bathhouse owner, Sila Sandunov, was among the first to introduce the innovation. After a successful acting career at Catherine the Great's court, he and his wife, a favorite of the empress's, moved to Moscow. Sandunov sold a diamond that his wife had received directly from Catherine and used the money to buy land and fund the building of a new banya on the Neglinnyi River, in the center of Moscow and only a twenty-minute walk from Red Square. Sandunov was a Georgian who associated the banya with comfort and leisure. In Georgia, "eastern baths," which had roots in the baths of Byzantium, emphasized the social aspects of the public bathhouse. At his new banya, Sandunov offered patrons in Moscow the option to bathe in more socially exclusive and luxurious conditions in isolation from the masses. Poorer patrons could continue to pay a few kopeks to go to rudimentary sections of the building, while the better-off could pay more money for private rooms with leather couches and personal attendants.[32] The Russian sweat lodge further melded with the transnational tradition of luxurious bathing in large urban buildings.

Sandunov's banya was also constructed of stone and built to last. When Napoleon occupied the city in 1812 and Moscow burned, many of the city's old-style banyas were destroyed, including many communal banyas and those that had been on private estates. Sandunov's banya survived. Like the city itself, the communal banya stock recovered—but the new elite sections became more common. They had the added incentive of providing services to elites, many of whom could no longer bathe at home.[33]

By the 1840s, the Imperial Senate, at the recommendation of the Ministry of Internal Affairs, began to codify the tiered service system. The state's goal was to ensure that conditions for the poor clients met a minimum standard at an affordable, consistent, and clear price. A decree in 1843 formally divided the capital's commercial banyas into four sections with strict price regulations. Three years later a similar decree regulated the standards and pricing for variegated services in Moscow banyas.[34] The new system made clear which patrons should go where and what conditions they might expect to find.

The first section had an entry fee of 3 kopeks and typically had room for 50 to 120 bathers at a time. It remained rudimentary and catered to the poorest patrons. The main attraction was the steam room—entrances, washrooms, and water supply were sometimes nonexistent. Those who could afford 8 kopeks could visit the second section, where they could find less crowded steam rooms and washrooms. The third section cost 15 kopeks and catered to those from the "middling estates" who rarely had bathing facilities in their homes. It was sometimes called the "noble" banya, because the high price meant that it was prohibitively expensive for the common folk. It provided semiprivate sitting areas with couches and servants; lavishly appointed washrooms, sometimes with swimming pools; and a less crowded steam room.

Finally, in the fourth section patrons could rent a private room for a few hours for rates starting at 75 kopeks and going up to a ruble and a half. This section was sometimes called the "family" banya, because unlike the common sections, men and women could bathe together there. It was also called the "numbered" banya, because each room could be rented out for personal use, like a numbered hotel room. While the steam rooms there often looked like smaller, private versions of the steam rooms in the other sections of the bathhouse, the changing rooms and washrooms, at least in principle, were filled with more comfortable furniture, nicer services, cleaner basins, and much more space for the clients.[35] The wealthiest clients, who went to the most expensive sections, provided the bathhouse workers with their greatest opportunity to make money from tips in exchange for services.

The family banyas soon attracted the attention of the Ministry of Internal Affairs. An 1846 decree about Moscow banyas insisted that the fourth section no longer be called family banyas—because operators were allowing men and women to enter the banya together under the pretense that they were husband and wife when they were not. Echoing an earlier ruling, the decree emphasized that under no circumstances were adult men and women allowed to bathe together in commercial bathhouses.[36] The effort proved futile: both the name "family baths" and the custom of mixed-sex bathing in them persisted.

Health was not entirely irrelevant from the state's point of view. However, they saw banyas more as a potential threat to public health than a salve. In 1841, when a group of soldiers fell ill after visiting a banya in St. Petersburg, the city inspected thirty-five commercial banyas and found that the sections for the "simple people" often did not have soap and that bathers rinsed themselves off in open courtyards, because there was no room indoors for washing. This had been perfectly normal forty years earlier. But the government decrees of the 1840s called on banya owners to incorporate enclosed washrooms into their 3-kopek sections. At this point neither the state nor doctors were paying much attention to water quality, temperature regulation, air quality, or controlling the behaviors of people, aside from mixed-sex bathing.[37] The medical literature had yet to identify the importance of those standards. In any case, most owners and operators could not afford the capital outlay for even basic upgrades, failed to abide by the decrees, and continued to keep their businesses afloat by providing rudimentary services to the "simple people."[38]

By the middle of the nineteenth century variegated banyas could be found in some of the major cities of the empire. A few had four tiers of service, while many had only one or two. This system—designed around class distinctions and luxury in order to generate wealth, not health—remained in place for the next seventy-five years. Working-class men and women tended to go to the least expensive sections. As one observer later noted, "clerks, coachmen, cabbies, sweepers, street vendors, postmen, watchmen, trash men, conductors, unskilled workers, and servants" went to either the first or second sections.[39] One doctor reported that "real lovers of the banyas and admirers of the 'sport' of the banya" understood that the "best steam" could often be found there. Evidently carters, butchers, and Finns were particularly fond of a well-run steam room and took pains to ensure that the heat and humidity were to their liking.[40] Though the elite found the first and second sections loathsome, the urban lower classes went because they thought it was good for them.

Water was usually hauled in from a nearby river; waste water was often sent back into the same river or into a swamp outside the bathhouse. Only a few Russian cities in the nineteenth century had city water and sewage systems, and these too relied on local rivers both to supply water and to wash away refuse. Washrooms were furnished with benches and tubs (usually wooden) and, in the first section, were often crowded with those trying to wash their clothes. Clients used hand-held basins with water, along with a sponge and soap, to wash and rinse themselves. They often also whisked themselves and one another with switches made from the branches and leaves of young birch or other trees. Sometimes people added a shampoo or a massage administered by an acquaintance or paid extra money to be attended to by a *banshchik* (bathhouse attendant).

The increased importance of *banshchiki* was another major innovation of the nineteenth century. This too had more to do with service and luxury than health. *Banshchiki* were responsible for conditions in each of the four sections of the bathhouse. As a rule (that was sometimes broken), male bathhouse workers served the men's sections and female workers served the women's sections. Doctors considered *banshchiki* of both sexes important to a well-functioning banya. How thoroughly *banshchiki* cleaned the banya and the quality of the services they provided went a long way toward determining whether a banya was healthy or dangerous. But *banshchiki* were not agents of public health. Like the banya owners and their operators, their goal was to make a profit. They did not receive a salary. Instead they paid operators for the right to work. They often formed cooperative associations that pooled both responsibilities and revenues. *Banshchiki* often came from outside of urban areas, got jobs in the city through kinship networks, and, when they could, sent earnings back home. Ultimately, their livelihood depended on pleasing their clients, not inspectors.

Even if *banshchiki* wanted to prioritize health, circumstances presented serious obstacles. The *banshchiki's* job was arduous and time consuming. They would begin heating the steam room around midnight on nights before the banyas operated, when they would stoke stoves using wood or coal as fuel. Because of drafts and poor ventilation, smoke inevitably filled the steam room and surrounding rooms even in banyas with chimneys. Early in the morning, when the stones glowed with heat, the fire would be dosed, the ashes dispersed, and any smoke that had built up in the room in the process was aired out by the cross-ventilation created by opening both the door to the washroom and a little window in the corner of the steam room. Finally, when the smoke had cleared, the *banshchiki* closed the door and window and tossed water, sometimes mixed with herbs or essences in solution, onto the hot stones to create steam and intense heat. The heating and steaming process would also warm the washroom and would be used to heat vats to provide hot water for bathing.

The morning sessions could start as early as 5 a.m. and usually lasted until mid-day. In the afternoon, when the stones had cooled too much to create enough steam to heat the room, the process would be repeated—*banshchiki* would clear out the steam room for a few hours, then restoke the fire and reheat the stones. On some days the operators might get away with heating the banya only once, meaning that those clients who came later in the day might get access to warm water, but no real steam. Crowds were biggest on Saturdays and holidays, often making it difficult in the common sections of the banya to find a seat or basin in the washroom and a spot to stand and whisk oneself in the steam room. This was true in both men's and women's sections. Women's sections were generally smaller than men's sections, in part because cities tended to have fewer women than men and in part because women were better able to spread their use of the banya evenly throughout the week, whereas workingmen tended to go on Saturdays.[41]

Not only were *banshchiki* responsible for the overall upkeep of the baths, they also had to haul in fuel, tend to the fires, and monitor the steam. Female bathhouse workers performed most of the same duties as their male counterparts—but were usually spared from hauling fuel or manning the stove. They all hoped to receive tips (or "a little something for tea") from clients who appreciated the overall atmosphere. They could also profit from selling *veniki*, soap, and sponges. But they made the most money in the form of tips exchanged for services provided to individual clients. The cooperative association might include barbers who could cut hair, attend to corns and minor ailments, and cup and bleed clients. Some attendants provided personalized attention to individual clients in the steam room—soaping them, whisking them with switches, and hauling and pouring water for them. They also provided massages on tables in the steam rooms or in private rooms in the more expensive sections. A "bath day" would end for the *banshchiki* as late as one or two in the morning, when those on the night shift would stoke the fire for another day's work. On off days the *banshchiki* cleaned the facilities and resupplied the banya for upcoming sessions.[42]

Duties unrelated to direct service to clients could be skipped or done haphazardly with little loss of income for the cooperative. This meant that conditions in bathhouses, particularly in the first and second sections, were poor while profits in the third and fourth sections could far exceed the limits the state attempted to impose on ticket prices.

The tiered system improved the financial viability of urban commercial banyas. By the middle of the nineteenth century there was a banya boom that outpaced the growing urban population. In 1833 St. Petersburg had twenty-nine commercial banyas for approximately 450,000 people (approximately one for every 15,500 people living in the city): by 1865 it had fifty commercial banyas for 600,000 people (approximately one for every 12,000 people.)[43] In Moscow the number of banyas also increased faster than the population during the middle of the century. The banya boom was driven by market forces and sustained by the potential for profits. Owners, operators, *banshhiki*, and clients—not doctors or the state—had spurred the redesign and expansion of urban banyas.

* * *

Centuries of foreign disparagement had asserted that steaming in the banya typified Russian eternal backwardness. Seen in another light, this adherence to an age-old custom could be taken as a sign of national resilience, not a lack of civility. The fact that at least traditionally, Russians bathed and Western Europeans did not may have been a point of embarrassment to some Russians in the years before bathing became recognized as potentially healthy. But that same sense of difference could also be used to point out the degree to which Russia was following its own path and could defend its own customs. Because it was peculiar, the banya could be trumpeted as a positive marker of national identity. Approval from the medical materialists of the West was irrelevant if the banya was primarily a symbol of Russia, not a harbinger of health.

Napoleon's invasion in 1812 brought to Russia an upsurge of nationalism similar to that spreading throughout the continent. That trend took hold in Russia quickly and helped turn foreign—and particularly French—ridicule of Russian bathing habits into a cultural asset rather than liability. The defeat of Napoleon challenged the elite's assumption that the West was by definition superior and more civilized than the simple Russian people. The *narod*, it now seemed, had proved their true value. After the century of Westernization begun under Peter the Great, returning to Slavic traditions and customs seemed to be the best way to set Russia on its proper historical path.[44] Educated Russians in search of authentic folk wisdom could recast the banya as a point of national pride, precisely because it was popular with the common people and had been crudely disparaged by so many foreigners. A peculiar phenomenon resulted: just as Westerners were beginning to embrace bathing for its forward-looking promise of universal health, Russians were solidifying their attachment to the institution because it represented their empire's unique and seemingly timeless character.

The French Revolution and the Napoleonic Wars destabilized existing discourses about bathing in different ways in Western Europe than they did in Russia. In the wake of revolutionary upheaval in France and the government reforms that followed around the continent, cities and states began to take on responsibility for the well-being of their citizens. Discovering that bathing was healthy slowly led experts to see support for public bathhouses as a sign of progressive governance.[45] In Russia, however, bathhouses had never ceased to be popular in the first place and the progressive medical discourse would not take firm hold until after the Great Reforms of the 1860s. In the meantime, the banya's reputation as a positive symbol of Russianness had time to mature.

Ivan Terebenev's popular broadside printed in 1812, after the Grand Armee had been decimated in Russia, displayed an early example of Russian pride in the banya. In it Napoleon appears in the steam room of a banya, surrounded by three Russian soldiers. The banya—with its steam, heat, and birch switches—was clearly a Russian and, to outsiders at least, exotic institution. Terebenev did not avoid the clichés about the banya, but instead

FIGURE 3.1 Ivan Terebenev's broadside showed soldiers beating Napoleon in the banya. Courtesy of New York Public Library.

reworked them to Russia's advantage. The banya allowed Terebenev to use caricature and popular imagery to convey a sense of patriotism and positive Russian identity.[46] Napoleon, like a stereotypical foreigner, abhors the banya. "I've never withstood such torture in my life! They are scraping and roasting me like in Hell," he complains. The Russians, in contrast, are diligently adding to the heat and steam and whisking Napoleon with a traditional *venik*. "You were the one who entered the Russian banya," one solider reminds him. Another suggests Napoleon will long remember how the Russians beat him "from spine to flank." The banya was not embarrassingly backward. Instead it exemplified Russian resilience in the face of foreign occupation. The epic defeat of Napoleon signaled to elite Russians the importance of their own folk and national traditions. The banya highlighted Russian superiority to Western Europe. This Romantic and patriotic vision of the banya emerged far less from its association with hygiene than from its association with the victorious and pure *narod*.

The contradictory possibilities exemplified by the banya caught the attention of writers as well. Some turned to the banya as a space that allowed specifically Russian qualities to endure. The banya nourished and protected traditional ideals from a harsh world. In *Ruslan and Ludmila*, Alexander Pushkin's epic poem set in medieval Rus', the "magnificent Russian banya" distracts one of Ruslan's rivals. The steam, the *veniki*, and the nudity of young maids in the banya drain the khazar khan Ratimir of his martial resolve and make him forget about Ludmila. As was the case with Napoleon, the mythical Russian banya protected Russia from an outside threat because it was no place for a foreigner.[47]

If the banya was traditional, it was important to trace its lineage. Nikolai Karamzin, a favorite historian of the Emperor Alexander who participated in a new wave of conservatism after 1812, declared with some pride that ancient Slavs considered going to the banya an important rite.[48] Again, the point was not hygiene. If anything, for Karamzin and other members of the elite in the period, bathing continued to be associated with physical danger and perhaps an extreme medical remedy. The banya, instead, was a defining characteristic of Russianness.

Over the course of the nineteenth century, as medical opinions about the banya gradually became more favorable, some sympathetic doctors began to superimpose ideas about proper hygiene on top of the seemingly ancient tradition of going to the banya. The banya was both deeply intertwined with Russia's past and indicative of the Russian people's intuitive wisdom about health. This was a strange amalgamation that grounded legitimacy in both popular tradition and new medical ideas. Russian advocates of the banya traced its Russian roots to pre-Christian Slavs and also saw it as an outgrowth of Greek, Roman, and Byzantine bathing customs. It was uniquely Russian and, at the same time, comparable to baths and showers. The lingering folk customs associated with it proved its authenticity; yet doctors assumed, as Sanches had, that those very customs would soon die out. Tradition and history were supposed to give way to hygiene and science.[49] The banya's contradictions were Russia's contradictions: it originated in and evolved toward something unique and incomparable and it simultaneously shared in a common European heritage; it was a hybrid, neither wholly exceptional nor wholly typical in its history or its destiny. The banya encapsulated the paradoxes of a socially, politically, and culturally conservative empire confronting the modern age.

References in Pushkin, Karamzin, and elsewhere notwithstanding, it was not until later in the century that the banya as a place representing a traditional way of life made its way into fiction. The writer Fyodor Dostoevsky saw the banya as a place that could potentially both rejuvenate and befoul and where dirt could make things transparent. In his work it is often impossible to be certain whether the characters represent the author's views or ones that he is struggling against or whether the point is the struggle itself. The banya, as it had developed as a symbol over the nineteenth century, helped give those ambiguities a physical presence. Dostoevsky addressed the banya in his *Notes from the House of the Dead* (1860–1862), a semiautobiographical story about a nobleman in prison in Siberia in the 1850s, where Dostoevsky spent four years in exile. Alexander Petrovich Gorianchikov, the narrator of the story, comes into contact with common folk, for whom he develops respect and admiration. The banya tests the limits of his understanding. One Christmas, the convicts receive permission to go to the banya, which they consider a special treat. Gorianchikov is apprehensive. Guards march the chained prisoners out of their barracks and across town. They do not go to the noble banya, which was expensive and is tainted, at least in Gorianchikov's mind, by the fact that it is "run by a Jew." Instead they head to the town's simple people's banya. The thick layers of filth on the floor, the crowded space (eighty to one-hundred convicts squeezed into a twelve foot by twelve foot room), the heat, the steaming, the banging and entangling of their chains, and the shouting all horrify Gorianchikov. He is reluctant to take part. Echoing centuries of upper-class disgust with the banya, he narrates, "when the door into the banya opened, I thought we had entered hell . . . Steam blinds your eyes; there's soot, dirt, and human flesh packed together so densely that there was not room to put one's foot down. I was frightened and tried to step back."[50]

A fellow convict, Petrov, takes responsibility for Gorianchikov and helps him with the process—he disrobes him (a challenge for anyone with chains on one's body), helps him navigate his way through the crowded steam room, and pays others for a small space on a bench for Gorianchikov to sit. Gorianchikov finds the traditional steaming and whipping with *veniki*, which the commoners clearly wallow in, too unseemly to undertake himself. The character who seems to enjoy the steam the most is an outlandish Jewish convict. He enthusiastically withstands the hottest part of the *parilka* and remains there long after the heat has forced others to withdraw, earning the admiration of the other prisoners. Observing all of this, Gorianchikov finds it repugnant. Petrov looks around, but does not respond. His actions suggest that he disagrees or perhaps is drawn to the hellish quality of the banya: after helping Gorianchikov out of the *parilka* and washing him with soap and water, he returns unencumbered to the steam bath, to undertake his own, more traditionally Russian, ablutions. What was "hellish" to the nobleman was a delight for the lower-class convicts.

Later in the story, in a chapter called "Akulka's husband," a prisoner tells a gruesome tale of how he came to be arrested. He married a woman of questionable repute, beat her mercilessly, and finally murdered her. After the crime, he hid in an unused banya, where he was eventually caught.[51]

These references depict the banya as a place of contradictions: a place of Russian tradition, favored most by a Jew; a place for cleaning that is filthy; a place that was hellish to some and relished by others. Dostoevsky's Siberian banya was a no man's land, a liminal place, beyond good and evil and thus well suited for his exploration of morality.

The bania reflects this same ambiguity elsewhere in Dostoevsky's writing. In his first major novel, *Crime and Punishment* (1866), the main character, Raskolnikov, struggles to make sense of the magnitude of the crimes he has committed. He notes that because he does not believe in the afterlife, he cannot seek solace in a heavenly eternity. Svidrigailov, his alter ego, suggests that perhaps imagining eternity as vast and inconceivable was the problem. "What if, instead of all that, there is nothing up there but a little room, like a rural banya, grimy and sooty, with spiders in every corner, and that is all there is to eternity." Raskolnikov is taken aback. This scene clarified the religious question that remained at the center of Dostoevsky's work from that point forward. If eternity was nothing more than a rural banya, there was no guarantee that heinous crimes would be punished or that virtuous acts would be rewarded. What, then, would serve as the lodestar for morality? Dostoevky's subsequent prose grappled with this question. The ambiguous banya was the backdrop against which the moral quandaries that haunted Dostoevsky played out.[52]

Given that context, it is not surprising that Dostoevsky turned to the banya in his final masterpiece, *The Brothers Karamazov* (1880), as well. Lizaveta Smerdiakova, literally "Stinking Lizaveta," is the village idiot who receives alms from the townspeople and turns them over to others. She is filthy and grimy. She ends up getting pregnant; the implication is that the drunken Fyodor Karamazov has raped her. One night people in the Karamazov house hear noises coming from outside. Lizaveta has crawled over the wall of the Karamazov estate and given birth in the family's banya. Lizaveta dies in child-birth, but the baby survives. The illegitimate son of Fyodor, he is greeted with taunts his whole life, including that he "grew from the mildew of the banya."[53] There are reverberations of the story from the *Primary Chronicle* in which the devil created man out of the straw that God had tossed out from his heavenly banya. Lizaveta and her son, who at first glance appear devilish and revolting, can be read as holy fools, not caught up in the vexing moral quandaries dog-ging other characters and all humanity. Again, Dostoevsky's banya represents ambiguity—a place of sinful birth and disgust, as well as unrecognized sanc-tity and wonder.[54]

━━◆━━

Until the last few decades of the nineteenth century Russian doctors assigned a relatively muted significance to the banya—it was not particularly note-worthy in the broader history of bathing, it was not recommended as a pro-phylactic, and it could serve as a potential remedy for only a few illnesses. More often than not doctors thought banyas posed a danger to those who went to them. The robust assessments of the banya's potential in public health that Sanches had offered in 1779 took almost a century to catch on in Russia.

The government was also slow to see the banyas as quasi-medical institutions. Laws continued to regulate social activity in banyas and sought to assure that banyas were charging the right amount for the services they rendered. But by mid-century the notion that banyas might be a tool for public health remained undeveloped. Meanwhile, Western European doctors and governments had a newfound appreciation for the physical benefits of bathing—and sometimes even the banya. Western Europeans, who had long ridiculed the banya, came to see its potential value when Russian doctors did not. One reason was because the banya in Russia had entrenched meanings that Russian doctors had a hard time overlooking. It was difficult to see the

banya as a modern hygienic tool of a well-ordered state if it was also kn
as a place of comfort, social mixing, and private profit. The banya's assocıa-
tion with the peculiar habits and preferences of the Russian *narod* hindered
doctors' ability to see it as a tool for treating physical ailments.

The same factors that stood in the way of Russian doctors recognizing the
banya as a worthy variation on the healthful bathhouses that were emerging
in Western Europe made others see the banya as a symbol of Russia itself. It
was a peculiar habit that bucked comparisons and an intractable institution of
the *narod* that successfully resisted modernization. As a potential instrument
of modern hygiene, the banya could be remade the world over. Its benefits
were as applicable in London as they were in Podolsk. As a Russian tradition,
however, it was firmly planted in native soil, resistant to transformations. The
banya was a universal remedy and a peculiar habit. It promised bourgeoning
luxury and age-old soot. It provided respite and elicited horror. The banya
transformed bodies and purified spirits, a place of extremes in a land of
extremes.

4

Our People Love the Banya But Nothing Good Comes of It

ON THE SURFACE, the end of the nineteenth century was a Golden Age of banyas in the Russian empire. Russian doctors came around to the opinion of their Western peers and celebrated the banya as an efficient and practical way to sanitize the population. The people's love of the banya could be harnessed for the benefit of all. Municipal governments passed ordinances prescribing behavior in the banyas that was safe, healthy, and respectable. Peasants continued to go to banyas in the countryside and the working class continued to flock to them in cities. Businessmen, sometimes in coordination with city governments, erected luxurious banyas that catered to expensive tastes. The challenge, from the doctors' perspective, was to make sure that the activities people undertook in the banya comported with modern medical notions of proper hygiene. If the banyas could be uniformly designed and constructed, their water supplies cleaned up, the temperature in them controlled, and the activities undertaken in them closely regulated by medical personnel and state inspectors, then the age-old peasant custom could be converted into a thoroughly healthy institution.[1] Steam bathing was good—even essential. Bloodletting, sex, cupping, defecating in wash buckets, sharing linens, doing laundry, washing with unfiltered water, breathing unventilated air, and lounging on unwashed furniture were not.

Those who envisioned the banya as a modern palace of hygiene in line with the bathing boom underway in Western Europe had to contend with a Russian approach to bathing that had never been solely about getting physically clean. The technical challenges of harnessing private capital to build well-designed bathhouses in the right locations proved vexing. There was a cultural challenge too. People may have loved the banya, but they had their own ideas about how and when (and even how often) to bathe. Regulations and rules proved easier to write than to enforce. The more doctors and city governments demanded well-ordered banyas, the clearer it became that the existing banyas of the empire were not up to their standards. It had been ironic in the first half of the nineteenth century that the medical acceptance of bathing was taking off in Western Europe at the same time it was stagnating in Russia. At the end of the century a different irony emerged—Russian doctors had joined their Western peers, only to discover that the long and rich history of the banya stood firmly in the way of efforts to refashion it as a purely hygienic pursuit.

The Great Reforms of the 1860s—when Tsar Alexander II decreed among other things military, judicial, and administrative reforms and the emancipation of the serfs—indirectly contributed to changing Russian medical ideas about the banya. The growth of local governance in particular created new opportunities for physicians. Prior to the reforms, doctors were in short supply and almost always tied to the military or other sectors of the imperial bureaucracy. The reforms created *zemstvos*, or local institutions of self-government, that encouraged medical personnel to improve public health in villages, towns, and provinces. This work brought them into closer contact with the peasantry and their customs, including the banya. They also led to the growth of more medical journals that more consistently integrated Russian medicine into European medicine.[2] By the 1870s, Russian doctors took advantage of their new positions to advocate for state support for banyas. In doing so, they hoped to bridge the gap between progressive notions of medical hygiene that had emerged in Europe and the age-old custom of the banya in Russia itself.

In Western Europe, bathing was a new discovery that trickled down slowly from the elite, via municipal governments to the poor. Medical experts and city bureaucrats had an opportunity to shape bathing habits almost from scratch.[3] But in Russia, bathhouses had never ceased to exist. For the banya to become an institution of modern hygiene—along the lines of bathhouses as they were emerging in the Western Europe—Russian elites would have to reposition a custom already beloved among the laboring classes.

Accepting and even promoting the banya's role in hygiene meant rediscovering its connection to the past. Russian doctors acknowledged in their writing the degree to which the banya had been embedded in Russian national history and identity. Medical dissertations and articles emphasized the prevalence of banyas in Kievan Rus' and during the supposed founding of the Russian state.[4] They also highlighted the fact that the "false Dmitrii" of the Time of Troubles revealed himself as a foreign usurper in part because he did not go to the banya. In their new interpretations, banyas were by no means exclusively a lower-class institution. Doctors reported that banyas played key roles in the marriage rituals of the tsars.[5] In an age when national myths required an emphasis on distinct traditions that cut across social strata, the banya emerged as a useful Russian identifier. One doctor even went so far as to declare that a love for the banya could confirm the "authenticity of one's Russian ancestry."[6]

The Russian peasant, in particular, was hygienically precocious, the experts declared. Doctors quoted folk idioms to emphasize the *narod's* inherent wisdom and natural understanding of bathing's role in health: "The banya steams, the banya cures"; "Elixirs are good but the banya is better"; "The banya's steam will make you feel reborn"; "On the day you go to the banya, you will not age"; "Steam your bones and your whole body will be cured"; and "Without the banya, we would perish."[7] Many of these idioms had been recorded as early as the 1830s. What changed was the extent to which doctors and other authors repeated them with enthusiasm and newfound admiration, rather than curiosity or disdain.[8]

The emphasis on the uniqueness of the banya and its rootedness in the Russian past and culture was supplemented by an effort to place it within the broader context of a positive world history of bathing. Russian doctors emphasized the degree to which the banya was the rightful heir to a long and venerable tradition among the "civilized" nations of the world, from the Greeks and Romans in antiquity through Byzantium in the Middle Ages. The fact that Western Europeans had ignored this tradition was a sign that they, not Russians, were backward. One doctor even blamed the "Latins" (i.e., the Catholics) for erroneously banning bathing for centuries wherever they went.[9] With bathing back in fashion in Europe, the banya could be lauded as a sign of Russia's pure heritage and the wrongfulness of those who had forsaken bathing before. The recent interest of foreigners in the banya provided further proof of its importance. Articles and dissertations cited foreign doctors, kept abreast of foreign opinions and breakthroughs, and situated their own arguments within the context of a transnational conversation about the benefits of bathing. Pride in the banya as the highest form of bathing was couched in the language of medical discourse. A single article could praise the uniqueness of the banya as a distinctive Russian tradition, while situating it within a longer history of bathing going back to antiquity, while at the same time eagerly engaging with Western European doctors about how bathing contributed to hygienic modernity.[10]

Ultimately, Russian doctors' defense of the banya rested on its relationship to health. That was their central, professional concern. Changing ideas about how diseases spread aided them in the effort. Germ theory, which came to prominence in the last decades of the nineteenth century, seemed to prove that microscopic organisms, sometimes living on people's skin and in the filth that surrounded them, were responsible for contagious illnesses. The shift from a concern with miasmas or smells to a concern with germs further justified the attention to cleaning individuals' bodies in the service of a greater public good. Bathing could root out the microbes that apparently caused diseases.[11] When these new ways of understanding disease emerged, urban banyas were already well established and doctors were well prepared to make the case for their utility. A century after Sanches had written, the time had finally come to defend systematically the banya as essential to modern medicine.

Doctors turned to medical experiments and engagement with foreign scholarly literature to show the direct relationship between going to the banya and health.[12] Dissertations, books, and articles in journals such as *Physician (Vrach)* and *The Bulletin of Public Hygiene and Practical Medicine* reported on the use of banyas in treating a full range of conditions. Chronic muscle pain, dysentery, emphysema, hemorrhoids, influenza, obesity, rabies, rheumatism, scabies, scrofula, syphilis, typhus, and typhoid fever were just a few of the diseases that doctors believed could be treated or prevented by visiting the banya.[13] Many scholarly works in this era were based on controlled experiments in which doctors closely monitored their patient-subjects as well as the temperature and other conditions in the banya. The specificity of the circumstances in which they tested their hypotheses did not prevent them from reaching broad conclusions about the benefits of bathing for the population as a whole. The challenge was to get people to bathe in ways that doctors deemed appropriate. Doctors tended to disparage private, rural baths because the populations' access to them was often limited and the resources required in time and fuel to prepare them meant that they were not consistently heated or used. Most rural bathhouses, they noted, had been built without chimneys and doctors presumed that poor ventilation posed significant health risks. The hope lay with the urban baths, designed by architects and monitored by health inspectors.[14] Like Sanches, then, these doctors praised the banya in principle, at the same time that they emphasized that it had to be used carefully and according to the rules of modern hygiene.

Another logical conclusion would be to replace banyas with showers and bathtubs, along the lines of those cropping up in Western Europe. The dual loyalty of Russian doctors—to the customs and traditions of the Russian people and to the broader European medical discourse in which they participated—potentially pointed in different directions. A consensus among their foreign colleagues found banyas less effective than other forms of bathing. Public showers appeared less expensive to build, cheaper to operate, and quicker and more efficient at cleaning masses of filthy people than a steam bath.[15] Further, the conditions in communal banyas often caused considerable contact between bathers—increasing the likelihood of the spread of infections.[16]

Others held fast to the relative benefits of the banya—compared to water baths or showers—for disinfecting the body. Only the intense heat of the banya killed all the living things on the body that could spread disease. One doctor declared that the wisdom of "our rural predecessors, the Slavs" was more hygienic than the foolhardiness of urban dwellers "in western dress" who had lost their instincts for going to the banya.[17] True cleanliness, another publication declared, was only attainable with the banya. Baths and showers removed visible dirt. Only banyas, the argument went, caused the body's pores to open enough for various poisons from deep within to exit along with sweat.[18]

Whether or not showers or water baths were more effective than steam baths was a matter of entrenched and persistent debate. But almost everyone could concede that practical concerns favored the banya, at least for Russians, who, as one doctor concluded, would be reluctant to give up their firm "attachment to the banya as a way of getting clean."[19] Even in the military, where presumably it would have been easier to introduce and enforce new forms of bathing, doctors had little confidence that common soldiers could be convinced to take showers. Showers or tubs may have been rational and cheaper, but Russians were accustomed to, and preferred, the banya. The most reasonable goal, then, was to combine the "old habit [of the banya], with new medicine."[20]

Bathing was clearly connected to public health more broadly. As one doctor stated in an article on the banya in the journal *The Archive of Forensic Medicine*, "All governments . . . pay special attention to the health and general state of their citizens, knowing what an important role they play in the political and economic fitness of the state." The banya, he argued, was the main tool for hygiene for the majority of Russians. It kept the population clean, fortified the nation's health, and served as both the clinic and the treatment for those who suffered from illness. It followed that the banya was essential for maintaining the strength of the army.[21] Foreigners evidently concurred. "The use of the banya is the most widespread in the Russian army," a German military hygiene textbook asserted, "and as a result no other army suffers less from skin ailments in general or rashes in particular." A Russian military engineer admitted that the actual conditions of the military banyas did not always live up to his foreign colleague's praise, but he fully endorsed the view that the banya was essential for the proper functioning of the Russian army.[22] Modern medical research seemed to prove what peasant idioms had long asserted: banyas—at least in principle—were healthy.

The professional appreciation for the steam bath was trumpeted in countless scholarly books and articles. The state of the field had clearly evolved since Pliushar's encyclopedia had been published in 1835. F. A. Brokgauz and I. A. Efron's *Encyclopedic Dictionary* of 1891, the most up-to-date Russian-language compendium of knowledge, neatly displayed the new ideas.[23] According to the dictionary, bathing was no longer strange and not necessarily dangerous. Bathing was eternal, natural, and universal, for everyone, not just the peasantry. It turned out that "[bathing] had always been a necessary requirement of man" such that "man instinctively resorts to cleaning the body with the goal of stimulating the skin, eliminating dirt, and restoring lively energy." Among the various forms of bathing, the "Russian banya" deserved pride of place. The encyclopedia entry briefly described banyas in the countryside, but urban, commercial banyas garnered the most attention. City banyas had various sections—entry rooms, changing rooms, washrooms, steam rooms, warm rest rooms and, sometimes in "the better sections," large pools for water baths. Ideally, banyas were well heated throughout, well ventilated, had hot and cold water, and were designed with domed roofs and high windows.[24] In 1835 experts had been leery of the banya. By the end of the century, the ideal banya was urbanized and modernized to meet medical standards.

Doctors even tried to codify the conditions of all banyas across the empire. Basic standards included the amount of time for a complete bath, including steaming and washing (1½ hours), the amount of water each bather required to get clean (15–20 buckets), the best sources for the water (city water systems, when possible), and the temperature of the pools (70–75 degrees F), the steam room (130–145 degrees F), and the washroom (77–100 degrees F).[25] Uniformity was essential. Brokgauz and Efron's encyclopedic dictionary specified the proper way to construct the floors and even the type of furniture that best suited the damp environment. The entry was in part aspirational; the author conceded, "these standards were met only in Petersburg, Moscow, and Warsaw" and not in other cities of the empire. But the author confidently assumed that the banya was an essential part of the urban landscape and a critical tool in the maintenance of public health. The imperial state evidently concurred. It had passed laws pertaining to "construction, medical matters, and police matters" and insisted that "prisoners were taken to the banya once a week," that men and women were separated, and that bloodletting was not performed without a doctor's oversight.[26] New rules would supplant older habits.

Health and medicine justified the attention architects, inspectors, and doctors gave to the banya. As the encyclopedic dictionary's entry explained, "the skin is one of the most important organs of our bodies" and "its normal function is absolutely necessary . . .for the normal development of extremely multifaceted and diverse reflexive phenomenon in the area of the head and the spinal cord." Doctors understood this. But so, instinctively, did Russian peasants, who "mainly through the use of the banya" had been able to "impressively surpass their European brothers in terms of their care for the cleanly upkeep of their skin." The banya was patriotic and medically progressive.

In 1835 Pliushar's encyclopedia had relegated the banya to a footnote in the broader story of bathing. In 1891 Brokgauz and Efron's encyclopedic dictionary lauded the banya as the best means of getting clean. Bathtubs and showers, popular in Western Europe and the United States, were clearly inferior. The only comparably effective way to bathe was the Turkish bath, which had slightly less impressive medical applications. Both the Turkish bath and the banya relied predominantly and effectively on steam to warm and clean bathers. But according to the latest experiments, the banya had particularly strong physiological effects: the skin turned red, the number of the red corpuscles grew, blood pressure rose, the pulse quickened, the pace of breathing increased, body temperature rose, digestion slowed, and, with the use of birch whisks, the blood went from the internal organs to the body's periphery. All this meant that the banya aided "skin functioning and the healthy exchange of internal substances." Its habitual use was crucial to hygiene.

The medical benefits of the banya went well beyond prophylaxis. In 1835, bathing was highly circumscribed as a treatment. By 1891, trips to the banya could help cure people suffering from "chronic muscle pain, rheumatism, gout, syphilis, scrofula, obesity, and hyperemia caused by rich food or a sedentary lifestyle." They could also aid people "at the early stages of all catarrhal illnesses in the nose, jaw, throat, bronchial tubes, lungs, urinary track and bladder" as well as "during chronic catarrhal illness of the ear canal, throat, tonsils, and nose." But that was not all. Proper use of the banya could address "chronic inflammation of the spinal cord and its membrane; neurosis and hypochondria; rheumatoid neuralgia and paralysis from chronic hyper-emia and the stagnation of blood in the liver, spleen, stomach, and intestines; [and] cholera during the period of the chills"; "ailments of bones, caused by scrofula, rheumatism, and syphilis"; "intermittent fevers with the chills"; "pleurisy, Bright's disease, [and] psoriasis," as well as "some heart diseases." The banya was fully integrated into the Russian doctors' toolkit.[27]

The encyclopedic dictionary noted a few limits on the banya as a pan-acea, but these served mostly to justify the importance of medical oversight, thereby emphasizing the banya's role in official medicine. People with blood in their lungs or arteriosclerosis, pregnant women, and young children were warned against indiscriminate use of the banya. Specific restrictions further buttressed the underlying message that the banya had made the leap from a peasant custom to a fully integrated tool of modern medicine, best understood by the experts. Over one-hundred-and-twenty years after Sanches had written about the banya, the gist of his argument returned in full force, even as the number of ailments and details about their treatment had grown. The banya belonged under the purview of doctors; its proper use required a standardiza-tion of conditions; and the state was crucial in making sure those conditions were met. In the first half of the nineteenth century Russian encyclopedists and doctors ignored Sanches. But by the end of the nineteenth century the acceptance of bathing as essential to personal and public health had be-come nearly universal. This new appreciation of the medical importance of the banya did not travel from the peasants to the Russian doctors directly. Instead, the banya gained official acceptance only after Western professionals had spent a half-century giving it an imprimatur of respectability.

In keeping with scholarly custom, the 1891 encyclopedic dictionary entry contained a long list of references, summing up the evolution of medical re-search on the banya over the course of the previous 140 years. The references showed the banya going from a mostly Western European topic of scholarly interest to one fully integrated into Russian thought and policy. The shift happened abruptly. The entry cited nearly thirty scholarly articles on the medical uses of the Russian banya published between 1760 and 1850. Only one was in Russian. The others were in Latin, German, English, and French and written by non-Russians. In mid-century that began to change. The entry cited nearly thirty scholarly articles on the topic published between 1850 and 1890. Almost all of these were published in Russian by subjects of the Russian empire. Russian doctors had discovered the significance of the banya well after their foreign peers had discussed the subject at length. But they also pushed that research further and understood their work within a national project of bringing together tradition, medical expertise, and government oversight. Like few other elements of Russian culture, the banya was both clearly of the people and just as clearly modern; clearly rooted in the Russian past and just as clearly a hopeful sign of things to come.

———

After Russian doctors came to understand bathing as a key component of health, they naturally turned their attention to the actual conditions in the empire's banyas and the habits of those who went to them. In the countryside, problems abounded. It was almost a truism that Russian peasants loved their bathhouses. Foreigners, of course, remarked on the importance of banyas for the rural population. Westernized Russian doctors and writers took it as a given that the peasantry bathed at least once a week. Initially, newly solidified faith in the benefits of bathing led doctors to laud the banya as a form of folk medicine—one that with some refinement and oversight could become crucial to public health. But as they gained greater access to the peasantry, their enthusiasm waned. Doctors soon discovered that banyas were not as consistently used as they had assumed. Nor were they necessarily healthy. What had appeared a few decades earlier to be a quaint custom now seemed an embarrassment because it was horrifyingly out of sync with modern hygienic ideals. Doctors wanted peasants to go to banyas. But they wanted those banyas to be cleaned up versions of those that existed in the countryside.

Banya use varied considerably among Russian peasants. Reports from rural provinces compiled by the Ethnographic Bureau of Prince Viacheslav Tenishev suggested that many peasants in many areas went to the banya on Saturdays, at least for part of the year.[28] But in some places families were too exhausted from the chores and routines of the week to heat the banya consistently. In one region of Tver Province, banyas were used primarily for drying and dressing flax, not for cleaning bodies. In the Kalushka province ethnographers discovered, "The banya for a peasant is a joy, but unfortunately, they have very few of them" and "they heat those that they do have only on holidays."[29] It turned out that some peasants did not bathe weekly after all.

Reports from Minsk Province suggested that the problem there was not the absence of banyas or even the absence of resources to put toward banyas. Instead, the problem was that peasants there refused to bathe. The danger they associated with the banya outweighed any benefits. In some places, the fear was hard to overcome. Beginning in the 1870s, the governor of the province propagandized the health benefits of going to the banya. Where peasants had no banyas the regional government stepped in and built them. Still, peasants in the area resisted. In 1901, some thirty years after the governor's campaign to promote banya use had begun, the habit had still not caught on. A doctor reporting on the situation in the *Russian Medical Bulletin* remarked, "We tend to think (and Europeans do too) that Russians in general love the banya, that the further you go into Russia the more prominent they will be . . . And yet I found that the people [in this province] not only don't love the banya, but are even scared of it." This fear led, in his estimation, to a high rate of skin disease in the region. He speculated that people living in other regions without banyas would suffer similarly.[30]

The doctor was right: the situation in Minsk was not unique and his peers across Russia agreed that there was a link between the absence of banyas and the appearance of various skin ailments. A *zemstvo* physician in Kursk Province reported that "it is deeply unfortunate that banyas are completely unknown to the rural population of the province," which he cited as the primary reason why such large numbers of people in that region suffered from scabies and other rashes.[31] The *Bulletin of Public Hygiene* reported, "Not one hamlet in the Podolsk Province has a single private or even public banya and therefore typhus, that constant satellite of overcrowding and dirt, will never leave the province."[32] In Iaroslavl' Province a doctor and sanitary inspector noted that most families there did not have their own banyas and even those that did used them no more than once per month.[33] Reports from around the empire made clear that rural banyas of the late imperial period were inconsistently used, were avoided in at least some communities, and often failed to combat diseases.

The vast majority of peasants, however, had access to banyas and seemed to want to go to them, under the right circumstances. In those cases, doctors feared that the potential harm to health from the banya could easily outweigh the potential for good. One doctor concerned with skin disease reported, "In the whole of Perm Province nearly every home has a banya." But, he continued, the peasants "use it only once every two or three weeks . . . and steam in it while wiping themselves with radish juice and other muck . . . and [men] often go with their wives [rather than to get clean]." Because peasants did not change their shirts very often—he estimated at most once every few weeks—the hygienic effects of the banya were further muted. Lice and mites, now associated with typhus, returned to bodies as soon as bathers dressed. He found that merchants and bureaucrats were also unlikely to go regularly to the banya or to wash their clothes and as a result also suffered from skin disease. "Under these conditions," he asked, "what kind of meaning can the banya have? What good could it bring when it is used this rarely and in contradiction to the rules of hygiene?" The banyas that did exist, he concluded, were *memento mori* (reminders of the inevitability of death) and places to catch a cold rather than places to get clean.[34]

Using banyas on a consistent basis did not necessary bring about hygienic results either. A physician in Pskov noted, "Our people love the banya and go often to clean, steam and cure themselves," wryly adding, "But nothing good comes of it." As a rule, the doctor observed, benches and floors were unwashed, water gathered in pools on the floor, the air was thick with smoke, ventilation was poor, drafts were strong, and water often came from questionable sources. Furthermore, sick and healthy people bathed together, often sharing water and sponges. The impact on the overall community was negative, even for those who avoided bathing. Banyas often emptied their dirty water into rivers, exposing populations downstream to contaminants and increasing the number of cases of diarrhea and other stomach problems. And yet people, in that region at least, continued to go to the banyas often.[35] Doctors also expressed concern that peasants almost always built "black banyas," where they inhaled smoke and became covered in soot. The same was true of the peasants who steamed themselves by crawling into the large bread baking ovens in their huts after the temperature had died down. Ethnographers and doctors concluded that the smoke and soot made these practices unhealthy.[36]

Health and hygiene were not always the point for peasants anyway. In some regions banyas were heated for marriage ceremonies, but were otherwise used inconsistently.[37] Peasants reported that the banya was a dangerous and "unclean" place inhabited by "devils" who bathed at midnight and beat to death those who dared to enter at that time or those who bathed alone. Peasants associated the banya with sex. One popular idiom declared: "On Saturdays they heat the banya, cook the pancakes, and fuck the women." Peasants did not accept the doctors' view that going to the banya was unambiguously about the preservation of health.[38]

Time and again doctors believed the solution to the problems with rural banyas was to build new ones, where positive effects could outweigh the negative.[39] One doctor suggested that new banyas should be prioritized alongside other crucial public institutions such as schools and hospitals. "The love of the people" for the banya could be put to good use. The key, he thought, was to compel private investors to build new, updated banyas.[40] But other observers noted that private enterprise was unlikely to work, since the peasants rarely had enough money to pay for the banya anyway. Another doctor supported building free banyas at the community's expense—an investment that he argued would pay for itself indirectly by limiting infections.[41] For another doctor, the problems posed by skin diseases "justified the need to strive to build public rural banyas."[42] Yet another doctor proposed that local *zemstvos* build large, public banyas to replace the filthy banyas run by individual households.[43] All concurred that the existing rural banyas more often than not posed a threat to health and offered little hope of fulfilling their hygienic potential. The doctors held firm, however, to their conviction that banyas were healthy in principle and that they could be and should be improved.

—•—

Urban banyas could not keep up with doctor's ideals any better than rural banyas. In cities, as in the countryside, long-established habits ran counter to new theories of hygiene. Failures of design, construction, and upkeep caused poor ventilation, tainted water supplies, and inconsistent heat. These problems were hardly new, but attention to them grew in proportion to doctors' expanding expectations. Municipal authorities, it seemed, were in a better position than rural ones to assert some direct control over banyas. But they faced strong resistance. Urban bathhouse owners and workers, who were crucial to upgrading banyas, had little motivation to adhere to new rules and regulations. And the common people did not demand the conditions doctors saw as essential. If anything, they even seemed to be drawn to the very things that doctors abhorred.

St. Petersburg became a focus of attention, in part because it was the capital and in part because city administrators and many doctors assumed its banyas were exemplary. It was civilized, cosmopolitan, and European. Surely its banyas would reflect the city's standing as the political and cultural capital. In terms of sheer numbers, however, St. Petersburg's banya situation was about average.[44] As elsewhere, its banyas were not always well distributed across the population or well positioned to serve the population. In the Moscow neighborhood of the capital, to take one example, there were eight banyas for approximately 130,000 people, meaning that there was a banya building for every 16,250 people, which was about average for the city as a whole. According to statistics at the time, in the year 1895 the eight bathhouses of this neighborhood provided 2.34 million bath sessions. Given that many workers could only go on Saturdays, it followed (and is corroborated by witnesses at the time) that during busy times the bathhouses sold tickets that put them well over capacity. But even assuming maximum efficiency, people could bathe on average only eighteen times per year, or once every three weeks. The customary Saturday bath was hardly possible for the population of this neighborhood or of the city as a whole. Inspectors, if not doctors, considered these numbers respectable. They took some solace from reports they had seen from foreign doctors that suggested that members of the working class in Western Europe sometimes went years without bathing.[45]

The inspectors, though, were less concerned with the raw numbers than with the filthy conditions and dangerous behaviors they consistently found in the banyas. From the initial push to see banyas as a tool of public health in the 1860s to the end of the empire in 1917, authorities confronted seemingly intractable problems. In the early 1870s the Petersburg police chief and Adjutant General Fyodor Trepov ordered an inspection of all Petersburg baths, with the goal of determining deficiencies in both sanitation and construction. Engineers and medical police applied hygienic standards that they now deemed essential to a well-ordered banya. The results were not good. Only a few banyas had fire-fighting equipment such as hoses, water barrels, and ladders. Stairs and railings were rickety and dangerous, which was an acute problem for banyas where the changing room, washroom, and steam room were not on the same floor. Many banyas had stoves that were poorly ventilated so that the smoke from them filled not only the steam room but also the other rooms and sometimes even surrounding buildings, causing complaints from neighbors. The problems were not all technical. The inspectors found that the *banshchiki* responsible for creating and maintaining the steam were often incompetent.[46]

In the most expensive sections, soiled sheets covered deteriorating couches. In all the sections inspectors remarked on "the lack of attention to the clients" exemplified by the ubiquity of broken glass and constant drafts of fresh air that entered the washrooms and that overwhelmed the heat and steam from the banya. The paint on walls was often peeling; floors were slippery, dirty, and smelled of heavy clay. The benches were covered with stagnant water. Some steam rooms were heated only two days a week and it was not clear if they were cleaned between uses. The changing rooms, where they existed at all, were dark and dank.[47]

Most banyas did not have latrines and the ones that did were "so filthy that it would be impossible to imagine anything worse." One had the bania workers' kitchen located right next to a cesspool. In another there was a terrible stench at the only door in or out of the bathhouse. The inspectors concluded, "One can say that in almost all, if not all, of the common banyas there is no attention paid to the entrance." As was common in other cities, the *banshchiki* lived either in the banya's wash or changing rooms or sometimes in the basement, in a state of dampness that "sometimes shocks the clients."[48]

"Banya monopolies" compounded the problems in the various neighborhoods of St. Petersburg. A lack of competition allowed banya owners to shirk on even basic services. Because travel across the city was time consuming, working-class bathers had little choice but to put up with the local conditions. Some banyas sold tickets even when there was no water in the family or numbered sections. In 1866, one newspaper pointed out that the situation was absurd. How could a banya make money without providing the services for which the money had been exchanged? The obvious answer was that people rented the rooms to do something other than get clean. The implication was prostitution. The newspaper deemed this a serious problem because of the centrality of the banyas to maintaining public health. The newspaper noted, "in our climate banyas can not be skipped because they serve basic hygienic functions and are a necessity of life" and added, "given the importance of keeping the body clean in order to guard against epidemics" the city needed to keep in check banya monopolists who overcharged the poor.[49]

One report summed up the situation: "With these inadequacies the capital's banyas are not in the condition they should be. Good baths are in the minority. The ones that are both good in terms of their public and sanitary requirements are rare and even exceptional."[50] Banyas provided a particularly vexing challenge that was different from other private enterprises like pubs or exchange kiosks where competition forced poorly run establishments to reform or go out of business. The complexity and cost of running a banya— buying the wood for fuel, heating the steam rooms, securing water, disposing of waste water, maintaining the furniture, and repairing the building's infrastructure—created very high barriers to entry into the business. Profit margins were low. Remodeling an old building could be prohibitively expensive, with no guarantee the investment would pay off. Building new banyas required even more capital and even higher risks. Even if a banya could be built and operated according to the highest standards, competing bathhouses could eat into profits by undercharging, providing rebates for workers, or offering free *veniki* or other incentives to encourage clients to put up with poor conditions. Observers concluded, "Only the strongest enterprises capable of improving the banya on all fronts could provide reasonable competition." Individual investors were hard to find. Yet if the banya had a clear public importance, a solution had to be found. Municipal authorities and doctors insisted that banyas needed to be improved: "They need help from science to create the new ventilation systems, new steam machines and to improve conditions."

As it was, poor construction meant that myriad problems persisted. One inspector lamented, "nothing good comes from such a banya."[51]

At that point, the city remained confident in its ability to instill some order in the banyas. Trepov's commission hired the architect Pavel Siuzor to design bathhouses that could meet sanitary and technical requirements. The goal was to make it possible for the poorest members of the population to keep their bodies clean and to maintain their health. Siuzor had designed his first bathhouse in the city in 1870; over the next twenty years he designed at least ten more, earning him domestic and international architectural prizes and fame. Soon architects in other cities modeled their banyas on his large "health complexes." Facilitated by the city, but funded by private businessmen, the new banyas were supposed to meet the hygienic needs of the poor, while providing luxury to the rich. Among Siuzor's most famous undertakings was the design of the Mal'tsev banya and the remodeling of the Egorov banyas. These had ornate interiors with Russian and Turkish steam rooms, pools, hydrotherapy rooms with medicinal tubs, gymnastics rooms, separate numbered baths, hair salons and even libraries, canteens, tea rooms, restaurants and billiards rooms. In 1876 Mal'tsev banyas opened at the cost to the owners of 200,000 rubles.[52] By 1880 one newspaper noted, "in every region of the capital new public commercial banyas have been cropping up like mushrooms after a rain."[53] Many of these banyas were clearly designed both to serve the masses in the cheaper, simpler sections and to cater to the demands of the elite in the numbered rooms, which rented out for anywhere from 75 kopeks to 5 rubles, depending on the accouterments and lavishness of the interior. The owners insisted that the banyas were designed as public enterprises that would support and develop "one of the most important elements of public health—cleanliness." They presented their capital investment as a matter of public affairs as much as business.[54] They also, presumably, were designed to conform to yet another ordinance the city passed, this time 1879, with the goal of bringing conformity and order to the capital's bathhouses.[55]

Municipal oversight and private investment created the hope and expectation that banyas could be both profitable and healthy. City ordinances, like those in St. Petersburg and elsewhere, attempted to spell out the hygienic standards that would strike a balance between the banya as a business and the banya as an institution of public health. To address the well-founded fear that fires might begin in the bathhouse, ordinances in St. Petersburg, Moscow, and Odessa required that banyas be built from brick. Excess wood for heating the stoves, as well as the extra *veniki* and washbasins, were to be stored in a separate, brick building. Moscow required banyas to have water hoses and ladders

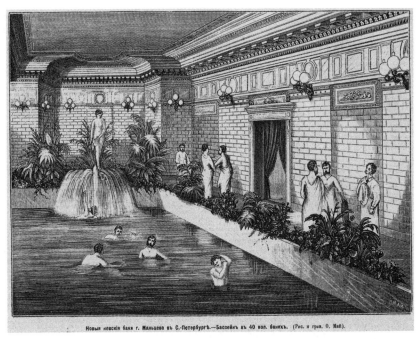

Новыя невскія бани г. Мальцева въ С.-Петербургъ.—Бассейнъ въ 40 коп. банихъ. (Рис. и грав. О. Мей).

FIGURE 4.1 The pools in the Mal'tsev banya in St. Petersburg, designed by P. Iu. Siuzor, idealized the intermingling of luxury and health. *Vsemirnaia illiustratsiia*, no. 410 (1876), 353.

as a precaution. Also for safety, doors from the steam room were supposed to be wide, to be easily operated, and to open out, making exiting easier in the case of an emergency. Cities insisted that banyas be properly ventilated to prevent the build up of carbon monoxide and that stoves used for heating the steam room be permanently connected to chimneys that would allow the smoke to exit.

Another concern was water quality. Regulations required water to be taken from clean sources and stored in vats made of metal or brick. Dirty water was either dispersed into the city's sewage system (if one existed) or into vats from which it could be filtered. The banyas' cesspools were supposed to connect to a separate piping system than the one used for the soapy and dirty water from the washrooms. Clean walls, floors, furniture, and washbasins (preferably made of metal rather than wood) also were considered normal standards for urban banyas. The goal was limiting potential physical danger to the community.

Regulators assumed that the banya posed a potential risk for clients. Ordinances declared that people with visible skin diseases, communicable diseases, or injuries should not be allowed to use the common sections of the banya. Bloodletting, cupping, and other medical procedures were to be conducted only with the oversight of doctors and the medical police and in areas separated from the common sections of the banya. Shaving and haircutting as well were supposed to take place outside of the regular changing and washing rooms.[56]

Other restrictions clearly had to do with comfort, propriety, and consumer protections—but not health per se. Banyas normally operated four days a week (Monday, Tuesday, Thursday, and Saturday). Leading up to holidays, when the demand was particularly high, they were open six days a week. Ordinances called on banyas to list the cost of the various sections and note what items (water, basins, soap, veniki, etc.) were and were not included in the price. City rules also called on banyas to have separate areas for checking outer garments safely and securely, boxes for storing clothes and valuables, and heated entryways and changing rooms so that people entering the banyas from the cold street did not bring drafts in with them. Also to limit drafts, double-paned windows were required by many municipalities.

Regulations required banya employees to deny admittance to drunken people. Odessa's regulators felt it necessary to stipulate that dogs and other animals were also not allowed into the banya. Washing and drying clothes was forbidden in the banya, due to the foul odor that inevitably emanated from the clothes. Keeping separate bathing facilities for men and women was clearly a major priority. So was making sure that the two sections were not visible to one another or from the street. Most regulations required that women's and men's sections have their own entryways and swimming areas (where they existed), not to mention changing rooms, washrooms, and steam rooms. It did not go without saying that the employees of each section were supposed to be of the same sex as the clients. Finally, any swimming area or outdoor wash area had to be built so as not to be visible from the outside. One city even regulated the height of the first floor windows and insisted that they not be transparent.[57]

Ordinances outlining standards for banya construction and behavior proved difficult to enforce. According to inspections by the St. Petersburg Medical Police in 1887, the problems persisted. As one doctor pointed out, banyas were run for profit and not in order to improve clients' health. Bathhouse owners rarely prioritized improvements or even basic upkeep because they understood that they were unlikely to get a decent return on their investments. Bathhouse operators, workers, and clients simply ignored the ordinances when they could. In the cheapest sections, doctors noted that if the clients wanted to wash their clothes, the *banshchiki* let them, for a price.

The stench from the drying clothes was unbearable to medical observers, but evidently not a major deterrent to the banya goers themselves. The contrast between the standards set by doctors and the expectations of clients practically hit the inspectors in the nose.[58]

After one set of inspections, the St. Petersburg police denounced a number of city banyas as "dens of unlimited debauchery manifest in an entire series of phenomena of the most immoral character."[59] Open site lines between men and women bathers, fighting, theft, and "unimaginable filth" all plagued the commoners' sections. But inspectors' major concern was the prostitution that was rampant in the family baths. Banya operators pleaded ignorance of any wrongdoing, claiming to be unaware of the activities that were going on behind closed doors and citing their unwillingness to discriminate against paying customers who wanted to rent a room. Their claims appeared dubious—reports suggested that turf battles between prostitutes were not uncommon and that operators oversaw and profited directly from the practice. Operators who ran afoul of inspectors and had their bathhouses shut down found themselves in desperate situations. One operator applied to reopen his bania, claiming that he had lost over 1,000 rubles and risked losing his 3,000-ruble rental deposit to the owner. The size of his claimed losses, however, was big enough to suggest that he had been running his banya as both a bath and a brothel.[60]

The newer, more luxurious banyas were not exceptions. Liudvig Geidenreikh, a bacteriologist working in Vilnius, wrote: "Despite all of the rich trappings—the marble, the chandeliers, and carpets and the grand buildings—and despite the millions of rubles spent on them, the luxurious [banyas of St. Petersburg] are at a low level hygienically ... The Egorov banyas are grandiose, rich, something in the nature of the Egyptian pyramids; its one building could compete with the Winter Palace ... But just the same these baths were built according to common measures and clearly without the advice of doctors with so many key features missing that it was hard to use the word 'hygienic.'" The fabrics on the walls and grooves in the floors may have been pretty, but they were certainly not easy to clean. The elaborate columns and ornate statuary created corners liable to collect dust and dirt. Dirty water gathered in the crevices of the leather couches. In the washroom, the floors were not slanted to allow water to run into a drain—a feature that had become common in the baths of Europe. In short, Geidenreikh claimed, "attention is paid to comfort, not hygiene."[61]

Conditions did not improve over time. A Medical Police report in 1897 suggested inspections and regulations had not successfully reformed

Petersburg's banyas.[62] Owners consistently bypassed rules about ventilation, the height of the banyas, the thickness of walls, and other matters of basic design. The medical police reported that in the "poorer banyas the subfloor becomes filled with liquid, dirt and various other things." Construction problems were matched by problems with the activities undertaken in the banya. People continued to wash their clothes there. The Medical Police conceded that for thousands of people the banya provided "the only real opportunity to do laundry." The *banshchiki* seemed to have no incentive to prevent this practice—indeed, they could make money on the side by washing people's clothes for them. The fact that clients smoked tobacco in every room of the banya only added to the odor. Finally, barbers continued to cup and let blood without doctors' supervision. "The doctors rarely show up in the banya," which meant that those who asked the barber to use "cups, bloodletting, or leeches" on them could do so without fear of getting caught. Efforts to control the use of ointments in massages had also failed—the medical police recognized that tradition meant that even in the public sections of the banya the practice continued on the side. That *banshchiki* used ointments in the numbered rooms was accepted as a given. The problems with banya infrastructure had clearly not been resolved by the 1879 ordinance or by the inspection regime that followed it.[63]

Banshchiki remained highly unlikely to help enforce regulations. A report on the banyas of the Kazanskii neighborhood of Petersburg in 1897 provides some insight into the arduous life of the banya workers. There, *banshchiki* generally came from the provinces surrounding the capital, with Tver providing the most. Any profit they made they would send home to families that they might not see for years at a time. It was not uncommon for children to follow their parents into the professions. But staying on the job was not easy. Over two-thirds of banya workers in the neighborhood had been working for less than ten years and only two out of eighty-seven workers had been on the job for longer then twenty-five years. The difficulty of the job diminished their overall health and ability to work. *Banshchiki* were prone to certain diseases. One doctor suggested that medical examiners should examine banya workers regularly, because they worked so closely with so many clients and because "among them you often find those sick with syphilis, diphtheria, and other contagious diseases." The male attendants who worked in the numbered baths were especially vulnerable and evidently had "a disproportionate number of cases of venereal disease."[64] *Banshchiki* who earned tips in exchange for sex with clients were more likely to get sick. But they determined that providing services for money on a day-to-day basis outweighed long-term health considerations.

Male bathhouse workers were generally younger than their female counterparts. Of the 105 male bathhouse attendants in the Moscow neighborhood of St. Petersburg, for instance, only 14 percent (15 workers) were over the age of forty. In contrast, of the sixty-five female *banshchitsi* in the same area 74 percent (48 workers) were over the age of forty. The discrepancy was not just a result of women taking up the work when they were older; they also lasted longer on the job. Fewer than half the male attendants had been on the job over five years in the region. But over two-thirds of the female attendants had lasted at least that long. Inspectors explained this in part by pointing out that men did more heavy work in the banyas and had lost their strength by forty, whereas women over forty without family found it difficult to find other work and were willing to keep the hard, but well paid, job. Inspectors also noted that both male and female attendants often took on debt to the owner of the banya, making it "very difficult [for them] to leave before [they] die."[65] But other factors in the relative youth of male workers and the relative longevity of female workers included physical hardships and exposure to sexually transmitted diseases that was routine for the boys and men. It may also have been the case that clients preferred younger men in the numbered baths, where the biggest tips could be earned. Despite progressive ordinances, inspections, and architecturally complex bathhouses, the conditions in the St. Petersburg baths failed to keep up with the standards set for them.

The results in St. Petersburg appear to have been typical of the major cities of the empire. For example, Kharkov, a city of approximately 175,000 people at the turn of the century and the sixth largest in the empire, had well documented, though hardly unique, problems. The city had four commercial banyas in average condition. All four were located in the center of town making it difficult for the poor, who tended to live on the city's outskirts, to make the trip to the banya on a weekly basis. Since getting there took too much of their very limited free time, many bathed at most once every few weeks. To make matters worse, two of the four banyas were often closed down in the fall and spring because mud made them practically inaccessible. They were only open during deep freezes in winter and dry, arid days in the height of summer.[66]

One observer noted that the banyas in Kharkov were in such "disorganized condition that only our national habit of rushing to them" had kept them occupied. The poor crowded into the banyas on Saturdays and put up with filth, stench, and "all kinds of inconveniences and certainty of illness." He concluded, "We don't have a banya . . . worthy of the name. Even though the best cities of Europe have 'Russian baths,' foreigners would not be able to imagine what the actual baths in Russia look like." Entranceways to the four banyas either did not exist or were unheated, meaning that when clients walked into the buildings a draft blew through the changing rooms and even into the washrooms, chilling those who were already mid-wash. The cement walls were clammy and dirty. The ventilation was poor—indeed attics became so damp that they brought cold air and condensation into the washroom through the ceilings. Single paned (and sometimes broken) windows added to the drafts.[67]

Filth accompanied the cold. The floors and benches were wooden, porous, and rarely cleaned. Because they were often uneven, dirt and refuse built up in the corners. One doctor reported seeing a man defecating into a wash bucket and using it in other ways that had "nothing in common with cleaning." All four of Kharkov's banyas provided dirty water for their customers to rinse themselves. Kharkov's rivers were shallow and moved slowly, meaning that the water from them was not particularly clean to begin with. But industrial and human waste polluted them even more. Up the Kharkov River from one of the banyas was a soap factory and an iron casting plant, each of which emptied their waste into the river. A brewery, which used the river for refuse, was thankfully down river from one banya. But it was upriver from two others. In addition, people used the river to wash clothes and to dispose of their personal waste and garbage; during rainstorms it was customary for the citizens of Kharkov to empty their trash pits into the street so that their waste could be washed into the river. In one banya, the bath water was drawn from a spot in the river directly across from what had recently been a manure pit.[68]

One popular adage stated, "The commercial banya scrubs everyone clean, but the banya itself is filthy."[69] The *banshchiki's* heavy workload rarely left them time to clean the couches, sheets, benches, and walls, particularly because they did not receive extra pay for doing so. Owners seemed content to make cleanliness a lower priority than immediate profit. Bloodletting and cupping added to the unsanitary conditions as blood spilled and pooled on the floors and benches. An article in the medical journal *Physician* concluded, "It is not surprising that clients return home with uninvited guests in their coats and at times unwanted infections."[70]

To make matters worse, the banyas were heated inconsistently. It was costly to procure wood or other fuel and banya owners often did not want to incur the expense. As a result, steam rooms were often only heated on Wednesdays and Saturdays. The rest of the week they only provided hot— or even lukewarm—water and no steam at all. The more expensive family or numbered banyas were in no better shape than the common sections. The leather couches were rarely, if ever, cleaned, even though the sex that took place in those rooms suggested that perhaps they needed to be cleaned even more often than the common sections. Doctors and inspectors were well aware that prostitution was taking place in many urban banyas. One observer noted, "It is understood that the numbered rooms in the bathhouse serve not as family bathing facilities, since they are not heated every day [but remain open nonetheless.] Instead they are like hotels where each person can go freely for rendezvous and to carouse." Some clients took prostitutes to the banya; others solicited sex from the *banshchiki*; in other instances the *banshchiki* provided prostitutes as a service. When asked about the less than hygienic activities in the numbered rooms, a *banshchik* explained, "But it is our only profit." In addition to tips, sometimes *banshchiki* were plied with cold *kvas*, beer, and vodka, which they purportedly could drink in immeasurable quantities. Stomach ailments were not uncommon. Doctors openly discussed the fact that the *banshchiki* were involved in sexual acts, noting that they "washed over the visitors in the family banya as they would people with questionable intentions." Yet the *banshchiki* themselves were not willing to put a stop to the sex—a *banshchik* could make upward of 15 rubles a month at the banya, which was a considerable salary for the working class at the time.[71] Clients' desires and *banshchiki*'s profit motives outweighed health considerations, time and again. The *banshchiki* did not even have time to clean themselves. One doctor in Kharkov asked them, "Why are you so dirty?" They responded, "We don't have time to wash; if we can clean up with real steam once a month or even every two months that is good."[72]   *debauchery!*

Doctors did not condemn banyas in general— the medical literature was too clear by that point about the necessity of public hygiene for that. Instead they called for the sanitary conditions in the actual baths to be improved so that the health benefits could begin to be felt by the population as a whole. For the "rich and poor, healthy and sick," for the physically active, and for "those who sit in offices all day," the banyas remained essential institutions. Doctors called on the city administrations to support the banyas and not to simply rely on the whims of owners, who did not consult medical experts or engineers even on such basic questions of water quality, where to build banyas, and what sorts of behaviors should and should not be allowed in them.[73]

Kharkov was typical of cities across the empire. As the editor of *Physician* noted, "We are certain that the problems [in the banyas of Kharkov] *mutatis mutandis* exist in all Russian banyas in general: at the very least, from personal observations we can emphasize that the problems exist in the majority

FIGURE 4.2 The elaborate designs in the elite banyas, including this "Gothic" changing room at the renovated Sandunov banya, belied the poor working conditions for *banshchiki* and the filth that built up in the changing rooms, steam rooms, and washrooms. From Otto Renar', *Illiustrirovannoe opisanie Sandunovskikh ban'* 1896.

of banyas of Petersburg, Moscow and Kazan'; the difference is only that in some of the banyas of the capital brilliant exteriors mask the true filth."[74]

Other reports suggest that he was right to extrapolate about Russian banyas in general. In Voronezh, the cesspool from a vodka factory and a nearby dung heap dirtied water upstream from a banya, which in turn dumped soapy water into the river. A doctor speculated in the *Bulletin of Public Hygiene* that the poor sanitary conditions explained the high occurrences there of typhus.[75] Doctors in Nizhnii Novgorod reported that the banyas there had been inspected four times and that while some of them were acceptable, others had mud floors, damp and grimy walls, and rotting doors. Even in the numbered rooms "filthy water flowed under the floors in the hallways."[76] In Vyborg and other areas of the Northwest, a region where going to the banya was a particularly in-grained tradition, the urban banyas, according to one doctor, were "incredibly crowded," unlit, with clay walls, and clay floors on which water gathered in puddles. Terrible drafts were common in changing areas, even as the lack of well-engineered ventilation meant that dangerous gases built up in the steam room and washrooms. People rushing out of the banya to cool off in the river swam where the unfiltered water from the banya itself was emptied out. It was not uncommon for minor medical operations to take place in the banya. Yet basins were rarely cleaned. One doctor concluded that as a result of the unsanitary conditions in a public banya, a whole military regiment had caught a serious infection.[77]

In 1895 the Ministry of the Interior's Medical Police conducted a broad survey of sanitary conditions across the empire. Inspectors gathered information about over 1,200 banyas from over 700 communities, ranging from towns with a population of less than 200 people to St. Petersburg, with a population well over 1 million people. Local bureaucrats responded to a questionnaire about the conditions in commercial and municipal banyas. Because hygiene was the focus, some included information on Jewish banyas (in some cases, referred to as *mikvahs*) and Eastern Baths (sometimes referred to as *hammams*). The report thus provided a complete, if not systematic, picture of the Empire's bathing establishments. It deemed conditions "unsatisfactory" in a majority of banyas they surveyed.[78] Reasons were by now easy to identify: reports cited poor construction, filthy interiors, foul water, and unregulated behavior of clients. Bathhouses of all types came under criticism. Even those banyas deemed "satisfactory" often met only minimal hygienic standards. There may have been Russian banyas that warranted the faith doctors had placed in the institution, but clearly those banyas were the rare exception.

As unsanitary as they were, at least commercial banyas were regulated. Factories sometimes ran their own baths and could do so with much less government oversight. Although many factory workers went to commercial banyas, if none existed nearby they were forced to go to the company banyas where they were particularly vulnerable to predatory practices. An observer's report noted that well over half the factories in the Moscow region charged a fee for access to their banyas that tended to cost more than the price-restricted commercial banyas. Workers often also had to pay additional fees for hot water, sponges, soap, and even the wood used to heat the banya, increasing their debt to the owners.[79] In the Vladimir region only a minority of the factories even had banyas and those that did almost always used them for cleaning laundry as well as people.[80] Workers would occasionally run the factory banyas that did exist. In one Petersburg factory a banya that served three hundred people per week operated without specially employed *banshchiki*. Instead the workers organized themselves so that five people at a time would run the facilities and take in laundry for money.[81] But this was clearly the exception. Most factories either ran banyas as a means of charging the workers or left the workers to fend for themselves, either in commercial banyas or by whatever other means they could find.

Not surprisingly, factory banyas were in no better condition than the commercial banyas. They were not heated consistently, making them exceptionally crowded when they were open. Factory owners had little incentive to keep them in good condition.[82] In the last years of the empire, complaints among workers about the conditions in the bathhouses were common enough to warrant action. But efforts by municipal authorities to intervene and subsidize factory bathhouses as part of an effort to improve conditions for the workers got bogged down in bureaucratic disputes. The existing system failed to address even the most basic hygienic concerns of the masses.[83]

——•——

Despite the harsh conditions in banyas everywhere and the paucity of banyas in some places, doctors continued to praise going to the steam bath as an essential element in the maintenance of public hygiene. Some conceded that the conditions in commercial banyas would not improve and that the effort to build new ones would prove too daunting. Doctor V. V. Rudin hit on a possible solution. He proposed a mobile banya that was cheap, easy to use, and accessible even to the remotest communities.[84] Other entrepreneurial doctors sold units that would allow well-off urbanites to avoid the dangers of the commercial banya by using a system that allowed them to steam themselves in the privacy of their own apartments. On sale for anywhere from 60 to 120 rubles, these private washrooms were clearly too expensive for the poor, who most needed respite from the dirtiest sections of the public baths.[85] These efforts never caught on, further convincing doctors and health inspectors alike that well-run communal banyas were a necessary feature of modern hygiene in the countryside and cities alike.

Banyas were considered central enough to health to be subject to city rules and regulations. Yet they were also businesses, run for profit. Cities inspected them and retained the power to close them down or prevent them from opening in the first place.[86] But owners wanted first and foremost to make money, as did operators and *banshchiki*. Upgrades to the physical infrastructure were costly and even when they were undertaken, capital expenditures were hard to earn back. The price scales set by the state—with the purpose of making banyas accessible to clients—made it even more difficult for banya owners to make money. Petitions to allow banyas to charge more for each

FIGURE 4.3 Doctors came up with creative solutions to allow people to enjoy the medical benefits of a steam bath without having to go to the potentially dangerous public banya. Stanislav Glinskii designed a "home banya system." Stanislav Glinksii, *Komnatnaia bania sistemy Stanislava Glinskogo* (Warsaw, 1896).

section made little headway.[87] The boom in banya construction associated with the innovation of the tiered system faltered in the face of regulations and restrictions.[88] The population overwhelmed the banya infrastructure in many cities. But the incentives to enter the market were not good enough to justify investing in them. Without options, clients, even if they were so inclined, could not demand better conditions. Owners, operators, and *banshchiki* were left to squeeze as much money out of the institution as they could. The obvious option for them was to continue to support activities that would keep money coming in, even if these were the very habits that state regulations had hoped to do away with. Prostitution, cupping, bleeding, and the washing of fetid clothes continued unabated. Problems with ventilation, heat, water quality, and building materials persisted.

In 1910 the city of St. Petersburg recognized that the number of banyas in the city had not kept up with popular demand, especially among the working class, and set out to rectify this. The city's Sanitary Commission reported that the poor were forced to go to ill-equipped, poorly run, and overcrowded banyas. Exasperated by banya owners' drive for profits, the Commission took it upon itself to build an affordable, well run, and well-located "people's banya." It solicited designs from architects based on specifications determined both by technical experts and based on the needs of the workingmen and women of the city. The standards used to judge the plans emphasized that projects should prioritize both the "preservation of the traditional national, Russian banya" and health and not profit, "since bodily cleanliness (and clean clothes) were key to protecting the capital's poor from all manner of disease." Work on the publicly funded banya continued through the fall of 1916, but never panned out. The people's banya was never built in the capital of the Russian empire.[89]

Reconciling modern hygiene with the banya tradition as it was actually practiced was not so straightforward after all. Once doctors determined that banyas were crucial for public health, the nonhygienic activities that people undertook in them and their poor condition became more visible. Doctors had in mind banyas that were designed and built to allow for consistent heating to specific temperatures, with clean water supplies and sealed sewage pipes, and modern ventilation systems that prevented the build-up of carbon monoxide in steam rooms and washrooms. They called for sanitation inspectors to ensure that new standards were followed and to monitor practices in the bathhouses to minimize potentially unhealthy medical procedures and prostitution. Laws and ordinances, they hoped, could compel bathhouse operators and bathhouse workers to prioritize health over profits and to enforce the new rules instead of providing remunerative, but unsanctioned, services.

Plans for healthy, hygienic banyas were imposed on an existing physical and cultural bathhouse infrastructure that had emerged haphazardly with little, if any, guidance from medical experts. The empire's banyas had not necessarily deteriorated over the century. Some design innovations suggested that at least some of them had improved in ways doctors welcomed. But new ideas about the positive impact bathing could have on public health raised standards and heightened scrutiny. Habits and customs that had not been particularly troublesome could, on closer inspection, be deemed dangerous. Deciding that banyas were healthy in principle meant that the degree to which they were unhealthy in practice became apparent. In the postreform era, regulators endorsed the banya's new, higher, purposes—to prevent the spread of contagious diseases, to limit skin ailments, and to keep the population healthy. In that context, they discovered that the physical state of the actual baths and the behaviors undertaken in them posed serious problems.

Everywhere experts turned, banyas were failing to serve the functions now envisioned for them. Increased contact with the peasantry contributed to doctors' skepticism about rural banyas. The "ignorant peasants" simply could not be trusted to forego dangerous practices and learn to integrate modern medical know-how into their ablutions. Urban banyas were often no better, but for different reasons. Profit-seeking owners, poorly paid and syphilitic workers, decrepit and filthy buildings, and a dangerous mix of various social strata, each seemingly drawn to the banya for different unhealthy reasons, all undermined the banya's potential. What could advocates of bathing do? Some called attention to the problem by describing in medical journals the conditions they found in the rural and urban bathhouses. In an attempt to compel owners to clean up their banyas, city ordinances outlawed behavior that egregiously put patrons and the community at risk. Some municipal governments designed and supported the building of banyas as public institutions geared toward increasing health, not profit. These efforts all more or less failed. Key constituents could not be swayed. Owners did not want to invest in improving conditions in banyas without a good chance of financial rewards. Operators and bathhouse workers benefitted most from the very activities doctors hoped to eradicate. And many clients ignored regulations against "unhealthy" pursuits that they strongly associated with the banya. By the eve of the First World War, from a public health perspective, the actual banyas of the empire still needed to be radically reformed. From that same perspective, the goal of building and running healthy banyas was stronger than it had ever been. Health standards had been clarified and codified; they just had not compelled owners, operators, and patrons to comply.

Experts understood that spending time in damp, poorly ventilated spaces with ubiquitous and filthy objects (such as towels, couches, sponges, and laundry in various states of wash) while in close proximity to dozens if not hundreds of other human beings whose bodies housed parasites was not so good for public health. The problems, according to doctors, stemmed from owners and operators who resisted costly improvements and *banshchiki* who held fast to unhealthy but profitable activities. They rarely blamed clients who determined, according to their own standards, that they would rather accept the conditions that the doctors condemned than reform or forego their trips to the banya altogether. By the end of the imperial period, cities had accepted doctors' hygienic standards and inspections showed that the empire's banyas failed to live up to them. But rather than turn to alternative means of cleaning the population, doctors and municipal officials trusted that more regulation and greater attention to proper construction and behavior would finally allow the banya to play its destined role in washing away the health problems of an ailing empire. The solution was not to abandon the banya, but to modernize it once and for all.

5

The Onslaught of Civilization

THE BANYA IN late imperial Russia was more than a popular mainstay, a potential boon to public health, and a damp and drafty place full of latent dangers. It was also an institution closely intertwined with Russian identity and the fate of that identity in a rapidly changing society. Vladimir Giliarovsky, the great chronicler of late imperial Moscow, observed: "Not a single Muscovite abstained from the banya. No one—not a master of trade, not an aristocrat, not a poor man, not a rich man could live without the commercial banya." Extant statistics bear out Giliarovsky's observation and suggest that at least in this case, what was true for the old capital was also true of many cities, towns, and villages across the empire. Commercial and municipal banyas, from rudimentary huts for workers to elaborate establishments catering to the wealthy, were consistently overcrowded, especially on Saturdays and before holidays. Men and women did not visit the banya just to promote physical health. In Giliarovsky's estimation even aristocrats, who had marble baths in their palaces, went to the banya because they had a "hereditary love of steaming themselves with *veniki*, relaxing in the changing rooms, and 'wagging their tongues' with their companions."[1] As the empire went through the profound social transformations unleashed by the Great Reforms of the 1860s and the subsequent drive toward industrialization, the banya remained a salient and seemingly unchanging institution, a traditional place for relaxation and social interaction that was open to all.

Beginning with the reforms of Peter the Great, Westernized Russians had often taken the banya for granted or presumed it was somehow an outmoded habit of the common people that would recede in the face of modernization. But beginning in the early nineteenth century a process of reappropriating the banya as a specifically Russian and thereby praiseworthy institution took hold. By the second half of the century, books on the banya insisted that it had been integral to everyday life for tsars and peasants alike in Russia since "time immemorial" or at least since the very emergence of the idea of Rus'. "The origins of the banya are synchronous with the origins of Russian history," one doctor explained in 1888, adding, "The banya is closely tied to the people, having always been a persistent satellite of the life of the Russian man. . . It is directly connected with the conception of 'Russian.'"[2] The banya's persistence had long been cited as evidence of Russian backwardness. But its consistency across time could also be reformulated as evidence of Russian resilience in the face of instability seemingly emanating from abroad. When the educated and Westernized elite looked to the common people for the features of an authentic national identity, the banya stood out. The late imperial period was a golden age for the banya not simply because doctors had decided that it could clean bodies. Writers and artists also discovered that the banya reflected the complexities of fin-de-siècle Russia.

The banya linked the rural and urban, the past and present, and ethnic Russians with the various nationalities of the empire. Large commercial bathhouses in cities like St. Petersburg, Moscow, and dozens of provincial capitals across the empire provided the setting for people of various backgrounds to gather and interact in ways that seemed reminiscent of the interactions taking place in the more numerous rural banyas strewn across the country. The banya united a disparate empire.

The banya also exposed the contradictions and paradoxes of the age. Elaborate palaces of hygiene presented new opportunities to develop urban identities, even as they invoked timelessness. The movement of people of all walks of life to cities created new opportunities to mix social classes, ideas, religions, and even bodily fluids. Stripping off clothes in turn stripped people of much of their public identity, creating an anonymous space rife with social possibilities, sexual tensions, and a hint of physical violence and risk. Like late imperial Russia more generally, the banya was a place in flux, a place of mingling, a place governed by an uncertain amalgamation of modern social norms and traditional habits.[3] The imperial city was a steam bath—sweaty, overcrowded, dangerous, and exciting. Yet those wary of Westernization, urbanization, and reform could not target the banya for ridicule in the same ways that they could target other seemingly unprecedented phenomena of modernizing Russia, such as hooliganism or prostitution.[4] The banya was neither novel nor alien. The disdain it had periodically received from foreigners only reinforced the idea that the banya—even in the cities—made Russians distinct and even superior to unwashed Westerners.[5]

When writers and artists self-consciously confronted the meaning of everyday life in the modern age, the banya, in all its incarnations, came to the fore. Literary figures like Anton Chekhov, Mikhail Kuzmin, and Vasily Rozanov, as well as the artist Zinaida Serebriakova and the photographer Karl Bulla, turned to the banya to help them confront fundamental questions. Lowbrow publications also featured the banya, although usually to scare, titillate, or entertain their audiences. When read together, these sources suggest that writing about the banya became a way to address Russia's relationship to the West, modernization, and the changes under way in Russian society.

The banya emerged as a stand-in for genuine Russianness even as it was undergoing changes of its own. State-of-the-art banyas in cities with elaborate pools and changing rooms could be seen as the manifestation of "Russian tradition." The banya was clearly Russian—and exotic—even as bathing, bathhouses, municipal pools, and Russian baths became regular features of the major cities of Europe and the United States. The banya was an "egalitarian" and anonymous place, even as it became increasingly segregated in its services. And it remained a comfortable place for homosocial camaraderie, even as its reputation as a place of same-sex relations, mixed-sex prostitution, and violence became increasingly visible. All of these attributes, whether regarded as admirable or deviant, reflected key aspects of Russian identity more generally.

The banya brought focus to some of the defining characteristics of late imperial Russia: a search for an authentic Russia unsullied by the West and Westernization; the desire for community amid the destabilizing effects of rapid urbanization and modernization; and the sense that sin and cultural degeneration were on the rise.[6] The era saw a flourishing of attention to and pride in a seemingly authentic and untarnished Russian culture that contrasted sharply with the West and that provided a clue as to how Russia might be able to thrive on its own terms. Doctors saw banyas as a means of modern hygiene analogous to baths and showers. Nonmedical sources highlighted the degree to which the banya created a uniquely Russian social space.

Representations of the banya in the late imperial period were contradictory and complementary. Its privileged place as a marker of Russian identity reinforced the idea that urban people might go there to assert their traditional values. But unlike in rural settings, where baths were usually taken with family, urban banyas obscured identities and required people to strip down with strangers. Going to the banya granted access to the Russian past, but doing so in the city exposed people to the disease, debauchery, and anonymity associated with modernity. The fundamental acceptance of open nudity in the banya remained strong, inviting in turn both vulnerability and the possibility of the exploration of sexuality and sin. The late imperial Russian banya was about "hereditary love" of Russia and about sexual and moral transgressions. By the end of the empire, the contradictions inherent in this sweeping view of the bathhouse were becoming more difficult to reconcile: the banya was healthy and dangerous, purifying and sinful, socially leveling and exploitative, the symbol of all that was right with imperial Russia and all that was wrong with it as well.

———•———

Writers concerned with defending authentic Russianness associated the banya with tradition and the people, while draining it of the negative connotations propagated by Westerners. In one poem, written in 1876, the humorist Peter Shumakher turned to the banya to describe his—and by extension the Russian intelligentsia's—effort to overcome their long-standing dismissal of the *narod*. Drunkenness, fear, and outside forces, he worried, threatened the foundations of Slavic brotherhood. The banya could set things right. "Bereft of sweet dreams / in impotent rage and anguish / I went to the Volkovskie baths / to steam my bones on the bench / And what then? Oh, the joy! Oh, the pleasure! / My lifelong ideals at last! / Freedom, Equality, and Brotherhood / Were found in the commercial baths!" The banya enveloped the Russian spirit. By its nature, the banya liberated, leveled, and created social bonds, but in a personal, visceral, emotional way, not through logic or the mind. The *narod* had something to teach the Europeanized elite.[7]

The effort to equate the banya with Russianness reached its apotheosis in the essay "On Writers and Writing (notes and sketches)," written in 1899 by the brilliant, eclectic, mystical nationalist, chauvinist, and anti-Semitic Russian literary critic Vasily Rozanov.[8] Considered "the greatest writer of his generation," Rozanov was fixated on the Russian past, Russian identity, and the qualities that made Russian culture resistant to and superior to the modern West.[9] He discovered the banya was a place that exemplified Russia's best qualities. Like much of his work, "On Writers and Writing" addressed a wide range of topics, including literature, religion, Slavophilism, sexuality, modernity, and decadence. The banya illustrated Rozanov's broader point about the importance of maintaining Slavic traditions in the face of the persistent pressures of Westernization. He began by referring to the oft-cited passage from *The Primary Chronicle* about the Apostle Andrew's exposure to the peculiar

bathing habits of the Slavs. Rozanov used the foundational story to highlight an admirable resistance to change. Nearly a millennium had passed since
Kievan Rus', he pointed out, but "the banya remains." The rise of Muscovy did
not alter that basic fact: "princes went to war, Moscow quelled them," but the
banya remained. Neither the foreign occupation during the Time of Troubles
nor foreign ridicule more generally could dislodge the banya from its central
place in Russian tradition: "They strove to 'smoke out' the banya, the false
Dmitry [a usurper] ignored it, native writers laughed at it, pointing abroad
and noting that 'there, abroad [they have no banyas] . . .' But the banya stood
firm." Even Peter the Great's reforms did not weaken this resilience: "Moscow
itself then faded, but the banya remains. All of Russia was transformed, but
the banya was not transformed." That the banya had witnessed a resurgence in
the West could not dislodge its fundamentally Russian character: "The banya
itself went abroad, demanding attention from doctors," but it could not be
rationalized and modernized. Instead, he concluded, at the end of the century
the banya remained "even less likely to give way to the onslaught of civilization."[10] The banya, according to Rozanov, exemplified a kernel of consistency
in Russia that survived for centuries, from Kievan Rus' through Muscovy,
Peter the Great's revolutionary transformations, and the self-loathing of the
Westernized intelligentsia. Modernization, which led doctors to attempt to
recast the banya as a medical tool, did not so much rescue the banya from
obscurity and obsolescence as it threatened to strip away the deeper qualities
that made the banya a permanent fixture of Russian identity.

Rozanov pushed the argument even further, suggesting that the banya
embodied the very characteristics that made Russia unique and admirable.
Where others saw beatings and disgust, he saw Russia's greatness. He whimsi-
cally proposed that the banya was a "far more marvelous historical phenomenon" than the English constitution, the well-worn symbol of all that was
sophisticated about European society. Comparison only showed the superiority of the banya and, by extension, Russia. Rozanov reasoned that with
its roots in Kievan Rus' the banya had been around longer than even the
earliest traces of the constitution. It was also more democratic: "the constitution provides for the satisfaction of . . . [only] those who vote, [whereas]
the banya provides for the pleasure of positively every Russian, the whole un-
broken mass of the population." Further, as an everyday activity, the banya
united the people on a basic level; elections, in contrast, were relatively rare
and came with the "fuss, filth, un-cleanliness, [and] alarm" of democratic
politics. This disdain for democracy fit with Rozanov's preference for emo-
tion, sincerity, and desire over the rationality of the West. His concern with

"filth" and "cleanliness" had less to do with physiology than with the soul. Europeans lauded the English Constitution because it was always evolving and modernizing. Rozanov's banya was consistent, timeless, and traditional. It was not to be judged by standards imported from the West; it—like Russia—was to be celebrated for its imperviousness to cultural erosion.[11]

If anything, Rozanov insisted, the West had much to learn from Russian institutions and habits, not the other way around. Pushing the connection between the banya and Russian greatness further, he continued: "The banya has deep roots in the people. I want to say that it is impossible to imagine the Russian people without the banya, just as it is also impossible to imagine any sort of banya except a Russian's banya, that is, in its proper appearance and with the proper colorful acts associated with it." Rozanov articulated the banya's centrality to Russian identity as a cultural institution. "Colorful acts" had long been the target of ridicule from those who welcomed the "onslaught of civilization" from abroad, but to Rozanov they spoke to the banya's Russian authenticity and unselfconsciousness. Anything but prudish, Rozanov welcomed the banya's association with sex, extreme heat, and beatings that so shocked foreign observers.

For Rozanov, the banyas of the Empire were islands of community and authenticity within a sea of dehumanizing modernization. A person's appreciation of the banya was indicative of his trustworthiness. "If you would like to make friends with someone, but are wavering, ask him if he loves the banya," Rozanov advised. "If [he says] 'yes', then you can confidently stretch out a hand to him and welcome him into your family." The banya itself created the right environment for discussion: "The banya in its very meaning is conducive to good will . . . it is simple, innocuous, and clean . . . it is a stream of human contact and a sort of wonderful world."[12] Rozanov's banya nourished a Russian love of community and disdain for deceit.

Rozanov's discourse on the meaning of the banya for Russian culture encapsulated the key contours for thinking about the banya that had emerged over the course of the century: it was Russian, it was superior to Western institutions, and it was a place of trust, good will, and communication. Foreigners, such as Adam Olearius, Chappe D'Auteroche, and the Marquise de Custine, had suggested the banya was a clue to what made Russia different and, to their minds, inferior. For foreign doctors, beginning with Sanches, the banya was first and foremost a medical and hygienic tool—its popularity could be used to encourage cleanliness. By the second half of the century Russian doctors basically agreed, even as they fretted that entrenched bathing habits might act as impediments to the banya's effectiveness. But Rozanov dismissed the hygienic potential altogether, instead describing the banya as essential to Russianness, intertwined with Russia's history and the identity of the empire's subjects.

———•———

The communal nudity, the chance to mingle with strangers, the beating of one another with birch branches, the extremes of the hot steam room followed by a cold pool or pond or a roll in the snow: all this made the banya exotic to foreigners and to those Russians who dismissed it as a regressive artifact that hindered the blossoming of modern culture.[13] But as Rozanov noted, rather than fade away with the Great Reforms, banyas had become even more prominent in Russian cities, even the ostensibly Western-oriented capital. Newer banyas were not only—or even primarily—places to get clean. People gathered in the restaurants, billiard rooms, and the well-furnished changing rooms to relax, read journals and newspapers, play cards, and socialize with familiar faces and anonymous peers.[14] This was obviously true in the more expensive sections of the bathhouses—the so-called noble, family, or numbered baths. But even in the cheapest sections of the new bathhouses the washrooms, pools, and steam rooms became social, crowded spaces where some would chat while others washed themselves or their laundry. In the banya, people could be together or could go about their personal business without interference, whether they actually got clean or not.[15]

Given his keen attention to the quotidian details of Russian life and the erosion of traditional society, it makes sense that the writer Anton Chekhov would turn his attention to the banya. In the early 1880s he wrote two vignettes titled "In the Banya." Each emphasized how relaxation mixed easily with private and semiprivate discussions in the commercial baths.[16] On the one hand, the banya brought people together and through nudity erased the outward distinctions that were so salient in the surrounding urban spaces. But on the other hand, the banya exposed the danger of not really knowing who was who. In the first Chekhov story, a large, pale man yells through the steam to a tall, skinny man with a thin beard and a big copper cross on his chest, "Hey, you, fellow! Add some steam!" But, as the big man soon learns, he has misread the situation: the skinny man is not responsible for the steam. He is, instead, a barber and makeshift surgeon named Mikhail, who only the week before had sliced away corns on the big man's feet in the banya. With the misunderstanding acknowledged, Mikhail proposes that this week he place bloodsucking jars on his client. No doctors monitor the situation; no discussion of physical ailments precedes the treatment. Within minutes, Mikhail has rushed off for his instruments, returned, and placed jars on the big man's chest and spine. While they wait, the two begin to chat. Conversation was an essential part of the experience of going to the banya. Evidently taking up a topic they had discussed the previous week, the barber ridicules the social changes underway in Russian society. He complains about young women in particular. In the past they looked for solid, strict men with money, the ability to judge things, and respect for religion. But lately, Mikhail laments, they seem to want "education" above all else. Recently, he reports, an educated telegraph worker could not even afford soap in the banya, let alone provide for a family. What good, then, was education? Suddenly a low voice interrupts the conversation: "Poor, but honest! We should be proud of such people. Education combined with poverty is evidence of a high quality soul. You boor!"

Taken aback, Mikhail looks up to see that the words have come from a man on the top bench slapping himself with a *venik*, his face obscured by his long hair dangling down. The barber dismisses the man as a radical, an "educated" man who exemplifies the deterioration of society. Mikhail turns back to his client and recounts a disparaging story about a "stingy" writer. Again the "longhair" interrupts with his low voice, this time accusing Mikhail of slander and dismissing his words as "nonsense." Mikhail responds by saying if he were not devout and preparing for communion, he would really put the longhair in his place.

After another brief exchange, Mikhail gets upset: "It is not for nothing that you have hair like that. Not for nothing. We understand everything very well and now we will show you what kind of person you are." He leaves the steam room to report to the banya's operators that a "longhair with ideas" was causing trouble. But once he is in the dressing room, his complaint makes no sense. A boy attendant informs Mikhail that no such longhair went into the steam room. There were only six bathers in total: two Tatars, a man undressing, two merchants, and a deacon. Mikhail doesn't believe him until he spots the deacon's clothes. Soon, he realizes his "sin": he has mistaken the deacon for a radical. He rushes back into the steam room to apologize. The deacon, who was already down from the bench, dumping water over his head, asks the reason for the apology, and Mikhail responds without any sense of irony: "For thinking that you had ideas in your head." The banya both encouraged casual conversation among strangers of various estates and increased the possibility of misreading social clues.

The second Chekhov story centers on two men in a steam room discussing the difficulty one of them is having finding a suitable husband for his daughter.

It turns out that her various plans for marriage have always broken down at the last minute. One would-be groom got nervous; in another case the daughter decided she did not like the man she was supposed to marry; and in yet another case the father and potential groom could not come to terms on a marriage contract. The dialogue is framed by references to the banya—to the fact that they are lying next to one another on the top bench, that they are slapping themselves with *veniki*. Chekhov describes one man as "naked like any naked person, but on his bald head he wore a cap. Fearing a rush of blood to his head and a apoplectic attack, he always steamed with a cap." The discussion is unusually frank and it is the banya that allows it to be so: the man telling his story is letting down his guard and sharing his thoughts openly.[17]

The stories reveal Chekhov's skill as an observer and humorist. The atmosphere of the urban banya allowed him to reflect on the changes underway in society. The banya was a place to tell stories; a place for men to talk about women; a place where relaxation predominated; and a place where people's identities in the world were stripped bare. The client cannot tell a barber from a *banshchik*; the deacon looks like a radical. Conversations take place between strangers who know little about one another, beyond the subtle and perhaps falsely understood clues provided by the naked body. The deacon has long hair, the client is big, and the barber is skinny. Using soap or not and ordering extra services or not may or may not suggest a bather's station in life. People of all sorts enter the banya. Chekhov mentions telegraph workers, nobles, and merchants, but those identities, which would have been more or less obvious on the street, are not easy to discern in the washrooms and steam rooms of the banya. Tatars may have been equally identifiable in the bathhouse as out, but their presence is not particularly noteworthy. The banya is open to the people of the empire, not just to the ethnic Russians. The *banshchiki* discuss things with their clients and clients also have conversations with one another. The discussions are informal and leisurely but touch on important topics. The banya is like a club, but without the exclusivity. It's a place to chat, a place to relax, but not necessarily a place to get well or for the body to heal.

The banya's role in public health was often overshadowed by its role as a setting to explore the social dimensions of the new city. The banya was traditional and conservative, a beacon in the disorientating storm of urban life. Etchings from 1871 of the changing rooms of the Voronin's People's Banya in the center of St. Petersburg, published in the popular magazine *World-Wide Illustration* (*Vsemirnaia illiustratsia*), accentuated the urban bathhouse as a place of social interaction. They show people relaxing either before, after, or in between their trips to the steam room.[18] In the men's changing room, a well-dressed man leans forward from the front right corner of the image to see one man relaxing in a sheet (his clothes evidently laid out next to him on the common bench) while a bathhouse attendant stands with a towel and sponge, prepared to assist his client. The curtains are pulled back on a number of semiprivate stalls, with mirrors and couches. In one stall, a man is lying casually on his back, smoking a cigarette, with his head turned slightly to a naked roommate, who is dressing. In another stall two men, dressed in sheets, sit shoulder to shoulder with one man's hand on the other's lap. The image conveys both a sense of intimacy among those who are together—and a sense of privacy from everyone else. Even though the curtains are open, the men do not look at one another. Their eyes are open but do not meet. The exceptions are the bathhouse attendant, who appears to be approaching a client, and the onlooker in the corner, whose gaze suggests to the magazine's viewers that they, too, can satisfy their curiosity. To modern eyes, the intimacy between men in the relative privacy of the banya may hint at a blurring of the lines between homosocial behavior and sexuality. But it is unlikely that a widely read illustrated journal in the 1870s meant to suggest that. Rather, the point seems to be comfort and ease.

An image of the women's changing room similarly invites the viewer to look while projecting a sense of intimacy: Women lounge and dress either together or alone in the semiprivate stalls; one woman appears to be folding a piece of cloth, while in the far right corner a shadowy figure in a sheet heads toward the door to the steam room. In this drawing, the woman entering the scene from the lower right, in contrast to her male counterpart in the other drawing, averts her eyes, hinting at a greater sense of privacy than was apparent in the men's room. The eye is drawn, however, to a private stall in the far distance where a woman with long hair has her back to the viewer. Her dress is halfway off and her arms are up above her head in a classical pose. A second woman eyes her from a lounging position on a couch in the same semiprivate room. Looking may not have seemed entirely appropriate, but the magazine offered an opportunity to explore the scene nonetheless.[19]

By the turn of the century, depicting social interaction in the urban banya was commonplace. The weekly humor journal *Fiskal* (*The Sneak*) ran a cartoon that played on the idea of the banya as a place of political agitation. A woman in the image calls her peers together, presumably announcing that the steam room is ready for bathers. "Comrades," she says, "I invite you all to come together." But in the aftermath of the 1905 Revolution, a gendarme mistakes this as a political call to arms. He enters the women's banya and announces the need to undertake a thorough inspection. The humor came

С.-Петербургъ: Народныя бани Воронина. Раздѣвальня мужского отдѣленія въ 30 копѣекъ. (Рисов. на дер. Г. Броллингъ, грав. К. Вейерманъ).

С.-Петербургъ: Народныя бани Воронина. Раздѣвальня женскаго отдѣленія въ 30 копѣекъ. (Рисов. на дер. Г. Броллингъ, грав. К. Вейерманъ).

FIGURE 5.1 Images of the men's and women's changing rooms at the new Voronin banya in St. Petersburg highlighted comfort, intimacy, and luxury. *Vsemirnaia illiustratsia*, no. 148 (1871), 280.

from both the gendarme's mistaking a typical call to bathe for a revolutionary act and from the image of a man walking freely into a women's banya to undertake an inspection.[20] Yet there was some reason for authorities to be concerned about what was being discussed in the banyas. Banyas allowed large groups of people to meet without necessarily calling attention to themselves. The social legitimacy of gathering in the banya made it difficult to discern what was happening there, and at least in some cases the banya's ambiguity did provide an attractive cover for political organizing.[21]

Political humor could target the highest echelons of society as well. A cartoon in *Ovod* (*The Gadfly*) made just that point—it depicted members of the Tsar's Council in the banya in early 1906. Titled the "Manchurian Banya," the image showed General Aleksei Kuropatkin, the incompetent leader of the disastrous Russo-Japanese War, getting his hair washed, with Sergei Witte, Chairman of the Council of Ministers, facing him. Others in the bathhouse include Konstantin Pobedonostsev, reactionary advisor to the tsar in pince-nez; Pytor Durnovo, the Minister of Interior, with head bowed; and Governor General of Moscow, Fyodor Dubasov, standing straight and tall on the right. None of them appear to experience the banya as the hell that Napoleon encountered; they all appear quite comfortable in the banya. But the absurdity of the gathering is obvious—they retain their identifying sashes and insignia, even as they bathe. The toga-like sheets may suggest a parallel to the decline and fall of the Roman Empire. These powerful and serious men are in the banya, but the message appears to be that they have been "taken to the cleaners" because of the situation in the Far East. The juxtaposition of nudity with serious decision-makers is farcical and ridiculous, even if the rest of Russia considered it normal to "wag their tongues" in the bathhouse with their companions.[22]

Depictions of male banyas often shifted the focus from the changing rooms, where clothing could conceal bodies, to the washrooms and steam rooms, where nudity was the norm. Images revealed the physicality of the banya and the intimacy clients shared with *banshchiki*. A cartoon in the satirical journal *Sprut* (*Devilfish*) from 1906 labeled "In the banya before the banya" shows two *banshchiki* with towels around their waists, brushes and tools at their side, scrubbing and massaging their clients. One client is lying down; the other is sitting with his feet in a bucket. The juxtaposition of the two working *banshchiki* in physical contact with their relaxing, naked clients suggested a comfortable social mixing. This could almost be an illustration of the scene from Chekhov's stories. By 1906 the idea that bathhouse workers could be paid for sex was not a well-kept secret. The image subtly hinted at

Маньчжурская баня.

FIGURE 5.2 The tsar and his cabinet depicted in the banya after the disastrous defeat in the war with Japan in 1905. *Ovod*, no. 1 (1906), 5. Beinecke Rare Book and Manuscript Library, Yale University.

homoeroticism. The *banshchiki* are muscular and masculine; the seated client is rounded and feminine, seemingly lacking male genitalia.[23]

Still, communality, not sex, was often the salient feature of the banya. Bathing with others was essential for curing the soul as well as the body. Ivan Shmelev, the émigré who described prerevolutionary merchant culture in Moscow, portrayed a romanticized version of the banya. A son gets incomparable joy and excitement from a trip to the banya with his sick father. The enthusiasm of the other bathers and the camaraderie of the time spent steaming and relaxing seem to cure the father of his illness and restore vitality to the family. The communal nature of bathing was at the heart of what gave the experience power.[24]

Socializing in the banya was crucial for women as well. Eugenie Fraser recalled the banyas of the late imperial period with delight. Like others, her mother and grandmother brought her to the banya. After she was thoroughly cleaned, she was free to walk around the room. She recalled, "I delighted in a happy orgy of splashing and throwing basins of water over everybody. Babushka, with a cold cloth over the forehead, lay stretched out on the top shelf. Kapochka [her nanny] stood in the middle of the floor and chastised

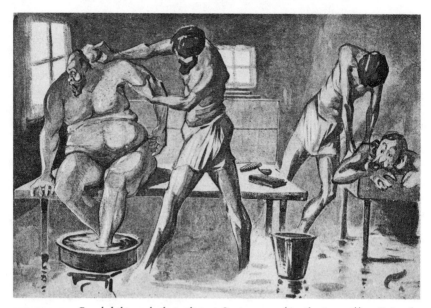

FIGURE 5.3 *Banshchiki* scrub their clients, *Sprut*, no. 15 (April 26, 1906)), 7. Beinecke Rare Book and Manuscript Library, Yale University.

herself with her switch until she glowed like a boiled lobster. The small leaves stuck to her body and she emptied countless basins removing them. Everybody sweated, soaped and scrubbed and all around us was this hazy curtain of heat and steam."[25]

In the imagination of male artists, the "happy orgy of splashing" in the women's banya was about titillation more than camaraderie. In the nineteenth century male artists including Pierre-August Renoir, Gustave Courbet, and Paul Gauguin painted women in nature and naked. As the art historian Linda Nochlin has argued, the French emphasis on the naked female figure in or near water was in part related to the late nineteenth century's growing number of public pools and its newfound emphasis on bathing and swimming within a broader discourse that disciplined, regulated, and governed the body.[26] Renoir's *The Great Bathers* (1884–1887) was a classic of the genre. In it, he depicts a younger, slender woman with a boyish figure who looks hopefully toward two more voluptuous women— one blond, one brunette—sitting at the water's edge. In the background another figure shoulder-deep in water looks up at the front of a slender women who has both arms raised, fixing her hair, chest high and exposed to her companion. The women in the painting regard one another, inviting the viewer of the painting to look as well.[27]

In this respect, Firs Zhuravlev's 1885 painting *Bridal Shower in the Banya* followed the Western line. His choice of topic and depiction of a scene from everyday life constituted a break from the strict rules of the Academy where he was trained, but he did this without radically changing the view of bathing and the female nude. Traditionally, a bride went to the banya with her attendants on the eve of her wedding. In Zhuravlev's painting, women in various states of undress lounge around a well-appointed room, relaxing. The naked bride sits in the center of the picture, with one naked attendant whispering in her ear, while another brings her fruit, and a third rests, head back, holding a *venik* above her. This is clearly a place without men, but as Zhuravlev has imagined it, it has less to do with the banya or bathing than with fulfilling a fantasy of what a naked bridal shower might look like.

Within a few decades, the conservative elements of Zhuravlev's approach became obvious. Zinaida Serebriakova, a path-breaking female artist, was attuned to how her rendering of the banya could challenge the male obsession with female bathers. The daughter of the sculptor Evgeny Lansere and grand-daughter of the architect Nicholas Benois, Serebriakova was a generation younger than Zhuravlev and, like others in her cohort, rebelled against the realist style he represented. Her uncle, artist and critic Alexander Benois, was one of the founding members of the highly influential World of Art move-ment, with which Serebriakova became associated and which helped arrange

FIGURE 5.4 The Academy painter Firs Sergeevich Zhuravlev depiction of a bridal shower in the banya jibed with Western European depictions of women bathing in the nineteenth century. *Devichnik v bane*, 1885.

the exhibition of her work. With Sergei Diaghelev acting as the driving force behind the movement, Silver Age artists like Leon Bakst, Boris Kustodiev, Nicholas Roerich, Mikhail Vrubel, and Wassily Kandinsky came to the attention of the European and American art world. Though the movement was eclectic in its goals and styles, it sought to revolutionize aesthetics while emphasizing the importance of a distinctive nationalism in Russian art and music.[28]

The Banya (1913), Serebriakova's first large canvas, fit squarely within the campaign to emphasize Russian themes while reinventing artistic possibilities in the modern age.[29] She used the bathhouse both to conform to and to challenge accepted notions of art and object. Her work, like the bathhouse itself, highlighted the instability of many of the dichotomies of the day, such as Europe/Russia, modern/traditional, urban/rural, and male/female. By choosing to depict women bathing, Serebriakova inverted the themes that dominated paintings of baths in Western Europe. Her banya was a modernist conceit that called into question male dominance in visual art, European efforts to exoticize Russia, and the elite's mistrust of the Russian peasantry.

The Banya conforms to the artistic tradition to a point: naked women are shown in various stages of their bathing. In some sense, the painting was a sensation simply because the artist was a woman and so the painting's subjects were not conjured by a male artistic gaze. But it did much more than that. Serebriakova's perspective challenged much of what made female bathing so attractive to male artists. In her painting eleven women more than fill the canvas as their figures extend beyond the boundaries of the frame. They overlap with one another in a dark, dense, and crowded washroom. The women are undertaking various utilitarian, not frivolous, activities: scrubbing themselves, pouring water, and carrying their wash buckets. Dirty washrags are strewn about. The figures are all red, rounded, and approximately the same age and same height. They share the same skin tone and body types. The impression is almost as if the eleven subjects are all the same woman, at various stages of her bath, depicted at once. V. N. Dudchenko, a peasant woman from Serebriakova's hometown who posed for the painting, recalled that the artist preferred "strong, strapping, [women so that she could give] them power, vigor, a diligence for work, and a tidiness."[30] A 1912 study for the painting shows a very similar scene, with fewer women in similar poses. Serebriakova focuses the viewer's attention on the heat and the naked women's bodies; there are no architectural details and only the wooden buckets and washrags suggest the specific setting. The figures in Serebriakova's painting are crowded together and appear to have been caught unawares, going about the business of bathing without playfulness or frivolity. A woman carrying a bucket on the right hand side of the picture glances back at the viewer with a blank impression.

Unlike staples of Western painting of women bathing, the figures at Serebriakova's banya convey indifference and distraction rather than allure. In Renoir's painting the water is a place where a variety of women can have flirtatious fun without men. (Of course, the absence of men is limited to the canvas itself: the male painter is presumably just off stage and those men who view the painting do so from a similar vantage point.) Serebriakova's banya, in contrast, appears to be a place where women can be comfortable and candid with one another in the absence of men. Her painting disrupts the sexual undertones and erotic possibilities so prominent in men's paintings of female bathers in general and of Western pictorial and literary descriptions of the Russian banya more specifically. For her, the banya stood in for feminine strength and was a direct challenge to a central tenet of social norms. This was a tableau vivant—a theatrical, highly stylized and carefully arranged scene, with no steam, no wetness, no pubic hair, and no attempt at rendering motion. It was the opposite of sociability.

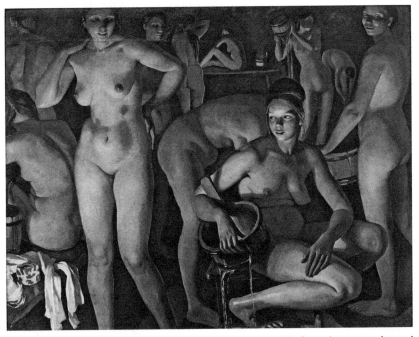

FIGURE 5.5 Zinaida Serebriakova's tableau vivant was notable for eschewing traditional female flirtation in the banya in favor of power and vigor. *The Banya*, 1913.

Karl Bulla, perhaps the most famous photographer of the late imperial Russian city and one of the empire's first photojournalists, also chose to depict the banya. But he emphasized the social nature of the banya. Where Serebriakova rendered static women seemingly in isolation from one another, Bulla focused on active male sociability. His innovation was to show naked men interacting in a way that almost dared his viewers not to see sex. He carefully staged a series of images of the Egorov baths in 1910 to emphasize intimacy and community.[31] In one photograph more than a dozen men are in the process of rinsing themselves and one another. Many of them are in pairs, and even those who stand alone are clearly and unapologetically watching others. At the center of the photograph is a man with a sponge washing the lower abdomen and crotch of a man lying on his back on a bench with his head on a switch and his arms above his head. The two men stare at one another intently. Other pairs of men in various stages of their own baths frame the scene. On the left, one man is in the process of pouring water from a basin onto his client or bath partner while another man watches and waits with his own basin. Behind them, dressed *banshchiki* stand back watching the activities and waiting to be of service. Along the back and up the right side of the photograph are men showering and massaging one another, in one case with a *venik* and in another with hands. One man, apparently returning from the steam room, carries a *venik* and a basin, while another man fills his basin with water. Nearly everyone is looking at someone else. The emphasis is on interaction and comfort with the bodies of others and the process of going through ablutions either with friends or with the help of a *banshchik*. The back half of the room is crowded, but given the ample space at the front, it appears that the crowding is by choice. A bench at the very front of the photograph is empty except for an upside down bucket and basin with an unused switch. As a result the viewer sees the scene from a slight distance and, in turn, is invited in with the recognition that there is room for at least one more pair.[32]

For Bulla, the banya brought to the fore an obvious comfort with open nudity and intimate social interactions in a public space.[33] A tub or shower could not do the same thing. In another Bulla photograph from the same bathhouse, a man showers while looking at an angle at another man showering. The second man has his back to the camera and is shielding his backside with his hands. A boy controls the faucets of the shower for him, while a third man, shoulder deep in a tub, stares off blankly in the distance. This photograph reveals isolation and shyness about the body rather than contact, interaction, and comfort. There are no switches or other

FIGURE 5.6 Bulla's photographs of the Egorov banya emphasized social interaction, with the empty bench at the front suggesting that there was still room for more bathers to participate. Courtesy of TsGAKFFD SPb.

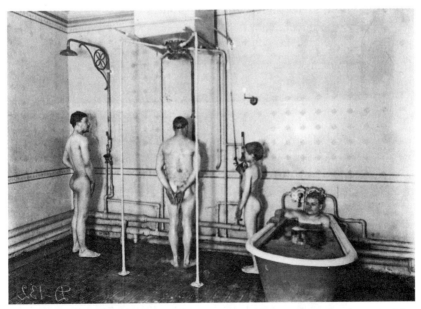

FIGURE 5.7 In contrast with the banya, tubs and showers suggested isolation and discomfort with nudity. Courtesy of TsGAKFFD SPb.

indications that this is a Russian banya. The sharp contrast only serves to further emphasize the social nature of the other, more Russian, activities. The banya is social, open, and interactive; tubs and showers isolate people and invite feelings of shame. While Serebriakova questioned the implicit sexuality of the homosocial space of the women's banya, Bulla hinted at the sexuality of the homosocial space of the male banya without talking about it openly.

In 1910, some viewers of Bulla's photographs would have seen more than asexual camaraderie in his bathhouse scenes. Only four years earlier the Symbolist poet Mikhail Kuzmin had published *Wings*, the first sympathetic literary exploration of same-sex love in Russia. The novel was not explicit about sex—no men embrace or even kiss in the story. Instead it approached attraction and desire through discussions of Greek mythology and aesthetics. Critics recognized the radical nature of the story, though, and were quick to label it "pornographic." They fixated in particular on a brief reference to men who paid for sex with *banshchiki*.[34] In the story a teen-age boy, Vanya, is just beginning to discover the world of same-sex desire through his attraction to an older, sophisticated man named Larion Dmitrievich Shtrup. At one point, while waiting for Shtrup, Vanya overhears from behind a wall a young banya attendant named Fyodor describing how he first learned about "messing around" with men. As a young and inexperienced *banshchik*, he greeted a young nobleman in the banya, who in turn told the boss that he wanted Fyodor to wash him. The boss hesitated, knowing that this nobleman liked to "mess around." Explaining that Fyodor was not experienced in those matters and didn't know the ropes, he suggested that Fyodor bathe the client along with Vasily—the experienced *banshchik* the nobleman usually requested. He agreed to hire both and after some haggling over the price, Fyodor found himself alone for a moment with the nobleman. While Fyodor undressed, the nobleman laughed and reached out to touch his face, asking "What do you have on your cheek there, Fyodor: Is it a birth mark or some sort of dirt?" Fyodor turned red and stood mute, unsure how to respond. But soon Vasily returned and "off they went." Fyodor's initiation into the supplementary role of the *banshchik* had begun. Vanya continued to eavesdrop on the story and when Fedor left the room and walked past him, Vanya sized him up with curiosity. The episode is less than a page of text and yet the scene clearly struck readers as scandalous.[35]

The book elicited derisive responses from Zinaida Gippius, Maksim Gorky, Leon Trotsky, and other critics shocked by its "decadence" and "anarchism of the flesh."[36] Review after review fixated on the bathhouse as the site of debauchery and pornography, grabbing attention at least in part because Kuzmin showed "fine gentlemen" corrupting "pure" and "innocent" peasants. Parodies fixed their attention on the bathhouse scene, while writers such as Andrei Bely were aghast that Shtrup had "satisfied his sexual needs with a bathhouse attendant." " 'Bathhouse,' *Wings*, and Kuzmin," the literary critic John Malmstad pointed out, "became synonyms for vice."[37]

In part, readers were upset that the Russian institution of the banya had been besmirched. Among the critics was Vasily Rozanov, who wrote in his review of *Wings* that "Hadrian and Antinous [the Roman Emperor and his male lover, associated with homosexuality and mentioned in *Wings*] would probably throw up from the disgusting *banshchik* [Fedor] and his banya adventures: can it be that the ancients like *that*?!!"[38] Rozanov was notoriously untroubled by sexual desires, whether homosexual or heterosexual—but he struggled to maintain the distinction between the banya as "simple, innocuous, and clean" place and one where sex could be bought for a few rubles and some beer.

Kuzmin's novel made clear to the uniformed in Russian society that the banya could be the setting for sex between men. Many people, of course, did not need Kuzmin's story to learn this. Ivan Pokrovsky noted at the time that the conversation that Vanya had overheard in the novel was similar to ones commonly aired in certain banyas in St. Petersburg and especially in banyas in the south of Russia where "the matter is looked at very simply."[39] This fact was even obvious to visitors to Russia. Maurice Magnus, who accompanied the dancer Isadora Duncan on her tour of Russia in 1907, recognized the sexual possibilities of the banya. In St. Petersburg his host, after vainly attempting to find him a female prostitute who was to his linking, finally realized, "But probably you don't like women; probably you prefer men." Soon Magnus was taken to the banya. Although he did not seem to have sexual encounters there, he did report that a pleasure seeker in Duncan's entourage appears to have been robbed in the banya by a man with whom he evidently had undertaken "various indecencies." On the tour, Duncan went to the banya twice. Once she went to calm her nerves. The other time, though, she went to relieve—evidently just through steam and cold water—the unsatisfied sexual tension that had built up from a crush she had on Konstantin Stanislavsky, with whom she was working. Magnus concluded that Russians "treat what we Westerns consider morals so lightly, letting the heart and instinct rule, irrespective of sex and conventions."[40] He was onto something. High rates among *banshchiki* of syphilis and other venereal diseases, especially among those working in the numbered or family sections, led Russian doctors and inspectors to conclude that sex was common in the banya.[41]

The connection between the banya and sex was often explicit. Historian Dan Healey noted, "Male bathhouse attendants appear in a range of sources of the 1860s to 1880s as sexually serving a male clientele." One merchant recalled in his diary visiting a male bathhouse in Moscow where he encountered "onanism and *kulizm* (anal intercourse)." Older *banshchiki* recruited young *banshchiki* to provide sexual services for clients. They formed a cooperative association where tips and earnings were divided up after a portion was given to the boss. One banshchik reported to a doctor that when a customer went to the banya for sex he would ask for a specific banshchik. Then "I can see that he doesn't need to be washed and he begins to hug and kiss and ask my name and then he does with me as he would with a woman, in the haunches, or, depending on what he wants, he sits while I stand in front of him, or he lies with me like with a woman, or orders me to do with him as with a woman, only in the anus, or else leaning forward and lying on his chest, and I [get] on top of him." It was not unknown for clients to see other clients having sex with *banshchiki*, even on the benches of public sections of the banya, albeit behind curtains.[42]

Entries in Kuzmin's diary make it clear that the scene in *Wings* was based on personal experience. He often went to the banyas in St. Petersburg. On October 23, 1905, he wrote about a visit to the Basseinaia Street banyas, "In the evening I had the urge to go to a banya simply to be stylish, for the fun of it, for cleanliness," and not to seek out sex.[43] The man who showed him into the banya asked Kuzmin if he would like a "good little female bathhouse attendant" but Kuzmin said that he'd prefer a *banshchik*, uncertain at that point even why he was saying it. But when the *banshchik*, Aleksandr, entered the room to bathe him, Kuzmin immediately noticed his "bold and uninhibited gait. . . He was very tall, very well built, with just a hint of a black mustache, light-colored eyes, and almost blond hair." Kuzmin noticed that "he stared straight at me, motionless, with a kind of mermaid look, not quite drunkenly, not quite insanely, almost terrifyingly, but when he began to wash me there was no room for doubt." Soon they begin "talking like thieves" and discussing the price. The *banshchik* asked him directly, "How do you like it?" After they have sex and the *banshchik* has dressed, he informs Kuzmin that he is twenty-two years old, had been working in the baths for eight years and that his principal client was a thirty-four-year-old prince.[44] Kuzmin returned to the banya a number of times. He was surprised to learn that Aleksandr had gotten married, but pleased to hear that he had discovered that Kuzmin was a poet and musician. When Aleksandr was away other *banshchiks* bathed Kuzmin instead. The diary shows that Kuzmin had sex with *banshchiks* many times between 1905 and 1913.[45]

While it seems difficult to reconcile the same-sex liaisons that Kuzmin and others highlighted with the idealized banya of patriotic lore prominent in so many other sources, Vasily Rozanov gave it a try. In the summer of 1916, Rozanov, who had found the banya references in *Wings* disgusting a decade earlier, headed to the same Basseinaia Street banya that Kuzmin had once frequented. "A very masculine seventeen-year-old" named Ivan cleaned and steamed Rozanov. In the process Ivan rubbed up against Rozanov's knee and hand so that "the lightness of the touch aroused [Ivan's] anatomy." Rozanov recounted that he was not offended and accepted Ivan's arousal as a natural fact. After some casual discussion, Rozanov washed soap out of his eyes and finally took a good look at Ivan and could not help but notice his penis. "Opening my eyes, I saw something exceptionally beautiful and magnificent, that, I have to admit, I became aroused myself. He was built larger than usual . . . it was shapely and unspeakably expressive." Rozanov reported that he immediately thought, "now there's a worthy man" and recalled an expression "a husband for seven wives"—suggesting that a man built like Ivan could make seven women happy. "In the presence of such beauty (and such shapeliness) I unintentionally began to love it and by no means withdrew my hand when he touched it. And he touched it every minute. He had washed my head twice already." The experience offered Rozanov insight into how women could be "rashly in love with very unattractive and even hideous men. Now I understood that they were not in love 'in general' but instead were in love 'in part.' One look in front of me convinced me of the definite circumstances in which that was possible." After more washing Rozanov reported feeling comfortable lying on the bench with the man's torso next to his face. As Rozanov finally began to get up he caught a clear glimpse of "something massive passing near his cheek." The experience spurred Rozanov to speculate about how wonderful it would be to breed such beauty.[46]

Rozanov lamented that Ivan, who was bound to be drafted into the army, would likely be killed in the Great War. In that context, Rozanov was no longer taken aback at the combination of homoeroticism and the idealism— even sacred nature—of the Russian bathhouse. In some ways, the war made Rozanov appreciate the banya—and the male physique—in a deeper way. In an earlier essay, written at the beginning of the war, he had noted that seeing the soldiers marching off to battle invoked erotic feelings in those watching them—including him. He observed, "the essence of the army is that it turns us all into women—weak, trembling, air-embracing women. Some experience it more, some less, but everyone does to some degree."[47] Rozanov's understanding of gender posited that everyone had masculine and feminine aspects to their psyche and even their body.[48] In the presence of such clear masculine beauty, he had no problem celebrating his attraction to the male organ—even in a mixture of pornographic detail and philosophical musing.[49] The "wonderful world" of the banya remained heroic and patriotic even when the "colorful acts" that took place there included men's attraction to the power and beauty of other men. For the Russian attuned to his emotions, the banya revealed all; no infatuation was inhibited; no transgression unfathomable. To be Russian was to be social, to be social was to be sexual. Modern sensibilities were checked at the door, along with one's clothes.

———×———

The connection between pure Russian identity, the banya, salvation, and sin were most explicitly articulated in Andrei Bely's first novel, *The Silver Dove*, published in 1909. In the novel, a young poet leaves the Westernized city and goes to a Russian village, where he is lured in by a simple peasant woman who is part of a mystic sect—the Doves—that is dominant in the village. The Russian peasantry appears crass and base, but pure and full of spirit, whereas the West and Westernized Russians appear sophisticated and knowledgeable but soulless. The village sectarians treat the banya as their makeshift church— it is there that the high priest of the sect gives sermons and it is in the banya that the people gather to pray. "[The banya] was full of people now, brightly lit, and locked, as though now quite cut off from the world; here was a new world, everything here was different, their own, of the Doves." In the banya, ecstatic revelations take place. The walls of the banya "would become a white expanse with neither end nor limit; on that day the walls of that city would move apart; and the people would start to live freely and easily in the new kingdom, the land of silver, under dove-blue skies. And in that kingdom, in that land of silver who would shine upon the land?—The Spirit." The scene is dreamlike—when a night watchman attempts to enter the banya, he finds it locked, as if all the worshipers had slipped out by "some secret passage and now were strolling in heaven, plucking the flowers of paradise, conversing with angels." There was no clearer indication that the banya was sacred to the people and, at the same time, appeared diabolical and even inexplicable to the helplessly Westernized elite.[50]

The mystical darkness of the banya was taken up in lowbrow literature as well. There too the banya appears both sinful and enticing. In the 1879 story "Murder in the Puzerevskii Baths" a man and a woman check into a private banya. This in itself is not so strange, but what followed surely was. The man—wearing a bearskin coat and carrying a bag—soon checks out, giving the attendant money and leaving the woman inside. Hearing nothing from inside the room and unable to make out anything by looking through the keyhole, the attendant lets himself into the outer room. Still seeing no evidence of the woman, he calls the police, who break into the steam room. They find a headless woman in the bathtub. They cannot identify the woman and have only the slightest description of the man. The privacy of the banya and the anonymity that it fostered could be dangerous and precarious.[51]

In another short story, "Ghastly Drama in the Moscow Banyas" (1909) a Russian man kills a Jewish man and his daughter in the banya. Once again a women's head gets chopped off. The murderer leaves a note confessing his responsibility. When the inspector tracks him down, the killer admits to what he has done. But, he explains, the murder was justified as an act of revenge for what the Jew had previously done to the man. The inspector reluctantly throws him in jail. At trial, the defense explains the murderer's reasoning to the jury, which votes to acquit him.[52] In this case, the banya serves as a space where the various elements of a deranged city come together with horrific results.

The banyas in the "The Murder" or in the "Ghastly Drama" or even in Bely's *The Silver Dove* hardly resembled Rozanov's "wonderful world." They were dangerous and fantastical; women were particularly vulnerable; and horrendous acts could be perpetrated away from prying eyes. The semiprivate and semipublic space gave the criminal elements a chance to act behind the guise of respectability and with the protection of anonymity. And yet it also promised a world of emotions, fate, and faith that was incomprehensible in purely rational terms.

The sin explored in fiction reflected sins taking place in real banyas. Rumors spread, for instance, that the banya had been the site of one of Dostoevsky's own egregious transgressions. Nikolai Strakhov, one of Dostoevsky's closest collaborators, his confidant, his mentor in the 1860s, and his first biographer, sensed with horror that "Dostoevsky would go down deeper and deeper into the spiritual abyss, into the frightful abyss of moral and physical corruption."[53] In the 1880s, Strakhov wrote to Leo Tolstoy that Dostoevsky was debauched.

He claimed Dostoevky had once raped an underage girl in a banya. Strakhov appears to have been repeating reports that had circulated in literary circles in the 1870s and were likely based in part on a passage from the *Devils* that was banned in which a similar event occurred. Strakhov's accusation also brings to mind Fyodor Karamazov's rape of Lizavet. Whether the rape in the banya occurred or not, the story lingered. After Strakhov's letter was published in the journal *Modern World* (*Sovremennyi mir*) in 1913, the literary world was left to wonder whether the greatest sin of the Russian writer who had probed the nature of sin most deeply took place in a banya.[54] The banya was at the unknowable core of Dostoevsky, just as it was at the unknowable core of Russian identity more generally.

The sex that seemed to flourish in banyas only reinforced its reputation as emblematic of basic desires and the danger and the overall degradation of modern Russian society. Kuzmin displayed no remorse about his desire to have sex with *banshchiki*. But others had a harder time escaping the sense of guilt that came with the ready availability of sex in the banya. This dynamic played out in the diary of the tsar's cousin, Grand Duke Konstantin Romanov, who closely associated commercial banyas—and his own private banya—with the temptation to have sex with other men. Unlike Kuzmin, Konstantin appeared to be tortured by what he considered to be his "great sin." He was both desperately drawn to the banya and desperately hoped to avoid what he considered amoral acts. "In my soul I am again unwell, again sinful ideas, memories, and desires come to me. I dream of going to the banya on the Moika Canal or order one at home and summon a familiar *banshchik*, Alexei Frolov or especially Sergei Syroezhkin," he wrote on April 19, 1904. Even when he was able to resist the temptation to stop by a banya, he was tormented by his desires. On one occasion, to conceal his destination, he asked his coachman to let him off at the corner so that he could secretly walk to the banya on the Moika. "I walked up and down twice past the banya doors; the third time, I went in," he wrote, adding only, "And so, I have once again sinned in the same way. My moral condition is awful."[55] His entry on June 17 of the same year came after a few days of resisting the temptation: "This morning I washed in the banya at home. And thus again I was unable to keep up the struggle." On June 23, he added, "At night they heated the banya for me. Sergei Syroezhkin was busy and sent his twenty-year-old brother Kondratii, a young lad who works as a *banshchik* at the Usachevskii baths. And I took this lad in sin. It is possible that I was the first who made him sin this way and only when it was too late did I remember the terrible words: woe to those who seduce one of the little ones."[56] Three days later he wrote, "Morning banya. And again, like a hamster in his wheel, I found myself again in the same place." The Grand Duke's diary entries speak to how closely he associated the banya with amorality and the sinful temptations of the modern city, even as it forced to the surface something elemental and irresistibly, genuinely human.[57]

Both Kuzmin's guiltless enjoyment and the Grand Duke's agony over trysts in the bathhouse remained hidden away in private diaries. But the "sexual decadence" of the banya entered public discourse as well. The Petersburg doctor Vladislav Merzheevskii described sex in banyas as indicative of degradation and defilement. He complained in his 1878 book *Forensic Gynecology* of a fully organized blackmail ring in the numbered baths among "disgusting pederasts." He declared that the key role was played by opportunistic *banshchiki*.[58] Same-sex relations were clear targets of ridicule, but so were the female prostitution rings run out of bathhouses. There was a decidedly negative spin in public about the sexual activity rampant in the banyas.[59] Doctors hoped the banya would play a positive role in public health. Rozanov saw them as an emblem of Russia. But they also facilitated sex and sin.

Perhaps the era had no greater symbol of both a mystical, anti-enlightened Russia and of the debauchery of the teetering regime than Grigori Rasputin. The spiritual advisor to the tsar and tsarina was an object of fascination and ridicule among the St. Petersburg elite, who saw him as the embodiment of all that was mysterious and dangerous about the reactionary autocrat.[60] That Rasputin, originally a poor peasant from Siberia, liked going to the banya was hardly a surprise. That he would go with prostitutes and sometimes even aristocratic women was a scandal. Police reports stated that Rasputin would walk along Nevsky Prospect, the main boulevard of the capital, and pick up prostitutes and take them either to a banya or to a hotel. On February 4, 1912, for instance, he went with a prostitute to the banya on Konyushennaia Street. Two days later he took another prostitute to the banya on 26 Moika Street, the same baths that the Grand Duke occasionally attended. His sexual appetite appeared insatiable.[61]

Rasputin's behavior made him the object of tremendous fascination. The elite appeared obsessed with him, some condemning him and others falling under his sway. Rumors, such as those that placed Rasputin in the banya with prostitutes and trusted members of the tsar's court, contributed to the pervasive sense of moral corruption and autocratic decay washing over the empire in 1917.[62]

Rasputin admitted to going to the banya with noblewomen, although denied that he took prostitutes. "I don't go with them [the noblewomen] on my own, but we go as an entire group," Rasputin told a man whose wife later accompanied the mystic to the banya, alone.[63] It is not known whether this explanation put the man at ease. Rasputin's reasoning was that temptation was the greatest sin and that elite women needed to be humbled. Corrupted by Western notions of shame and modesty, going to the traditional banya with a "dirty peasant" was a magnificent way to peel away their unhealthy propriety and remind them of their Russian bodies and souls.[64] Rasputin may also have been testing his own resolve. At one point he explained that the great saints of Byzantium went to the baths to see if they could resist, or not, the temptation of the flesh.[65]

The banya was Russian and Byzantine, a place for sinners and saints. In the end, it did not really matter whether going to the banya revealed Rasputin's hypocrisy and insatiable sexual appetite, was a test of his spiritual purity, or was instead meant to denigrate noblewomen who seemed, to him at least, to be in dire need of humility. In all of these cases, the banya was primarily about an indefinable cultural essence that encompassed national pride and national shame, authenticity and deceit, sex and murder, the permanent past and the emerging future. It was the ideal gathering place for an imperial society gone mad.

6

Either Socialism Will Defeat the Louse or the Louse Will Defeat Socialism

"MARX DID NOT write anything at all about the banya," philosopher Vasily Rozanov lamented while watching the Russian Revolution of 1917 unfold in Petrograd. This was more than a humorous aside in the midst of unprecedented upheaval. The fate of the banya in the Revolution, Rozanov suggested, could help clarify exactly what the Russian Marxists hoped to achieve. Would the revolution eradicate all vestiges of Russian tradition and history? Would there be a place in revolutionary culture for everyday activities such as going to the banya? Rozanov readily admitted that he was ignorant of Marxist theory and the economic issues Russian Marxists put at the center of their world view. But he wondered whether their fixation on political economy distorted their vision. He believed that they underestimated the powerful influence of the Russian past on the people for whom the revolution was ostensibly taking place. If a distinctive Marxist culture were to emerge, what would it look like? For Rozanov, the question of how people spent their free time and resources revealed just as much about them as economic exploitation or political repression. "What kind of 'developed' age would [the socialist future] be if there were no banyas, no prayers, no holidays?" he asked. What role would specifically Russian traditions play for the proletariat in the future?[1]

The Bolsheviks—the faction of the Russian Marxists that eventually took power—agreed with Rozanov more than he realized: the revolution was supposed to be about everyday life. Only unlike Rozanov, Soviet Marxists disdained engrained Russian traditions. They supported the banya, but only because they saw it as a crucial tool for making the working class healthy and hygienic. Under capitalism, they held, the working class lived in filth and squalor. Their homes and lives were surrounded by debris, refuse, and contagions. A socialist revolution would radically reorganize everyday life. Socialist culture would eclipse bourgeois culture, transforming its institutions and traditions for the benefit of the proletariat.[2] Greater access to facilities for personal hygiene would naturally follow the revolution. Banyas would benefit public health. Socialism would be clean. The workers would rule and when they did they would also wash.

In Russia after October 1917 the Bolsheviks had the opportunity to execute their agenda and create a new kind of banya. The steam room and changing rooms would basically be the same—at least for the time being, old imperial bathhouse buildings would remain in use. But Bolsheviks held that the activities undertaken within them would be transformed. They would no longer be sites of decadence, violence, and sex as they were under the Old Regime. Nor would they be spaces infused with "backward" peasant customs. They would no longer be miserably dark and dank huts, as likely to spread diseases as cure them. Nor would they evoke a timeless Russian past, as Rozanov would have hoped. Instead, socialist banyas would be sites where workers could thoroughly clean themselves without concern about access or exploitation. The community of the banya would be based in social class, not country. In principle, this would come about when banyas ceased to be run as businesses for profit by greedy owners and would instead be run by the state for the benefit of the workers. Immediately following their seizure of power, the Bolsheviks emphasized the proactive and medical approach to the bathhouse that had been prevalent among doctors in the late imperial period and took it a step further. The banya was a tool for preventing epidemics and promoting public health. Municipally run bathhouses would be modern and efficient and replace the exploitative and poorly run bathhouses of the capitalist, imperialist past. Personal hygiene had been elevated to a matter of state concern and therefore state control. Banya culture would adapt to Bolshevik priorities.[3]

As in countless other spheres, the Revolution did not quite bring about the expected results. It proved difficult, if not impossible, for the Soviet state to create the sort of institutions their ideology called for. Writing in *Pravda*, Bolshevik leader Grigory Zinoviev suggested that the "fate of the revolution" would be decided by quiet battles taking place in the "quotidian economy and in everyday life."[4] Providing access to the banya was one of these quiet battles—one that in the 1920s the new socialist state lost. Banyas never became fully Bolshevik. The conditions in them did not improve and there were too few of them to serve the population. A banya culture driven by profit and decadent behavior persisted. But banyas did become partially Bolshevik. By the 1920s Soviet leaders and citizens accepted that supplying people with access to well-run banyas was the new state's responsibility.

Government-run bathhouses were hardly a Bolshevik innovation or monopoly, of course. The hygienic ideals that the Bolsheviks emphasized could be traced to principles of modern medicine and state responsibility for public health more broadly. Municipal bathhouses flourished at the time across Europe and the United States. Nonsocialist states prioritized creating up-to-date bathhouses and pools where the working class could bathe.[5] But for the Bolsheviks, providing for the needs of the working class was also a political goal. The regime's legitimacy rested on providing things like well-run and accessible bathhouses for the proletariat. If that cultural superstructure was not forthcoming, it reflected poorly on the socialist economic base. Their own propaganda about the importance of going to the banya raised the stakes. It is hard to measure whether Russian workers were any cleaner after the revolution than they had been before, but it is clear that under the Bolsheviks, they expected to be cleaner. The Bolsheviks never managed to build banyas quickly enough and equip them well enough to satisfy either their own goals or the demands of the workers and peasants living in the Soviet Union.

They also failed to fully transform banya culture. The sex, socializing, and crime associated with the banya never disappeared, despite the Soviet state's efforts. Other Russian traditions that lingered on after the Revolution and were decried as either backward or bourgeois or both could be said to be dying.[6] But that could not be said of going to the banya. The new state needed banyas; propaganda urged people to use them. The banya was supposed to evolve, not disappear. The Soviet state sought to retain the banya's hygienic function while abolishing its culturally questionable features. The banya proved resistant to this effort to disentangle its official purpose from its popular appeal. People after 1917 continued to go to the banya for the same reasons they had prior to 1917. Some hoped to get clean, of course, but they also went because of tradition, to seek out company, to conspire, to thieve, to hire prostitutes, or to sell sex. The revolutionary state—at least in its first decade—proved incapable of molding bathing practices to its own vision of socialism. At the same time, rampant famine and disease and vocal demands from workers for more access to banyas meant that the new government could ill afford to abandon the institution altogether. Convinced of the centrality of banyas for its purposes and in the eventual power of economics to transform culture, the Soviet state inadvertently buttressed traditions that it had hoped to destroy.

Rozanov need not have worried that his beloved banya, symbol of old Russia, would disappear. The banya held its place. More than that, it came to epitomize the ambiguity of the Soviet impact on everyday life. The Soviet experiment involved layering—sometimes awkwardly, sometimes imperceptibly—Marxist aspirations on top of a resilient Russian past. Amid the tremendous cultural, economic, social, and political changes that accompanied the Bolshevik assumption of power, the banya remained prevalent and popular. Old meanings never fully disappeared even as new meanings were inscribed in their place. As a result, the banya managed to be unquestionably Soviet on the surface even as it remained quintessentially Russian at its core.

———•—•———

Before the Revolution, the Bolsheviks saw banyas as emblematic of economic exploitation. The imperial Russian state did little to manage bathhouses. City governments regulated them and tax codes attempted to generate a profit from them, but they were not state institutions or major state priorities. When conditions in the banyas were bad or access was hard to come by, industrial workers focused their ire on their bosses, the owners of the factory-run banyas. Not surprisingly, these imperial-era industrialists saw little need to keep them in good shape and continued to line their pockets by charging the workers for the privilege of going to them. Some owners automatically docked workers' pay, purportedly to support the factory-run banya. In other cases workers received stipends from their bosses to use a municipal banya, but the amount was usually too small to cover the cost of admission. Commercial banyas were often beyond the reach of workers for a variety of reasons. They could be expensive, located far from working-class neighborhoods, and not open at times that would allow workers to make use of them. Those workers who managed to make it to the banya—and long lines suggested that the effort was a priority for millions of them—often complained about the conditions they found there. Many if not most banyas were too small to accommodate demand. Lack of soap, buckets, heating materials, and clean water made them deplorable.[7]

Pravda, the official organ of the Bolshevik party, declared that workers desired accessible, clean, well-run, and affordable banyas. Labor unrest, which peaked around the empire in the early 1910s, was based in part on everyday concerns. In 1912, some workers struck to demand enough pay to be able to afford to go to public banyas.[8] In 1914 carriage builders protested that they were able to go to the banya only once a month.[9] Other workers bathed far less—construction workers complained that they could go months without access to a banya.[10] In many towns and cities across the empire, the one or two publicly accessible banyas were small and poorly run. In other cases, going to communal banyas made bathers sick. The Bolsehviks clearly thought that workers clamored for greater access to high-quality bathing facilities.[11] Presumably, a socialist revolution would provide them with that access.

If meeting the hygienic demands of workers was hard before 1914, the onset of the First World War made things far worse. Refugees from the front overcrowded cities. Shortages of heating materials and soap made supplying banyas even more difficult than it had been during peacetime. Workers in the cities were hit particularly hard by the demands of war—hours increased, discipline became more strict, and the threat of being sent off to the front hindered collective action.[12]

Lack of access to banyas and proper hygiene was listed among the workers complaints heading into the revolutionary year of 1917. In February, strikes on the streets of Petrograd (the newly Russified name of St. Petersburg) targeted the moribund autocracy, which soon fell. The Provisional Government, which quickly emerged, sought to run the country until a Constituent Assembly could be elected. Dominated by liberals and moderates, the Provisional Government, by its very nature, tabled major policy decisions, such as negotiating a separate peace in the ongoing war with Germany and enacting significant labor or agricultural reforms. At the same time, the Petrograd Soviet of Workers and Soldiers Deputies—modeled on the Soviet of the 1905 revolution—formed to represent what it saw as the interests of the workers and soldiers. Its leadership came from various socialist parties, who staked out a radical alternative to the middle-of-the-road approach of the Provisional Government. The result was "dual power," in which the Soviet kept the Provisional Government in check, particularly when it came to issues of direct concern to workers and soldiers.

Conditions did not improve over the course of 1917 for many peasants, soldiers, or workers, even as the toppling of the autocracy increased their expectation that their demand for peace and economic justice would be met. Even in the hectic and confusing summer of 1917, while the war continued and revolutionary demands in the Soviet became increasingly radical, securing access to banyas remained a pressing need. At the massive Putilov factory in Petrograd, for instance, workers complained that despite the "collective ownership" instituted after February, their wages were in fact being docked because new workers' organizations charged them high rates for basic

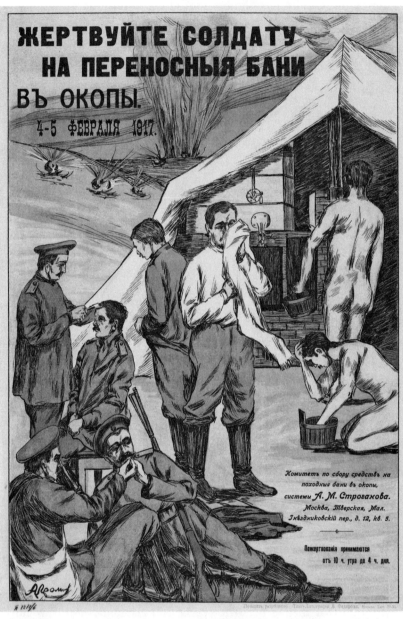

FIGURE 6.1 A poster from early 1917 urged soldiers in the trenches to use mobile banyas at the front. The imperial government recognized the importance of bathing, even as the conditions in the country made it challenging for most people to go to the bath. Courtesy of Lenin Library.

necessities, such as access to the banya.[13] Towns, factories, and villages without banyas could hardly address the problem on their own. The priorities of local and central government were simply elsewhere. Those banyas that did exist often remained in the hands of private owners, who could not have improved conditions even had they made doing so a priority. Under the Provisional Government, workers and peasants' demand for access to banyas went unmet.

Meanwhile, running a banya in the midst of the political unrest and World War proved nearly impossible. Owners found it increasingly difficult to maintain and supply them. They often passed on the hardships to their *banshchiki*, who stood to make little money if clients could not be compelled to come to bathe. Banya workers felt emboldened by the revolutionary atmosphere and protested the conditions of their employment. They joined a wave of workers' unrest in the summer and fall 1917.[14] In Petrograd a representative group of banya workers forced their bosses to negotiate with them, appeared to have reached an agreement about fair pay and conditions, and then were frustrated as the owners reneged at the last minute. On October 27, 1917, the day the Bolshevik leadership coordinated their revolutionary takeover, banya workers in Petrograd threatened to strike, potentially closing down all of the city's municipal banyas.[15]

In the immediate aftermath of the Bolsheviks' seizure of power in October, *Izvestiia*, the official paper of the new government, proudly proclaimed that a plan was underway for an enormous housing complex that included a free banya for the workers. This would be "the first shot in the battle for the people's right to exist in a bright future, on the eve of the destruction of all injustice."[16] Many workers did not wait for gifts. In factories, workers' councils moved to provide open access to the banyas now under their control. In cities in the winter of 1917–1918, neighborhood workers' councils "municipalized" existing banyas and in many cases began to run them as public institutions. Banya management was localized, with no uniform rates, quality controls, inspections, or centralized administration. In the rush of the revolution, neighborhood councils often granted workers, soldiers, students, and invalids free access to banyas. Some city councils distributed tickets to the poor so that they too could bathe for free. Meanwhile, in the countryside the new leaders encouraged the peasants to make their personal bathhouses "communal," allowing access to all workers and soldiers. The banya, at least in principle, became more of a public good than a private business or an independent social space.[17]

Making access to banyas free, however, meant that no revenue was generated to pay for their maintenance, let alone for the improvements that many workers had demanded prior to the revolution. The Russian Civil War that emerged in response to the Bolshevik takeover made matters worse. From 1918 to 1921, epidemics and mass starvation increased the demand for access to banyas, just as the disintegration of the economy and state institutions made provisioning them more difficult. The social dislocation unleashed by occupying armies and relocations of millions of people created optimal conditions for the spread of bacterial infections like typhus and relapsing fever. Doctors understood that lice transmitted these diseases; the vermin excreted rickettsia onto the skin while biting their hosts, who scratched the bites and rubbed the louse's fecal matter into the open wounds. A hot banya, the doctors contended, could kill the lice and stem the transmission of the diseases.

Propaganda posters attempted to explain the vector of diseases in a succinct manner. One simply declared: "The Fight Against Typhus is The Fight Against Lice!" Another showed an image of a louse with words explaining that typhus was a "very vile and dangerous disease" and that a "female louse lays its eggs in the folds and seams of clothing." The eggs hatch and in turn the new lice lay more eggs. "One female louse," the poster explained, could "within two months produce 5,000 offspring." The solution was straightforward: wash clothes, iron them, and "go to the banya more often!"[18] What seemed simple on the posters proved more challenging on the streets.

Desperate conditions made disease more likely and banyas more necessary. But it also made operating them more difficult. Few governmental organizations at any level had the resources to take on the great expense of maintaining and running banyas. Building new ones was out of the question. In Moscow, beginning in 1918 shortages of heating materials forced many banyas to close. Many broke down to the point that, as an official government publication later admitted, "one of the basic demands of a wide spectrum of the population went unmet at the very moment that all-powerful epidemics were on the rise."[19] In most places across Russia, government authorities had limited power and little incentive to invest in banyas. By 1918 Russian workers, soldiers, peasants, and other citizens could only hope that the same worn-down banyas that had been in disrepair even before the Great War, Revolution, and Civil War were still open. When they were, long lines quickly formed. Party leaders, such as Joseph Stalin, attempted to intervene to help

Red Army soldiers access banyas where they existed. The "extremely difficult sanitary conditions" on the front required crucial resources to be diverted toward building banyas.[20] Meanwhile, Leon Trotsky, the War Commissar, had a armor-plated train that included a banya so that at least he and his staff could remain clean and healthy while criss-crossing the country in the Civil War.[21]

The new government emphasized the banya's importance for public health, even as it could do little about the shortages of supplies or the horrendous conditions. In 1918 the Moscow Soviet, for instance, took measures to provide free or cheap laundry services and soap near banyas and standardized admissions fees for banyas at a rate it felt most workers could afford.[22] Newspapers and medical commissions implored all people to go to the banya, which officials considered crucial for controlling the spread of disease.[23] Banyas were to be used as "disinfection chambers" to combat typhus and typhoid fever in particular. The Bolsheviks also hoped to obtain privileged access for certain populations that appeared to be more likely carriers of disease, such as prisoners of war, runaways, and students. *Izvestiia* called on the construction of banyas in key locations where diseases might spread, such as train stations and checkpoints around Moscow to try to protect the capital's residents from being infected by those entering the city.[24]

Controlling epidemics depended on adherence to hygienic norms. The Bolsheviks were eager to establish basic procedures. An article in *Izvestiia* clarified how an ideal banya would be managed. The unwashed entered the banya and immediately went to a room for undressing. After handing over dirty clothes for disinfection, laundering, and ironing, clients would proceed to the banya, where they would clean their bodies with soap and steam. When that was done, they would exit the washroom through a different door than the one through which they had entered, keeping the newly washed people separate from the unwashed. The exit led to a separate dressing room, where they would retrieve their newly cleaned and pressed clothes, and leave the banya. Yet another separate room for the barber would ensure that quasi-medical procedures were done in isolation.[25]

Modern, ideal, socialist banyas, like the one described in *Izvestiia*, could not exist in the middle of a civil war. No funds for such institutions existed. Most citizens were forced to settle for the banyas that remained from tsarist times—and these often had only two rooms: one room for washing and another room for steaming. In the washroom, new bathers undressed while those finishing their baths got dressed. Many people hand washed their clothes in the same room. If they did not, their clothes remained in piles, unwashed. Either way, lice and other carriers of disease could spread from one set of clothes to another, and thus from one bather to another, making it immaterial whether or not people successfully cleaned their bodies in the steam room. These sorts of banyas predominated. Not surprisingly, then, access to "free banyas" had not prevented millions of people from getting sick. Even if people managed to go to the banya, the conditions more often than not failed to rid them of lice.[26] The rush of potentially sick and infected people to poorly run and organized banyas was a deadly serious problem. Officials reported that popular demand overwhelmed capacity. Waiting in line for the banya, of course, was nothing new. But in the context of rampant disease and famine, the urgency with which people sought to clean themselves increased, as did the likelihood that lice would spread from one client to another.

At the very moment when banyas were desired and needed the most, private owners had little incentive to keep them open. By the summer of 1918 the situation had become untenable. The Bolshevik response was to attempt to assert state control. A ruling from the Central Executive Committee of the Russian Soviet Republic (RSFSR) on August 20, 1918 officially shifted banyas from private owners to the communal affairs divisions of town executive committees.[27] In Moscow, banyas fell under the lax supervision of the city's utilities division. But because that division had no money to invest, no ability to obtain credit for investments, and no administrative tools for overseeing banyas, the work of maintaining them fell to the whims of each neighborhood. Neighborhoods often had even fewer resources than the city government and could hardly prioritize the upkeep of the banyas that fell under their charge.[28]

Those banyas that did remain open in these conditions did so because they figured out how to run independently of government oversight. Banya owners charged people money for access, while minimizing how much they provided in terms of heat, water, and other services. Those few commercial banyas that remained open were overcrowded, with little competitive economic incentive for those running them or working there to do their jobs well. Bolshevik municipal leaders later admitted that despite the Central Executive Committee ruling, they had no choice but to allow the preservation of the private control of the banyas in 1918 and 1919.[29] One worker complained that at the same time that prices in the banyas were doubling, articles in the papers were demanding that people wash themselves as frequently as possible.[30]

Many banyas simply shut down. In Moscow by the spring of 1920 only 26 of the 46 banyas that existed prior to 1917 remained open. In Petrograd by 1921 only 21 of 75 pre-Revolutionary banyas were in operation. The capitals were in better shape than many cities across the empire. The town of Iaroslavl', for instance, had a population of well over 50,000 people and went from having four working banyas before the war to zero working banyas in 1918 to only two in 1919.[31] Shortages of heating materials meant that working banyas were open only three or at most four days a week. Towns and cities fought over heating materials. In an effort to stay warm, people burned anything made of wood they could get their hands on, including floors, doors, and furniture. In Moscow alone some 50,000 apartments (or 22 percent of the total) were dismantled unsystematically for heating supplies.[32] This environment explained both the desire for access to a warm banya and the difficulty of actually keeping the banya heated. Some banyas as a result were evidently open "only for show"—they were officially open, but had no heat. In any case, even if all of them had been in full operation, extant urban banyas could only accommodate a small fraction of the demand. At best, Muscovites could bathe once every three months.[33] Even considering other bathing options that may have existed—which frankly were few in the middle of shortages of clean water and heating materials—it is unlikely that people were able to bathe that often.

Memoirs and diaries about the situation in banyas during the Civil War back up the statistics. Princess Sofia Volkonskaia, who returned to Russia in 1919 in an effort to reunite with her imprisoned husband, gave a particularly vivid account of a public banya in Petrograd. After countless ordeals lasting many months, Volkonskaia was desperate to bathe. No longer able to bathe privately on her former estate, she decided to try a communal banya for the first time in her life. She went to one associated with the Alexander Theater where "all artists and theatre workers could get a free wash." Friends helped her obtain a ticket. She was horrified:

> How to describe it? A medium-sized room, the air heavy with steam and the exhalations of human bodies; a crowd of naked women standing in various postures on the slimy, bespitten wooden floor; some nondescript bloodstained rags and cast-off bandages lying in an untidy heap in a corner. . . . The room filled with the noise of angry words and protests for a place near the hot water tap or vacant seat on one of the benches. . . . Hideousness and deformity in every imaginable form and variety. . . . Underfed bodies, meagre, pendant breasts, crooked legs, legs swollen with oedema, legs with big knots of varicose veins, like blue worms moving under the skin; big flat feet deformed by the ugly angles of inbent toes; itching scabies; necks and shoulders powdered with the pink patches of syphilitic roseolas, innocently

peeping out from under the thick gray coat and lice of many months' accumulation. . . . If hell exists, it surely resembles that bathing room of the Alexander Theatre.[34]

Volkonskaia might have written something similar about a pre-Revolutionary banya had she ever visited one. The banya as a sort of hell was by this point a cliché for some members of the upper class. And yet her account conveys the sense that the situation in Petrograd during the Civil War was particularly bad. The scale of the nightmare she described suggests that the banya stood in for the situation in the country more generally. She needed to bathe, the Socialists had promised to improve banyas, but the results were in fact horrific.

Turning to the diary of an "average Muscovite," Nikita Okunev clarifies just how much the situation in the banya had deteriorated during the Civil War. Okunev—employed at a Moscow steamship company—was the son of a small trader and was only one generation removed from the peasantry. He visited the banyas in Moscow regularly and shared none of Volkonskaia's aristocratic elitism. But he too was appalled. In September of 1918, he recorded in his diary a trip to the banya. Calling himself "an unreformed bourgeois," he sought out a few minor luxuries: a *banshchik* to soap him down, shave him, and clip his nails. These services cost many times more than they had before the war. By 1920, the prices had risen again and the conditions had gotten even worse. "Before being able to enter that humid place," he complained, "I was required to stand outside in line for an hour and one half." He also encountered nothing but contempt from the banya workers. His conclusion? "Cramped and filthy (in the banya no less!)—it was unbearable."[35] This was hardly the socialist banya that Bolshevik rhetoric promised would be forthcoming after the Revolution.

The banya crisis was not simply a matter of unmet promises, which in the end could be explained away by the conditions of the Civil War. Especially because the banya was now seen as essential in defeating typhus, the problems plaguing it threatened the stability of the regime. In December 1919 Lenin famously declared, "Either socialism will defeat the louse or the louse will defeat socialism."[36] From 1917 to 1922 over 5 million people reported cases of typhus and relapsing fever and approximately 3 million people died from epidemics. The problem was particularly acute in urban areas that relied on commercial banyas for hygiene: in Moscow in 1919 over 65,000 people died. The mortality rate rose to 461 per 10,000 people, 150 percent higher than the mortality rate in Moscow in the 1860s. In Petrograd in 1920, 64 out of every

1,000 people died from typhus and 31 out of every 1,000 people died from relapsing fever. Prior to the revolution the rates had been almost negligible.[37]

Lenin had hoped that an increase in the number of doctors attempting to tackle the epidemic would help. Banyas were also key to the struggle. By the end of 1919, the Bolshevik leaders decided to use Red Army forces to build banyas.[38] In September 1920 Lenin and the Council of People's Commissars, the supreme administrative body of the fledgling state, passed a decree intended to "provide banyas to the population of the republic."[39] The stated purpose of the decree was "decisively fighting epidemics of typhus and relapsing fever and with the goal of widely disseminating to the population the means to attain cleanliness." Once again, Lenin turned to centralization to attempt to tackle the pervasive banya problem. The decree handed over control of "all banyas of the public type" to local Communal Departments under the supervision of the People's Commissariat of Health and its local organs. This decree targeted all town and village communal banyas with the capacity to service twenty or more people at a time. The People's Commissariat of Internal Affairs (NKVD) was put in charge of coordinating activities to provide workers access to banyas, including helping to build them, reconstruct them, renovate them, and ensure that all were used to their full capacity. Local units of the centralized commissariats were charged with general oversight.[40]

Within a month the People's Commissariats of Interior and Health had further spelled out the meaning of the decree, clarifying that they would thenceforth oversee all banya affairs in the country. They centralized control over all commercial and public banyas, including those located in former municipal organizations, under private control, and in monasteries. They clarified that the decree included banyas that were operating, those that were no longer in operation, and even those that might one day begin to operate.[41]

Socializing banyas proved at least as challenging as socializing other sectors of everyday life. Who would pay for the heating materials or the salaries of the banya workers? In the midst of a feverish effort to build communism while also fighting a Civil War such questions were brushed to the side. In the spring of 1920, the city of Moscow declared a "Banya Week": everyone was granted free access to the city's banyas.[42] At least for a week, banyas were a free public good. Again, Lenin had put the issue succinctly: "How can you run an economy when 70 percent of the people suffer from typhus?"[43] Most weeks, however, the banya was not free. Making bathers buy tickets, even under tight government oversight by the Commissariat of Health, restricted access and reeked of capitalism. The government balanced socialist promises, state needs, and economic circumstances, tipping the scales in favor of the state when necessary. In late 1920 Politburo member Zinoviev had suggested that building public banyas would clarify to the trade unions that the Party had the concerns of the people in mind. Trotsky mocked the idea only to have Lenin lecture him that building public banyas would help stave off workers unrest because doing so clarified what trade unions can do "in plain and intelligible terms."[44] In August 1921 the Central Executive Committee ordered that in response to mass starvation all laundries and banyas were to work at maximum capacity in order to fix shortages and to provide for the masses.[45] Theater performances designed to educate the masses in revolutionary morality emphasized that going to the banya was a civic, communal duty. Preventing the spread of typhus and lice helped keep workers healthy and the economy going.[46] The welfare of the regime was at stake.

In many cases, the measures taken after the assertion of centralized municipal control worked no better than the initial attempt at "municipalization" had worked in the immediate aftermath of the revolution. Banya goers quickly discovered that money they saved on "free" admissions was spent on other basic services. Okunev, who returned to the banya in 1921, clarified just what "free banyas" meant. Although he avoided an entrance fee into the banya building itself, he reported excessive fees to receive treatment for his corns, to use a *venik*, to get water, and even to enter the steam room. The banya employees "attentively watched you to make sure you did not steal your neighbor's filthy pants (which very often happens)" and then demanded a tip for their vigilance. Okunev continued, "This is your free banya. And to hell with it! It is now so filthy, lousy, and cold that it would be better not to go at all. At home I can somehow wash with a bucket."[47]

In 1921, the Moscow city government had done its part to assert control over the capital's banyas. An Administration for Small Municipal Organizations formed to oversee banyas, cleaners, and hairdressers. The city could now attempt to provide free use of the banyas for the entire population on a regular basis. The centralization of the banyas and the assumption of responsibility by the government seem to have had an impact. According to official statistics, the average number of bathers per month nearly doubled to over 900,000. It was a minor victory. On average Muscovites could still only bathe once every forty days. Still, the Bolsheviks finally showed the desire and ability to wrest banyas from private owners.[48]

Creating socialist banyas, however, had to wait. In the spring of 1921, just as Moscow and other municipalities were finally bringing banya management under government control, Lenin and the leadership of the country reversed course and announced a New Economic Policy (NEP). In response to the harsh economic conditions around the country in the aftermath of the Great War and Civil War, NEP was intended to give the new regime some breathing room on the economic front. While the state remained in control of the "commanding heights of the economy" (international trade, communication, banking, large scale industry, etc.), smaller sectors of the economy were reprivatized. A full-fledged effort to make the leap to socialism would have to wait until some unspecified date when the country was better prepared for the effort. Banyas fell in a category of municipal organizations that could be rented out to private entities, once again to be run for profit. Banyas remained a public good in principle. But the overburdened Bolsheviks conceded that perhaps allowing them to operate as private businesses would at least restore them to the deplorable but functioning conditions of the pre-Revolutionary period.

Under NEP, communal banyas did not automatically revert to previous owners, as was the case with some other de-nationalized industries. Instead, municipalities had a range of options. They could run banyas themselves, they could rent them out to others to manage, ostensibly according to rules outlined by the municipality itself, or they could allow fully private baths to operate within their cities. In many places, all three types of administrative structures emerged. Generally speaking, city governments kept control of the banyas in the best shape and leased those that were in need of renovation. By the end of 1921, for instance, the Moscow Soviet directly oversaw the three largest and most popular (and profitable) banyas in the center of the city.[49] Neighborhoods nominally remained in charge of the rest. Ill equipped to run them, they usually rented them out instead.[50]

NEP-era banyas were economic hybrids, often run for a profit but also subordinated to the greater needs of the state. Bureaucrats in the Main Administration of Municipal Services (GUKKh) issued guidelines to cities across the Soviet Union about how to lease their banyas. In 1922 it attempted to impose some order on utilities that had been only haphazardly run during the Civil War. GUKKh administrators wanted functioning banyas, but they also wanted to limit the degree to which the new operators prioritized profit by catering only to wealthy clients. Their rules limited the amount of space a banya could dedicate to luxury services, pegged ticket prices to the amount operators paid in rent to cities, and insisted that even private banyas meet obligations to the public, as determined by government authorities. For instance, "in cases of extreme need, such as the appearance of epidemics," renters were obligated to keep banyas heated for longer than usual and to allow the local medical administrations access to them. Operators were also supposed to provide soldiers and students with free or at least steeply discounted access. Nominally "private" banyas were subject to government oversight.[51]

Under the new system banya owners had little incentive to toe the socialist line and a lot of incentive to return to a profit-motive system. The new rules of NEP allowed for, even encouraged, such profits. Laws compelled cities to keep leasing rates low. If a banya required "colossal renovations" or the "expenditure of tremendous amount of resources and energy"—and many did—then it was permissible to lease out banyas for free, so long as the "interests of the working population" remained a priority.[52] But more importantly, rules said nothing about the amount banyas could charge their customers for the various ancillary services that had been a crucial source of income for banya operators. Banyas ran cafeterias, charged for checking a coat, and added fees for maintaining the steam room. Traditional services quickly returned, as small private businesses took back up their positions inside banya buildings. In the Sanduny banya—in the center of Moscow—massages, access to the pool, and hair cutting were all available for a fee on the spot. Businesses that repaired banyas, provided buckets, and built new banyas also cropped up.[53] Just as "free banyas" were not really free, price restrictions led operators (and *banshchiki*) to make money other than through the sale of tickets.

Banyas had to be profitable enough for operators to want to run them. But they had to be accessible enough for members of the working class to be able to afford to go to them, especially if an epidemic lurked. The state sought to strike a balance. What constituted the right balance was a matter of debate, even within the Soviet bureaucracy. In early 1922 the directors of a banya in Vologda claimed that because their banya provided free access for the unemployed, invalids, orphans, and others, it should not be taxed as a business. Central tax authorities disagreed. They determined that the banya was being used at least some of the time by private, paying citizens and therefore was not exempt. They argued that even banyas that provided some free baths were still businesses.[54]

The NKVD, which oversaw GUKKh, however, estimated that economic pressures had forced over a quarter of the country's banyas to cease operation. The tax was increasing the burden of operating banyas and would no doubt mean that even more would close down. This, according to the NKVD, was "completely unallowable from a sanitary-hygienic and social point of view."[55] When the *Journal of Municipal Services* reported on the debate, it noted, "in the face of unrelenting epidemics this is a serious threat that is necessary to consider carefully." It suggested, "as institutions that carried out sanitary-hygienic functions, communal banyas should be included on the list of enterprises which are freed from the obligation to pay a business tax." The distinction, the article asserted, between trade enterprises seeking to make money and communal banyas seeking to service the mass of workers in the cities, should be clear.[56] Yet the distinction was not clear. Those operating the banyas sought to make money too. Their drive for profits had been integral to getting the country's banyas back up and running after the Civil War. And central tax authorities were trying to fill their coffers, not trying to cut banya operators a break. The banya's ambiguous position—it served state-mandated functions and operated as a business—reflected the ambiguous nature of the economy under NEP more generally. Banyas were socialist in principle but capitalist in fact.

The NEP-era arrangement tipped the scales back in favor of privately-run banyas. Just one year after NEP had been announced, only half the operating banyas in the Russian Soviet Republic (the largest, most populous, and most economically advanced of the Soviet republics) were state-run. The rest were rented out to people who were able to run them for a profit. Even city-run banyas relied on market forces to stay afloat. By 1923 the Bauman neighborhood in Moscow, for instance, had its banya up and running, even as it allowed Red Army soldiers and militiamen to bathe for free. Citywide leaders considered taking it over but decided against it, recognizing that the neighborhood had figured out how to bring in revenues and feared that centralizing control would impede profits.[57]

Like other municipal expenses, the costs of operating a city-run banya were borne in part by a specific tax on workers' wages. But ticket sales and fees for specific services also kept banyas afloat. Municipal banyas were subject to market forces. In principle, Soviet workers were supposed to make enough money to be able to afford to pay their own way to the banyas. But because they often could not, even during the NEP era, city governments periodically instituted "free banya days," echoing the "banya weeks" of the Civil War era. These throwbacks to universal access, however, were increasingly restricted to certain segments of the population (like soldiers) and for limited times.[58] This meant that people hoping to bathe regularly had to have the money to do so. In many cases, workers' wages could not keep up with inflation. The less expensive—and less profitable—banyas that served the poorest parts of the population were the most likely to be shut down or rented out to private entities that would either undertake repairs and raise prices or use the space for something else entirely.

The combination of market forces and municipal regulation stabilized the banya business but stymied the aspirations of Bolshevik leaders, who remained convinced that under socialism workers should have access to cleaning facilities. In 1922 an official statistical study administered by GUKKh found that a majority of the cities, towns, and villages in the Russian Soviet Republic did not have a single communal banya of any kind. Extant banyas often did not operate. Technical, mechanical, and financial problems persisted because neither the cities nor private operators had the means to address them.[59] The problem was acute in some places. Seventy percent of towns with a population below 10,000 people did not have a single banya. Big cities faced problems too. Twenty percent of urban areas with a population of 50,000 to 100,000 did not have a banya either.[60] Leasing banyas to private operators had succeeded in getting some imperial-era banyas reopened. But the goal was to go further—to build new banyas or at least to refurbish run-down banyas at a rate that could keep up with demand.

Municipal service administrators could not solve the problem without a broader shift in economic policies. On the plus side, banyas were profitable. By one calculation, in 1925 they provided 14 percent of the net receipts from municipal enterprises for cities across Russia.[61] NEP had created the conditions in which banyas, especially those rented out to private operators, brought in much-needed revenue. But on the negative side, NEP had also created the conditions in which operators had little incentive to improve conditions and cities had little wherewithal to reinvest their earnings into new or improved bathhouses. Central administrators could publish articles outlining standards and instructions for how to build banyas. They could emphasize the banya's role in combatting disease and, therefore, strengthening the state. They could note that people demanded banyas and recognize their importance for hygiene. But under NEP, administrators could not finance them from above or compel cities or operators to invest in them from below.

To the extent possible, banyas were doing what they were supposed to do. But under the existing system at least, they could not offer anything close to the universal access to hygiene that the Bolsheviks had envisioned and promised. Without additional investments, they could not even reach prewar levels of accessibility and efficiency. In 1898, 75 percent of towns in the Russian Empire had a banya. Medical administrators, politicians, and towns people had deemed the numbers insufficient to meet the hygienic needs of the population. Clearly things had gotten worse in the First World War and Civil War. The burst of banya openings provided by NEP did little to make up for the lost ground. The percentage of towns with a communal bath jumped from 47 percent in 1923 to 53 percent by 1925. Growth soon flattened, with only 56 percent of the towns having a banya by 1926.[62] Put another way, 44 percent of the towns in the Russian Republic did not have even a single communal banya almost a decade into Soviet rule. The limited access to cleaning facilities that had appeared unacceptable to many urbanites and workers before 1917 had become worse, not better.

Just as disappointingly, the conditions in many of the banyas that did exist remained poor. In Moscow, administrators reported that "poor ventilation, dampness, peeling walls, crumbling wooden sections of the buildings" were common. One solution was to figure out a way to compel municipal administrators to reinvest banya profits back into banya infrastructure. GUKKh administrators worked with the People's Commissariat of Health and city-level health and construction administrators with the goal of developing model projects and rationalizing the banya business to meet the needs of the people.[63] But many of the challenges were beyond the capacity of even this broad group of interested parties to solve. For instance, improving bathhouses depended in part on improving water works. But by the mid-1920s nearly forty towns with populations of over 20,000 people (including eight towns with populations over 60,000 people) did not have waterworks.[64]

The market forces fostered by NEP helped reopen some banyas, but that did not guarantee access to them for the poorest members of the population. By 1922, Okunev reported that heating materials had reappeared in the banya. But the price of services was still too high for him. Ticket prices had once again skyrocketed. Apparently, workers were no more satisfied with banya conditions than they had been before the revolution. Many people in the banya could not even afford soap. They would either ask their neighbors for some or attempt to steal some when another bather with soap was washing his eyes or headed off for water. Okunev overheard a conversation in front of the ticket office that seemed to suggest that access to banyas was indeed part of the reason workers had supported the revolution in the first place—and why they remained unsatisfied with the direction things had taken since. One person in line said, "I'm a fool. [In 1917] I marched on Tverskoi Street [the main thoroughfare of Moscow] with a red flag and yelled, 'down with the tsar'. But no matter what you yell, our banyas remain in sorry shape . . . And such rudeness is rampant now." Another person in line added, "Wait, by Easter [going to the banya] will cost a million [rubles]," to which the first responded, "And so what? It already costs nearly that much." A third added a idle threat, "Let them continue to fight us, it'll just make us angrier!"[65]

Banyas failed to meet the expectations of the workers on whose behalf the Bolsheviks claimed to rule. The abysmal conditions were obvious to bathers and government officials alike. In the middle of the 1920s, banyas around the Soviet Union were poorly organized, in disrepair, and could not come close to meeting basic hygienic requirements. The paradox remained— authorities saw banyas as essential in the fight against diseases even as they admitted that existing banyas were clearly not up to the task assigned to them. But not much could be done in the circumstances. Workers protested both the absence of banyas in certain locations and the conditions in those that did exist. An article in *Izvestiia* in July 1926 summed up the difficult situation for banyas in Moscow. No new bathhouse had been built during the previous twelve years. Those that had been were built before 1914 were in need of renovations. *Izvestiia* also noted that the work conditions for the *banshchiki*—which had been the impetus for strikes in 1917—were hardly good either. The paper called for unemployed workers to seek out work in the banyas and for engineers to help fix-up old ones. But renters felt little compulsion to improve conditions. One fired all of his employees. Another faced lawsuits about work conditions. And *banshchiki* in at least one place struck in protest.[66]

Meanwhile, Party authorities began to worry that complaints from workers about banyas and other everyday necessities were drowning out "more important" issues.[67] NEP, as a compromise with capitalism, was not yielding great support among the workers, at least when it came to banyas. By 1927 the Party seemed to accept that the complaints were legitimate and re- quired attention. Leaders conceded that a socialist state should indeed build banyas for the masses. In October 1927 Moscow leaders organized a banya- laundry fund to oversee activities in Moscow, including building one banya a year.[68] The modest goal would have been an improvement on the first ten years of the revolution but would not have kept pace with population growth. It was at best an incremental plan to solve a colossal problem.

—◦—

By Bolshevik logic, NEP's capitalist economic relations were bound to foster bourgeois elements in the culture writ large. Behavior in banyas proved the point. NEP-era banyas continued to be rife with theft, prostitution, violence, and other sorts of atrocities that socialism was supposed to eradicate. "It's not a banya, it's a place for thieves," one article in *Communist Labor* (*Kommunisticheskii trud*) noted about a typical banya. The author advised bathers to bring a trusted companion with them to the banya to watch over their belongings while they bathed. "If you walk in alone," he warned, "you'll walk out naked." The banya hired security personnel, but they were capricious and failed to prevent theft. Banya employees, the article reported, were more interested in making money than doing their jobs. The barber who worked in the banya, for instance, complained that his official work interfered with a card game he operated on the side. Theft, corruption, and leisure predominated, not health or hygiene.[69]

Fictional banyas highlighted the conditions in the actual banyas. In 1924 the humorist Mikhail Zoshchenko satirized NEP-era banyas in a story called simply "Banya," based on letters to the editor of *The Red Gazette*. Zoshchenko later explained, "[The letters] are helpless and comical. But at the same time they're serious. I should say so! They concern a human affair of no little importance: the banya."[70] In the story, an average *muzhik* (a simple man of the people) narrates in a working-class vernacular what happens when he goes to an urban banya on a Saturday, the traditional day for bathing in Russia. He runs into various problems checking his clothes, receiving linens, finding a bucket to wash with, figuring out where to store his coat check ticket on his naked body, and finally, retrieving his clothes after he's finished bathing. The story opens with the narrator describing an ideal banya, using an imaginary American banya as his foil:

> I hear tell, citizens, they have some excellent banyas in America. For example, a citizen just drives in, drops his linen in a special box, then off he'll go to wash himself. He won't even worry, they say, about loss or theft. He doesn't even need a ticket.[71]

The American banyas, in Zoshchenko's telling, were run the way that Soviet banyas were supposed to be run. "The American will wash himself, come back, and they'll give him clean laundry—washed and pressed. Foot-wrappings, no doubt, whiter than snow. Underwear mended and sewed. That's the life!"[72] The imaginary American banyas were all the more wonderful in comparison with the experience of going to a bath in Russia. "Well, we have banyas, too," the narrator concedes, "But they're worse." So much for the Soviet promise of providing for the everyday needs of the workers and for the triumph of socialism over capitalism.

Workers had little choice about where to bathe. The narrator explains: "I went to one of our banyas (after all, I can't go all the way to America)." Once in the washroom, he asks a fellow bather who is using three buckets if he could share one. The other bather accuses him of attempting to steal the bucket and threatens to hit him. The narrator responds with incredulity— "This isn't the tsarist regime"—before moving on. Meanwhile, those washing their clothes in the washroom splattered other bathers, such that "No sooner do you get yourself all washed up than you're dirty again." Zoshchenko made clear that his satire was not directed at a specific banya. "Of course, the reader might be curious to know: what kind of banya was this? Where is it located? What's the address?" The answer, "The usual kind. Where it costs [only] ten kopecks to get in."[73] For those who could not pay for the greater luxuries as-sociated with select banyas, the conditions remained poor—reminiscent of "tsarist times" and not the Promised Land associated with "American banyas." Zoshchenko recalled that while writing the story he laughed uproariously, but he also recognized the somber and dreary side of the story, the painful absurdity of not being able to bathe.[74]

By chance, Zoshchenko submitted the story, along with others, to a journal edited by Mikhail Kuzmin, the author of the famous banya scene in *Wings*. Kuzmin rejected Zoshchenko's story.[75] After it was published by an-other journal the story so resonated with readers that it helped him became one of the most popular Russian writers of the decade.

Other writers pointed out the problems with Soviet banyas too. In a short piece called "Banya Affairs," published in 1924 in *The Signal* (*Gudok*), the organ of the railroad workers' union, writer Mikhail Bulgakov highlighted the various challenges—bureaucratic, technical, and administrative—that confronted those who wanted to find a place to clean themselves. Near one rail station, he reported, "no living unwashed soul would even look in the banya" because it lacked a working boiler. The local bureaucrats blamed their superiors up the chain of command for simply not approving their request for repairs. Meanwhile, Bulgakov noted, "muddy workers itch themselves," while the local administrator "strokes his white body," having bathed else-where. Workers' complaints at meetings and exposés on the situation fell on deaf ears. Bulgakov noted that, "red tape triumphs" while the "people become encrusted in filth." Another banya had frogs and lizards in the water. In an-other town the local administrators did not allocate enough fuel, meaning that the banya could only be heated once a month. And in another town two thousand people had no banya at all. The administrators did not even con-sider building one, citing a lack of funds. On those occasions when a banya existed, tired workers had to wait for hours for a turn and even then it was often cold.[76]

Bulgakov ended his report with a final plea to the administrators that he held responsible for the situation. He emphasized that the health of the population was at stake, explaining "our body breathes not just with the lungs, but also through the skin, through countless pores." "All the poisonous substances released by our body," he continued, "are removed in the form of sweat through the pores." Sweat-inducing heat was essential. Administrators, he insisted, "must take this into account and take all necessary measures so that workers can use banyas." He made clear that workers understood the importance—and science—of bathing; the Bolshevik bureaucrats were the ones not taking the situation seriously enough.[77]

NEP-era articles made clear that Zoshchenko and Bulgakov's accounts were based on a set of experiences that were common in the Soviet Union. Across the country, the situation in many banyas bordered on the absurd. If technical and bureaucratic problems could be solved, other, social problems often emerged. In one banya, twenty workers were employed to watch over people's belongings while they bathed, to no avail. Theft remained common. In 1924 "bandits" stole some 400 rubles from a banya. In 1925 various household items were stolen at Moscow's famous Sanduny banya.[78]

As in Zoshchenko's "Banya" story published that same year, naked bathers found it hard to keep track of their clothes-check tickets. To make matters worse, thieves easily forged tickets to steal clothes. So even if bathers figured out a way to keep their tickets on their naked bodies—Zoshchenko's character tied his ticket to his leg with a string—there was no guarantee that their clothes would be there at the end. In the Zoshchenko story, the narrator received from the attendant another man's clothes instead of his own. One article—written in direct response to Zoshchenko's story—recommended that instead of a ticket with a number on it, bathers be given a basin with a number on it when they checked their clothes, which would be easier to hold onto and harder for would-be thieves to forge.[79] The practice never caught on.

Theft was only one of many problems. Banyas during NEP remained a focal point of all sorts of illegal activity. They were the site of suicides, murders, fights, and beatings, at least according to reports in the national papers.[80] Beyond violent crime, banyas became known as places for people to gather when they were "missing work or shirking their duties."[81] They were also commonly used for distilling alcohol, which was then consumed in the banya.[82] The carousing, drinking, and socializing made banyas potentially politically suspect as well.

Pravda reported that banyas were a potential site for political activity and agitation. Authorities called upon workers and Red Army soldiers to go to banyas in order to take arguments against "factionalism" to the people.[83]

Perhaps the greatest indication that the NEP-era banya remained mired in bourgeois culture was the continued prevalence there of prostitution. The Sanduny Banya in Moscow was a key case in point. Sanduny was officially one of the three banyas still run by the city's Municipal Services Division (MKKh). In practice, administrators at MKKh leased the right to run the banya. This meant that Sanduny, although officially run by the city, in fact operated in practically the same way as it had before the revolution. MKKh did not pay *banshchiki* any salary. Instead, the city collected rent from them in exchange for allowing them to operate the banya and make a profit in whatever way they could. With ticket prices regulated, tips from clients remained essential for the *banshchiki*. Some clients clearly expected to be able to pay for sex. A 1922 inspection by the Moscow Soviet revealed that the *banshchiki* in the Sanduny family baths brought clients prostitutes from the streets. For this service, the *banshchiki* received tips from both the clients and the prostitutes. In addition, the homosexual subculture that had existed in public places such as banyas before the revolution, with male prostitution and the bartering for sex, was partially reconstituted. Rather than confront the problem city bureaucrats evidently chose to look the other way.[84]

As *Pravda* reported after the prostitution scheme at Sanduny was uncovered, the case revealed the "depravity" that took place night and day in the center of Moscow. The court determined that the prostitution ring was a "holdover from bourgeois life" and declared the *banshchiki* guilty and sentenced them to five years in prison. The two overseers from the city government received five-year sentences for "abuse of power." Witnesses were less certain. One prostitute testified openly that "I strongly of my own free will and with pleasure give the *banshchiki* tips and no one can prevent me from doing that." The *banshchiki* defended their work on straightforward grounds: this sort of thing had been common during the tsarist regime and, in any case, people could find prostitutes easily enough without their assistance. They were just the middlemen.[85]

A few weeks later *Pravda* again addressed the "unseemly activities" in the family baths at Sanduny. Evidently the case had been used to teach a lesson to a large meeting of workers. Authorities explained that the professional prostitutes, the "pimps," and the "merchants" all shared responsibility for the situation. The workers in the audience were supposed to learn that this sort of "night time relaxation," which had been part of street life in the tsarist era, was

Historian Sheila Fitzpatrick has suggested that a Muscovite who left the city before the Revolution and returned in the middle of the 1920s would find his surroundings familiar.[91] The Revolution had yet to leave a strong mark on the city. This was certainly true of banyas—their addresses had not changed, many of the people working in them remained the same, and, after a period of intense distress during the intervening world war, revolution, and civil war, they were once again run more or less according to the old rules. *Banshchiki* worked for tips, which encouraged them to meet the demands of their paying clients rather than the state. Superstitions continued to hold sway.[92] Many banyas were more run down than they had been before the end of tsarist rule. The service in the poorer sections remained deplorable, while people with more means could pay for greater luxuries. Little had changed in rural banyas either. Peasants still heated them mostly on holidays, still used birch *veniki* to slap one another, and still seemed to prioritize ritual over the "principles of hygiene and sanitation."[93] Overall, Bolshevik banyas looked a lot like imperial banyas.

In 1917 Rozanov had asked how banyas would be transformed under socialism. Neither he nor the Bolsheviks expected the answer to be "not much." Rozanov may have been relieved to learn this, but the news irked the Bolsheviks on both a theoretical and practical level. The tremendous sacrifices of the revolution were undertaken to improve the everyday lives of workers. The laboring classes expected more. They had revolted in part because of the horrendous conditions of their lives. Poorly run communal banyas were an obvious emblem of poverty and neglect—and their lack of improvement suggested the revolutionary promise had not been realized.

The official reason why things had not gotten markedly better during the NEP years was that the tsarist and capitalist past impeded the steady march toward socialism. Others believed that NEP itself had made it difficult to eradicate the very evils of Russian society that the revolution had originally targeted. The immoral behavior of the Moscow administrators who oversaw the prostitution ring at the Sanduny banya and the fear of "factionalism" festering in meeting places such as banyas suggested another element of blame: bureaucrats and opportunists had infiltrated and corrupted the system. A purge was in order.

In 1924 Zoshchenko's story "Banya" had satirized the conditions, clients, and employees in the average Soviet banya. His target was clear and localized. Frustrations with banyas were commonplace. The absurdity of losing one's ragged clothes or arguing over a wash bucket or small piece of soap was the stuff of humor, even as people understood that access to a good banya could be a matter of life or death.

The decade ended on a more sour note, with the publication and performance of the play *Banya* by the revolutionary poet Vladimir Maiakovsky. Despite the title, the banya did not appear in the play. When asked why it was called *Banya* Maiakovsky responded, "Because it is the one thing that isn't there." Instead, the title invoked what was needed—a symbolic banya that could rid the society of its problems. Maiakovsky implied that the Soviet Union in the wake of NEP desperately needed to be washed clean. As with his earlier plays, *Banya* used metaphors of hygiene and purity. The 1920s had made parasites only more difficult to attack, germs only more challenging to exterminate. Maiakovsky's goal was to take society to the cleaners—a phrase rendered in Russia as "to organize a banya" for society. "What is *Banya?* Whom does it wash?" Maiakovsky asked. His answer: "*Banya* washes (it simply launders) bureaucrats." Later he added, "*Banya* cleans and washes. *Banya* defends horizons, inventiveness, enthusiasm." A well-organized and operated banya could prepare the country for the leap toward socialism. These metaphors were integrated into the advertising that accompanied performances of the play. Posters stated, "We can't clean the swarm of bureaucrats right away / and there are neither enough banyas nor enough soap for us."[94] The Soviet Union needed more and better banyas to attack both real and metaphorical parasites. The play was performed during the first few months of 1930. Critics in the Soviet press panned it. On April 10 Maiakovsky attended a performance of the play at the Meierhold Theater. Four days later he committed suicide. But the idea that socialism would eventually prevail over parasites lived on. All that was needed was more banyas.

7

Things Are Bad on the Banya Front

THE SUCCESS OF Joseph Stalin's effort to transform the Soviet economy and society is often measured in pig iron and steel. Its failure can be measured in banyas. To be sure, the millions of people needlessly killed by famine and disease, the loss of countless others in industrial accidents, and the violent arrest and execution of national minorities and "harmful elements" from society at large and the Party in particular are striking demonstrations of the costs of Stalin's rule.[1] Examining banyas reveals something else about the Soviet Union in this period. The woeful state of construction and upkeep of banyas exhibit clearly and unequivocally the failure of the Stalinist system to meet its own goals. The Party and state leadership wanted to build banyas—it made them a part of the plan, it funded them, it propagandized on their behalf, and it chided local administrators to construct and maintain them. When these initiatives did not produce enough banyas in enough places, the next step was to find people to blame.

Socialism was supposed to be clean and modern. A lack of personal hygiene could not be ignored by either the state or those desperate for a bath. Yet despite the demands of the people and the imperatives of the Party, banyas went unbuilt and undersupplied in the Stalin years. Studying banyas in the 1930s helps expose the challenges of getting things done in the Soviet planned economy. It also lays bare the often dismal consequences of the effort to "build socialism" on the everyday lives of Soviet citizens. Attempting to fulfill (or overfulfill) high-profile state priorities, such as heavy industry or "heroic projects"—such as the Moscow Metro—came at the price of lesser priorities—including meeting citizens' and the Party's standards for basic services.[2] The state grew more powerful, but the people did not get much cleaner.

During NEP the deteriorating banya infrastructure could be blamed on the imperial legacy or on the remnants of capitalism in society. But the poor state of banyas in the age of socialism was less excusable. Stalin inherited the NEP system from Vladimir Lenin and oversaw the state and Party as its troubling results unfolded. By the second half of the 1920s the economy seemed to be enriching petty traders and entrepreneurial farmers at the expense of workers and the state. Political leaders seemed incapable of bending the economy to their will. Banya operators, for example, were more interested in making money than in providing a public service to the working population. Many, if not most, Party leaders hoped that NEP would somehow slowly evolve into socialism. By 1927 Stalin, however, feared that the continuation of NEP would lead to the strengthening of capitalist forces in society and a weakening of the drive toward achieving the goals of the revolution. Rather than preparing the society for socialism, NEP seemed to be making the possibility of true socialism even more remote. The situation outside the USSR made the contradictions of NEP even more pressing. Stalin saw the existential need to build up industry so that the USSR might defend itself from what he viewed as a "capitalist encirclement." Rapid industrialization required greater state control of the economy, which seemed to require a break from NEP and renewed revolutionary fervor, with the Bolshevik state itself setting the pace.[3]

Beginning in 1928, Stalin led a "revolution from above"—a three-pronged approach to radically restructuring the economy and society. Each prong affected the function and place of banyas in society directly. First, Stalin oversaw a violent campaign to requisition grain from the peasantry, who had been increasingly reluctant to sell their produce on the market. In turn, to better control and monitor the agricultural sector, the state forced all peasants into large collective farms (*kolkhozy*), overseen by the Party apparatus. Most other Bolsheviks had been reluctant to undertake these steps—they knew that chaos would ensue, as an entrenched peasantry would resist their efforts. But Stalin insisted, fearing that a failure to act decisively would lead to regime-threatening results. When peasants predictably fought back, Stalin insisted that the state respond with violence. Over a remarkably turbulent three-year period, the countryside was forcibly collectivized and the Party firmly established its presence on the newly formed collective farms or *kolkhozy*. It finally had control over the peasantry and the harvest—or what was left of it. It also took responsibility for providing social services—like banyas—to the population. At least in principle, the rural banya went from being a family affair to being run directly by state agencies.

The assertion of authority came at a heavy price. Millions of peasants fled their rural villages in search of work in cities; millions more were arrested and deported. The struggle and vindictive state policies against perceived threats in the countryside resulted in the man-made famine of 1932–1933, which affected the USSR's most productive grain growing regions most severely, leaving approximately 7 million dead in its wake. The famine also fueled epidemics that accompanied sick and weakened people as they dispersed across the country.[4] The spread of infectious diseases underscored the importance to the state of scrubbing the population (and their clothes) clean. As had been the case during the famine of 1921, building banyas—always at least a nominal aspiration of the socialist state—became a much more urgent matter. In the context of typhus, scrofula, and other highly infectious skin diseases associated with dirt and malnutrition, banyas could save lives.

Collectivization alone caused a demographic and health crisis of colossal proportions. The economic disruptions were exacerbated by the second prong of the revolution from above: the push for the rapid industrialization of the economy. Not only did the Bolsheviks believe in the necessity of industrialization as a prerequisite for socialism; Stalin and his associates also thought that industrial capacity was necessary for the USSR to be able to defend itself in an inevitable war with capitalist powers. The first Five-Year Plan (FYP) replaced NEP's small-scale capitalism with a system in which the whole economy was "planned" from above. The idea was to liberate the system from the vagaries of capitalist forces that seemed to produce and distribute goods and services in ways that prioritized the whims of the rich over the needs of the working poor or of the state. The plan would change all that, demolishing the remnants of the market and harnessing the whole economy toward the state's (and therefore the proletariat's) goals. In terms of hygiene, this meant the state would organize and build well-equipped banyas in highly populated workers' neighborhoods throughout the country. According to the plan, they would operate at hours that allowed workers to make use of them. The plan called on the state finally to accomplish what NEP had failed to bring about. It would ensure that working-class banya goers had enough soap, sponges, buckets, hot water, and steam to clean themselves according to the standards of modern hygiene.

The totalizing effort on the economic front worked better on paper than it did in practice, however. The movement of people, urgency to meet far-fetched plans, and the need to build new industries from the ground up led to uneven production, poor quality products that had to be reworked down the line, clogged or disrupted supply chains, and gross mismanagement. Even basic necessities became scarce. Indeed, by 1931 the Party accepted a restructured market for basic foodstuffs.[5] While small-scale entrepreneurship and individual initiatives could bridge the gap for small-scale necessities, the state alone could provide the infrastructural support required to build and maintain banyas. Banyas required too much investment and government co-ordination to benefit from the small-time trading that cropped up in legal and semilegal spheres of Soviet life. There were no "private" communal banyas in Stalin's Soviet Union. But building state-run-and-operated banyas was also not a very high priority compared to the state's overarching industrial goals. In principle, building banyas fit solidly and comfortably within the Stalinist effort to modernize. In fact, banyas required more resources than the state was able to provide in the midst of rapid industrialization.

"Cultural revolution" represented the third prong of Stalin's revolution from above.[6] Laying the foundation for a socialist economy and society would finally break the backs of the "kulaks," "Nepmen," and "old intelligentsia" who presumably stood in the way of the socialist offensive. A socialist culture would replace the last vestiges of bourgeois life. The elimination of capitalism in the countryside and the establishment of a socialist economy geared to-ward meeting the goals of the state made it possible to build a fully socialist society and culture—a process that had been hamstrung during NEP by a lack of resources and the contradictory policies of the state itself. A 1928 ar-ticle in *Izvestiia* titled "Leninism and the Problems of Cultural Revolution" pointed out that the state had made too little progress in bettering the workers' living conditions, particularly in such "small" but significant areas like banyas. *Pravda* later stated more clearly that building socialism required building amenities such as banyas for the workers.[7] The banya associated with the Russian past, sin, and exploitation would finally be eliminated. The state would no longer be indebted to market forces to keep banyas open. What remained was the utilitarian goal of providing enough banyas to clean the population.

Stalin aimed for a cultural revolution that would offer the workers an op-portunity to taste the sweet fruits of revolutionary power and modern culture. This took fantastic forms, as state-sponsored writers, architects, filmmakers, and artists attempted to reshape people's minds and souls with grandiose visions of a better world in the making. The promised land of communism may not have been a reality, but literature showed the process by which sacri-fice, loyalty to the system, and hard work made its realization in the not-too-distant future inevitable. The cultural revolution also took concrete forms, as the state promised workers access to education and upward mobility, institutional support for ethnic minorities, and banyas for hard-working people throughout the USSR. Countless articles made clear that keeping oneself (and society) clean was a key component of the new, cultured, socialist system.

The first FYP took for granted that a modern state would provide its citizens with easy access to public banyas.[8] Konstantin Ukhanov, a representative on the Moscow City Soviet, declared at the beginning of the FYP, "it will be necessary to build a series of new banyas and laundries, and to organize and supply them with the newest technological equipment. . . . This task will be a very important way to ease the living conditions of the workers."[9] Providing the public access to cleaning facilities was vitally important for a socialist country that proclaimed its commitment to the well-being and health of the working people. The push for more banyas was not just a question of modern public health; it was also a question of building socialism. A 1930 review of the conditions on the "banya and laundry front" declared, "Under the conditions of the Cultural Revolution and under the conditions of building socialism in our country, they [banyas and laundries] have and should have tremendous meaning."[10]

With very few exceptions, Soviet cities did not have waterworks. Filling buckets at a well and hauling them back to living quarters proved difficult, time consuming, and often insufficient to get people clean. Banyas were a necessity. Articles in *Pravda* and *Izvestiia* made it clear that responsibility for providing workers with access to banyas lay with the state and Party. Only state-run banyas could make clean, progressive citizens. In the USSR (as in many places), physical purity implied internal moral purity as well. Articles emphasized that people on the collective farms wanted to bathe regularly and that "cultural living" in villages and in cities involved in no small part getting clean. *Pravda* informed its readers that a "love of cleanliness" pervaded the USSR and emphasized the need to build more banyas. Collective farm workers declared that the banya was central to living a modern life. One article asked what a cultured worker needed in his factory. The answer in part: access to a working banya. What did miners on the Donbass region want to improve their conditions? A banya. *Izvestiia* cited going to the banya as an ideal example of socialist behavior.[11] Bathhouses existed in other modern countries—but in Soviet socialism banyas would be so prevalent, so accessible, and so well used that its citizens would soon be the cleanest and healthiest on earth. The

USSR set for itself the goal of catching up and surpassing the West not just in the production of steel but also in its ability to keep its population clean.

The banya was significant both in actual terms—the workers demanded them, the state promised them—and in metaphorical terms—the whole society needed to be cleaned up. The language of cleanliness (and its opposite, such as filth and parasites) was prevalent in the society in the 1930s more broadly. The goal of the FYP was to modernize society—and that modernity would be clean and efficient. In keeping with the thrust of the revolution from above the soul and body would be cleansed of the tsarist (and capitalist) past. Any remaining layers of dirt from earlier eras had to be washed away. Any people who remained filthy had to be excised from the society. As the brigadier of a collective farm explained to *Pravda* in 1936, "The 18 years of the revolution have scrubbed [society] clean like a banya, we have washed all the parasites down to the smallest one clean off of ourselves."[12] The metaphorical filth and parasites hampering the body politic was analogous to the filth and parasites ravaging the bodies of Soviet workers.

The state trumpeted banyas in part to meet workers' demands for the very conditions that the state itself had insisted were forthcoming. In 1931, when banya construction and other public services had made little progress, Stalin emphasized the extent to which the state had to be responsive to workers' needs: "[The worker] demands that all his material and cultural requirements be met, and it is our duty to fulfill this demand of his." The state required tremendous sacrifice from workers—it only made sense to Stalin that the "workers in their turn demand that the Soviet government should fulfill its obligations in regard to further improving their material and cultural condition."[13] Stalin's words were readily applied to banya construction, further emphasizing the state's intention of providing people with the wherewithal to bathe. Daniil Sulimov, the Chairman of the Council of People's Commissars of the Russian Soviet Federative Socialist Republic (RSFSR), for instance, cited Stalin's speech when discussing the need to build more banyas in Moscow and Leningrad.[14] Hundreds of articles in national papers furthered the sense that demanding a banya was the right of workers not just in the Russian Republic, but in every republic of the USSR.[15]

Stalin understood that the promises had not yet become a reality. He liked to go to the banya as a form of relaxation, but he knew that others did not have the same sort of access he did.[16] In 1931 Iakov Matiukin, an old revolutionary who had known Stalin before the revolution, penned a personal letter to the leader explaining the need for greater attention to the country's sanitary conditions. He wrote, "You know that I am a cultured person and culture

FIGURE 7.1 At the opening of Usachev Banya in the Khamovniki neighborhood of Moscow a banner quoted from Stalin's 1931 speech acknowledging Soviet workers' legitimate desire to have their material and cultural requirements met. Courtesy of RGAKFD.

more than anything requires cleanliness." The problem was that cleanliness was hard to come by when workers lived in apartments without running water and when there was "no soap, there are long lines to go to the banya, and the banya is filthy from overuse." Matiukin evidently wrote a similar letter to another old revolutionary acquaintance—Mikhail Kalinin, the Politburo member and Chairman of the All-Russian Congress of Soviets Executive Committee.[17] Socialism required cultured workers; cultured workers required cleanliness; cleanliness required banyas.

Banyas were desirable for another practical reason. State administrators and doctors argued that bathing helped stem the spread of infectious disease. One report of the People's Commissariat of Municipal Services of the Russian Republic stated, "The sanitary defense of the country and the fight with epidemic diseases both in conditions of peace and war require in the coming years that the people of the RSFSR have banyas ... We must build new ones that can treat the whole population."[18] In regions where typhus was rampant and upward of 20 percent of the population was infested with lice, banyas were considered an essential element in maintaining public health.[19]

If the goal was to prevent disease, why did the Soviets insist on banyas instead of showers? The issue came up in March 1932, in the midst of the effort to rapidly industrialize the economy and at the outset of the catastrophic famine. Experts met in Moscow to discuss the future of Soviet bathing. Representatives from the Banya-Laundry Administration (*bannoprachechnogo upravelenia*), the People's Commissariat of Health, the military sanitation department, the sanitary institute, and construction engineers gathered to debate whether the country should build showers or more steam rooms for the woefully underwashed masses of Soviet citizens. Technical experts, who had recently toured Germany's bathing facilities, concluded that showers were easier to operate, allowed more people to clean themselves in a shorter amount of time, and were more sanitary. Shower stalls separated people more successfully than the banya, where bathers came into constant contact with one another and shared soap, basins, and sponges. A military sanitary expert pushed further: steam rooms in certain circumstances were even damaging to people's health. The defense of the country, he argued, called for the building of showers, not traditional banyas.[20]

The idea of substituting showers for Russian banyas, however, did not even make it out of committee. An engineer from the Banya-Laundry Administration pointed out that in places where there were not enough showers, Russian-style banyas would remain necessary. And even where showers had been built, he added, the Soviet population continued to prefer Russian-style steam baths. New, expensive showering facilities sat empty while old, traditional facilities, even those in need of repair, were overworked and in high demand. Finally, he noted that if either water supply or heat was inconsistently available (as it was throughout the USSR at the time), the alleged benefits of a shower would be lost: "[One place] has sixty shower stalls but the population avoids them. Following the Berlin example we build showers, but we can't forget the Russian banya." At the very least, the Soviet state needed to invest in mixed style facilities, with both steam rooms and showers. Another like-minded participant in the discussion questioned whether showers were in any way more hygienic than banyas. Russians, he reasoned, needed banyas to really get clean.[21] This also seemed to be the consensus among those on the local level in charge of public hygiene. Where showers had been planned, municipal authorities often insisted on building Russian-style banyas anyway—and, when pressed, would simply overreport the number of shower facilities relative to banyas in their region to appease central authorities.[22]

The committee tacked toward a compromise. Whether banyas were good for health and hygiene or not, there was no question they were more popular than showers. The question was whether the influence of customs and the strong association of the banya with "age-old habits" should hold sway or whether the population should be taught to appreciate the shower. The debate in the end was moot. The committee concluded that the possibility of eliminating steam baths was only theoretical. Two issues stood in the way of changing the policy: first, Russian banyas constituted too big a percentage of the cleaning facilities in the country to be done away with; second, popular proclivities meant that steam baths, especially for the rural population, would remain essential for Soviet hygiene. The committee called for a study of the comparative health effects of the various bathing methods, but in terms of immediate plans it equivocated. Recognizing the difficulty of instituting a whole new construction plan, the committee conceded that the best the USSR could do was to emphasize showers in the unspecified future.[23]

Even if a state committee could agree on the type of bathing that was ideally desirable, the physical realities of existing buildings and plans combined with the apparent preferences of the people, made any change difficult. German public shower pavilions may have set the standard for hygiene and cleanliness, but the USSR was going to have to come up with its own answer to the question of how to provide the proper bathing facilities for the maintenance of public health. The breadth of the Soviet state's aspirations was clear

FIGURE 7.2 The first citywide conference in Leningrad in 1933 on banyas and laundries took place under the images of Marx, Lenin, and Stalin. Courtesy of TsGAKFFD SPb.

in this area as it was in all aspects of public (and most aspects of private) life. But so too were its limitations. When push came to shove, in this sphere at least, the state adapted to the preferences of the people.

Once bureaucrats determined that banyas were the way to go, they carefully charted the number of baths citizens across the USSR could take and made centralized policies accordingly. They monitored the types of bathing facilities that existed in each region and city of the USSR and it set out to determine where and how often a person would bathe. Visions of hygienic modernity, however, could not overcome limited bureaucratic and administrative capacities: actually building banyas to meet the state's plans proved a vexing challenge, particularly in the midst of a maniacal economic drive that emphasized other priorities over the immediate needs of the people.

There was no predicament, however, when it came to extoling the benefits of the banya to the population. Propaganda posters clarified the degree to which state agencies saw banyas as a crucial feature of cultured living and an essential element in the fight against disease. These posters targeted everyone: men and women, rural and urban populations, and ethnic Russians and non-Russians. The most basic poster showed a worker—most likely a miner—with his face covered in soot and a sponge in his hand under the imperative "Go to the Banya." (This was a play on words: in Russian the phrase can be taken literally or can mean something like "go to hell.") This poster was widely distributed in Russian and other languages as well. Leaving the image the same, but changing only the language suggested that the poster-makers saw going to the banya as a habit that was easily translatable to all the nationalities of the empire.

Through images and text, the posters propagated ideal behavior in ideally constructed banyas. An exemplary poster from 1935, titled "For Each Collective Farm a Well Built Banya," echoed the print media's suggestion that banyas were both a sign of cultured living and a tool in fighting disease. The poster was divided in three sections top to bottom. The top displayed a drawing of the interior of a banya, with a young man smiling and toweling off. Men in the background are shown in various states of washing: going and coming from the steam room, filling a bucket with water, and rinsing. An official quotation at the top of the page listed going to the banya as a cultured activity alongside things such as reading books and newspapers and establishing libraries.

FIGURE 7.3 The "Go to the Banya" poster of the early 1930s was translated into many languages, including, in this case, Ukrainian. Courtesy of the Lenin Library.

Achieving bathing bliss required well-built banyas. The middle section of the poster displayed two drawings. On the left hand side was a rendition of the exterior of a banya on a collective farm, with a woman and her child approaching in the snow. Next to that was the floor plan for the banya, complete with separate rooms for dressing, undressing, cutting hair, disinfecting clothes, washing, and steaming. The entrance was marked off from the exit so that dirty and clean people and clothes would not mingle and lice would not spread. The poster established the goal; real banyas rarely resembled the clean, organized depiction.

FIGURE 7.4 This poster, from 1935, titled "For Each Collective Farm a Well Built Banya," suggested the ideal features of a cultured and well-ordered banya in the country-side. Courtesy of Lenin Library.

Finally, the lowest section of the poster contained text, informing readers that "each kolkhoz needs to have a banya" and that "banyas should not be erected haphazardly, but according to norms worked out by engineers and doctors." The sanitary doctor of the region was supposed to help the collective farm pick the location and size of the banya and make sure that it was built to be durable, beautiful, and inexpensive. Ideally, it would service the needs of the population living within a kilometer of the selected location. The text also pointed viewers to resources—such as a book on building banyas and on "sanitary culture" in state and collective farms. Fifty thousand copies of this poster were printed and distributed in 1935 alone. To put this figure in perspective, there were enough copies for this poster to have been distributed to one in five collective farms throughout the USSR.[24] The posters helped to spread the word that each collective farm could expect to have a well-ordered banya.

Other posters conveyed the same themes, but to other sectors of the population. A 1934 poster quoted Stalin about the need for shock workers and activists to lead cultured lives and to help others to do the same. It implored them to clean up their homes and displayed the exterior of a banya with three men walking into it. The caption read: "Fix up the banya, expand it, organize a disinfection room in it for the elimination of parasites."[25] "For the Sanitary Maintenance of the Banya" urged the urban population in the banya to check their outer garments, hang dirty clothes in the locker on a separate hook from clean clothes, refrain from spitting, keep the facilities clean, use individual lockers, avoid bringing glass into the washroom, avoid sharing basins, refrain from smoking (and keep others from smoking), not enter if they had skin disease, skip the steam room if they had a heart condition, and go every six days.[26]

The main thrust of the posters was to address the threat of diseases and public health concerns. Posters instructed people to wash with warm water and soap and to put on clean clothes after washing so that they were not reshrouded in lice. The connection between personal cleanliness and tidiness and the struggle with typhus was explicit in many posters. One read: "Have you been to the bath today? . . . Liquidate typhus and pox in our region by the end of the first FYP!" Since disease seemed to travel along the major transportation networks, other propaganda posters told travelers to go to a hot banya en route. "Dirt that settles on the body and skin on the road encourages lice, that carry typhus," a poster explained. Another simply stated, "Dirt is an enemy of health." The banya was a key tool of the state—one poster touted it as "our best ally in the fight for cleanliness and health." Other posters were explicit about the dangers of filth, magnifying ticks and lice for all to sense the menace that unclean bodies represented.

The message was clearly meant for all ethnicities of the USSR, with the assumption that the science of human hygiene superseded any cultural differences. In many cases, posters were reprinted in various languages. The sign on a drawing of a building might be switched from "banya" to "hammam," for instance, but the message was essentially the same. A cultured Soviet citizen visited the banya at least once a week in the city and once every ten days in the countryside. Often the propaganda posters presumed that the Russian tradition of the banya—replete with birch switches and steam rooms—would be easily assimilated by other nationalities. Posters targeted "small peoples of the north," Ukrainians, Buriat-Mongols, Turkmen, and other nationalities with identical messages.

The posters, like the enthusiastic support for banyas found in speeches and in newspaper articles, represented idealized Soviet banyas—ones that worked according to plan. They invariably had steam rooms and showers. Buckets, soap, and hot water were readily available. And they were not overcrowded. They conveyed the message that banyas were necessary for cleanliness, for a cultured life, and for building socialism. They also suggested that going to the banya was a matter of individual choice—failure to go was clearly a sign of uncultured people neglecting their own hygiene and the demands of public health.

Propaganda posters about hygiene had two additional features that need to be explained, because of their absence. First, they invariably showed only men in the interior of banyas. This was not because banyas were exclusively male domains—most were either split in half, with one side for women and one side for men or alternated the days of the weeks that the banya was open to men and women. Official calls for greater attention to personal hygiene were directed at both men and women. The choice to show more men in banyas reflected social attitudes about the depiction of the female nude. Perhaps to make up for this, women were overrepresented among (dressed) people entering or leaving the banya. Second, despite the occasional quotation used from a political leader or a Party decree, the usual symbols that would mark the banya as a specifically socialist space were missing.[27] There was a striking absence of state or Party symbolism, particularly in comparison with other propaganda posters of the 1930s. There were no Soviet flags, portraits of Stalin, or use of the color red to symbolize the banya's place in the broader Soviet project. The message seemed to be that proper

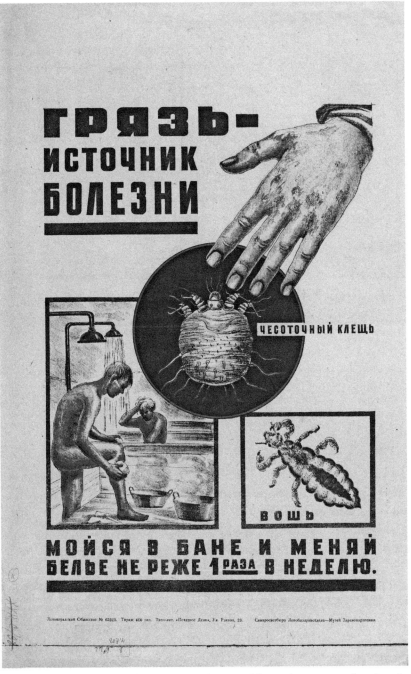

FIGURE 7.5 Some posters emphasized the dangers of dirt and parasites, rather than the joy of cleanliness. This poster, from 1931, warned: "Dirt is the Source of Illness: Wash in the Banya and Change Clothes No Less Often than One Time a Week." Courtesy of the Lenin Library.

FIGURE 7.6 An excerpt from a poster "For a Healthy Collective Farm" (1932) has a caption written in transliterated Buriat-Mongolian telling people to "Go to the Collective Farm Banya." Words for banya, *venik*, basins, and procedures for using a banya were translated into various languages used in the USSR, implying the Russian custom had unproblematically become a Soviet custom. Courtesy of the Lenin Library.

personal hygiene was not a matter of propaganda at all. Instead the posters emphasized public health in the context of cultured living and the eradication of disease.

The Soviet press, of course, echoed the posters in trumpeting plans to build banyas for the masses. An article titled "Path to the Development of Soviet Banyas," in the journal *Socialist City*, placed Soviet banya building in historical perspective and offered blueprints for plans for banyas for populations of various sizes. Among them was a "round banya" that not only had separate facilities for men and women, but also accommodated mothers and children. Plans such as these suggested that the Soviet state was in the process of building up-to-date and innovative bathing facilities for the people.

This optimism was echoed in the USSR's top newspapers. At the beginning of the FYP readers of *Pravda* and *Izvestiia* learned that Moscow would use the latest technology and material to make banyas that were far

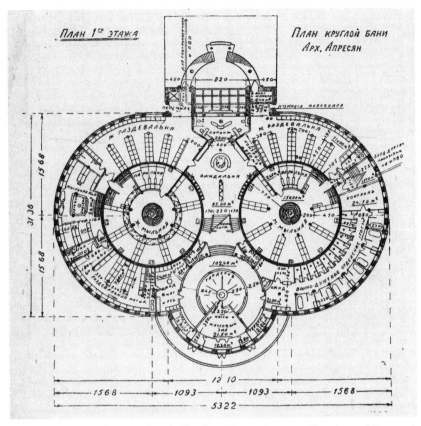

FIGURE 7.7 "Plan for Round Baths" by the architect Apresian. The plan and Smetnev's article suggested that Soviet banyas would be innovative and attuned to the needs of the people, by providing a separate bathing area for children to bathe with their mothers, for instance. The plan also incorporated showers and tubs into a building that maintained the Russian steam room. Published in N. I. Smetnev, "Puti razvitiia sovetskoi bani," *Sotsialisticheskii gorod*, no. 1 (1936), pp. 30-37. Widener Library, Harvard University.

superior to the existing stock of outdated imperial-era banyas. These plans reflected the state's goal, at least in principle, of improving the everyday lives of workers, including meeting their desire for basic sanitation. The first year (1928–1929) of the First FYP called for spending 110 million rubles on improving workers' living conditions, including building banyas. After an initial evaluation of the results suggested that not enough had been done, the Sixteenth Party Congress in 1930 doubled that amount to 220 million rubles for 1929–1930.[28]

How much of the money dedicated to improvements of the daily lives of workers was dedicated to banyas? It is hard to say for certain. But the results of the first Five-Year Plan hardly matched the aspirations of either the state or the population. The raw number of banyas in the Russian Republic went up by 133 banyas, from approximately 505 in 1928 to 638 by the end of the first FYP. The overall capacity of these banyas went from 100,000 to 114,000 spaces. At first glance this seemed like an improvement, albeit not one in line with the ambitious goals of the plan. But the key factor that interested bureaucrats was the number of baths a person in any given region could take in a year. The goal—as indicated by propaganda posters and in internal memos evidently based on the determination of doctors—ranged from 36 a year (one every 10 days) usually in rural regions to 52 a year (one a week) usually in urban or industrial regions. In this respect, the increase in the number of banyas and total number of spaces failed to keep up with the population, let alone the influx of people from rural areas to cities at the time.

———•———

Converting propaganda and plans into banyas was no easy task. This had less to do with banyas per se than with the challenging conditions of the planned economy. What did it take to build a banya in Stalin's Russia? First, the pressure to build banyas was rarely as high as it was to fulfill other aspects of the plan that were more directly related to the functioning of the overall economy. Funds, personnel, and supplies designated for banyas were often diverted to more pressing needs.[29] Second, local leaders often lacked the resources to plan and build banyas. Some sort of urban planning had to be done to determine where capacity was most needed and to justify using land and resources to build a banya instead of something else. Yet municipal authorities rarely had the expertise or authority to undertake such evaluations and decisions on their own. To do so amidst the rapid economic changes and population movements of the period made the task particularly challenging. The needs of the workers and peasants who rushed to industrial centers could be ignored at little cost to municipal leaders. The result was both a shortage of working banyas and their poor distribution in relation to the living quarters of the rapidly expanding urban population. Identifying a suitable location for a new bathhouse—one near water supplies, close to workers' housing, on land not needed for some other pressing purpose—often proved elusive. In one instance a long-awaited banya was built, but was unusable because it had been constructed in a flood zone.[30]

If a location could be found, other challenges emerged. Most competent builders were too occupied with other projects to be assigned to bathhouse construction. The Banya Trust—the state agency created for the task of building banyas—faced challenges tracking down the appropriate building materials. In the countryside, it was conceivable that wood could be felled and milled into straight lumber. But where that was possible, other priorities took precedence. Where lumber could not be extracted from the surrounding area, it had to be ordered and delivered—a daunting prospect in an economy in which building materials were in great demand and short supply.[31]

Construction delays were commonplace. Bureaucratic roadblocks compounded resource allocation problems. The problem was so acute that Politburo member Lazar Kaganovich brought up the topic in his speech to the XVII Party Congress in 1934. Noting that the Party was supposed to care for the workers, he cited a plan to build banyas in the far east. Despite the recognition of the importance of personal hygiene for public health, eighteen months had gone by without any sign of the proposed banyas. The task was supposed to be straightforward, but the various bureaucratic entities involved in the process had complicated things beyond belief. "In a word," Kaganovich concluded, "it was like something out of Gogol's Dead Souls: 'the Committee for Supervision of the Committee of Management'" had brought the urgent task to a standstill.[32] The problems were not isolated to the far east. In the Donbass, where banyas were desperately needed for miners, banya construction had stretched on for two to three years. Delays of up to five years or more hindered people's ability to bathe in numerous other towns across the USSR.[33] One banya that took three years to build remained unusable because no internal equipment had been procured or installed.[34] Another banya lacked a boiler to heat the water or the air. A review of banyas in *Pravda* in 1934 noted that in Saratov, where long lines for the existing banya suggested the need for a new one, four years of construction had yielded a building with four walls, but no place to bathe.[35] At least construction had begun there—in other areas, plans for banyas never even got off the drawing table. One city council had been at the planning stage of a new banya for six years.[36]

Running and maintaining a banya in Stalin's Russia proved just as hard as building one. One of the biggest obstacles was finding enough heating materials. Wood, coal, gas, and oil were all in high demand and, even if found and procured for the banya, could easily be diverted to other sectors of the economy.[37] Most Party organizations, municipalities, or factory managers prioritized something other than consistently heating the banya. They could reassign a banya's limited resources. In one instance, a banya itself was dismantled so that its wood could be used to heat other enterprises.[38] Materials earmarked for banyas were often diverted to other pressing needs that were themselves hampered by the chaotic supply chains of the command economy. Leadership in a town or factory or kolkhoz often had to prioritize. On the one hand, they faced pressure from an industrial or agricultural commissariat demanding they fulfill an order; on the other, they faced disgruntled workers desperate for a bath. It was far easier for them to ignore or clamp down on the latter than it was for them to stand up to the former.

Even when there was heat, there was often not water. The water supply for some banyas was taken directly from local rivers without filtration, much as had been the case in the imperial period. Banyas not near a water supply were dependent on city water systems—which as often as not were nonexistent, insufficient to meet demand, or broken. Here too, factories received top priority. When water did make it to the banya, it was not uncommon for only a single pipe to be installed with a single faucet. Water could either be hot or cold, but poor construction and materials made it difficult to have both at once. In many cases there was neither.[39] As in the imperial period, banyas often flushed used water directly into rivers, in some cases causing significant pollution. In one case, after *Pravda* noted that a banya in Astrakhan had been doing this, the local leaders shut it down, rather than solving the problem of what to do with the water refuse. A month later *Pravda* made clear that this was not an acceptable solution—the banya needed to be reopened and the pollution problem had to be solved another way.[40]

Shortages of basins and soap were common. Bathers assumed that a full basin was in use and therefore unavailable to them. Abandoning a basin filled with water was not just taboo, it also brought a 100-ruble fine.[41] Soap was considered a luxury. Sponges were in short supply and often shared, with no attention paid to the possible health effects. Services were notoriously poor. The hours of operation were inconsistent—with many banyas open only a few hours a day. Long lines formed at any banya that managed to be in operation. Many remained closed for long stretches.[42]

Pravda and *Izvestiia's* critical articles about the situation on the "banya front" were interspersed with more optimistic ones, touting the success of certain banyas in certain areas. Clearly some banyas had been built—even if they did not keep pace with the needs of the population. Hardly a month went by in the 1930s without an article in either *Pravda* or *Izvestiia* announcing the completion of a banya in some part of the USSR. A 1934 article in *Pravda* about an election campaign suggested that one candidate noted, "Well you asked that we build a banya. A banya has been built!"[43] Those who read in national papers about new banyas that had been constructed in Minsk and

Murmansk, Uzbekistan and Turkmenistan, Vladivostok and the Caucuses, the Jewish Autonomous region in the Far East and throughout Ukraine, could be excused for thinking that the poor banya conditions in their own town were atypical for the USSR. They could read that banyas had been built in collective farms and factory towns, in cities, on submarines and on the Northern most polar station in the Arctic. One in Tashkent could even boast that its water was heated entirely with solar energy.[44] Sulimov, the Chairman of the Soviet of People's Commissars of the RSFSR, announced hopefully in 1936 that 151 bathhouses had been built during the first three years of the second five-year plan—and that 112 more were planned for 1936 alone. As he suggested, Stalin's promise of bringing a good, cultured life to the masses was coming to fruition. In Stalin's terms, "life was more joyous."[45] By implication, if that joyous life had not yet found its way to each corner of the Soviet Union, it would certainly do so soon.

The general consensus held that Moscow was the model socialist city in banya affairs (as in all things related to "socialism"). Some of that reputation was based on the opulent imperial era bathhouses like Sanduny that remained in working operation. The elaborate pools, cafes, massage rooms, and showers stood as exemplars of what a banya could be—even if the newer versions would be more austere, utilitarian, and hygienic. One of the most widely acclaimed banyas built in this period was the banya on Usachev Street in the Khamovniki neighborhood of Moscow. *Izvestiia* declared that it was the "best banya in Moscow." In other words, this banya was supposed to be the best of the best.[46]

The celebration of the banya on Usachev Street masked just how hard it was to build a banya in the USSR, even in Moscow. The neighborhood had been desperate for a banya for most of the 1920s. According to official estimates, at the beginning of the Stalin period citizens of this neighborhood could bathe at best five times per year, well below the city average of eleven baths per year and not even remotely close to the "hygienic norm" of fifty-two baths a year.[47] The banya for Usachev Street was first commissioned in the middle 1920s. By 1929, *Izvestiia* was already voicing complaints that its construction had been inexcusably delayed.[48] The building was not open to the public for another four years. Yet even when it was complete and running at capacity, it hardly came close to meeting the overall demand for bathing facilities in the neighborhood or the city.

Despite the investments, the country's banya infrastructure at the end of the First FYP remained poor. The vast majority of citizens still lacked a way of bathing at home and yet using a public banya remained difficult. Buildings were old and drafty, their location far from the working population, and their equipment was unsatisfactory and not in keeping with the demands of modern sanitation. Would-be patrons wasted time in hours-long lines only to find themselves in cramped washrooms and steam rooms without soap or basins. Laments about the banyas did not let up over the course of the 1930s. In 1934 a satirical article in *Izvestiia* compared the opulence of the Roman baths with the deprivation of the Soviet banya. "Where are the sponges? Where are the basins? Where are the birch whisks?" the author asked, "One day, the water from the spigot is boiling, the next it is ice cold." Some patrons walked out of the banya covered in soot from the furnace. The long lines led administrators to force people to bathe quickly, even to the point where patrons did not always have enough time to rinse soap off their bodies. The article concluded that it was impossible in most Soviet banyas to clean oneself in a civilized manner. In terms of bathing, the author complained, the socialist state had not made any advancement on the ancient Romans.[49]

Even beyond their unhygienic conditions, Soviet banyas could be dangerous places. Fires were common. Theft and other crimes were rampant. While some statistics and many articles suggest the situation in Moscow may have been better than elsewhere, it was hardly good there either.[50] Moscow banyas too suffered from problems with water supply, a lack of basins, poor management, and fires.[51] In one instance, a father and son evidently teamed up to try to swindle a Moscow banya. They entered the bathhouse together. The son reportedly bathed first, and before exiting the bathhouse dressed in both his own clothes and his father's clothes. The father then came out of the washroom, claiming that his clothes had been stolen. He demanded either new clothes or money from the bathhouse administration, which was ostensibly responsible for crimes committed on its premises.[52] While *Pravda* assured its readers that this scheme failed, theft in banyas remained a serious problem. That year also saw a drowning in one of Moscow's main banyas, as well as the arrest of a man who had been using the "private rooms" at one banya to perform illegal abortions.[53]

Moscow may have been more equipped with better banyas than the rest of the USSR, but that was not saying much. In 1931, three years into the first FYP, an internal report in the Commissariat of Municipal Services of the RSFSR noted that before the revolution there had been 84 active banyas for 1,700,000 Muscovites. As of 1931 there were 2,750,000 people in Moscow but only two new banyas and one new, but evidently underutilized, shower pavilion. Of the old banya stock, 34 remained open to the public and 12 more were affiliated with factories that limited the public's access. The other 30 odd banyas from the imperial period had been destroyed or converted to living or production space. The report concluded that even if the city's banyas ran at full capacity all year, Muscovites on average could bathe only 18 times a year; in fact, the People's Commissariat for Municipal Services recognized that the banyas were running far below capacity and that the average Muscovite could expect to bathe less than once a month. Inspectors reported that the situation in specific neighborhoods was even worse. In some areas of the capital, workers bathed fewer than six times a year—and even the best neighborhoods only provided their citizens with 19 baths a year. Making matters worse, according to their estimates, many of the remaining imperial banyas were breaking down or were on the verge of breaking down. To compound the problems, the technical specifications of existing banyas did not meet recent standards. Sanduny—often lauded as a model banya—used unfiltered river water in the washroom. Another took its water unfiltered from a swamp. Ventilation was deemed unsatisfactory in all but the two new banyas. Indeed, half the banyas had no ventilation system whatsoever. When basins could be found, they were used for weeks without being cleaned. But building new banyas, even in Moscow, was disastrously slow: the report lamented, "in all the other neighborhoods in which banyas were to be built, there are no plans, no plots, no orders of building materials, and no workers." Those that had been built were quickly falling apart because they had been built poorly or incorrectly.[54]

The situation in the area surrounding Moscow was worse—and more in keeping with the rest of the country. There the capacity only allowed people on average six to seven baths per year. The same Commissariat of Municipal Services report concluded, "In the conditions of Cultural Revolution and the building of socialism in our country, the defense of the health of the workers takes on exceptional meaning." Building bathhouses was "one of the principal challenges of municipal affairs" but this "political issue" was not receiving enough attention.[55]

The report did not seem to have much of an impact, however. In 1932 the conditions in the extant pre-Revolutionary banyas had deteriorated further—they were broken down and filthy, floors were cracked, paint was peeling, and the need for major repairs was almost universal. Even after the Moscow Soviet had spent nearly 13 million rubles on banya construction and repairs in the city and region in 1931, the problems, if anything, had gotten worse. The Commissariat somewhat hopefully issued a set of instructions on improving the sanitary situation in towns and regions. It called for banyas to increase their hours of operation, to add more workers to shifts, to make sure their hours conformed to the schedules of the workers. It insisted that the banyas be cleaned consistently and that inspections be regularized. It also sought to minimize disease by insisting that if banyas could not disinfect people, patrons had to receive a sanitary inspection before using the banyas. It is hard to imagine these instructions being followed. Neighborhood banya directors were not running their banyas poorly out of spite or lack of recognition of what needed to be done; their decisions were being dictated by poor conditions, high costs, and low priorities of the local bosses. The center seemed to concede this in part—it accepted that even simple banyas or the "chimney-less systems" (i.e., the black banyas that remained popular in some rural areas) should be used to clean the population if necessary, even though medical practitioners warned that this could be less healthy than not bathing at all.[56]

By 1935 considerable investment had only produced 134 new banyas across the whole Russian Republic—raising the maximum number of baths per person per year to a little over twelve—about one-quarter to one-third the minimal norm called for by public health officials. The problems persisted throughout the 1930s: banyas were old and in need of repairs, dozens were closed, there was no money for renovations, and those that were open were often cold and under supplied. The banyas in Leningrad were in similar shape to those in Moscow; even presuming maximum efficiency, people there could bathe at around sixteen times per year on average. But in other major cities the situation was far worse. In Saransk, the average was four baths per year; in Tambov, less than four; and in Lipetsk, under three baths per year. The plan in 1935 called for sixty-one new bathhouses to be built across the Russian Republic, which had a population of over 100 million people. But the obstacles to building even this limited number of banyas remained. As internal reports made clear, there was not enough equipment such as pipes and cement, cost overruns were common, construction delays lasted years, a shortage of capital made the purchase of necessary equipment a challenge, and the use of inferior materials and low technical expertise meant that those bathhouses that were built broke down quickly. To top it off, heating materials continued to be diverted to other concerns.[57]

The spread of typhus and the effort by the state to eradicate it put increasing pressure on local leaders to build banyas. Yet one report to the Peoples Commissariat of Health of the USSR in 1936 noted, "The building of banyas in the RSFSR and other republics is proceeding at a very weak pace, without a plan, and the regional and neighborhood committees with rare exceptions are taking an extremely weak participation in the organization of the issue. Plans remain only on paper, many can not be built because of the absence of certain materials that are in low supply (nails and pipes), banyas that have been built are being used for other things (such as a Collective Farm office, apartments, for housing animals or bread, etc)." Further, the report pointed out that the use of traditional rural banyas persisted even though they were "backward" and could "aid in the spread of typhus, not the eradication of it." Once again, the plan called for building thousands of banyas across the USSR with the goal of each person being able to bathe once every ten days. Given the limited waterworks infrastructure in even capital cities like Moscow and Leningrad, the plan somewhat optimistically assumed that only 75 percent of the population would rely on the banya for personal hygiene.[58] Again, plans did not pan out. In 1938 the All-Union Sanitary Inspectorate reported that the situation on the banya front had not improved across the USSR. Their laments were by now familiar. Construction of banyas was delayed because of the absence of necessary materials such as pipes, ventilation systems, and faucets and because of the lack of necessary attention from political authorities. Even where banyas were desperately needed, construction was at a standstill.[59]

Statistics on the overall number of banyas in the RSFSR suggest that capacity at best stagnated in relation to the population over the course of the 1930s. Between 1928 and 1939 the state had added approximately 25,000 new banya spaces. In ideal conditions, each space could bathe 40 people a week (documents assumed a person took an hour to bathe and that bathhouses were open 8 hours a day, 5 days a week) or 2,000 people a year (40 per week per space x 50 weeks a year.) Even if problems of heating and water supplies, poor construction, delays, and inconsistent hours of operation are set aside, this new capacity of 25,000 spaces would add a total of 50 million washes per year—that is, on average about one-half an extra bath per person per year. They were still nowhere near meeting even in principle the minimal standards of hygiene that the propaganda suggested was the norm. In 1938, Moscow still had only 42 banyas with a little over 19,000 spots for over 4 million people.[60] The building of the Usachev Baths and other new banyas did not keep pace with the rising population or the deterioration of other bathhouses. Even if all the bathhouses were running at capacity, well distributed, and efficiently processing bathers, the best case scenario would have allowed Muscovites to bathe approximately ten times a year. Ten years of investment in the 1930s hardly made a dent in the average. Banyas were emblematic of the broader problem in Stalin's Russia of providing for the basic needs of the population.

Individuals' capacity to bathe most likely dropped over the course of Stalin's vaunted era of socialist construction.

——◦——

The myriad problems facing public bathing facilities in the period could hardly be kept secret from the population, which knew all too well how hard it was to find an open, working banya. More often than not, articles in major publications such as *Pravda* and *Izvestiia* revealed the challenges of constructing and maintaining banyas. In some ways, these articles carried with them the message that the authorities recognized the problems in everyday life that Soviet citizens faced. They also attempted to place the challenges within the broader context of the system's progress and accomplishments. When things went well, it was to the credit of the Soviet system. But when they did not, local administrators took the blame.

This message was sometimes conveyed in gallows humor, which called attention to areas where reality had not kept up with rhetoric. The humor magazine *Krokodil* became a forum for biting critiques of workers' struggles to satisfy their most basic needs. A few rules obviously applied: first and foremost the responsibility for any problems lay with local bureaucrats—not with the center and certainly not with the Party. When it came to banyas, almost all of the humor magazine *Krokodil's* cartoons, stories, vignettes, and published letters to the editor were critical of the situation in the country. *Krokodil* highlighted the long lines at banyas—to gain access, to check one's clothes, to get a turn in the steam room or washroom. It lambasted the lack of hot water, or cold water, or any water, and the shortages of basins, soap, and sponges. It commented on the lack of heat for the banya buildings as well as the theft that often occurred there. It targeted local leaders who either did not work to improve the conditions in their towns' banyas and those who clearly used them for their own personal benefit at the expense of the working people, who were sometimes literally left out in the cold. In short, *Krokodil* made fun of the long list of problems that were evident to banya goers and had vexed state officials hoping to rectify the situation.

Konstantin Rotov's 1934 cartoon satirizing one of the most famous Russian national paintings of the mid-nineteenth century, Alexander Ivanov's "The Appearance of Christ Before the People," provided a prime example of *Krokodil's* message that local officials were responsible for the conditions in the banyas. In Rotov's version, titled "The Appearance of the Deputy Before the People," an official arrives at the banya with birch switch in hand. But the people—cold and unable to rinse off—greet him with anger and contempt. The poem under the image reads, "Once a deputy went to the banya . . . but misfortune awaited those that bathed there, because the neighborhood banya had no water. It was cold, without any steam, except for that which came out of people's mouths. The defining feature of the neighborhood banya is the absence of baths and basins. . . . The deputy stood quietly with his *veniki*, surviving the loud onslaught from the people. Why was he steaming and red? They gave him a hot banya!!" Not only had Rotov substituted a bureaucrat for Christ; he also showed people greeting the bureaucrat as anything but a savior. Clearly, those stuck in the cold, cobwebbed banyas were being instructed to direct their ire toward local officials.

Krokodil articles suggested that pointing out the shortcomings of the Soviet banya was not just allowed but even a sign of integrity. Blind praise for everything Soviet was a dishonest and unrealistic; some criticism (though how much was clearly a distressing question) was warranted and even marked people as more deeply committed to the socialist cause.[61] The anonymity of the banya—and its less-than-ideal conditions—made it a natural place to situate a lesson in speaking one's mind, Soviet style. In the 1930s *Krokodil*

FIGURE 7.8 K. Rotov's "The Deputy Appearing Before the People" offered a satire of Aleksandr Ivanov's nineteenth-century painting "Christ Appearing Before the People." In Rotov's version angry citizens in the cold, waterless bathhouse, plan to give a deputy a "hot banya." *Krokodil*, February 1934 (no. 32–33), p. 12–13.

published two satires on the famous Anton Chekhovstory "In the Banya." In Chekhov's original story, a banya worker circa 1880 assumes that a man with long hair and unusually frank ideas must be a radical. When the *banshchik* runs out of the steam room to hand over the radical to the authorities, he is shocked to discover that the long-haired man is actually a priest. The *banshchik* returns to the steam room humbled and apologetic. In *Krokodil*'s reworking, the story becomes one about the duty (at least in principle) to point out what was wrong with the Soviet system.

In one *Krokodil* version, when an anonymous bather encourages workers to criticize the Party, another bather takes offense at what he takes to be anti-Soviet behavior. But it turns out the first bather is more politically astute than the second—he cites Lenin, Stalin, and Nikolai Bukharin about the benefits of honest criticism.[62] In yet another riff on Chekhov's story, a worker gets upset with a "fat man" who is openly complaining about the lack of water and heat in the city's only working banya. The brand new banya in the city has yet to open because its pipes had frozen the previous winter and priority in the meantime had been given to building a park instead. The fat man declares that life was better under the old regime—at least in terms of banyas. The worker runs out of the *parilka* to denounce the fat man to the authorities for "un-Soviet" statements. But once outside he realizes that the fat man is a representative of the neighborhood committee who is in town on important business.[63] The banya had concealed someone's powerful identity which in turn led someone else to misread honest criticism for open hostility. Again, the message was that at least in principle workers were not supposed to simply defend all aspects of life in the USSR as good. It was important to be honest (to a limited extent, of course) about things that were not in order. It made no sense to say everything was going well when clearly and undeniably they were not.

Krokodil was consistently critical of the situation in the banya. A 1928 story complained about the fact that it took three years to build a banya in Novgorod. It operated for four days before the walls collapsed, the oven cracked, and the roof beams became twisted.[64] In 1934, the magazine claimed that in Tula there was only one banya for the whole population. In order to process people, it used a bell to admit new people and expel those whose time was up—no matter what state of washing they were in. The image accompanying the story showed men being rushed out of the back of the banya naked, half-dressed, or covered in suds while a line of dressed citizens marched into the banya's front door. The caption read, "The session is Over! Finish cleaning, Citizens!"[65]

By far *Krokodil's* most common banya theme was about shortages. Articles noted that in some regions there was either no water in the banya or only cold water. Another lambasted a neighborhood administrator for requiring peasants to provide their own wood for heating the communal bath. A poem about Magnitigorsk mocked the hours-long lines for the bathhouse. "We stand dejected and packed in / at the hygiene center / my neighbor hot and sturdy / laughs, 'Protest, don't protest [it makes no difference].'" When workers finally make it into the bath they were quickly ushered out, some dressed and some naked. It turns out there is no water. The poem juxtaposed the ideal with the reality of Soviet everyday life, "They say it is important, that we have earned our banya / but each day comrade, it the same poor scene." Another humorous poem titled "It would be good to get clean" pointed out long lines, lack of buckets, theft of soap, and the fact that water came out either too fast or not at all.[66]

Lack of supplies also posed a particularly challenge that underscored how difficult it could be to adhere to the authorities' hygienic demands. One letter noted that the imperative "'Go to the banya!' which is heard everywhere, was made difficult by basins that had holes, or no handles, or indeed even no bottoms." The result was that people ended up "walking around unclean while reading slogans about the need to be clean: 'We are all Muscovites! Maintain your health.'"[67]

Irony was common in *Krokodil's* critiques of the banya. One cartoon on the back cover titled "Modern Warning" showed a man with his birch switch walking toward a modern building labeled "Banya." A man sitting outside in an ice bath says, "Stop! Are you nuts? Going to the banya! You'll freeze in there."

Another article titled "Comments on Cleaning" used satire even as it lamented the fact that humor alone would not make the banyas any better. It started with the simple proposition that bathing did not require much. Yet in the USSR essential items were in short supply. "Take the sponge," the article posited,

> We don't export them to English Aristocrats. We don't import them from Germany. They are purely a domestic affair. And just the same in [one town's] banya on a lone nail hangs the one sponge in the region. It is rented out to bathers for a short period for a ruble. Those that have reached an understanding with the banya administration get to use it. Others stare jealously. Then they clean it and rent it to the next person. Maybe on off days it is shown to the younger generation as a scientific

Рис. Кукрыниксы

— Все говорят: шаек нет. Обходятся же люди без шаек!

FIGURE 7.9 The lack of basic supplies in the banya was hardly news, but could be fodder for humor. The artistic team of Mikhail Kurpiyanov, Profiri Krylov, and Nikolai Sokolov (known by the collective name Kukryniksy) showed people using vases and pitchers to substitute for the lack of basins. "Everyone says: there are no basins. The people can get by without basins!" *Krokodil*, August 1938 (no. 24), p. 13.

specimen! We don't know. But they should—kids should be exposed to and get to know such rare things!

The article noted that other places had sponges but that faucets did not work or absurd rules limited people's ability to go there. In one case, the article claimed, even a local prosecutor had his possessions stolen at the banya. It concluded, "Things are bad on the banya front. There are many satires, but few basins. It isn't as though you can wash up with a satire!"

FIGURE 7.10 Banyas also lacked heat. K. Rotov's cartoon on the back cover of *Krokodil*, January 1935 (no. 2) shows a man in ice speaking to another man who is on his way to the banya, "Stop! Are you nuts? Going to the banya! You'll freeze in there."

Another 1935 article about how to behave in various situations included a mock plea for the acceptance of the conditions in the banya. It instructed its readers that "If there is no hot water, accept it. Don't ask for the impossible. You can wash with cold water, if they have that. If no water at all, an educated person can wash with a dry sponge; do not ask for services from the *banshchik*, who will in most cases refuse service (because service is a remnant of the difficult past). So just sit dressed on a bench and chat. After ½ hour get up and go. Because there is a line of people waiting!" The lesson continued: "If [you find yourself in] a well-supplied banya—that even has water" you should try not to sleep in the shower, wash your clothes in the tub, or take a neighbor's soap or basin. These mock instructions seemed to suggest that these were, in fact, behaviors that one could readily witness in Soviet banyas.[68]

So what was one supposed to do in the banya? Why were there endless lines for banyas without water, soap, or heat? One 1939 *Krokodil* image made fun of the paradox of what people did "When there is no water in the banya." It depicted men singing in a choir a famous Russian folk song, "The Storm Roared, the Rain Pounded," perhaps as a sort of rain dance in the waterless banya. Booths had been set up in each dry shower stall, including one selling ice cream. Other people were playing chess, dancing to the accordion, reading, or simply waiting for water to appear. The banya remained a meeting place, whether one could wash there or not.

Perhaps the clearest sign in *Krokodil* that the situation on the banya front had not improved was the publication of another article by Mikhail Zoshchenko about the banya. His popular story on the banya in the 1920s had pointed out the absurdities of the process by which one checked one's clothes at the banya and the difficulty of getting the right clothes back. In 1935 *Krokodil* published a second Zoshchenko story about the bathhouse. The absurdities had not receded amid the effort to build socialism. Indeed the situation circa 1935 closely resembled the situation circa 1924, despite the

FIGURE 7.11 Banyas also often lacked water. I. Semenov's "When there is no water in the banya." *Krokodil*, April 1939 (no. 11), p 6.

Five-Year Plans and promises of improved conditions. Zoshchenko began his 1935 "A Story of the Banya and Its Patrons" with reference to his earlier story: "In our time we wrote a thing or two about the banya. We noted its dangers . . . Some years have passed. The problems we touched upon have generated heated discussions in the banya-laundry trust" about how to keep possessions safe. Zoshchenko, however, then described an incident "in one of Leningrad's banyas" that suggested that not much progress had been made. In the story a man's clothes are stolen while he is steaming himself. The public informs him that "every day in this banya people steal." His troubles escalate when he is forced to confront the female bathhouse administrator with only a hat and belt covering his naked body.[69] In the end, the police drag off a man (although for a different crime). Zoshchenko concluded that something still needed to be done to keep people's belongings safe in the banya.

As was the case in *Pravda* and *Izvestiia*, references to the banya in *Krokodil* sometimes took a sinister turn, where the banya was referred to metaphorically as a place where those responsible for the situation should be sent for a cleaning. (The rough equivalent in English of "giving someone a banya" would be to take a person out to or behind "the woodshed.") A 1928 article called on the banya administration in a local town to be given a cold shower. Another, in 1930, called for the Neighborhood Governmental Council to be "taken to the baths." The 1930 poem about the poor conditions in Magnitigorsk suggested that the Municipal Services Division "needed a good hot bath" and concluded, "And [the people] cried, no fooling (what is there to proud of?), A good hot banya is what somebody surely needs." A letter to the editor in 1938 complained about a banya that was only open a few days a week, evidently because of both a lack of banya workers and basins. The letter writer suggested that the local banya director did not respect the needs of the workers in his region and that if he was "taken to the banya," he would "find all that he needed."[70] Such calls for punishment in the context of the terror that was raging in 1938 suggests that even as *Krokodil* articles and images poked fun, the failure of local leaders to solve the problems on the banya front was clearly a serious matter.

———

Calling for someone to be "taken to the banya" could clearly imply calling them on the carpet, having them arrested, and perhaps shot. Soviet authorities could admit that Soviet banyas were not working; that fact was too obvious to hide. But when it came time to assigning blame, "traitors," "enemies," and "spies" at the local level took much of the share that surely belonged to the system itself. In March 1938 a commission of the People's Commissariat of Health of the USSR undertook a review of various regions of the country and concluded that "enemies of the people" were responsible for the poor sanitary situation.[71] A review of the Banya-Laundry Cleaning Division reached similar conclusions. The division was responsible for the construction of banyas, technical specifications, organizing workers, and maintaining banyas across the RSFSR. On top of all of its technical challenges, the division was plagued with personnel issues, ranging from people skipping work to those who were on the job conducting their work in an "undisciplined manner."[72] In the context of the late 1930s, these accusations could easily be followed up with arrest.

Problems with banyas were no secret to the most powerful people in the country. In 1936 Stalin had begun the systematic purging of political rivals or even those who could be construed as rivals. At the Central Committee Plenum of February–March 1937 Stalin began to turn on rank-and-file party leaders suspected of heinous political and economic crimes. A speech at the Plenum by Nikolai Shvernik, the chairman of the All-Union Central Council of Trade Unions, cited "wrecker-saboteurs from a Trotskyist group along with right[ist] restorers of capitalism" for failing to meet the demands of workers. As Stalin peppered him with questions, Shvernik reported that in the Donbass workers had consistently complained to their superiors about the poor conditions in the banyas. One banya was woefully short of basins, functioning waterworks, and heat during the evening sessions. Local party leaders, according to Shvernik, ignored the complaints and swept the issue under the carpet. That sort of behavior was hardly unusual in the 1930s. But now it was being exposed at the very top. In 1937, failure on the banya front was tantamount to treason.[73]

Similar vigilance followed at the local level. In the spring of that year the Moscow City Council took up the question "How well was municipal affairs construction going in the capital?" Addressing the "special question" of banyas, Maria Shaburova of the Party Control Commission of the Central Committee informed the city council of the "neglected conditions of Moscow banyas."[74] In the fall, Moscow Party boss Nikita Khrushchev raised concerns about the work of the city's municipal construction division and called for the city council to "give the most serious attention to the liquidation of the influence of enemies in the city's affairs."[75] In the midst of the political terror—in which the Party Control Commission played a key role—*Pravda* reported that despite tremendous investments in banyas in Moscow, the situation remained "unsatisfactory." In 1938 the city of Moscow spent six million rubles on boilers, ventilation, upkeep, and improved water systems for the banyas. It spent another one million rubles on sheets, furniture, and basins. Yet despite the expenditure, the Moscow Soviet continued to raise "sharp criticism of the work of the administration of municipal affairs."[76]

The terror swept through the various organizations involved with administering banyas, just as it swept through the rest of society. In early March 1937 *Pravda* published a critical article accusing the authorities in Saratov and Gorky of neglecting banyas and allowing unsanitary conditions to persist there. A few months later, on June 29, 1937, Alexander Grinshtein, the head of the city council in Saratov, was arrested. On January 20, 1938, he was tried and convicted of anti-Soviet agitation. He was shot on the same day. Ukhanov, the Moscow City Soviet member who had spoken at the outset of the Five-Year Plan about the need to build banyas to meet the demands of the workers, was arrested on May 21, 1937. He was convicted on October 26, 1937, of participating in an anti-Soviet terrorist organization and was shot the same day. Sulimov, the Chair of the People's Commissariat of the RSFSR, who in February 1936 gave a speech cited in *Pravda* touching on the state of country's banyas and quoted Stalin on the need to meet the needs of the workers, was arrested on June 27, 1937. On November 27, 1937, the Military Collegium tried and convicted him of economic sabotage, espionage, and participation in an anti-Soviet terrorist rightest organization. He was shot on the same day. Mikhail Poliakov, the representative of the State Administration of Municipal Services of the RSFSR, who had pointed out the need for greater attention to banyas in the 1931, was arrested on February 2, 1938. On May 9 the Military Collegium of the Supreme Soviet convicted him of participating in a terrorist organization. He was shot on the same day. Matiukhin, the old revoluationary who had written to Stalin in 1931 mentioning the poor sanitary conditions in the banyas, was arrested on June, 28, 1939, convicted of anti-Soviet terrorist activities and sentenced to eight years in prison. He was shot on September 15, 1941.[77] Rotov, the *Krokodil* illustrator who drew "The Deputy Appears Before the People" and the cartoon "Modern Warning," in which a man in ice warns a would-be bather that it was too cold in the banya, was arrested in 1940 for being a German spy, a traitor to his country, and a producer of anti-Soviet propaganda while working at *Krokodil*. He spent eight years in a Soviet labor camp.[78] Shaburova, of the Party Control Commission, who had targeted the Moscow City Council, came under suspicion at the end of the terror but evidently escaped arrest. Kukryniksy, the collective name of the three artists who drew the 1938 cartoon in *Krokodil* explaining how to make do without basins, became Heroes of Socialist Labor. There was not necessarily any rhyme or reason to who was arrested and when. And while banyas may or may not have played a direct role in the fate of these people, it is certain that the persistently bad conditions in the country's cleaning facilities were both impossible to ignore and necessitated assigning blame.

Arrests and executions did not improve the conditions in Soviet banyas. Typhus remained a persistent problem through the 1930s, although the end of famine conditions alleviated some of the pressure on the system. Still, it was clear there were simply not enough banyas across the country to meet the demands of citizens or to reach the hygienic norms set out by health care experts and adopted by the state. In 1938 a report from the State Sanitary Inspection division to the People's Commissariat of Public Health outlined familiar problems with banyas throughout the USSR: there remained a severe shortage of building materials and equipment, poor inspection protocols, a lack of heating materials, uneven distribution, and the complete absence of banyas from entire communities.[79] Long lines for the banya persisted even in those areas that had received significant resources over the course of the first two Five-Year Plans. In 1939, at the XVIII Party Congress, Vyacheslav Molotov singled out banyas as part of the third FYP's goal of raising "the material and cultural standard of the working people." As Molotov informed the Congress, "There will be a considerable increase in government expenditure on cultural and public services for the working people of town and country . . . There must be a real improvement in the building of new public banyas, a matter which has been unpardonably neglected."[80] In 1941 Stalin put things a bit more crudely in a meeting with economists who were perhaps a bit overeager to make the leap to communism, "We have dirt in the factories and want to go directly to communism. And who will let you in? They are buried in rubbish but desire communism. . . . Dirty people are not permitted into communism. We need to stop being pigs."[81] Communism was going to be clean—people and society had to "go to the banya" before the good life could be attained. The idealized banyas of the USSR were supposed to be an essential stop on the way to a good, cultured life. The actual banyas, however, like the Party's policies, appear to have been as likely to spread parasites as to eliminate them.

8

Here Nobody Is Naked, There Is No Need for Shame

DURING AND AFTER the Second World War two visions of the banya in Soviet society coexisted. To government bureaucrats and to Soviet citizens with few bathing options, banyas were utilitarian. Their purpose was to clean bodies and the socialist state's responsibility was to ensure that they did so. At the same time, in the context of war and recovery, the banya's role in forging a communal identity and restoring vitality found renewed acceptance, which was reflected in literature and art. The two approaches were not contradictory in theory—a banya could be both physically cleansing and spiritually restorative. But in practice long lines, poor infrastructure, insufficient financing for public works, shortages of essential equipment, and inadequately trained technical and service personnel made municipal banyas challenging places to get clean and in turn unlikely spaces for people either to bond with fellow bathers or to feel rejuvenated. Instead, rural banyas, seemingly untarnished by Soviet plans, emerged as authentic spaces capable of healing a population devastated by war.

The utilitarian, top-down approach to banyas as instruments of hygiene had its origins in the public health movement of the nineteenth century, became Soviet and state-driven after October 1917, foundered during the Civil War, retreated during NEP, gained renewed energy and focus during the 1930s, survived intact during the Second World War, appeared even more pressing in the Cold War, and persisted right through the 1960s and 1970s, albeit with waning confidence and enthusiasm from the bureaucrats in charge of executing the plan. There appeared to be a fundamental flaw in the system. Those who held that banyas were integral to a healthy communist society were left with a conundrum: the Soviet Union was unable to build and maintain enough banyas in enough places to allow the population to clean itself regularly.

At the same time that state institutions struggled to implement their plans, the banya's importance to communal identity and as a unique social environment conducive to soulful human interactions became more pronounced. This way of understanding the banya—especially the rural banya—existed in ancient Rus', had survived the disparagement of foreign and Russian medical doctors, symbolized the innocence and backwardness of the peasantry in the late imperial period, and became officially out of date after the Bolsheviks took power. Even after the revolution, the sense that going to the banya could be a deeply meaningful experience did not disappear entirely. During and after the war, the banya's association with old Russia and tradition became more prominent. Going to the banya—experiencing the heat, the steam, the birch branches, the openness, the conversations—united people with their fellow bathers and with the generations who had bathed before them. There was a catch here too. The danger and potential for transgression in the banya remained as well. When people spoke of the banya as a meaningful cultural space, they transposed pre-Revolutionary themes into a Soviet key. But the fact remained that even as the Soviet state built, supplied, and regulated banyas in the name of hygiene, people went to them to purify themselves (at the risk of defilement) and to find fellowship with others (at the risk of estrangement). Unsafe or accursed banyas became symbols of all that had been lost or corrupted by the cataclysms of the mid-twentieth century. The instability of the war, the horrors of the Stalinist system, the cultural "thaw" that followed Stalin's death in 1953, and the retrenchment that followed the thaw all heightened the appeal of seeing the banya as a place either of innocence or of redemption and apart from the vicissitudes of politics. Seemingly untransformed by Soviet plans, the rural banya in particular became a place to go to become whole again.

Key characteristics of the Soviet battle on the banya front of the 1930s remained salient in the 1940s. Good personal hygiene was a sign of one's socialist bona fides. But most Soviet citizens had too few opportunities to bathe. The state saw this as a liability—unclean people were uncultured and susceptible to infectious diseases, which drained resources and reduced economic productivity. Few cities had sewage systems in place to remove waste, so people lived surrounded by filth, refuse, and the health threats they posed.

Opportunities to clean oneself at home were limited. Where city waterworks existed, pipes rarely reached apartment buildings. Public banyas were supposed to provide what other municipal services could not: a place for people to clean themselves.[1]

The Second World War made poor conditions considerably worse. The German invasion and the chaotic Soviet retreat left public infrastructure in occupied territories abandoned or destroyed. Behind the lines, upward of sixteen million Soviet citizens evacuated east, relocating to towns and cities that were already hard pressed to provide for the needs of their own populations. The new arrivals only increased the burden.[2] Because the priorities of local administrators focused first and foremost on the direct war effort, basic services, like banyas, suffered from even greater neglect than they had before. As had been the case during the Civil War, economic turmoil and demographic upheaval made it difficult to keep banyas open. At the same time, war made it even clearer that cleaning bodies was essential for public health.

Central authorities were desperately frustrated by how difficult it was to keep banyas running. From Moscow, it was pretty straightforward to decree, for instance, that everyone living in areas liberated from the German army was supposed go to the banya at least two times per month. But putting that into practice was next to impossible. In most cases state-run banyas were the only places to wash, but were in disrepair and suffering from neglect. A government memo ordered regional leaders "to establish quickly a working banya" in areas where they had been destroyed. The desperation was clear. Bathing might prevent outbreaks of diseases from spreading from vulnerable civilians to Red Army soldiers.[3] Devastated and war-torn communities were especially susceptible to typhus. The Red Army leaders understood the importance of the banya to the health of its soldiers. When troops were stationed in places where banya buildings were not available, makeshift banyas on train cars and even in dugouts were built. State publications attempted to provide guidance to rural communities seeking to build banyas quickly and efficiently. Yet time and again, word came back to central administrators that these efforts were not effective. Banyas were often not functioning at all or were functioning poorly at best.[4]

Desperate circumstances increased the population's demand for banyas. During the nearly 900-day siege of Leningrad, banyas served as a crucial weapon in the fight to stay alive, particularly as springtime thaws unleashed parasites that had been dormant during the deep freezes of winter. Despite tremendous hardships, Leningraders waited in long lines to crowd their way into the city's few open banyas with the hope that they could stave off illness.

FIGURE 8.1 A mobile banya on the Western Front, 1942. Banyas were deployed to keep soldiers clean and to limit the spread of disease. Courtesy of RGAKFD.

Once inside, starving people came face to face with one another and those who had access to food and privilege. They went for hygiene but they experienced a social reckoning.[5]

The banya, like the war itself, was a hellish place that made transparent things that might have been obscured elsewhere. One Leningrader in the Siege, Olga Berggol'ts, held that the banya forced people to confront how starvation and deprivation had come to define people's common identities. Nakedness revealed who people really were. True heroes, to her mind, were the weakest and weariest. Those who were well fed and healthy appeared grotesque to those who were suffering. The banya exposed the inversions caused by war:

> [In the banya] I had a look at women. Their dark female figures covered with rough skin—no, not even women—they ceased to be like women—their breasts had disappeared, their stomachs were sunken in, purplish and blue spots, from scurvy, covered their skin . . . And suddenly a woman entered. She was smooth, white, glimmering with golden peach fuzz. Her breasts were round, pert, with almost shamelessly erect pink nipples . . . We wouldn't be more frightened if a skeleton entered that room. Oh, how scary she was! Scary with her normal

impeccably healthy, eternal female flesh. How all this could have managed to survive? She was simply frightening to us.

She was nauseating, repulsive, disgusting... A frighteningly bony
woman approached her, gave her a slight smack on her butt, and said,
"Hey beauty—don't come here, we might eat you!" ... They spurned
her as if she had leprosy, not wanting to touch her silky, glowing
skin ... The woman screamed, threw away her bucket, and ran from
the room.[6]

The war turned the world upside down. The infernal banya made that obvious. But the banya also united those who were suffering; the banya could
forge solidarity out of starvation.

The fact that Leningraders could go to the banya at all was no small feat
in the conditions of the war. Keeping banyas open proved difficult even far
behind the front lines. The municipal infrastructure of overcrowded cities in
the country's interior was pushed beyond capacity by waves of refugees and
the demands of war, despite government efforts to ameliorate the situation.
In December 1941, the Council of People's Commissars of the Russian Soviet
Federative Socialist Republic (RSFSR) passed a decree, "On Measures to
Improve the Operation of Banyas and Laundries," only to find a few months
later that its impact was minimal. Even when facing outbreaks of typhus,
municipalities were unable to find the resources to keep banyas open and
allow the population to bathe regularly.[7] Again, central decrees did little to
improve conditions at the local level. Banyas across the USSR suffered from
a lack of heating materials, periodic water outages, and shutdowns that limited operating only a few days a week. Those that remained open were filthy
and broken down. Even in Moscow, the banyas had deteriorated considerably, leading Vyacheslav Molotov, First Deputy Chairman of the Council of
People's Commissars of the USSR, and Aleksei Kosygin, Chairman of the
Council of People's Commissars of the Russian Republic, to intervene.[8]

Soldiers seized upon the chance to bathe whenever they could. They did
so to get clean, of course, but also as a rare respite from battle and a moment
to contemplate the events of the war.[9] The banya evoked patriotism. Official
propaganda had placed the USSR's struggle against the Nazis in the context
of Russia's long history of combatting foreign invaders. Stalin himself had
suggested that Soviet citizens fighting for the liberation of the motherland
were following in the footsteps of heroes who had over the centuries defended
Russia from Teutonic Knights, Mongols, Poles, and Napoleon.[10] The Soviet
Union assumed Russia's martial past as its own. The banya's value as a unifying

and defining national custom became more powerful, particularly in the face of foreigners confident in their cultural superiority. Nowhere was this more clearly on display than in the Soviet writer and correspondent Alexander Tvardovsky's widely celebrated and beloved story in verse *Vasily Terkin: A Book About a Soldier* and its chapter "In the Banya."[11]

The poem tells the story of Terkin, a grizzled veteran making his way through the war. Official newspapers for soldiers at the front printed each new chapter as Tvardovsky wrote them. National papers, like *Pravda*, *Izvestiia*, and *Krokodil*, also reprinted portions of the poem. Its popularity was further enhanced by readings aired on national radio by Tvardovsky, Yuri Levitan (the greatest Soviet radio voice of the era), and actor Dmitry Orlov.[12] Readers valued its apparent authenticity. Ignoring the conventions of Soviet wartime literature, Tvardovsky never referred to Stalin or the Party in the poem. Terkin's loyalty was to his homeland, not to socialism. After publishing the first few chapters, Tvardovsky received hundreds of letters from soldiers asking him to write more. These letters convinced him to do so and helped sway his reluctant superiors to continue publishing it. To Tvardovsky's credit as a writer, his poem was acceptable to the censors and appealed to literary figures and regular soldiers alike.[13] Aleksander Solzhenitsyn, who served as an artillery commander in the Red Army, later wrote, "I remember how soldiers at the front knew to a man the difference between Terkin, which rang so miraculously true, and all other wartime books."[14] In contrast to other officially sanctioned wartime literature, Tvardovsky had managed to create a character that earned broad appreciation across the USSR.

In March 1945, as the Red Army approached Berlin, Tvardovsky noted in his journal, "This morning I was spurred on by last night's banya to remember all of the various banyas where I had cleaned myself in the war, and I suddenly decided to write a chapter [of the Terkin poem] 'In the Banya.'" He continued:

> [The banya is] half-fantastic, forgiving, and softening of the sharpness of the discussions and thoughts about who counts for what in war and what the differences are between this and that contribution. Since ancient times Russian people have spoken in the banya (I mean the rural banya, the kolkhoz banya—not the commercial urban banya) about strength, often about a specifically masculine strength, they have spoken in aphorisms, in exclamations, in short breaths.[15]

Tvardovsky realized that the rural banya was an ideal setting for his purposes because it made possible difficult conversations and it did so in a way that evoked the Russian past. The association of "commercial urban" banyas with propaganda and official, top-down orders to use them undermined their value as an untarnished space for the people. The traditional, rural banya, in contrast, seemed unchanged and capable of uniting the Soviet people. As the Red Army made the final push toward Berlin and contemplated the transition from war to peace, a rural banya seemed like the right place to go to make sense of what was happening.

Tvardovsky's journal entries in the spring of 1945 clarify that he intended the chapter to celebrate both the soldier and those working on the home front. He sketched out positive lines about noncombatants like weapons producers,

FIGURE 8.2 Red Army soldiers outside a banya at the front, 1941. Courtesy of RGAKFD.

ship builders, and even writers like himself. He made notes about conversations that he thought might emerge in the banya. In one of them, Terkin tells a Tvardovsky-like correspondent that everyone's contributions to war were important. Writing about the war was a duty. Working through the lines of banya talk, Tvardovsky added, "It's true boys, this one and that one fought / And soldiers and generals / And tankists and even the clowns / behind the front lines / and at the front and in Siberia / In a word, everyone fought."[16] To strengthen national unity, Tvardosvksy even contemplated including a line about how poorly Hitler would have fared in the heat of the Russian banya.[17]

Tvardovsky's plans to celebrate all Soviet citizens, however, existed in tension with his desire to celebrate the soldier's body in particular. The banya did not so much make everyone equal as it clarified who people really were in a way that could be unapparent elsewhere. His notes suggest the degree to which he believed nudity helped reveal heroes. Stripping off uniforms and medals exposed hard earned scars that made it easier to size up another man's character. As many Red Army soldiers understood, some officers and grunts had not been brave and some medals had not been earned justly. The trick was to figure out another soldier's worth without resorting to state-sponsored markers of heroism, such as uniforms and medals. In the banya, with insignias and regalia removed, and party membership cards left behind, wartime injuries and scars made it clear who had been suffering at the front.[18]

In the final version of the poem, the conversations Tvardovsky had drafted disappeared. Terkin's banya was a victory banya, Deep in Germany Terkin comes across a German "house or castle, it doesn't matter" and quickly transforms it into a banya where the soldiers can undress without concern. A banya "whether Sanduny or any other one" is still the banya, even if a "Count's chairs" line the changing room. The steam converted a noble German house into a simple Russian banya, where a Russian soldier could feel at home, even in Germany.

Tvardovsky drew attention to Terkin's wounds and his unequalled ability to withstand the intense heat of the banya. The banya was revealing of "who counted for what in war"—and it turned out the front-line soldier counted more than others after all. The banya was a place "without deceit," where the hero undresses slowly, and where "we can have a look at our stark-naked soldier."[19] The poem continued to size up the hero and, with it, the author's ideal of a soldier in a way that was only possible in the banya, where nudity was obligatory and therefore the body was relatively open to comment and contemplation: "Medium height but chest well out; / Body's clean uprightness / By four years in uniform / Tanned to lily-whiteness. And, although by now he's shed / All his grand regalia, / Still, with action you can tell / He's not unfamiliar. // And you'll simply be amazed / That he could survive it— / On the naked skin a star / Flaming bright and livid. // Like a medal that he's won, / And he always wears it, / Only it's his shoulder-blade, / Not his chest that bears it. // . . . What each mile he marched was like, / He needs no reminding. / To the steam room now he goes, / Leaves his clothes behind him."[20] A later verse made the exclusivity of the strength of men at the front explicit. Soldiers enjoy the high temperatures, but the average man is unable to take the heat and, in the process of going to the banya, even risks his ability to reproduce: "If some connoisseur and expert / Drops in—hardy though he be— / He won't stick it out, or rather / If he does, he'll be no father, / He'll be seedless presently! // No, it's useless, useless, useless / For a stranger in this place / Vying with a soldier: even / Satan couldn't stand the pace!"[21] Tvardovsky had managed to relay in poetry some of the ideas that he had sketched out earlier in his notes: a soldier's scars tell his story.[22] But hierarchy remained. Conversations in the banya may have "softened the differences" between people, but the heat separated out soldiers from civilians, patriots from adversaries, Russian heroes from everyone else.

The clarity provided by the banya was only temporary. As the poem ends and Terkin has dressed again, someone has the temerity to ask him if he bought his medals at a shop. Terkin laughs off the potential insult, explaining that he still had more medals to earn during the final push to Berlin. Again, Tvardovsky distinguishes Terkin from the soldiers who had gotten medals illegitimately. In a way that was impossible anywhere else, the openness of the banya made legible who fought bravely in the war, who had the scars to prove it, and who had been able to take the heat of battle. The "half-fantastic" banya, in Tvardovsky's phrase, allowed soldiers to do what Russian people had been doing since "ancient times." Steaming oneself, in keeping with Russian tradition, set things right, if only for a little while.

The banya emerged from the war as an institution tied to survival and victory. Horrendous conditions and circumstances thwarted the state's push for better hygiene. Those same conditions, however, also reanimated the popular sense that the banya provided a way to commune with an authentic past and was a space where truths could be revealed. The wartime banya made battle scars visible and emaciated bodies more normal than well-fed ones. It was a source of spiritual rejuvenation and a means of forging a common identity, rooted in the Russian past and flourishing in the Soviet present.

—•—

Authenticity and solidarity were important, but Soviet people also wanted to be able to clean themselves. After the war, citizens expected the state to prioritize improvements in everyday life.[23] The Cold War heightened attention to these priorities. In the middle of the twentieth century, the idea that people should have access to bathhouses was hardly peculiar to the Soviet Union. What made the USSR different was that the centralized state assumed responsibility for building, maintaining, and supplying those bathhouses and acknowledged that doing so was an ideological imperative. If a Soviet citizen could not bathe in 1936, saboteurs who had infiltrated the Soviet system could be blamed. If she could not bathe in 1946, it was because of the lingering effects of the war. But if she could not bathe in 1956, it reflected poorly on the system itself. As society recovered from the war and people expected to begin to receive some respite after years of sacrifice, the Soviet state was obliged to deliver on its promises. Banyas were part of a larger ideological investment in meeting the personal needs and desires of the people.[24]

Immediately following the war there was no opportunity and little reason to re-evaluate the assumption inherited from the 1930s that public banyas were essential for public health. The devastation of the war, crop failures, and political decisions that prioritized the state's reassertion of control in the countryside led to a famine in 1946–1947. With much of the population malnourished and living in overwhelming squalor, epidemics spread. Over a million people died.[25] In such circumstances, postwar efforts along what officials still thought of as the banya front quickly reverted to mirroring prewar efforts. Various republic-wide Ministries of Municipal Services took on the task.[26] Local executive committees in regions, towns, and autonomous regions of the USSR were in charge of seeing the plans through to completion. Bureaucrats continued to keep careful count of the number of banyas in operation, the number of bathing spaces those banyas represented, and the number of "cleanings" in total and per capita they could provide both in principle and in fact. The diligent and consistent keeping of these statistics, year in and year out, reflects the all-encompassing agenda of the Soviet state. Yearly—and even quarterly—reports detailed how often people on average were able to go to the banya in every republic, region, city, and community of the Soviet Union. It was the state's responsibility to monitor and improve the situation.[27]

Two familiar and related problems confronted bureaucrats in charge of the banya front after the war. First, there was the problem of capacity. On aggregate, the USSR still did not have enough banyas of the right size to allow people to bathe once every ten days. The problem was even worse at the local level. Some neighborhoods and even whole cities had no municipal banyas at all. The challenges posed by limited capacity were compounded by markedly unequal distribution of that capacity.

The second problem was operational. Banyas that did exist did not run consistently and efficiently. Just as it had in the 1930s, the vagaries of Soviet economics made managing a banya arduous. Costs far exceeded revenues. The use of faulty and inefficient equipment increased the difficulty of keeping banyas open and increased the likelihood that they would need to be shut down until repairs could be arranged. If banyas were unable to operate, revenues decreased further. The problem was hardly isolated. In 1946, across the Russian Republic, revenues were less than half of what planners had anticipated. Increasing ticket prices was not an option. The centralized plan determined how much banyas could charge for tickets based on a calculation of the average cost of a cleaning and on what workers could be expected to afford, not on supply and demand curves. This meant that banyas invariably depended on state subsidies for maintenance, repairs, and even to stay open.[28]

Increased support from Moscow did not directly translate into better-equipped banyas. As in the 1930s, heating materials were hard to come by, which made it tempting for local authorities to divert fuel designated for the banya to other sectors of the economy instead. Everywhere, infrastructural problems persisted: many banyas lacked running water or boilers for heating the water. Access to electricity was intermittent. Soap production in the country as a whole during the war had almost completely ceased and by 1947 was still not up and running. Bathers could not bathe without heat, water, and soap.[29] Personnel problems compounded the challenges. Municipal leaders had a hard time finding technical workers to run and repair furnaces and boilers, oversee construction, and manage the buildings. Without all the pieces in place, a banya would shut down.

Even at the federal ministerial level, there were not enough workers in the banya industry. Ministries of municipal services were responsible for public transportation, housing, sewage systems, waterworks, electricity, and count-less other services. Banyas were often not a top priority. In the whole Russian Republic, only twenty-one central administrators oversaw the plans and oper-ations for 866 municipal banyas.[30] This meant that most of the basic decisions were made on the local level, where the push for better-run banyas could be ignored. When resources were short—as they often were—there was little political cost to raiding banya funds, equipment, and personnel. Leaders in the town of Saratov, for instance, wanted to repurpose one of its banyas even though people in the city could bathe in a banya only once every forty days.

Administrators in Moscow denied the request. But they did not have the resources to build new banyas in Saratov or to refurbish the banya in question.[31]

Local decisions that did not prioritize bathing combined with a shortage of capacity to create serious problems. In 1946, if all the banyas were running smoothly, people could bathe in a banya only once every sixty days on average. The situation was far worse than that because bathhouses operated far below capacity.[32] In the city of Kaluga plans called for its only two banyas to provide 500,000 cleanings in the first half of 1946. Instead they provided 172. In Cheliabinsk, the three extant banyas reported that they fell over a million cleanings short of their goal for the year.[33] Capacity was woefully insufficient and efficiency was woefully low.

A few factors ameliorated the situation, although only slightly. Some factories and industries allowed their workers to access enterprise-run banyas after the workday and in some rural communities private banyas remained popular. Nonetheless, administrators understood that these other potential means of getting clean could not come close to making up for the shortfall from public banyas. Problems of access plagued the enterprise banyas too. In most cases, only people who worked in an enterprise could bathe in its banya and then only when the managers determined that heating the banya was worthwhile. Fuel shortages, breakdowns, and inconsistent electricity dogged enterprise banyas too. Furthermore, enterprise banyas had none of the local or federal oversight or support that communal banyas benefited from. Peasant banyas—operated privately by rural families—also did not ease the burden on communal banyas much. They provided little solace to the bureaucrats, who questioned how healthy it was to bathe in them and lamented that the peasants wasted many hours on Saturdays heating them when they should have been working. Building more public banyas was supposed to be the answer for the rural shortfall as well. Even when all the different kinds of banyas were taken into account, people in even major Soviet cities could bathe at best once every twenty to thirty days and at worst once every two months. "The results," an internal government memo concluded, "speaks to the unsatisfactory work of the communal banyas."[34]

The situation was very slow to improve. In 1947, the number of banyas and the number of spaces in operation in Russia actually went down.[35] In 1948 the ministry concluded that even humble goals for the number of cleanings banyas could provide were still not being met.[36] By 1952 the situation with fuel and water had stabilized somewhat, making it possible to get more use out of existing spaces. Overall capacity rose, but this could hardly mask the fact that the number of banyas coming online barely outnumbered those that had to be shut down for repairs and that those in operation still ran far below capacity. The plan itself set goals that were under what the state deemed the hygienic norm and even then many towns and regions failed to meet the targets.[37]

The newfound stability was precarious. In 1952, citizens in major cities such as Briansk, Gorky, Kursk, Rostov-on-the-Don, Saratov, Sverdlovsk, and Tomsk were only able to bathe once every fifteen to twenty days and even then only after waiting for hours in lines. The ministry concluded that 177 urban communities across the Russian Republic still had no banyas at all. The ministry now calculated that it needed to add 140,000 more spaces to provide the population with basic hygiene. To start down that road, the ministry suggested building 50,000 banya spaces by 1957, an incredibly ambitious plan that would entail a faster pace of growth than had been achieved at any point under Soviet rule. But even 50,000 new spaces would have been insufficient to meet demand or to address the problems caused by the unequal distribution of bathhouses. With little exaggeration, workers complained of a "banya famine."[38]

The extent of the problems was hardly a secret. Just as it had in the 1930s, the humor journal *Krokodil* openly criticized conditions on the banya front. Satirical essays, poems, cartoons, and letters to the editor lambasted banyas across the USSR for their lack of heat, lack of water, long lines, and general mismanagement. There were limits, of course, to what any state organ could point out. The journal's commentaries always accepted the state's utilitarian agenda as a given, even as they highlighted the problems that everyday life made obvious and that propaganda ignored.

In 1945, the journal published a satirical set of cartoons by Ivan Semenov on the development of modern services and their potential problems. In the modern banya, the water has run out. The caption reads: "Take communal services. The banya. Well, what good is a cold waterfall or a weak stream from a pitcher when compared to a modern marble-tiled, nickel-mirrored, and bronze-tubbed luxurious center of hygiene? Entering this castle of cleanliness, the visitors experience unspeakable ecstasy, which only dies down a bit with the absence of running water." A little over a year later, the magazine published a series of cartoons by Mikhail Cheremnykh suggesting outrageous places where dancing might break out. Alongside the "Hospital Tango" and "Library Rumba" was the "Banya Boston Waltz." Under a sign

FIGURE 8.3 Soviet policy called for improvements in basic municipal services, such as the banya. Ivan Semenov's cartoon on the modern banya suggested that conditions instead had deteriorated over time. From *Krokodil*, August 30, 1945, p. 6-7.

reading, "Due to the absence of water, today we will dance," a naked man sits on a stool playing the accordion, while two naked male couples dance arm in arm. The juxtaposition of the banya's legendary—but officially outdated—role in male sociability and the state's failure to provide water made for ironic humor.[39] (There were limits, however, to how much humor state-sponsored journals could find in the banya. In 1945, when Mikhail Zoshchenko published yet another a satirical story, Stalin was upset by his inclusion of a banya scene.)[40]

By the early 1950s, it was clear that the war could no longer be legitimately blamed for continued deficiencies in the country's banya infrastructure. A poem by Stalin-Prize winning writer Samuil Marshak took on the issue directly, suggesting that a local decision in Simferopol to take space from a banya and allocate it to a local building agency was a bad idea. The devastation of the war, he concluded, could not excuse such a gross and absurd misallocation of resources.[41]

Krokodil turned to local administrators to solve the problems—and found them wanting. The magazine lambasted municipal leaders for ignoring the banya and banya directors for their lack of concern for the population. Readers learned that in the Tagansky neighborhood of Moscow corrupt banya workers let friends and relatives bathe for free.[42] In the small town of Arzhanovo the banya was open during the day, when workers could not go, and closed at night when workers conceivably could.[43] Other banyas took years to build.[44] Humorous drawings suggested that this was a generally recognized problem, even if the blame remained focused on local administrators. A 1951 drawing of a recently remodeled banya that was already crumbling could have described the situation in any city in the USSR.[45]

FIGURE 8.4 The banya's roots as a social space were never far from the surface. In "The Banya Boston Waltz," by Mikhail Cheremnykh, men went to the banya even when there was no water. From *Krokodil*, May 20, 1946, p. 6.

The criticism of the banya front after the war in *Krokodil* accepted the state's formulation that banyas were primarily about hygiene. If men danced together in the banya it was because the water had run out, not because socializing was supposed to be the point all along. Communal banyas were supposed to provide for personal cleanliness. The jokes were about their failure to do so.

At their worst, banyas posed far greater dangers than the absence of water. This was most evident in banyas of the Soviet Union's elaborate prison system, which peaked in terms of arrests and incarcerations in the late 1940s and early 1950s. Since the late 1920s, millions of Soviet citizens had been imprisoned for a range of alleged crimes and forced into the Gulag—hard labor camps, labor colonies, and special resettlements. The Gulag banya, like all Soviet banyas, was nominally a place to get clean. It exemplified the modernist impulses of the Soviet system—purifying prisoners by excising diseases was akin to cleansing society of socially harmful elements. It also displayed the system's destructive abilities. The price of personal hygiene paralleled the price for social hygiene. Epidemics could spread easily from camps to cities and from prisoners to those who remained free. With the threat of disease rampant, prisoners were obliged to bathe. But if problems on the outside made banyas difficult to manage, in the camps they were often unbearable. The Gulag exaggerated and distorted "normal" Soviet life. *Krokodil* could make fun of a city banya without water. Inside the Gulag, material deficiencies suggested moral inversions. Pure things became vile. The banya went from being, at least in principle, about cleanliness to something debasing, from a place conducive to intimacy and contemplation, as it was for Tvardovsky, to a place of disgust, as it had been for Dostoevsky in *House of the Dead*.[46] *Zeks* (or Gulag prisoners) cited the banya as a place that accentuated their already extreme vulnerability in the camps.

In Solzhenitsyn's book *The Gulag Archipelago*, the prison banya is a sort of hell—the opposite of a place of redemption. It is where women are stripped down and humiliated and where authorities march prisoners off to be shot.[47] According to Varlam Shalamov, who had been arrested for the first time in 1929 and who remained a *zek* until 1951, the banya was "a negative event, a burden in the convict's life." "This observation," he added, "is a testimony to the 'shift of values,' which is the main quality that the camp instills in its inmates." Doctors and camp officials saw the banya as a hygienic process—a job for the "sanitation squad." The prisoners did not, joking instead that the banya was a form of "tyranny," not cleanliness. Outside the camps people, at least in the *zek's* imagination, could experience the "physical bliss" of a well-heated banya. But in the camps, it was best to resist going at all. Officials thought the prisoners' refusals to bathe were a form of protest. Imbued with the sense that the banya was a hygienic tool, they could not understand why a human being would "refuse to wash himself in the banya and free himself from the dirt and sweat that cover his body with its festering skin diseases." But *zeks* understood that the Gulag had turned the banya's role inside out. Instead of respite and cleanliness, the banya meant more work and increased exposure to danger. Guards made prisoners bathe during their precious free time, not work time. The banya was invariably located far away from the barracks. Not only did it take prisoners otherwise valuable personal time to get to them, they had to carry their own wood in the process. The banyas were overcrowded and often underheated. And the guards took advantage of the prisoners' absence to ransack their barracks. Upon entering a banya inmates handed over their dirty underwear; upon leaving they received wet underwear distributed at random. The rest of their clothes were sent to a "disinfection chamber," which more often than not failed to serve its purpose. Rather than restoring their health, the prison banya undermined the dignity and integrity of the prisoners.[48]

If the Gulag banya could turn purity into danger, Shalamov suggested, it could also turn strength and authority into weakness and submission. The "shift in values" could work both ways. Shalamov recalled the story of the demise of a powerful, but despicable *zek* foreman, Timoshenko. Timoshenko made a habit of going to the prison banya after his workday in the mines. One day, a prisoner who had recently served a stint in solitary confinement, because he refused to accuse a fellow *zek* of a crime, replaced the normal *banshchik*. When Timoshenko discovered who his new *banshchik* was, he mocked him for his high-minded morals and integrity, calling him a fool. Timoshenko had no qualms about ratting out his fellow *zeks* with impunity if it furthered his own cause. Meanwhile he instructed the new *banshchik* about the way he liked to bathe: after steaming, he would get in a tub of water and heat it with a faucet that drew boiling water directly from the banya's boiler. When the water was hot enough, he tapped on the faucet as a signal to the *banshchik* in the boiler room to turn the water off. With the system explained, Timoshenko began to bathe. When the water in the tub was hot enough, he tapped. The *banshchik* either ignored or did not hear the signal. Panicking about the increasingly hot water, Timoshenko tried to scramble out of the tub but the faucet trapped him. He was boiled alive. The prisoners' own system of justice had caught up with the arrogant Timoshenko. Shalamov's Gulag banya was a torture chamber but also, in this case, an instrument of divine retribution.[49]

Other Gulag survivors also turned their attention to the banya to describe the horrors of camp life. Janusz Bardach's memoir of the Gulag, *Man Is Wolf to Man*, described his first banya in the camps. As with Shalamov, a cleansing ritual was inverted into something that was befouling. After a brutal shave Bardach headed to the banya, where the "putrid smell of urine rose from the floor." The water was scum infested; the soap "smelled like an old dirty rag." As Bardach's grew accustomed to his overwhelming environment, he noticed two young men who "held each other at the waist and brushed their erect penises over each other's bodies. Sitting on a bench, another skinny fellow masturbated a friend, who held him in return." He soon realized that many others were doing similar things. When he went for more water, he witnessed a rape, with the rapist being cheered on by the prisoners. "Man is wolf to man" he recalled his mother telling him when he was a child as he realized that "I could be forced to lie on a bench in this or in another bathhouse and be repeatedly raped not by my oppressors—whom I considered to be the NKVD guards—but by my fellow prisoners." The hellishness of the banya was made even more extreme by the corruption of what, at least in principle, was supposed to be pure and the mockery of any hope of prisoners' solidarity.

Women's Gulag banyas were no less disorientating. Evfrosiniia Kersnovskaia wrote detailed notes describing in prose and drawings her twelve years in the

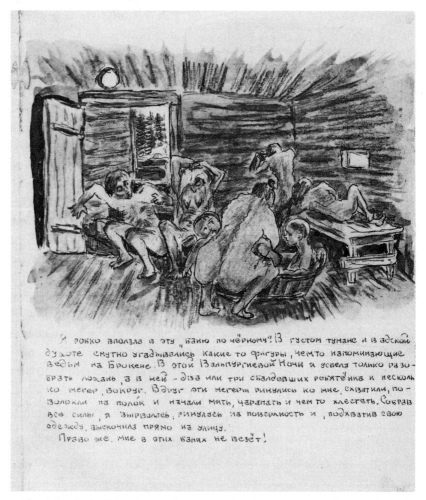

FIGURE 8.5 Evfrosiniia Kersnovskaya recalled going to a dugout banya, where she felt as though she were suffocating. Courtesy of E. A. Kersnovskaia and her heir I. M. Chapkovskii.

Gulag. Once, she came across a rural black-banya dug into the ground. She entered with trepidation and quickly became disoriented. Covered in soot, barely able to see, and "almost strangled by the hot steam," she could just make out two or three children in a tub on the floor and a group of women squatting while they splashed water from the stove. Soon the women grabbed Kersnovskaia, picked her up, and before she knew what was happening spread her on the shelf "like a skin on a ruler and began rubbing, kneading, and whipping" her. Kersnovskaia trusted the intentions of the women but could not help but feel as though she

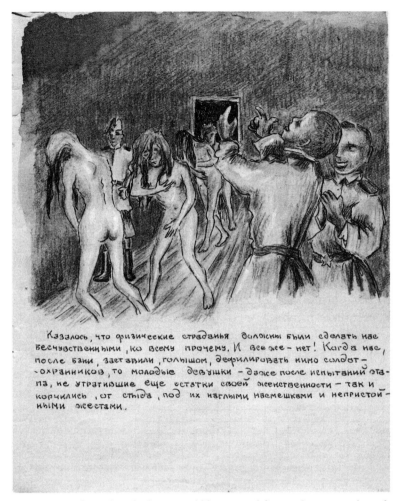

Казалось, что физические страданья должны были сделать нас бесчувственными, ко всему прочему. И всё же - нет! Когда нас, после бани, заставляли, голышом, дефилировать мимо солдат-охранников, то молодые девушки - даже после испытаний эта-па, не утратившие еще остатки своей женственности - так и корчились, от стыда, под их наглыми насмешками и непристой-ными жестами.

FIGURE 8.6 In the Gulag, the banya could be inverted from a cleansing and purifying activity into a humiliating and terrifying one. In Kersnovskaia's journal, a trip to the banya became yet another opportunity for male guards to taunt female prisoners. Courtesy of E. A. Kersnovskaia and her heir I. M. Chapkovskii.

were suffocating. She quickly jumped up and shot herself out of the banya "like a cork." "That's the banya," she sighed.

Later Kersnovskaia described the banya as a place that revealed that there was "no limit to bullying" and "no limit to human endurance." In the Gulag banya female *zeks* were huddled together in a cold room that provided no steam and only cold water to wash with. Afterward, a guard gave them cold, damp clothes to change into. "It was a wild image," she reported, "a tangle of wet female blue-violet bodies in constant motion, seeking out warmth by struggling to get to the center of the human huddle." The Gulag had turned the banya into a claustrophobic nightmare and a shocking challenge to the human will to survive and maintain dignity amidst immeasurable hardship.

——◆——

After Stalin died in 1953, the Gulag system was partially dismantled. The new party leader, Nikita Khrushchev, oversaw a cultural "thaw" that redefined the limits of what could be discussed openly in society, challenging the strict boundaries of discourse enforced while Stalin was still alive. In 1957 a group of hardliners, led by Stalin's close comrades Georgii Malenkov and Vyacheslav Molotov, balked at the reforms and attempted to oust Khrushchev as First Secretary of the Party. In the midst of the crucial meetings to decide the issue, Molotov excoriated Khrushchev for having accepted an invitation from the Finnish President Urho Kekkonen to go to a "Finnish" banya after formal meetings between the two had concluded. The idea of the banya as a potentially intimate and vulnerable place was palpable. Khrushchev countered that even though he was less familiar with steaming himself than others in the leadership, he agreed to go to the banya because he felt it would have been rude to turn Kekkonen down. Besides, he maintained that all they did in the banya was steam and joke around. Still, Molotov insisted that going to the banya with a foreigner was unbefitting of the First Secretary of the Party. Khrushchev's side responded that it was better to go to the banya with a bourgeois leader than undertake conspiratorial meetings with Hitler, as Molotov had done before the war. In the end, the effort to oust Khrushchev failed. The idea that it mattered who you went to the banya with remained.[50]

The thaw continued in fits and starts. As *zeks* began slowly streaming back into "normal" Soviet society, they may have recognized the dark humor in *Krokodil's* jokes about the conditions in municipal banyas. On the one hand, the Gulag banya and the troubled municipal banya were each related to the dark underbelly of the clean and modern goals of the system. On the other hand, *zeks* likely had more trouble comprehending an image of the banya as a symbol of purity and innocence that was re-emerging during the Thaw. The rural banya, which Tvardovsky had suggested in his diary was "forgiving" and where people could speak openly, appeared often in public. The contrast between the nightmarish Gulag banya, still talked about mostly in whispers, and the idyllic banya touted publicly could not have been more striking.

FIGURE 8.7 Aleksandr Gerasimov, known for his Socialist Realist paintings of the Soviet leaders, began painting a women's banya in the midst of the terror of the 1930s and continued to work on it through the 1950s. This is a study of a larger painting that he kept in his studio until after Stalin's death.

Even an ardent Stalinist understood the banya meant more than the steadfast emphasis on hygiene suggested. Aleksander Gerasimov, the head of the Soviet Academy of Arts, was famous as the court artist most responsible for portraying Stalin in propaganda paintings. In the late 1930s, as many of his fellow academy members were being arrested, sent to camps, or executed, Gerasimov served the state as an artist and bureaucrat. His public depictions of Stalin and others were masculine, strident, and ubiquitous. In the privacy of his own studio, however, he painted women bathing in the banya. This

FIGURE 8.8 Arkady Plastov's 1954 painting *Spring* turned to the banya in the country-side, and to feminine beauty, as symbol of purity. Courtesy of the Tretyakov Gallery.

was not the utilitarian banya of propaganda posters, the humorous banya of *Krokodil*, the diplomatic male banya of Khrushchev and Kekkonen, or the nightmarish banya of the Gulag. In a series of studies that he worked on through the 1950s, Gerasimov conjured a stereotypical women's sphere—intimate, relaxed, open, revealing, and interactive. Only after Stalin's death, when Gerasimov's role in propagating Stalin's personal power became clear, did the artist begin to show his banya paintings more openly. The woman who was "smooth, white, glimmering with golden peach fuzz" and whose "breasts were round, pert, with almost shamelessly erect pink nipples" who had appeared grotesque to Berggol'ts during the siege of Leningrad reappears with her girlfriends and has taken over the banya, at least in Gerasimov's imagination.

Gerasimov was not alone in representing the banya as a steamy, healthy, purifying, and female space. In an era where the tenets of the Stalin years were called into question, the banya was once again free to represent Russian purity and not just Soviet fastidiousness. The rural banya equaled uncorrupted Russianness. And the female rural banya was the most Russian and the least corrupt of all. The further one got from the male world of Soviet public life and from the Soviet city, the purer things became. Siberia, more than any other rural space, represented both an ucorrupted Russian past and evidence of Soviet superiority. In 1960, the film *Russian Souvenir* showed an American businessman learning the futility of capitalism in part through exposure to a Siberian banya.[51] That same year the young Thaw-era poet Andrei Voznesensky used a Siberian banya to evoke the innocence of female wholesomeness, citing the "cleanliness of fire and of snow with the cleanliness of nudity."[52] Arkadii Plastov's Thaw-era painting *Spring* (sometimes referred to as "Northern Venus") conveyed this sense of the banya as well. As snow lightly falls, a naked blonde woman squats down on golden straw outside a rural banya to comfort her daughter as if Kustodiev's *Russian Venus* had returned from the 1920s, with her innocence untarnished by famine, terror, the Gulag, or war.

Under socialism, goddesses walked the earth. Lest people think that this was only a fantasy, the newspaper *Soviet Culture* declared that Plastov's paintings, including *Spring*, had accurately conveyed the "simple, ordinary life of simple Russian people." Plastov painted the "modern kolkhoz workers" as "clean, bright, hardworking moral people bearing socialist humanism and beauty." He did not "idealize" his subjects, the newspaper informed its readers, but instead showed them "as they really are."[53] For Gerasimov, Plastov, and Voznesensky, bathing women were there to be admired and observed. City banyas were usually overcrowded and undersupplied and Gulag banyas were the setting for horrors. But in the countryside steaming oneself was still associated with personal innocence, spiritual survival, and rebirth. The rural banya was once again the "second mother" of all of Russia.

During the 1950s and 1960s, few banyas resembled the golden banyas of Gerasimov's and Plastov's imaginations. Instead, banya operators confronted the more mundane challenge of trying to remain open and serving a population desperate for opportunities to clean their bodies. In society and in cultural depictions of the banya, there was a thaw, but in banya administration there was no fundamental reform. Stalin's death did not alter the goal of building enough banyas to allow each citizen to bathe once a week. If anything, the rapid urbanization of the period further complicated the state's efforts. Over the course of the 1950s, the urban population of the country grew by 3.4 million people a year. Even taking into account the approximately 27 million Soviet citizens who died during the war, the urban population increased by 39 million people from 1939 to 1959. Natural growth accounted for only 14 million people—the rest came from massive in-migration from rural areas. Existing cities grew, putting tremendous strain on urban planning and infrastructure. And new cities and urban districts emerged where municipal systems had to be built almost from scratch. The demand for new banyas in urban areas was tremendous. Meanwhile, much of this migration was unplanned, leaving some communities overcrowded while others experienced labor shortages.[54] In this context, it was difficult for either central administrators or local authorities to predict how many banyas would be needed and where.

Some cities adapted to the growth relatively well. Greater access to fuel and better upkeep meant that the numbers of cleanings rose on aggregate. In some towns, banyas were well taken care of and remained in operation consistently. In some places, administrators were pleased to report that basic services were in place: benches had appeared, ventilation systems were in operation, special sections for mothers and children had been built, the steam rooms were functioning "normally," the snack-bars were open and had items for sale, the entrances were welcoming, and the furnaces were well stoked.[55] But these accomplishments still fell far short of the goals. The Ministry of Municipal Services of the Russian Republic, for instance, built only 20 percent of the banya spaces it had planned to build in 1957.

In the late 1950s, even when "enterprise banyas" were included in calculations, the urban population of the Russian Republic was still bathing on average once every eighteen days.[56] In many communities, banyas languished. In 1957 the number of cities without a single banya had jumped to two hundred. Over 250 cities failed to meet their specific plans. The need for renovations, breaks in supplies of hot water, the poor condition of the boilers, and other problems persisted. The Russian Ministry of Municipal Services blamed local administrators, noting that "where the communal organs and local councils pay attention to banyas, they are in good shape."

A scientific-technical committee admitted that city administrators often failed to "pay attention to the people."[57] Towns that relied on enterprise banyas were at the whim of industrial bosses who often concluded that running banyas for the whole community was not their responsibility, even as local government leaders thought it was. But the problems went well beyond that. The existing system was underperforming, the committee concluded, because there were still too few banyas, the pace of building new ones was still too slow, and those that did exist were still plagued by myriad technical problems.[58]

There was enough blame to go around that nobody had to take responsibility. Central administrators in Moscow found fault with local officials, who in turn cited poor technical support from the center and recalcitrant enterprise bosses in their communities. One solution, in keeping with Khrushchev's administrative ideas, was to shift even more responsibility to the local officials. The 1956 "plan for the development of municipal services" sought to make the conditions in banyas "reliant on the executive committees of the local Soviets."[59] Some communities seem to have responded. In the town of Vladimir, the Party and the union organizations created a "mobilized collective" to respond to "justified complaints from the population about the serious problems with the banyas." The town leaders concluded that banyas could become more cost-effective if they were not heated during times when workers were unlikely to use them. Their solution, essentially, was to shut down banyas two to three days each week.[60] But even this "breakthrough" in local initiative conceded that banyas ran best when they did not attempt to reach their overall capacity. Not heating banyas at slow times saved money, but it also meant that the total number of cleanings decreased. This approach also presumably increased the lines during reduced hours. The town of Kaluga took the opposite approach. There, operators discounted the cost of entry during nonpeak times, which encouraged people to bathe mid-day and mid-week. In this way, they had increased the number of cleanings. "From an overcrowded banya," they boasted, "they had created a cost-efficient enterprise."[61]

Most local leaders, however, did not follow Vladimir's or Kaluga's lead in taking on their persistent banya problems. In 1958 a chief engineer at the Ministry of Municipal Services concluded, "City Soviet executive committees give little attention to new construction of banyas . . . and don't even use all the materials designated for that purpose." The downside of shifting responsibility to local administrators became clear within a few years. Some regional and local leaders were unprepared to oversee the banyas and the banya workers they found nominally under their direction. Some factories and industries did not turn over control of their banyas. These enterprises often worked "according to the old rules" in which priority was given to fulfilling the production plan, not worrying about the conditions of the people. Other regions did not have sufficient heating material for banyas. Some regions had no money for repairs. For banyas that were already cost-effective, local control was potentially beneficial. But for the ones in the direst need of resources from central authorities, localization only compounded the difficulties.[62]

Another solution was to build bigger banyas, which, economists calculated, would cost less per cleaning than smaller ones. To assist local leaders, architects developed blueprints for banya designs that could be built in any place at any time with only slight modifications for regional variations. Experts suggested that building banyas with showers and baths could also clean more people more quickly. The downside, they admitted, was that while the "hygienic norm" for a banya was one cleaning every seven to ten days, people needed to shower or bathe more often than that to stay clean. The question of whether government officials were now allowed to count showers as a "cleaning" according to old norms or instead were supposed to apply a new norm was raised, but apparently never answered.[63]

Even if banyas were large and even if they included showers and baths, they remained a burden on local administrators. Poor infrastructure and a lack of repairs put banyas "in a state of neglect," according to a scathing article in the Ministry's trade paper. The article reported that banyas had "fallen sharply behind" other sectors of municipal services. People headed to banyas after work, but found them closed or running without water. Others were unheated, had inoperable furnaces, cold dressing rooms, or inadequate ventilation. Many banyas were "closed for repairs" more often than they were open.[64]

In 1965, an inspection of five hundred banyas sought to figure out "why are our banyas still not cost-effective?" The conclusions were familiar: over 25 percent of the banyas had poor ventilation; 90 percent had walls that were crumbling from the moisture; 25 percent of the boilers needed repair; reserve water was stored in open containers, which often flooded buildings and soiled the water; heating material was used inefficiently and poorly stored; and unqualified people manned the boilers.[65]

The situation in rural areas was hardly better. An urban journalist who headed out to the countryside was at first impressed with the echoing sound of peasants on collective farms singing the traditional call to prepare the bath—"Fire up, Fire up the banya! Take a wife, take a wife, my kind Vanya." On Saturday mornings, across rural communities, collective farm workers collected water, gathered wood, and prepared their banyas so that their family and friends could undergo their weekly steaming. The smoke emanating from thousands of chimneys on "banya day" suggested that in many rural communities the old fashioned banya had not fallen out of favor. To an urbanite, the journalist admitted, the idea of bathing in a peasant banya with "primitive wash buckets and the smell of birch veniki" might seem romantic. But clear-eyed analyses showed him that preparing the banya required a "colossal amount of labor and building material" and was a waste of valuable resources. The effort could hardly be justified in hygienic terms: many of the banyas were located next to fetid ponds. Local officials knew that the proper Soviet solution was to build large communal banyas for everyone on a collective farm. But they also decided that doing so was a low priority and questioned whether collective farm workers would give up their family banyas anyway. The argument that centralized banyas would save time and money did not seem to sway reluctant local leaders, who retorted that in any case, the state itself produced too few blueprints of modern banyas of various sizes, failed to produce the right equipment for them, and did not do enough work to propagandize the importance of building large public banyas for rural communities. The result was that people in the countryside continued to bathe in banyas that the Soviet state had deemed unhygienic.[66]

Banyas struggled throughout the USSR, not just in the Russian Republic. In the middle 1960s in the Belorussian SSSR plans went perpetually unmet. Internal reports conceded, "in the last few years the number of cleanings in the banya is not growing, but is actually going down." The situation was also considered dangerously bad in the villages, where neither plumbing nor banyas were available. The problem was becoming acute. As part of the preparation for the 50th anniversary of Soviet rule, regional administrators in Belarus committed themselves to having a banya in every community. But 1967 came and went without having met the goal. Banyas remained unevenly distributed across the population, were often open only one or two days a week, and were sometimes used for other purposes, such as storing grain. Head lice were a persistent problem. Each year the plan called for Belorussian Republic to build new banyas but each year the plan fell far short, rarely reaching even 50 percent of the goal.[67]

In the Moldovian SSR, the persistence of typhus focused attention on the capacity, efficiency, and location of the republic's banyas. In 1965, people living in the republic could bathe in a banya on average one time every 70 to 90 days, even though indoor plumbing was still rare. In the capital Kishinev, citizens could bathe on average once every 150 days—or a little over twice a year. Efforts to build new banyas could barely keep up with the pace at which

FIGURE 8.9 Despite limited capacity and poor conditions, posters continued to insist that people around the USSR should go to the banya. This poster, printed by the Ministry of Health of the USSR in 1955, used a stock image of the banya to encourage rural Moldovans to build banyas and bathe in them. Courtesy of Lenin Library.

existing banyas closed down for repairs. The new official goal was to build enough banyas so that people could bathe on average once every two or three weeks. Two years later, the actual number of cleanings the banyas could provide had barely budged. If banyas were so hard to build, perhaps they were not needed after all. One memo questioned the role of banyas in fighting typhus, suggesting that the population could learn to live without a bath without endangering its health. Moldovian bureaucrats balked at the idea and continued to assume that having access to a banya remained integral to public health and therefore Soviet socialism.[68]

Across the USSR, the situation was dismal. In the mid-1960s in Kazakh SSR only 35 to 40 percent of the rural population and only 52 to 58 percent of the urban population lived in communities that had even a single banya. Where banyas existed, broken equipment, poor sanitary conditions, and a lack of running water often forced them to shut down.[69] Even in the Baltic republics, where a high number of enterprise and private banyas helped make up for the shortfall in municipal banyas, officials worried about poor sanitation and indiscriminate use of water from questionable sources.[70]

———

Krokodil continued to mock the situation. One magazine cover in 1965, titled "Regional Leader Going to the Banya," depicted a man riding atop a horse-drawn wagon, equipped with his own *venik*, bucket, and full barrel of water. The exact location was not relevant: many rural Soviet citizens would have recognized both the ostentatious privilege of the local boss and the implication that he did not bother to make sure that the banya itself was well equipped, since he could afford to bring his own supplies with him.[71] Another image suggested that the problem was with the banya directors themselves. A drawing called "The Director of the Banya with His Bucket/Gang," by Anatolii Tsvetkov, played on the double-entendre of the word *shaika*, which means both the "wash bucket" and a "gang." The banya director sits naked, smoking a cigarette on a bench with one foot in a bucket, while three other men attend to him: one, holding a *venik*, lights his cigarette; a second places a towel/sheet around him; and a third offers him a drink. They all appear sinister.[72] The director's luxury in his personal fiefdom was all the more disgusting, given the long lines and poor functioning of banyas across the country.

The written and visual criticism was consistent. A letter noted that the town of Poronaisk in the Far East had a fancy new banya with

РАЙОННОЕ НАЧАЛЬСТВО ЕДЕТ В БАНЮ

Рисунок А. КАНЕВСКОГО

КРОКОДИЛ

№1(1759) • ГОД ИЗДАНИЯ 43-й • 10 ЯНВАРЯ 1965

FIGURE 8.10 Making fun of the lack of basic supplies at many banyas, a *Krokodil* cover titled "Regional Leader Going to the Banya" depicted a local boss traveling to the banya with his own basin, *venik*, and even supply of water. *Krokodil*, January 10, 1965, cover.

everything . . . except hot water.[73] The relatively well-supplied Moscow, where there were now fifty-seven banyas in operation, was contrasted with a town where the whole population had only a single imperial-era banya.[74] One cartoon in 1971 depicted a banya on the top of a hill with a large funnel on top of it: capturing rainwater was the only way to get water. A truck with a water tank appears to be "under repair," water pipes sit disheveled next to a sign reading "under construction since 1953," a well is "out of service," and a water barrel on a donkey cart has broken down. A sign at the

ИЗ СЕМЕЙНОГО АЛЬБОМА

Директор бани со своей шайкой.

Рисунок А. ЦВЕТКОВА

FIGURE 8.11 "The Director of the Banya with His Bucket/Gang" suggested that banyas were centers of corruption, even as average citizens had to wait hours for access to their facilities. *Krokodil*, March 30, 1965, 6.

entrance to the banya reads: "There is no water!"[75] The cumulative effect of reading *Krokodil* suggested that the problems were widespread. Readers understood well enough that long lines, a lack of heat or water, and poor conditions were par for the course. The drawings reinforced that image. The humor was dark. For those hoping to get clean, the poor conditions in the banya were serious, even as readers of *Krokodil* could take comfort in knowing that the challenges of finding a working banya in their community was not unusual.

An accident in 1969 in the town of Elets in the Lipetsk region, about 240 miles south of Moscow, made clear to government authorities just how poor the banya infrastructure was across the country. Founded in the twelfth century, Elets was located in the black earth region, on the main rail line connecting the capital to the Donbass. In 1969, two small banyas—each with space for about fifty people at a time—served a population of 100,000 people. The building for "Banya #1" was located at the corner of Pushkin and Cooperative Streets. In the late imperial period it had been a synagogue, after the revolution it was converted into a club, and in 1938 the town had appropriated it for use as a banya. Little care was given to the technical requirements that the banya might demand—builders did not account for humidity in the walls or the extreme temperature differentials that heating the banya created. In 1967 a city inspector had warned that the building was operating in "hazardous conditions." But the regional committee did not act on this warning. Closing down the banya would have left the town with only one banya, which even in ideal circumstances would have allowed for each person in the town to go to the banya once or twice a year. Besides, there was no indication that the banyas in Elets were really any worse off than those elsewhere in the USSR. Keeping rundown banyas, like Banya #1 in Elets, in operation was calculated to be a reasonable risk. In this case, it did not pay off.[76]

At 9:45 a.m. on Monday, April 28, 1969, part of an outer wall of the building, running the full height of the banya, crumbled and fell after being compromised by moisture. This, in turn, caused the attic and then the floors between the stories to fall as well. Faulty construction had failed to adequately secure the floors and ceilings to the other loadbearing walls. The whole building collapsed. Fire and military rescue workers soon arrived at the accident and worked until 8:00 p.m. trying to save bathers from under the rubble. They pulled seventeen corpses from the wreckage. An eighteenth victim died the next day. Eleven other people were injured and sent to the hospital, some in critical condition.[77] Had the accident occurred on a Saturday, the number of victims would have been much higher.

A Ministry of Municipal Services inquiry accused members of Elets' city executive committee and municipal services division of "unallowable negligence" for not taking action to close down the banya after the 1967 inspection. The chair of the executive committee, the chief engineer for the city, and the director of the banya were all fired. Regional leaders also took the heat. The head of the regional municipal services and the chief of engineers for the Litepsk region lost their jobs as well. The ministry sent their findings on to regional prosecutors so that they could press criminal charges.[78]

The ministry recognized, however, that the problems were not unique to Elets. Their report found that many of the country's banyas were old and that their walls and floors had not been built to handle damp, wet conditions. The sort of weak construction that characterized Banya #1 in Elets was likely common throughout the country. Internal reports noted that fewer than half of the communal banyas in the Russian Republic (not counting those in Moscow and Leningrad) had been inspected within the previous five years. The ministry wanted them all inspected to determine whether they were able to operate safely.[79] But it kept news of the accident and the overall condition of the banyas out of the press. It was one thing for articles in *Pravda* or cartoons in *Krokodil* to point out problems in one or another banya in some specific region; it was quite another thing to suggest that banyas were fatally hazardous across the country.

As dilapidated as the country's banyas were, national, regional, and local bureaucrats could not afford to shut them down. They remained essential, at least in principle, for hygiene in the countless communities around the USSR that did not have indoor plumbing. Replacing old banyas was too expensive and viable alternatives were not in place. Instead, the XXIV Party Congress in 1970 once again determined that more local control might help remedy the situation. A party decree called for banyas, along with other municipal enterprises, to shift to an independent economic footing. They were supposed to run a balanced budget. Those banyas where revenues already exceeded costs could make the leap. But many banya directors were stymied by the request and, according to a lead economist in the Russian Ministry of Municipal Services, they could not manage to "convert their enterprises to the new conditions of the planned economy."[80]

———

In some large cities, a few select banyas managed to be cost effective—but they did so less because they were considered centers of hygiene than because they catered to the pre-Revolutionary idea that the banya was a social space. In Moscow, for instance, Sanduny was known both for its imperial elegance and because people went there to relax as well as to get clean. Athletes went to heal sore muscles or to help them prepare for competition. Andrei Starostin, a Soviet soccer player and coach, wrote in the mid-1950s that "for an athlete, the banya is honorable institution." This had nothing to do with hygiene or the latest Soviet innovation in banya technology. Starostin went with his teammates to the banya because he had learned about the importance of "steaming" from his grandfather in rural Russia, who bathed on Saturdays in his "oven." He held that the steam "made aches and pains in the joints disappear and quickly healed bruises." This was true in the simple rural banya and in Sanduny, he claimed.[81]

Similarly, in Minsk the Zhelezka (Iron Rail) banya, which had been built in the late imperial period, remained in the 1950s a lively meeting place that stood out for reasons the state did not explicitly endorse. Different groups would take over the banya on different days. On Wednesdays, Jewish taxi drivers would gather from all over the city to wash and *kibbitz* in Yiddish. On Fridays, athletes dominated the banya to the point that only people in their circle could make their way into the *parilka*. On Saturdays, actors, artists, professors, and teachers took their turn. The system was clear. One bather recalled that an individual's authority on the outside was irrelevant inside. Even political bosses, once they took their pants off, lost their pride and privilege.[82]

Sanduny, Zhelezka, and other well-organized and well-supplied urban banyas were the rare exceptions that proved the rule. Time and again, Sanduny was celebrated because of its history and rarified environment. People traversed Minsk to go to the Zhelezka because it offered a sense of community that could not be found in any other banya in the city. These banyas served as a model for a banya that could be social and consistent with pre-Revolutionary, even ancient, traditions without undermining Soviet imperatives. But they were anything but average or typical.

For banya directors around the country who were dealing with broken boilers, dilapidated walls, water shortages, and power outages, creating a social environment was out of the question. Their problem was finding resources and administrative support that would allow the banyas to function, even at a rudimentary level. Sanduny, Zhelezka, and other urban banyas may have kept alive the notion of a social, healthy urban banya, but the banya industry more generally was in dangerous disrepair. In the late 1960s, Banya #1 in Elets, not Sanduny, more closely resembled the average urban banya in the Soviet Union.

Urban banyas had become so closely associated with Soviet urbanization and its failures to serve the needs of everyday life that many dismissed them as not "real banyas" at all. In popular renderings, Russian tradition and authentic interaction required rural banyas, the more rudimentary, simple, and wedded to the countryside, the better. As Tvardovsky had suggested in his journal in 1945, "the rural banya . . . not the commercial town banya" was emblematic of the open discussion that Russians had undertaken "since ancient times."

Gerasimov's and Plastov's paintings of the 1950s seemed to concur. Rural banyas were pure, authentic, innocent, and Russian; urban banyas were filthy, deceitful, corrupt, and cosmopolitan. In the 1960s and 1970s, celebrating the rural banya in particular and juxtaposing it with the urban banya meshed with the "Village Prose" literary movement. Village Prose writers emphasized Soviet rural communities, loss, memory, and cyclical time.[83] The banya fit naturally with that group's concern about the erosion of rural values and traditions in the face of Soviet urbanization and industrialization. As with Tvardovsky, in Village Prose stories, what people said in the banya was less important than recognizing that going to a banya was a critical part of Russian heritage. In Valentin Rasputin's story *Farewell to Matyora* (1976), Siberian villagers prepare for the completion of a new dam that will flood their village and end their way of life. The banya clarifies how different life in the modern city will be. Not only do some people in the city bathe in a small tub right next to the toilet, the urban banya there is large and communal. One woman asks incredulously upon hearing that there is only one banya for everyone in the city, "How could that be! One for so many people?... Can't we set up our own?" But of course there is no room in the city for people to have their own banyas. Later, it becomes clear that the city banya stands beside other "industrial concerns" such as the "garage, shops, welding unit, [and] boiler shop."[84] The urban banya is designed to process and clean people efficiently. To the villagers, the rural banya is part of what makes them Russian. In the city that identity and their individuality will be erased.

Some urbanites shared the sense that the rural banya was the more authentic banya, where genuine philosophizing and discussion could take place. In his 1980 movie *A Few Days in the Life of Oblomov* (based on Ivan Goncharev's 1859 novel about a "superfluous man") the director Nikita Mikhalkov added a banya scene to the story. Situated in the Russian countryside, inhabited only by two aristocratic friends, the banya elicits a discussion of the meaning of life, of the inability of the eponymous character to act or make concrete decisions. When his friend runs into the snow after steaming and relishes the vitality that flows through him, Olbomov sits still in the banya. His friend's efforts to shock him out of his malaise do not work.[85] For Mikhalkov, the rural banya was the natural setting for a heart-to-heart among friends because it seemed to provide a justification both for vigor and idleness all at once.

Appreciation of the banya was associated with being a successful rural man. For instance, Boris Yeltsin recalled in his memoirs that in the late 1940s before his "obstinate" grandfather would allow him to head off to the technical institute he had to pass one final rite of passage. He had to build a banya from scratch with his own hands. Only when Boris had passed this test did his grandfather grant him permission to enroll in classes.[86]

The ideal of the rural banya was most clearly described by Vasily Shukshin in his short story "Alyosha at Large" (1972). As an acclaimed actor, director, and writer, Shukshin was perhaps the best-known writer of the 1970s.[87] While his themes often paralleled those addressed by Village Prose writers, Shukshin's focus was on eccentrics and outcasts, rather than celebrating rural life for its own sake. In "Alyosha at Large" the title character refuses to work on Saturdays, opting instead to heat his banya. Alyosha is healthy and principled, "as strong as a horse" and a "robust muzhik [man's man]." He is a Terkin-like figure twenty-five years later. Alyosha, Shukshin writes, "had served [during the war], been wounded, recovered, fought out the war, and then for the rest of his life remembered it with loathing." His military service, unlike his Saturday banya tradition, hardly gave him a sense of self-worth.[88]

Shukshin clearly intends his hero to be a relic of an earlier ideal of Russian life. Stepping away from the pressure of the workweek and his endless chores and responsibilities, Alyosha establishes his own rules and rituals on Saturdays. He takes his time heating up the banya and enjoys each step of the process. He scorns other villagers who rush to the banya at the end of the day, burn themselves, and inevitably inhale smoke. He likes to bathe alone. He finds peace, solace, and integrity in his own private banya. Alyosha knows that working for the state has come to dominate the rest of his time and he accepts the responsibility of providing for his family. But Alyosha respects a tradition that set aside Saturdays for the banya. The weekly ritual had decidedly religious implications. The Russian word for Saturday—*subbota*—also means "Sabbath." Alyosha's Sabbath banya provided an escape from the world of labor and familial responsibility. The narrator reports that Alyosha's wife used to bother him about taking the whole day off. "She'd start in, 'You need to do this, you need to do that, you can't heat up the banya the whole livelong day!'" He would respond, "So what am I supposed to do, cut my soul up into little pieces?"[89] There was no getting away from the urbanized life that he saw destroying people's humanity. The best Alyosha could hope for was to restore his sense of identity and truth through his sacred bathing ritual.

When Alyosha has finished steaming himself his son appears. The young man has not taken an interest in the banya, does not like it too hot when he does go, and, following his mother's example, has never really learned how properly to steam himself.[90] Unlike Yeltsin's grandfather, the fictional Alyosha is unable to make the next generation accept the banya as an essential part of a Russian man's identity. The tradition that means so much to Alyosha, that defines him, will clearly be lost to modernization. He is powerless against the flow of time. As in *Farewell to Matyora*, the implication is that the old Russia of the peasant banya is slowly dying out, along with much of what defined rural life. *LMAO my dad*

Shukshin made it clear that he thought the rural banya had nothing in common with the urban banya. Alyosha once tried the crowded, public banya in town, only to conclude that it was a complete waste of his time: "In a banya like that, a public one, all you could do was sit around and drink beer. That's no banya, God only knows what it is." Later, in an interview, Shukshin emphasized the significance of the banya in the Russian village and contrasted it with the cookie-cutter banyas the Soviet state attempted to foist on rural communities. He wrote, "In the village it is necessary to preserve that ill-fated 'kind of patriarchy' which evokes among us a condescending smile or angry rebuff." For example, he added, "When a standard-design for a public banya is sent to the village, it is done in vain. Sending a standard-designed prison would have the same effect; I think it would be just as uninteresting and uncreative. Beyond that, there's no need for a public banya in the village anyway."[91] Urbanites may have believed that their banyas were similar to the traditional village banyas; Shukshin and many villagers thought otherwise.

The rural banya was fundamentally restorative, not interactive or conversational. It was a space conducive to contemplation and potential redemption. In the Soviet 1960s and 1970s, the war and the Stalin years still loomed large in the imagination and as the defining moments of people's lives, for better and for worse. As Alyosha prepares his banya, for instance, he recalls that on the way home from the war a woman took advantage of his kindness, trust, and lust to rob him. But even this does not seem to bother him terribly. It reflects poorly on the woman, but also leaves Alyosha's weekly decision to escape to the banya more comprehensible. The banya is a place where Alyosha cannot be tricked or fooled. In the banya he sings songs, thinks, and can safely philosophize about life, death, and war.[92]

In Boris Vasil'ev's 1969 story *The Dawns Here are Quiet* a rural banya is used to establish the prebattle wholesomeness of a battery of female soldiers in a small town in the Karelia region, not far from the German front in 1942.[93] Toward the beginning of the story, the women go to the banya, where they marvel at one another's beauty. They are soldiers, but the banya helps to emphasize their Russian femininity and virtue. Young, nubile, and nude, the women reveal to one another their deeply personal reasons for hating the

Germans invaders. They will trade their youth and innocence for a chance to avenge their family and friends who have suffered at the hands of the enemy. The banya scene establishes the purity of their motivations when, later, they find themselves face-to-face with the enemy and are called upon to act violently. War upended traditional gender norms, but only for a while and out of necessity.[94] The book was extremely popular and in 1971 it was turned into a play performed at Moscow's Taganka Theater. In 1972 it was released as a feature film, which was nominated for an Academy Award for Best Foreign Language Film. The rural banya's unique ability to confirm Russian identity, convey femininity, and expose deeper motivations for action meant that the film director, Stanislav Rostotsky, insisted on keeping the banya scene even though naked women had not been shown on screen before in Soviet cinema.[95] He evidently convinced the actresses to allow him to film them without clothes by insisting that the audience needed to see that their characters' bodies were "made for love and child bearing," not the military sacrifices they later endured.[96]

If the war in retrospect produced heroes of all kinds, the Gulag in retrospect created misfits, who no longer understood normal society. In "Snowball Berry Red," one of Shukshin's most famous stories (turned into a film in 1974), the recidivist Egor has returned from prison to village life. A broken man, he is lost in free society. Shukshin emphasized Egor's basic inability to fit in outside the camps by showing him entirely unaware of the rules of the rural bathhouse; instead of pouring water on the hot rocks, he poured it on his fellow bather, burning him in the process.[97] The rural banya helped people come to terms with both the patriotic war and the horrific Gulag.

How to understand the Stalin era as a whole remained a vexing question in Soviet society. Explicit discussions of Stalin were taboo, lest the accomplishments of the system be tarnished by the violence of his rule. Vladimir Vysotsky, an actor, songwriter, and singer who was by far the most popular entertainer of the 1960s and 1970s, implied that the Stalin period had ruptured Russian history. Postwar Soviet citizens were not free to redefine their relationship to the past as they saw fit. The scars of the Stalin era remained. Worn proudly, they reminded people that sacrificing oneself for the state and party had been a clear marker of one's value in society. These same scars, however, by the late 1960s also evoked a certain naiveté about that devotion and the identities that it helped to forge. Vysotsky's song "White Banya" (1968) suggested that the legacy of the Stalin years would be hard to overcome:

Fire me up a bath woman,
I'll forge myself, burn myself
At the very edge of the bench,
I'll destroy all my doubts.

I will become too soft.
A jug of cold water, and all will be in the past.
My tattoo, from the days of the cult of personality
Will turn blue on my left breast.

How much faith and forest has been felled?
How much grief and distance has been felt?
On my left breast: Stalin's profile.
On my right breast: Marinka straight on.

Oh, with my unconscious faith,
How long was I at ease in heaven?
But I changed my unbelievable stupidity
For a hopeless life.[98]

Those who constructed their identities in devotion to Stalin and who demoted their loved ones in the process were marked for life, but in a much more ambiguous way than the Terkin-like soldiers scarred by war or even the emaciated survivors of the siege of Leningrad. The tattoo of Stalin, not his lover Marinka, is over his heart. A woman, presumably not Marinka herself, re-emerges to fire up the banya and hold out the possibility that the broken Soviet man might yet forge a stable identity. The banya finally allows the man to talk openly, to think, to unfreeze his soul. The birch *venik* whips his body, holding out the promise that the remaining evidence of the old days could be washed away. Even though the tattoo remains, the banya might clean and redeem the bather's spirit.

Vysotsky's banya suggested that those who had lived through the Stalin years had negotiated identities that settled uncomfortably between two extremes: Some people internalized the "unconscious faith" of those marching in line with the state's demands, while others opted for the seemingly "hopeless life" of those who did not conform. The banya helped to expose the futility of either approach and suggested Soviet citizens could have been both complicit in the regime and dispirited by what they now knew about their past beliefs and actions.[99] Vysotsky's song served as a reminder that late socialist identity was defined both by the memory of the sacrifices of the Stalin years and by the lingering aftershocks that came later. So long as the system remained Soviet, any effort at restoring a connection to either the Russian past or a broader community in the present had to first come to terms with Stalin's rule.

A few years later, another Vysotsky song, "Ballad about the Banya" (1971), returned to the banya as the site of redemption. The banya was a place for rebirth, where a person could emerge not just clean, but remade. It was also a leveling place, where the outside world's standards were put aside. "All vices, sins and sadness / indifference, deals, and fights / are shot out like a bullet / by the steam that has been poured on." A few verses later he added, "here nobody is naked, there is no need for shame" and "Here all are equally wealthy / all can endure the heat / Here is freedom, equality, brotherhood / For those who feel the hellish steam."[100] He echoed Tvardovsky's initial sense of the banya as an authentic place, where differences melted away and where true character was revealed.

The rural banya, even in the stories of Village Prose writers, was not anti-Soviet. To the contrary, eradicating sin and vice, eliminating shame, and promoting equality and brotherhood were all tenets of Socialist morality. Rather than challenging the ideals of the system, the point of the rural banya was to press the system to live up to its promises. Municipal banya administrators and their critics in *Krokodil* after the war shared the assumption that banyas were supposed to be about health and hygiene. The rural banya of fiction, film, and paintings saw the banya, whether it was horrific in the Gulag or idyllic in the countryside, as fundamentally about either spiritual degradation or redemption. Whether they were tools of the state or a popular custom, banyas in the USSR after the Second World War and through the Thaw shared a common core: they were ideally a force for good that contained within them the potential for evil. The "hellish steam" of the Russian banya nurtured hope that a purer, cleaner life in the future might just be possible.

9

The Banya . . . Is It Still Necessary?

BY THE LATE 1960s, a possible solution emerged to persistent challenge of building and maintaining enough urban banyas in the USSR. If people could manage their personal hygiene by bathing at home, the problem of filthy bodies might be overcome not by making banyas Soviet—ubiquitous, state-run, well maintained, and universally accessible—but by making them obsolete for disinfection or delousing. The need for utilitarian banyas could eventually fade away. The annual state plans to build more banyas, though, continued for the simple reason that in many Soviet communities indoor plumbing and bathtubs remained far from universal.

Where people could bathe at home, however, the purpose of the state-run banya could be re-evaluated. Some imagined them as communal recreational facilities, evoking the sociability of elite pre-Revolutionary banyas and the legendary soulfulness of rural banyas. The old, imperial Sanduny, which had long been noteworthy for leisure, socializing, and relaxation, became a model to be emulated. Once they were liberated from the obligation to clean people efficiently, public banyas became places to talk and to commiserate with friends about the challenges of living a fulfilling life in late Soviet society. They facilitated open discussion and meaningful human contact without being explicitly Soviet, anti-Soviet, or Russian. They provided people with a public place to gather that allowed them to check their everyday responsibilities at the door. Nudity in the banya revealed all, including the paradoxes of Soviet life.

In the steam room the difference between a state-run banya and a family banya in the countryside melted away. Banya aficionados cared most about the quality of the steam. Creating it was an art form that involved mixing in herbs and adding water or beer or *kvas* to the hot stove at the right time to create conditions that would cause bathers to reach a point of euphoria. In the village, bathers made their own steam. In the city, making steam was primarily the responsibility of a *banshchik*. Everyone "has their own style and recipe," one *banshchik* reported, to create the right amount of humidity in the room, with the right medicinal aroma. In the Finnish sauna, Russian banya lovers knew, the rocks were heated first and water was thrown on only afterward. The heat was basically dry. But in the Russian banya the steam was added throughout the heating process, making the air "softer" but no less bracing. The process involved clearing out the humid air, reheating the room, creating just the right amount of humidity along the way. The steam room, it seemed, was where a banya came to most resemble the rituals and traditions of "ancient Russia."[1] The wisdom of the old was passed on to the young, in cities as well as in the countryside.

Whether rural or urban, female or male, traditional or modern, commonplace or luxurious, the banya during the last decades of the USSR was a hybrid institution: it was about hygiene and socializing; it was Soviet and Russian; going to one was a commonplace chore and a potentially transformative undertaking. This hybridity was also a nod to tradition. Protestations of the Village Prose writers aside, the city banya in Russia was in fact as old as the rural one. Sin, sex, violence, and corruption in the banya were not new either. Certain aspects of the banya's Russian roots were obscured beneath layers of Soviet soot. There was no way to preserve the banya's purity without also keeping alive the threat of danger that lurked in the corners.

Urbanites in the late Soviet period sought to have it both ways. They wanted their steam room to be authentic, even as the changing room served as a center for recreation and social mixing. The sociability of public, urban banyas was fundamentally different from rural banyas, at least in the public imagination. Rural banyas were purifying, personal, rule-bound, and seen as a place where Russians might hold at bay the crushing drive of modernization. They were fundamentally about returning to a more innocent past and restoring bodies and souls to a condition that preceded corrupting influences. Urban banyas, in contrast, were interactive, cosmopolitan, held out the potential for transgression, and offered a way of feeling at home in the modern world, even if that world was corrupt. They were oriented toward the present and future. The urban banya did this by providing a temporary escape to another world, where things were not as they appeared elsewhere. Bathers always returned from the banya to the here and now, but with their bodies reborn and their fates altered, for better or for worse.

The desperate shortage of well-run banyas in many areas of the USSR remained a persistent problem. It is remarkable that in light of the seeming impossibility of achieving even minimal goals in terms of either upkeep or construction that the banya bureaucracy did not abandon its efforts on the banya front. It's all the more remarkable that the banya bureaucracy did not declare bankruptcy when a viable alternative existed: indoor plumbing. The fact that beginning in the 1960s there were areas where most of the population could bathe in their homes might have made the state's efforts to build and run public banyas unnecessary. When given a choice, people evidently preferred to use domestic baths or showers. In theory, communism sought to overcome differences among the population. Banyas seemed to exacerbate them. The divisions between the rural and urban population were supposed to disappear over time. Everyday life in major cities was not supposed to be palpably more luxurious than everyday life in smaller towns. Access to banyas in one neighborhood, at least in principle, should be equal to access in any other.[2] Ticket prices, like milk prices and indeed the prices of just about everything, were supposed to be uniform, whether in Vladivostok or Yerevan.

Yet opportunities for Soviet citizens to bathe were clearly not equal. Those communities without indoor plumbing needed more banyas. Those with indoor plumbing might not need them at all. Either the future of Soviet hygiene was predicated on a shower in every home or it remained tied to the necessity of the public banya.[3] The Ministry of Municipal Services appeared to push in both directions at once. In 1966 its official publication, *The Journal of Municipal Services*, highlighted this tension. An article reiterated the need for both more and more efficient banyas across the USSR. At the same time, a technical commission noted a new trend: "In large well-built communities there has been a decrease in the demand for banyas among the population" because of "the massive construction of domestic apartments—with gas, hot and cold water, and bathtubs." The author did not concede that banyas should be shut down where they were no longer in demand. Instead, he reasoned that banya directors could try to attract clients by offering a "broad assortment of services" and creating "more comforts." Snack bars, relaxation rooms, barber shops, and kiosks with items for sale might attract clients who no longer needed the banya to get clean.[4] In the late 1960s there were still too few of these "large, well-built communities" to suggest that banyas were no longer necessary across the country. Indoor plumbing was far from ubiquitous, even as it was becoming more readily available in some cities. From 1959 to 1970 the percentage of state housing with a bath or shower rose from 30 percent to 65 percent. This meant that 35 percent of people living in the relatively well-furnished state housing still could not bathe at home. Housing owned by individuals, which constituted almost 30 percent of housing in Soviet cities, was far less likely to have bathing facilities. In rural areas, the percentages of dwellings even with running water were much lower still.[5] Furthermore, the availability of indoor plumbing was unevenly distributed across cities of the USSR. Some were well equipped; others were not.[6] Even though the presumption was that the percentage of the population living in homes with showers and tubs would increase, as of 1970, banyas could not be phased out. Where communal banyas were not up to the task of keeping the population clean, the state-sponsored solution was to build more and better banyas. The battle on the banya front continued.

The 9th Five-Year Plan, begun in 1971, called for banya capacity in the Russian Republic to increase by 31,500 spaces at a cost of 48.3 million rubles. Two years into the plan, construction was already hopelessly behind schedule. The reasons were familiar: central administrators had not given enough attention to the problem, leaving the details to local bureaucrats, who wasted or diverted material resources. Local organizations, for their part, treated banya construction as less pressing than other tasks. Plans were not well conceived or organized. The solution was familiar too: blame the local administrators. "Workers of communal organizations," the Deputy Minister of Municipal Services of the Russian Federation noted, "need to strive more energetically and persistently to fulfill the plan for banyas."[7]

In 1974, five years after the accident in Elets, there was an explosion "with serious consequences" (often a euphemism for fatalities) at a banya in Rostov. This time poor maintenance of the boiler equipment was the cause. Inquiries into the situation emphasized that this was not an isolated incident; similar problems plagued banyas in Astrakhan, Briansk, Chelyabinsk, Khabarovsk, Saratov, Volgograd, and elsewhere. In Gorky, Ivanovsk, Moscow, Tambov, and Voronezh, "major repairs of banyas" had gone "much too slowly."[8] What went unstated was that pressure on municipalities to meet their quotas for numbers of cleanings in a cost-effective manner created short-term incentives for ignoring warnings and putting off repairs.

In other communities, however, banyas no longer primarily served a hygienic function. By the late 1960s, people who had a choice preferred to bathe at home. A doctor in the journal Tourist (Turist) put the question succinctly: "So, what is better a banya or a shower?" "A long time ago," he continued, "when there were no baths or showers, the banya was, naturally, the best and only means of keeping oneself clean." (Many Soviet citizens, of course, could attest to the fact that even in 1969 they did not have baths or showers, but that was not the doctor's point.) "For everyday hygienic procedures," he reported, "[other means] are more convenient, accessible, and comfortable [than the banya]."[9] A few years later, a variation on the question headlined an article in *Health* (*Zdorov'e*): "The Banya . . . Is It Still Necessary?"[10] And the following year a scientist in the government organ *Izvestiia* asked: "What's the point of going to the banya, when now there's a bathtub in each new apartment? . . . Is passion for the banya a relic or artifact?"[11] If going to the banya was about hygiene alone, there was little doubt that baths and showers had rendered them superfluous in some communities. It was just a matter of time, and more modern housing, before everywhere else followed suit. To preserve the banya, the case had to be made that going to one was not really about basic hygiene after all. The banya had something to offer overall health beyond clean bodies. The doctor concluded that people continued to partake in the "age-old popular habit" because "unlike its modern competitors, [the banya] creates a health-promoting effect . . . it invigorates and rejuvenates [bathers]." The banya provided deeper, more profound sensations than a shower or bath could provide.[12]

Some claimed that the banya was the most effective means of treating people who were exposed to too many pesticides or other toxic chemicals; a tub or shower was less effective.[13] Another article in *Tourist*, titled "The Banya Makes Everything Right," suggested that the reason people continued to "steam at Sanduny"—and why there was continued interest in the traditional Russian banya and the Finnish sauna—was that the banya had "powerful healing capabilities."[14] In the "space age," banyas were once again popular with the people because they did more than showers and tubs.[15] Or as another publication put it: the value of banyas could be found in the Russian past and "their older function." Overall health and not hygiene alone, it turned out, was the original purpose of the Russian banya just as was the case with the Finnish sauna and the "Eastern banya of the Middle Ages."[16] Restoring the banya as a place of holistic medicine would help keep them relevant after their hygienic functions had been eclipsed. The banya's pre-Soviet origins illuminated its late Soviet purpose. Distinctions between the Russian banya, the Finnish sauna, and the Uzbek *hammam* that had been deemed insignificant in the 1930s started to matter again. When showers and tubs threatened the banya's purpose in the USSR, the "specifics of the national banya" re-emerged.[17]

Some banya operators in communities with indoor plumbing scrambled to adapt to the new rationale. In 1968, the head of Leningrad executive committee's banya and laundry section concluded that operating banyas "the

FIGURE 9.1 Men wait in line in the morning to get into Moscow's famous Sanduny Banya in 1984. As a survivor of a pre-Revolutionary Russia, Sanduny evoked the idea of an urban banya that was not simply about the utilitarian drive to get clean. Vladimir Sokolaev, *Morning Queue at the Sandunovskie Baths*, Moscow, April 20, 1984. Courtesy of Khristina Vladimirovna Sokolaeva.

way they did, say, twenty years ago" was no longer viable. Gone were the days when clients put up with disrepair and poor services because they had no other options. In order "to get people to go to the city banya when many of them live in apartments equipped with utilities," it was no longer enough, in Leningrad at least, to have water, heat, soap, and provide new customer services. Banyas that offered tailors, kiosks with the sale of soap and sponges, and express laundry services had a better chance of convincing those with access to showers and tubs at home that going to the banya was still worth their while.[18] "Advertising the work of the banya on radio, television, and in the newspapers" would also help "bring in clients." When people came into the banya, employees had "to do everything so that clients are not only satisfied with their visits, but that they also tell their neighbor or colleague" to visit the banya. One Leningrad banya director crowed that doing this allowed his banya to exceed its target number of cleanings cost effectively. But more importantly, providing extra services offered a glimpse into the future of the Soviet banya and served as an example to others for how they might help to "revitalize the glory of the Russian banya."[19] An article lauding increased luxuries must have seemed perverse to readers in towns where the capacity of banyas could not meet demand. But this was the nature of banyas in the USSR at the time: some were well-equipped but hard pressed to find clients; others were in disrepair but had lines out the door.

Architectural plans reflected the growing discrepancy between banyas that were required for basic hygiene and those that could serve "traditional" and "healing" functions. When the purpose of banyas was hygiene, designs had been universal and straightforward. The assumption was that bodies across the USSR needed more or less the same thing from a banya to get clean—a steam room, a washroom, and a changing room. Even though these sorts of banyas were still necessary, publishing blueprints for them was not. Old designs would suffice. "Medical recreational" banyas, however, required new designs and in the 1970s these started to appear in the press. Architects imagined massage rooms, swimming pools, and centers for relaxation existing alongside the basics. Logically, different parts of the vast USSR might expect different things from a recreational facility. It was not enough to apply plans from "the north" to other areas of the Soviet Union. Instead, "historically grounded" bathing traditions in Central Asia, the Caucuses, the Baltics, and Russia should inform local designs. "Social-demographic and city planning peculiarities" had to be taken into account.[20] In other words, the idea that everywhere in the USSR could build basically identical banyas based on a centrally designed plan did not work for the new kind of banya. When the purpose of going to the banya was recreational and traditional, cultural differences and tastes came to the fore. Cities would want banyas designed with local customs in mind. "Experimental" designs anticipated the direction public bathing in the Soviet Union was heading, not where it was.

Banyas designed for hygiene were not obsolete. Even in Moscow, indoor plumbing had not entirely supplanted the need for utilitarian banyas. Sanduny provided the sorts of amenities and services associated with a medical-recreational facility—but it was successful because it harkened back to the imperial era, not because it was cutting-edge and modern. Sanduny was unique. Most new banyas were still designed, at least in principle, to clean people efficiently. They reflected the Soviet present, not the communist future. Indoor plumbing was arriving unevenly, making the transition to medicinal-recreational banyas uneven as well. The 10th Five-Year Plan in 1976 called for "more, better, modern banyas that can keep up with the needs of the people" throughout the USSR.[21] But the "new type of banya" remained beyond reach. An article cowritten by an engineer and an economist in 1977 summed things up: "The development of the banya has seriously fallen behind modern requirements. The majority of active [banyas] and those that are planned do not bring in sufficient revenues. The pace of the building of private apartments with bathrooms can explain this. Banyas cannot compete with bathrooms when it comes to meeting hygienic requirements. And not enough modern banyas that can function as social and recreational places are being built or they are not being built at all."[22] Modern, recreational banyas had one important thing in common with all other postwar Soviet banyas—there were not enough of them.

In an age of indoor plumbing, the banya's place in Soviet visions of hygienic modernity was no longer clear. For every underutilized banya made super-fluous by waterworks, there were dozens more that remained undersupplied and overrun by popular demand. Despite the postwar surge, the percentage of people with hot water and baths in their apartments remained low not when compared to previous decades in the USSR, but in comparison with the rising expectations of the population, the promises of the regime, and the experiences of people living in the United States, the focus of Cold War comparisons.[23] In many neighborhoods in many towns and cities in the USSR, finding a place to bathe remained a serious challenge. In the 1970s people waited for hours in line for banyas. When their turn came they might find no hot water, no cold water, no water at all, or no heat in the steam room. The most consistent feature of the Soviet banya may have been a sign reading "closed for repairs."

At the same time, the rise of in-home bathing facilities left banya directors looking for a new way to justify their enterprises' existence. That they turned to advertisements to drum up support was not a sign of the return of a cap-italist business model, *a la* NEP. Advertisement and promotional articles sought to strike the proper balance between what the state provided and subsidized and what the people wanted. Since 1917, it had proven difficult to increase supply where demand was high. Now it was proving just as hard to curb supply where demand was low—banyas operated whether there were clients or not. Officials implored people with showers at home to go to mu-nicipal banyas anyway. They emphasized that the banya provided something that could not be easily replicated in a private apartment. Where banyas lost their strictly hygienic function they were repackaged as recreational, a nod to tradition, and a supplement to the more prosaic cleansing that took place in baths or showers. In this way, bureaucrats insisted, banyas remained rele-vant. Ironically, imperial-era banyas like Sanduny had an easier time fulfilling the demand for recreational facilities than those built in the Soviet period. The imperial past, at least in this instance, provided a glimpse into the Soviet future.

In 1976, the man in charge of overseeing Moscow's banyas did not despair that banyas were becoming obsolete. He sensed that "people will come to [our banyas] because the bath in the apartment will never be able to provide the kinds of services that a banya is capable of." Unlike doctors, he did not see the banya's superiority to the bath in physiological, medical terms. Instead, he saw the banya as a "place to spend a whole day off" relaxing in the "chess room, bar, cafeteria, or solarium." It was a place to socialize, see people, and get away from the crowded city. Where banyas were no longer required for hygiene and health, they could become social spaces that cleansed peoples' spirits instead.[24]

When indoor plumbing decreased demand, banyas had more resources at their disposal. American journalist Hedrick Smith described a Moscow banya in the 1970s as "the closest thing Russian males have to a 'men's club.'" He added, "There, they lounge around naked or wrapped loosely in their sheets telling jokes, arguing over last night's hockey game. . . . It is a pleasant place where people eavesdrop freely and butt into conversations, proffering

FIGURE 9.2 The banya was a place of leisure and intimacy, an oasis from the pace and pressures of domestic and professional life. Vladimir Sokolaev, *The Men's Section of the Baths on Dostoevsky Street*, Leningrad, March 17, 1982. Courtesy of Khristina Vladimirovna Sokolaeva.

unsought advice on how to handle women, where to find *defitsitny* [scarce] goods, or how to keep young in old age." Its official functions aside, the banya was a space where men could talk, procure goods, and wield power in ways that were not possible according to the formal rules of the Soviet economy.[25]

If banyas had been solely social spaces, the Soviet state might very well have ceased to support them when they were no longer required for hygiene. But so long as banyas' primary function was practical in some places, they remained unassailable everywhere. Going to a banya still meant fulfilling a Soviet commandment. The system enabled and sustained banyas but did not necessarily control how people used them. Officially people went to banyas to clean themselves; unofficially they went to interact. As playwright and screen-writer El'dar Riazanov noted in 1972, "Where else is it possible to chat comfortably? At dinner parties other guests are always interrupting, and everyone is always busy with eating and drinking. In public transport people are always shoving and the stadium is too loud. You'll not find a better place for intimate discussions than the banya!"[26]

This was true for women as well as men. Andrea Lee, an American who lived in Moscow in 1978 and 1979, was excited to go to Sanduny with friends. Once inside, it was clear to Lee that the women were there for camaraderie as much as cleanliness. In the washroom, Lee saw "a peculiar wholesomeness that is characteristically Russian." The act of stripping down revealed things that were not visible on the street. "The nude women here were the women I had seen carrying string bags on the metro . . . they were as I might have imagined them . . . but so unpretentious and unself-conscious that they had a powerful appeal." Women of all ages "chatted, strolled idly around, put on makeup, drank beer." Not all the elements of the idealized Russian banya were present—nobody used birch branches, which Lee's friend informed her were "uncultured" and for "hicks," not Muscovites. But to Lee, "there was a magical feeling of freedom in the air: the unhindered freedom of women in a place from which men are excluded." Lee noted that the chance to be only with women was doubly significant in Russia, because women's burdens there were great and the opportunity to gather without men was limited. "In the segregated world of the banya," Lee reported, the feeling of constraint that characterized women's behavior in Russia most of the time disappeared. Lee described the banya as a "self-enclosed world" in which the same women she saw on the street were transformed, not just because they were nude, but because the space of the banya was itself liberating and otherworldly. The banya provided a temporary respite from the outside world.

The transformation of the banya from a tool of hygiene to a magical space of rejuvenation and rebirth appeared in popular culture as well. The most well known banya of the period was the one depicted in the play and the film *The Irony of Fate or Enjoy Your Steam* (*Ironiia sudby ili s Legkim Parom*). The play, written by Riazanov, was performed to critical and public acclaim in over a hundred theaters. The film had an estimated audience of one hundred million people when it aired on January 1, 1976. It was then released in movie theaters, shown on national television three more times that year, and awarded Movie of the Year. One of the most popular films in Russian and Soviet history, it still airs many times each winter, serving a role in the Russian winter holidays similar to *It's a Wonderful Life* in the United States.[27] The banya in the film is the antithesis of the solitary banya of the countryside celebrated by Shukshin. In *The Irony of Fate*, men gather in an urban, public banya to drink and to socialize, not to display their bodies or to steam in stoic silence. The hero of the story, Zhenia, is an educated, sophisticated doctor with thick eyeglasses and a gentle demeanor—hardly a Russian *muzhik*. The banya serves as Zhenia's gateway to a different world, where things are not as they initially appear. It's a classic hero tale: Zhenia enters the liminal space of the banya with his friends, purifies himself through steam and alcohol, and leaves with his fate altered. True to form, having been transformed, he conquers all the challenges that come his way and ends up in love with the correct woman. Fantastically, the banya sets things right by mixing things up. *banys = truth*

The banya in this context is an urban getaway far from domestic concerns. Zhenia is thirty-six and living comfortably with his doting mother. They have recently moved into a new apartment that looks exactly like so many other newly built apartments popping up across the USSR in the 1970s. As the movie's narrator informs viewers, every city seems to have the same suburbs, the same apartment buildings, the same theaters, and the same street names. Obtaining one's own apartment in one of these new buildings brought both elation at achieving stability but also a corresponding fear of the banality and sameness that life inside these apartments might turn into.[28]

In its urban incarnation, the banya became a place to work through the troubles posed by modern life. It was particularly appealing for Soviet men, who tended to see the new apartment as a women's sphere where wives and mothers and mothers-in-law controlled decisions.[29] For sophisticated urbanites, the banya was a portal away from the city, but not into the past. Their goal was not to replicate an authentic rural banya, but to find a place where the materialism characterized by new possessions and things was kept at bay.

The banya provided an escape from official discourse as well. In a society saturated with reminders of Soviet priorities and symbols in almost all areas of public life, where Red Stars and portraits of Commissars predominated, the banya was surprisingly nonideological. The state propagated the drive toward cleanliness as natural and therefore beyond politics. "Building communism" required clean people, to be sure. But the imperative to bathe was deemed natural and universal.

As a space liberated from both domestic concerns and public discourse, banyas nurtured conversations leading to spiritual betterment. They distilled life down to basics: sweat, alcohol, and good friends. In *The Irony of Fate*, before heading to the banya, Zhenia comes face-to-face in his apartment with his long-time girlfriend, Galia, who wants to get married, and with his mother, who is afraid he will be a bachelor forever. He just wants to meet his friends Misha, Pavel, and Sasha at the banya to start the New Year clean. Emphasizing the contrast with the modern apartment, the banya scene opens with a brief conversation among Zhenia's friends about the benefits of the banya as opposed to the bath. While getting beers from a bathhouse vendor, Misha tells Pavel, "A bathtub in each apartment is right. That's civilization.

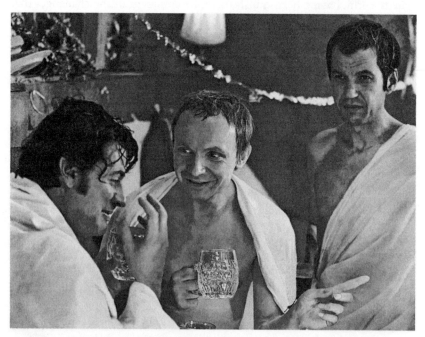

FIGURE 9.3 Zhenia with his friends at the banya in *The Irony of Fate or Enjoy Your Steam*. Dir. E. Riazanov. Programme One 1976.

But in the tub you can just get rid of dirt, but in the banya the process of cleaning oneself is an artistic endeavor." When they join their friends sitting around the changing room dressed only in sheets, Sasha pulls out a bottle of vodka as Zhenia tells them briefly about Galia. Despite Zhenia's protests, the group of friends drinks to him. Inevitably, another bottle appears. He cannot resist and must participate when they propose to drink to Galia. Then, drunk, Zhenia declares himself a bachelor and raises his refilled glass to friends. Despite its public setting the banya proves to be a better place to discuss true feelings than the private realm of the apartment. The friendship and fellowship of the banya alter Zhenia's fate. He will not return to meet Galia but will instead end up taking Pavel's seat on a plane to Leningrad. There he will meet another woman, disrupting the predictable domestic future that had been laid out before him. The banya cannot prevent the onslaught of civilization but it can be the lodestar for a new, moral orientation. To emphasize the significance of the banya—which is on screen for six-and-a-half minutes in a three-hour movie—Riazanov subtitled the story "S legkim parom" ("Go with a Light Steam" or "May a light steam stay with you"). These are the customary words shared while departing the banya and they remind the film's audience that the rest of the story takes place in the aftermath of the transformation that has taken place in the banya. The phrase itself implies that the spirit of the banya stays with the bathers long after they leave. The banya creates a state of mind—like the concepts of peace or faith in the phrases "peace be with you" or "Christ be with you." In the banya scene, Misha and Pavel laugh at how absurd it would be to exchange those words after washing at home. The steam of the banya was transformative in a way that a bath or shower could never be.

The power of the banya to alter people's dispositions was also crucial to the play (1973) and film (1980) *Old New Year (Staryi Novyi God)*, written by the acclaimed playwright Mikhail Roshchin. Once again, the challenges of Soviet identity in the context of late Socialist domesticity are played out as men retreat from their new apartments to the banya. The play was performed at Moscow's *Sovremennik* theater prior to *The Irony of Fate*; the film is also televised annually on Orthodox, or "Old," New Year (January 13) and continues to be popular in the post-Soviet period.[30] In it Peter Poluorlov is a typical member of the Moscow intelligentsia, with sophisticated and artistic friends, a new and well-furnished apartment, a son who takes piano lessons, and a wife who appreciates him. Peter Sebeikin is his working-class equivalent.[31] Sebeikin and his family—caring wife, daughter, mother-in-law, father-in-law—are moving into an apartment downstairs from Poluorlov on

Orthodox New Year's Eve. For them the domestic bliss of a new refrigerator and a telephone (even though they have nobody to call) is fresh and exciting.

Both men, however, are dissatisfied. Poluorlov has decided that all of his possessions and professional success have left him empty. He has quit his job as a writer, has denounced his friends and his wife for their shallow interest in material things, and has dismissed the petty bourgeois trappings that surround him. Meanwhile, in the apartment downstairs Sebeikin is proud of his new digs, but ashamed that they are not the products of his own hard work. In fact his wife's family has secured the new apartment by selling their rural home. Far from being a model member of the proletariat, Sebeikin drinks and watches soccer more than he works and provides for his family. Both Peters find themselves fed up with their families and lives on New Year's Eve. Both men end up storming out of their apartments, each with a male friend tagging along. Ivan Adamich, a wise old man who is the only connection between the two pairs of friends and who is the only character who sees the futility of their crises, joins them. The five men squeeze into Poluorlov's car and they drive across town in silence.

The film cuts to the men leaving the steam room and entering the pool area of an elite banya. The play's stage directions emphasizes that this is an urban banya and the film version makes clear that this is a non-Soviet space.[32] There are no signs or posters marking it as ideological. The banya exists in a parallel universe. As in *The Irony of Fate*, the banya provides a respite from the anxieties and pressure of life in a new apartment. In *Old New Year* there is the added element of escaping the frustrations of public life as well. The banya's timelessness and classless neutrality nurture cohesion and openness among the bathers.

The five men are relaxed, wrapped in towels, bespotted with birch leaves, and drinking beers while lounging by the pool. Poluorlov's friend Gosha refers to the banya and says: "Well that is how we do it here. That's the Russian way!" Sebeikin agrees. Waving his finger he says, "I bathed yesterday. But showers, baths . . . that isn't it. This is where we can really relax." The sort of urban banya that rural Russians disdained appears to be authentically Russian to the urbanites. For the characters in *Old New Year*, however, tradition and the steam room are not really the point. Conversation and intimacy are.

In the pool, the two Peters begin to chat, complaining about their respective stations in life. Adamich, who it turns out has steered the group to the banya in the first place, emerges from the pool, wraps a sheet around himself and delivers a speech. He reminds the younger men of how good their generation has it. He explains that life has become organized and regularized.

Everyone understands their roles. The present was the best of all possible worlds, even if the two Peters did not yet recognize it. The relevant past, for comparison, is the Soviet 1930s, not Muscovy or Imperial Russia. There is no nostalgia—only the recognition that things had improved. The wizened Adamich continues, "There was a time, dear comrades, of starvation and cold, of crowds of beggars, and we carried water up flights of stairs, and we heated the ovens ourselves." Sebeikin interrupts him, but Adamich pushes on, "And now? What do you need? The world is at peace. At home things are good . . . it's warm, clean, there's food, the children are well fed and dressed." The implications are clear: the two Peters, who came of age after the Great Break of the 1930s and were too young to fight in the Great Patriotic War, are struggling to figure out how to live meaningful lives in an age of relative calm and plenty.

Adamich's speech, though disjointed, serves its purpose. At first the two Peters have no idea what he is talking about. But slowly they come to realize that even though they come from vastly different milieus, their problems are pretty much the same. The goal is not to preserve some idealized past or to hold the modern world at bay. Sebeikin complains that no matter how hard he tries, his wife is not happy. But then he realizes that perhaps he does drink too much and watches too much soccer and concludes that the best members of the working class have advanced culturally and socially and left him and his poor habits behind. He and his friend Vasia should go back to school, get more training. Meanwhile, Poluorlov begins to regret having tossed away work and colleagues and the respect that he had earned. He realizes that writing is meaningful after all and, in his day and age, that is enough. They swim, they joke, they drink, they talk. "Our women are smart, principled," Poluorlov declares. He then looks meaningfully into Sebeikin's eyes, strokes his own mustache slowly, and asks with a drunken slur, "Do you respect me?" Sebeikin looks surprised: "We've shared our feelings! What kind of question is that!" As if to provide a definitive answer, Sebeikin puts his two big hands on Poluorlov's cheeks, and bringing their faces close together, he gives Polurolov a long, strong kiss on the mouth. The worker and the writer have affirmed their cross-class bond. The camera cuts away.[33]

Meanwhile, in a bit of comic relief, Vasia is now twisting Gosha's arms back, saying: "Do you respect me? So, do you respect me now?" Gosha, pleased with the vigorous massage, declares—"That is the way we enjoy a Russian banya!" Throughout the long scene the camera periodically lingers on a marble statue next to the pool of a woman draped in a sheet with one hand casually touching her own breast, in a way reminiscent of how Poluorlov's wife had tried to entice her husband the night before. The women are not at fault—they are as consistent as statues, grounded and principled. The days of working-class identity based on beer and football are receding, along with the intelligentsia ideal of anti-materialism. As new roles are carved out in relation to women and to families, men must work out their own responses to the challenges of modern life, preferably in an uncomplicated and homosocial place like the banya. There men can learn to appreciate their new apartments, their new furniture, and their social status. In *The Irony of Fate*, the "light steam" of the banya altered Zhenia's life; in *Old New Year*, it allowed the two Peters to recognize the value of the lives they were tempted to abandon.

The urban bathhouse of the late Soviet period was a place for workers and intelligentsia alike. It was less about the body than about conversations, less about who counts for what than recognizing that many different types of men (but not all—homosexuality, for instance, is never overtly addressed) count for something. It was urban and public. It was a place without women, but where women were always present.[34] It was a place to drink and a place to get away from it all. It was a place that was without overt ideology, so that the men themselves could come to understand their roles at home and in the world.

There was a potential downside to the socializing that took place in the banya, however. When the banya ceased to be a self-enclosed world and the troubles, vices, and transactions of the outside world permeated its walls, the atmosphere could quickly become more corrosive than cleansing. Conversation could devolve into something base and transactional. Stripped of deeper meaning, the urban banya might not be about the transformative heat or the magical steam or even soulfulness.. Instead it was just a club where like-minded individuals could wheel and deal there way through Soviet life.

Perhaps no person was more trusted and therefore potentially dangerous than the bathhouse attendant or *banshchik*. The *banshchik* heard everything and knew everyone and as such came to represent a crucial hub of unofficial behavior. The seemingly lowly *banshchik*'s intimate familiarity with people from all sectors of society made him the ideal go-between, a status that he could use to obtain an elevated importance in society. This, at any case, is the conceit of the 1976 film *You Scratch My Back, I'll Scratch Yours* (*Ty Mne, Ia Tebe* ").[35] Written and directed by Aleksander Seryi, one of the Soviet Union's most popular comedic filmmakers, the film's protagonist is Ivan Sergeevich or Vanya, a masseur at a prominent Moscow banya. His loyal clients include ministers, apparatchiki, and anyone else lucky enough to be able to get in to see him. His clients bribe him with foreign shampoo, caviar, and other hard-to-find items. He in turn uses these items and connections to advance his own status. To emphasize Vanya's authority, viewers see a policeman stop traffic to allow him to make an illegal turn across traffic—a privilege usually reserved for important officials. Well-dressed Muscovites wait in line at the banya for him to arrive at work, stand upon seeing him enter the building, and treat him with tremendous respect. While giving massages, he advises a diplomat on foreign affairs and a sports administrator on the problems with Soviet soccer. Even an important minister respectfully changes his schedule in order to accommodate Vanya. In short, he's a quintessential Soviet man of the 1970s—he has bartered, maneuvered, and literally massaged his way to success. He is more powerful in the pervasive shadow economy than those at the highest echelons of official Soviet life.[36]

A twist of fate forces Ivan to leave Moscow for his hometown on the Volga, where he has to take up his twin brother's duties as a fish and wild-life inspector. Vanya ends up running the inspection job in the same corrupt manner he had managed banya post. Soon he strikes a deal (in the local banya, of course) that allows the director of a local factory to continue polluting the river. Meanwhile, smugglers are after the caviar from the fish Vanya is sup-posed to be protecting. They hatch a plan to fool him and after a few drinks Vanya agrees to let them poach: "You scratch my back, I'll scratch yours," they wink to one another.

Soon, however, Vanya learns that the pollution in the river is catastrophic, that the sturgeons are dying, and that he has made a deal with dangerous criminals. Chastened by the experience and the realization that he has bartered in stolen caviar back at the banya, he returns to Moscow and his banya post determined not to let people bribe their way up the line for his services. He will stick by the official rules, which only confuses everyone who knows him. When Vanya comes across one of the smugglers from his home-town, he ties the smuggler's arms and puts him in his car, determined to take him to the police. The man begs to make a deal: "You scratch my back, I'll scratch yours." This time Vanya says no. The smuggler complains that he could get two years in jail for his crimes. The film ends after Vanya informs him, "Oh, you'll get more than that, I know the judge."

The last line leaves the impression that although Vanya will not continue to make deals with a caviar smuggler, he has not fully embraced communist morality either.[37] He is not above using his connections to sway a judge, whom he no doubt has met in the banya. It may have been unrealistic in the Soviet

1970s to expect a Soviet man to resist all bartering and influence peddling. After all, nearly everyone in the society, from ministers on down, relied on the parallel economy to distribute goods and services. Corruption, the film seems to suggest, will not end, but the state can hope that people like Vanya will recognize some limits. Likewise the banya as the ultimate place for making deals cannot be reformed entirely either.

Part of what made the film amusing was that the fictional banya reflected the manner in which Soviet men used the banyas in real life. Writing in 1985 in the journal *Soviet Culture*, a *banshchik* asked the question, "What's a banya?" First, he gave the official answer: "[It is] a public enterprise providing a communal service where one can bathe and steam." He quickly added, "But it is not just that." "It is also a place where you can relax well, wonderfully ease nervous pressure, get better from a cold," none of which he thought was possible in a bath at home. More importantly, the banya was a social space. "The beauty of the banya is also that it gives you the chance more than any other laid-back place to chat with friends and get together with people who have common interests." The banya allows people to talk about sports, work, home repairs, and even personal issues. "The very atmosphere of the banya is inclined toward informal interaction." The real-life Vanya conceded that there were problems with drunkenness and alcoholism. Smoking too, he had to admit, was rampant. And there was a shortage of *veniki* for sale in official places, so bathers bought them from "speculators" in front of the banya instead. But perhaps most tellingly, he had to admit that many *banshchiki* had entered the profession in search of illegal "tips" and that many of his coworkers unfortunately understood perfectly well what to do "to make a pretty penny."[38]

How, exactly, they "made that pretty penny" was left unsaid. He may have meant bartering. But some sources confirm that the tradition of having sex in the banya had survived the Soviet state's campaign to make bathing solely about hygiene. Even if *banshchiki* did not exchange sexual favors for money or gifts, they implicitly understood that bathers paid extra tips to rent out private or family rooms in order to have sexual encounters. For soldiers in particular, the banya remained a place where even outwardly straight men could have sexual relations with other men.[39] In one case, in the 1980s a deputy commander for political affairs chose to laugh off the formation of same-sex couples that gathered in the banya in his border unit, rather than confronting the situation.[40] The privacy and otherworldliness made the banya a convenient place for men seeking sex with other men to meet one another in the late Soviet Union; that same permissiveness, if acknowledged in public, threatened to undermine the idea of the banya as a space of either innocence or of publicly acceptable homosocial bonding. By the end of the Soviet Union, the urban banya as a symbol of the corrosion of society's values rivaled its reputation as a benign club. Rather than setting things right, the banya was where amoral behavior, from the state's perspective, flourished.

Same-sex liaisons would have been impossible to depict in a commercial film at the time. The licentiousness of men with women in the banya sufficed to show the potential vice the banya nurtured. The film *Emergency Situation at the District Level* (*ChP Raionnogo Mashtaba*) illustrated this powerfully, by pointing out the misbehavior of Komsomol (Young Communist League) members in Leningrad during the Brezhnev era.[41] The film was released in 1988, in the middle of Mikhail Gorbachev's campaign calling for greater transparency about political and social issues in Soviet society. The film featured a stunning lack of morality among the young elites who were supposed to be future leaders. In the film, Nikolai Shumilin is a regional Komsomol leader who has received word of his promotion to a prominent position in the Leningrad City Party Organization. To celebrate, Nikolai leaves his wife at home and gathers with his Komsomol colleagues at a banya. The banya scene begins with traditional activities—a friend gives him a whacking with a birch switch and they then sit around in sheets recovering from the steam and discussing party business. It soon becomes clear that they've rented out a private banya, where mixed sex bathing was possible. Komsomol women, also dressed in sheets, bring food and alcohol to the table. A colleague raises a toast asking Nikolai not to forget his colleagues when he goes on to great things. The men drink. The young women do too, although somewhat more reluctantly. Nikolai offers a toast of his own. He acknowledges the role that everyone in the room had played in making their district the best in the city. He offers a drink to the Komsomol, "Which has given us everything." One woman asks, "Can I kiss you, Nikolai Petrovich?" He agrees. His male comrade also kisses him deeply on the mouth. The third toast, in rapid succession, is raised to "those who make life beautiful"—our "girls." The alcohol completes the transformation that begun in the steam room. Traditional Komsomol songs follow, with men and women embracing and, soon thereafter, dancing, kissing, and coupling off. By the scene's end, everyone ends up naked together in the banya pool. The country's "best and brightest" are shown indulging in drunken debauchery.

The film's critique of the system made it controversial. At least one reviewer in the prestigious *Literaturnaia gazeta* thought that rather than depicting an "emergency situation" the film instead showed "our usual everyday reality which existed not long ago and still exists today." That young people would drink and have sex in a banya was hardly a surprise. Gorbachev's *glasnost* had allowed that reality to make its way into film.[42] But most reviewers were aghast. The city of Frunze refused to show the film in its theaters. In another town, protesters called for the town's movie theater director to be fired for showing it. For many, the camaraderie and intimacy in the banya went too far, leading to unspeakable corruption. A banya with friends was good. An "orgy"—the word some used by some to describe the banya scene in *Emergency Situation*—was not.[43]

Although far more cynical than *You Scratch My Back, I'll Scratch Yours*, the message of *Emergency Situation* was similar—the banya was the natural setting for corruption. In many cases banyas were a place for Soviet citizens to rejuvenate themselves and seek refuge from the outside world. But they also potentially revealed the ubiquity of the pollution that was eating away at society as a whole.

—•—

The chatty banyas depicted in *The Irony of Fate* and *Old New Year* and the corrupt banyas in *You Scratch My Back* and *Emergency Situation* were archetypes. Most Soviet banyas did not resemble them. Instead, they struggled to stay open. The discrepancy between the well-functioning (if corrupt) banyas of Soviet film and the banyas in most towns was striking. An article in *Sovetskaia Kul'tura* in 1979 pointed out that some of Moscow's banyas, like Sanduny, had become "comfortable palaces" where concern for clients was paramount. But that was hardly indicative of the banya situation around the country, where "under construction" had become a permanent condition. Despite a steady outpouring of funds year in and year out, some banyas had been "in the process of being built" for upward of ten years. (This included the banya that was slated to replace the one destroyed by the accident in Elets a decade earlier.) At Sanduny and a few other places bathers could buy *veniki* of various types, receive cutting-edge spa treatments, and swim in cold pools, but many other banyas did not have working steam rooms or even a cup of tea for sale at the café. The banya bureaucracy greeted complaints with obfuscating language that passed the buck to still other bureaucracies that had failed to produce the right equipment. Isolated cases of well-organized banyas obscured a system that was in disrepair.[44]

In 1979, the Russian Ministry of Municipal Services lamented that just over half of the banyas called for in the plan had been built.[45] Rather than demanding more vigilance, as had been the refrain for decades, goals became more modest. In 1984 the ministry hoped to build only eighteen new banyas across the whole Russian Republic—a far cry from the 50,000 spaces a year called for in the plans of the 1950s. That same year, the ministry concluded that "in many autonomous republics, districts and regions, the technical and sanitary conditions in the banyas are unacceptably bad."[46] In 1989, the Council of Ministers of the USSR looked into the conditions of the banyas in the country and found them "poorly developed and poorly functioning." The report could have been written in 1929 or 1939 or 1949: banyas were unevenly distributed around the country, plans for new ones continued to go unmet, conditions in them had been "extremely neglected," banya workers were uncultured, and efforts to introduce improvements had failed.[47]

The USSR continued to build new banyas and to assume that banyas remained an integral part of the everyday life of the Soviet citizen. Citizens evidently agreed.[48] During Gorbachev's *perestroika*, some banyas could begin to openly cater to the whims of those who paid the most money. This made them cost effective, but it did not mean that everyone could bathe as often as hygienic norms required. In 1988 Anatolii Rubinov, a historian of the banya and writer for the newspaper *Literaturnaia gazeta*, pointed out that old, pre-Revolutionary banyas like Sanduny remained open and profitable. In contrast, Soviet-era banyas often had to be shut down for repairs, which in turn made it next to impossible for them to break even financially. Sanduny had lines out the door. Others had no business at all. Sanduny's directors understood the new economic climate and recognized that if demand was high, they could raise ticket prices even without providing any additional services. Rubinov observed that prices went up not because services had improved. The water was not suddenly softer, the steam room was not suddenly hotter, he quipped. Sanduny was responding to supply and demand. Meanwhile, elsewhere in Moscow most banyas struggled just to stay up and running.[49] Popular and efficient banyas could afford upkeep and renovations. Without an influx of capital, broken-down banyas were destined to remain in disrepair. The old Soviet economy's support for them waned even as the leap to a market-based system remained beyond reach.

Judged by its own standards, the Soviet project ended in failure on the banya front. The state never built enough banyas in the right places with the right supplies to satisfy its own hygienic goals. In the nineteenth century, banyas in the Russian Empire were prevalent even before public bathhouses had become a focus of urban policy in Western Europe and the United States. At that point it appeared that Russians were ahead of a trend that prioritized prophylactic bathing on a regular basis. By the 1970s, most Western Europeans and Americans lived in private apartments or houses routinely equipped with hot and cold water, showers, and bathtubs. In the Soviet Union in the 1980s, the goal of building more banyas and keeping extant ones in operation, especially in neighborhoods without well-developed indoor plumbing, remained pressing. Egalitarian rhetoric made the stark discrepancies in services appalling and jarring. While some citizens bathed comfortably at home and headed out to Sanduny for some rest and recreation, others had no choice but to wait in long lines to enter dilapidated and poorly run banyas. Despite a concerted effort by the USSR in the postwar period to improve everyday life, many Soviet citizens could still not take bathing for granted.

The collapse of the USSR coincided with the eclipse of the official Soviet endorsement of the banya as the epitome of hygienic modernity. In the end, people could bathe at home, or at least that was the new goal. A strong sense of the banya's deeper, symbolic value re-emerged to fill the void. In 1917 V. V. Rozanov had asked what place there would be in revolutionary culture for everyday practices such as the banya. By 1991, the question became inverted: what was the meaning of everyday practices such as going to the banya when revolutionary culture collapsed? When the steam of Soviet hygienic aspirations cleared, two answers that had been there all along became more visible: banyas could restore society's connections to the Russian past and they could help individuals in their search for authenticity in the modern world.

10

In the Banya I Changed My World View

ισι

THE END OF the Soviet Union began in a banya. On August 17, 1991, the head of the Committee for State Security (KGB), Vladimir Kriuchkov, convened at a safe house in Moscow a group of hardliners from the Red Army, Communist Party, and Soviet President Mikhail Gorbachev's staff. They had come to settle on a plan to declare a state of emergency and to seize power from Gorbachev. The goal was to prevent what they saw as the further deterioration of the economy and state security. Specifically, they hoped to stop Gorbachev from signing a Union Treaty that would have ceded much of the USSR's centralized power to the various constituent republics, including Russia. To put his fellow conspirators at ease, Kriuchkov invited them first to the banya. The choice made sense. The banya was considered an ideal place for people to have frank, confidential discussions. The banya established trust. Afterward they drank alcohol and hashed out the details. The next day, they sent a delegation to Gorbachev in the Crimea asking him to feign illness and to allow a newly formed State Committee of the State of Emergency (GKChP) to assume control of the affairs of the country. When he refused, they proceeded without him.[1]

On August 19, the TASS news agency announced the establishment of the GKChP, adding that Gorbachev was ill and that the vice president (one of the conspirators) had assumed his duties. At first there was confusion. On the streets in Moscow, Leningrad, and other cities, people rallied against what they took to be a coup d'état. Military commanders were reluctant to open fire on their own people. Boris Yeltsin, the President of the Russian Federation, who had been in Kazakhstan for talks about the new Union Treaty when the plot was hatched, returned to Moscow. The coup leaders failed to have him arrested and he was quickly able to assert his authority. Within a few days Gorbachev was back in the capital, but his support had evaporated. Within a few weeks the various republics of the USSR, including the Russian Republic, had wrested enough power that the union seemed superfluous. The attempted coup failed miserably, accelerating the decentralization that the conspirators had hoped to rein in and delegitimizing the institutions they hoped to empower. On December 7, Yeltsin met with his counterparts from the Belorussian and Ukrainian Republics in a secure compound in the woods of western Belorussia. Together they worked out the details for what would become the Commonwealth of Independent States. To celebrate and consecrate what they had done, Yeltsin and a few of his aides joined their Belorussian hosts in the banya.[2]

The Soviet Union disappeared; the banya did not. The fifteen republics that had been only nominally independent under the USSR became effectively autonomous. Each had its own borders, its own institutions, and its own traditions, some predating 1917 and some cultivated during Soviet rule.[3] Each republic inherited banyas. Both the Imperial Russian state and the Soviet Union had built and maintained banyas across what had suddenly become fifteen independent states, each of which took over a ministry of municipal services.

The collapse of the USSR and the emergence of the independent country of Russia affected the banya in two ways. First, there was no longer a centralized state that took responsibility for banyas. Many city governments followed suit, allowing banyas to be privatized. The planned economy of communism gave way to market forces. While occasionally banyas could be seen as public goods, more often than not they were deemed commercial enterprises, just as they had been before the Revolution. Some banyas marketed their sparse authenticity and the quality of their steam. Some were more like clubs, a place to gather with friends away from home and work. Others sold luxury and the decadence of an older, imperial era. Some offered sex with prostitutes; others offered a meeting place for same-sex liaisons. None of these conceptions of the banya were new. What changed was that the state's bureaucratic support for banyas, its propaganda on their behalf, and its insistence on the primacy of hygiene wilted. Without an overbearing state presence, individuals could pick and choose the various cultural threads of the banya's past and weave them into the banya of the present. Banyas of the post-Soviet period were capitalist. What mattered was what sold and what sold was healing, tradition, sex, and community.

The second major change to the banya in the post-Soviet period involved the reassertion of the association of the banya with Russianness. National politics in the 1990s usually required the non-Russian states to reject outward expressions of Russian cultural dominance. But none attacked the banya. Instead, they found its Russianness inoffensive, or they reinscribed steam bathing as their own tradition, or they let it languish without much fanfare. Russians, however, claimed the long history of the banya—including the Soviet banya—as part of their patrimony. As Russian society attempted to reorient itself after the collapse of the USSR and the sudden absence of state-sponsored communist ideology, consistent, unproblematic markers of Russianness became more salient. While the other newly independent states could frame their national politics in opposition to what they viewed as the twin malignancies of the Soviet legacy and a resurgent Russian empire, the new Russian Federation had the more difficult task of disentangling the positive attributes of the Soviet and Russian past from the more troubling ones. After 1991, there were very few unifying traditions that the vast majority of Russians could rally around without ambiguity. Religion was problematic. Former communists, as avowed atheists, could endorse Orthodoxy only awkwardly.[4] Non-Christian Russians could not endorse it at all. History remained a thorny topic. Celebrating the Romanov dynasty required amnesia about the reasons for the Revolution in the first place. Stalin may have made the USSR an international power but he had done so by crushing the lives of millions of people. High culture seemed to ignore the masses. Drinking vodka was almost universal—more people than ever were drinking more than ever in the 1990s—but the downside of that tradition was obvious to anyone paying attention to the country's mortality rates.[5] The banya, however, emerged as a relatively unproblematic symbol of Russianness. Its longevity and stability—throughout Russian and Soviet history—made it resistant to accusations of being too Soviet or anti-Soviet, too modern or too backward, too imperial or too revolutionary.

In the 2000s, when a more sober and strident government asserted control of society, the banya's association with Russianness remained an asset. The banya represented integral parts of a Russian world view—it was communal, corporeal, social, traditional, and resisted marching in lockstep with the cultural norms flooding in from Western Europe and the United States. That it was also associated with sex, corruption, and illegal transactions furthered the sense that all of post-Soviet Russian culture—the good and the bad—was manifest in the banya.

The banya's status in pre-Soviet Russian history was celebrated like never before. The fact that it had been around since Kievan Rus' and had been popular with the people before the Revolution added to its allure and the sense of its importance. The close connection between going to the banya and Russian identity was not new. But during the Soviet years, it had been held in check by the same forces that held Russian nationalism in check. Sovietness had enveloped Russianness and the banya. After the collapse of the USSR, the banya served as reminder of an independent and resilient Russia. The tremendous investment of the Soviet period in modern, socialist banyas remained evident in thousands of banya buildings across the former Soviet Union. But new texts and films reanimated pre-Soviet habits and traditions for post-Soviet imaginations. In the countryside, family banyas remained a key feature of rural life. When the new rich built their dachas or cottages, they invariably included a banya. In the cities, the extant imperial banyas, like Sanduny in Moscow, thrived in no small part because of their association with a long history that seemed to straddle 1917—and 1991—easily.[6] Politicians went to the banyas, sometimes to restore their health or to make deals, but just as often to signal their affinity with the Russian people.

The transformation of the Soviet banya back into a Russian banya occurred abroad as well. The banya had first traveled to Western European and American cities in the nineteenth century, when public bathhouses were becoming commonplace there. With the rise of indoor plumbing across the United States and Europe, most bathhouses shut down. In 1960s and 1970s, those that remained open became even more openly associated than ever with gay sex and sociability. Russian banyas were different, at least outwardly.[7] Straight Soviet émigrés frequented banyas in Chicago, New York, London, and other cities where they saw them as a remnant of something the USSR had gotten right and that many sought to recreate in their new communities. They provided émigrés a place to gather. Like in Russia and the Soviet Union, people went to these steam rooms in diaspora to wash, talk, conduct business, and relax in a social setting.

Yet this was hardly the banya of the eighteenth century, when Chappe D'Auteroche and António Sanches had debated its merits and dangers. Chappe, the snobby Frenchman, had mercilessly ridiculed banya customs, even as he grudgingly accepted that a steam bath might have some medical value. Sanches, the Portuguese physician who was generally sympathetic to the Russian state, had insisted that overcoming the peculiar habits of the peasantry would allow the banya to flourish in the name of universal health. Over the next century, Sanches's argument had gained the upper hand and in the Soviet period it had been predominant. But by the late twentieth century the medical rationale was just one factor, among many, buttressing the banya either in Russia or the West. People were attracted much more to the culture of the place and its promise of an authentic Russian experience. More often than not, that meant following what they thought were the specific customs of the Russian *narod*, not the advice of medical experts. Producing the right sort of steam, properly using *veniki* to whack one another, and lounging around afterward in sheets helped ensure that the banya was in keeping with tradition. Being Russian after 1991 meant being visceral and connected to the soil, passionate about close personal interactions, and alive to the possibility of corruption, violence, and criminality. One surefire way to experience all of this was to go to the banya.

In the Soviet period, banya proponents in the state bureaucracy justified banyas by insisting that paying attention to personal hygiene was part of being a good socialist. After 1991, the state no longer had to justify banyas at all. The hygienic imperative had been eclipsed. Bathing, at least in principle, could be done at home. The banyas nourished people's spirits more than their bodies. Going to the banya became a way of establishing trust and asserting one's Russian identity at a time when other symbols of stability and tradition had vanished or were more problematic.

Yeltsin, the first Russian president, made clear the extent to which the banya had been set free from its association with the goals of the Communist regime. In the fall of 1989, he had still been a loyal member of the Communist Party. But his intense criticism of the system had led to his political exile and removal from the Politburo. Embattled by political rivalries and depressed about his prospects, his aides insisted he go with them to the banya. He later recalled, "It was an ordinary neighborhood banya, rather unpretentious, but they knew how much I love the banya and they wanted to help me defuse some stress." In the steam room Yeltsin came across other naked bathers waving their *veniki*. He recalled that they cheered him up and voiced their support for what he was trying to do. The location was ideally suited for the spiritual crisis he was undergoing. The nudity suggested vulnerability and openness. It brought Yeltsin palpably closer to the people he hoped to represent. "The fact that this occurred in the banya was symbolic," Yeltsin recalled, adding, "The banya, after all, purifies things. All feelings there are clean and people are exposed . . . Yes, in that moment in the banya I changed my world view, I realized that I was a communist by historical Soviet tradition, by inertia, by education, but not by conviction. The scene in the banya remains vivid in my mind."[8] The banya, rather than the church, was the most obvious place for Yeltsin, a nonbeliever, to undergo such a conversion.[9] The banya had survived seventy years of Soviet rule without being unduly tarnished by its association with the goals of the communist state. Yeltsin had entered a Soviet banya only to discover that it was in fact a Russian banya. He went into the *parilka* a communist and came out a Russian patriot.

After the collapse of the USSR, the infrastructure that supported the neighborhood banyas deteriorated. As president of independent Russia, Yeltsin's policies supported deregulation, liberalization, marketization, and "shock therapy"—all based on the assumption that capitalist economic relations would help secure material rewards for Russian citizens in ways that the planned economy could not. As the state receded—even disintegrated at many levels—existing institutions, such as municipal banyas, were left to fend for themselves. They survived in part because of tradition and in part because banyas remained places apart, where their familiarity gave people a sense of balance amid economic, political, and cultural unrest. The nudity of the banya and the contact with basic elements of heat and water helped it appear stable in a world that was seemingly unrecognizable.

Yeltsin continued to seek solace and companionship in the banya as president, but only with people he knew and only in private compounds. His bodyguard, Alexander Korzhakov, often accompanied him, in part because he made Yeltsin feel more like a regular person.[10] They took turns slapping each other with the *veniki*. With foreign leaders, Yeltsin forged trusting relationships in the banya. When he visited Finland in 1992 he took up an invitation from the Finnish Foreign Minister to bathe together. In the steam room they bonded and talked politics.[11] In 1997 he further solidified economic and political bonds with Finland by bathing with the Finnish president, Martti Ahtisaari. Yeltsin told reporters afterward, "I used a Russian birch switch to spank the president well." Ahtisaari did not seem to take offense.[12] Yeltsin also steamed with the German Chancellor Helmut Kohl. The banya allowed the two leaders to forget about politics and instead joke around "like old friends." Unlike Khrushchev, whose unpublicized trip to the banya with Kekkonen in the 1950s had been considered by Molotov and others to be a sign of gross diplomatic embarrassment, Yeltsin proudly told the media about the joys of bathing with foreign leaders. The banya, in his telling, was a place of deep contemplation, of fellowship, and of truth. He was less forthcoming about his habit of retreating to the banya during his most depressing moments.[13]

Most urban banyas remained communal in spirit even when discrepancies in pricing and services began to reveal growing class divides in society. In her study of Russian life in the early 1990s, anthropologist Dale Pesmen described a wide range of Russians (urban and rural, rich and poor, men and women) going to the banya as a way of nurturing the soul. She found that banyas served a "historically 'Russian' role" in society: "The fact that baths are a locus for meeting and promiscuity, dirt and purity, power and equality, heat and cold, sobriety and drunkenness, health and illness, communion with others and contact with one's own 'deepest' needs, as well as drink, song, and healing, makes them *dushevnyi* [soulful]—*anything* that unites things is." She added that "like *dusha* [soul], banya is a separate 'place' where you become aware of things and of oppositions (like inner or hidden cold, illness, and impurity, emotional pain, and various truths) as part of the process of them either leaving you or emerging into the light."[14] Russia itself was undergoing a tremendous transformation in the early 1990s. Social instability accentuated the power of the banya to set things right—to free the body and spirit of waste and to give meaning to a world where many old meanings had been upended.

The period was defined in part by the process of coming to grips with the more difficult aspects of the Soviet legacy and a search for meaning that could be salvaged after the collapse of the USSR. In this context the banya—especially the rural banya—was a convenient symbol of an uncorrupted Russia. In the film *Burnt by the Sun* (*Utomlennye solntsem*), the rural banya represented innocence, purity, and unapologetic sensuality. Nikita Mikhalkov, the film's director, producer, and costar, returned to the theme of the banya he had broached in *Oblomov* in 1980. Again, for Mikhalkov, the rural banya—not the city banya—encapsulated Russian authenticity. In contrast, the urban bathtub was wrought with complex emotions, intellectualism, and despair. The film takes place in 1936, on the eve of the peak of the Great Terror. Toward the beginning of the film, Division Commander and Stalin favorite Sergei Petrovich Kotov (played by Mikhalkov) is enjoying an idyllic rural banya with his wife Maroussia and their young daughter. The naked girl straddles her father's back, beating him with a birch *venik*, while he smiles and flirts with his charming wife. Kotov is a *muzhik* (or rural man's man) immersed in a Russian tradition. The effect is made all the more powerful through comparison with Maroussia's hopelessly bourgeois family back at the dacha. Kotov is active and strong. The family appears to be living the charmed life of the pre-Revolutionary elite, concerned with

frivolities and unimpeded by the terror around them. Kotov's enjoyment
of the banya is interrupted when he is called upon to save a local field from
being trampled by a nearby Red Army exercise. Relying on his military authority and self-confidence, he is heroically up to the task. To further the
sense that he embodies power and masculinity, he later makes wordless, im-
passioned love with Moroussia in an attic where the banya *veniki* have been
hung to dry.[15]

Despite his reputation, status as a military leader, charisma, and connection to Stalin, Kotov is not safe. He has a rival for Maroussia's affections,
in the form of a cosmopolitan intellectual named Mitya who had known
Marroussia in their youth and to whom she was briefly engaged. Kotov and
Mitya are studies in contrast. In the Civil War, Kotov was a Bolshevik mili-
tary hero; Mitya fought for the Whites. Kotov stayed and helped to build the
USSR; Mitya lived in exile, unable to return to his homeland. Kotov is trans-
parent and physically imposing; Mitya is a deceptive, delicate piano player.
Kotov is honorable; Mitya has made a deal with the NKVD. By the film's end,
Kotov has been arrested and shot and Mitya is a broken man. The film has
come full circle from the raw purity of Kotov's rural banya. In the final scene,
Mitya has returned to his apartment overlooking the Kremlin and slits his
wrists while sitting in a bathtub. In the film the banya represents the authentic
Russian spirit, which was crushed by the rootless intellectuals who hijacked
the Revolution. The country's journey from the banya to the bathtub may appear to some like progress, but to Mikhalkov it suggested degradation and a
nation that has lost its way.

The close affinity between the banya and Russianness was developed in
lowbrow films as well. In the popular cult classic of 1996, *The Peculiarities
of National Hunting (Osobennosti natsional'noi okhoty)*, a young Finn visits
Russia with the hope of experiencing a traditional Russian hunting trip.[16]
He imagines nobles on horseback, but instead finds himself among a rag-tag
group of friends who prioritize drinking, brotherliness, and high jinks. At
first the Finn has a hard time understanding what is going on, both because
he does not speak Russian and because the group shows little interest in
hunting. The banya, in this context, proves transformative for the Finn. He
enters as an outsider uninitiated in the peculiarities of Russian life. While
getting beaten with a *venik* in the banya, he says, in English, "I feel as if I am
falling to pieces. My hands, legs, head, and soul are all separated." One of
the Russians responds in Russian, "This is the banya, brother, the Russian
banya." They drink to brotherhood. They jump in the ice-cold pond. And
by the time the Finn leaves the banya, he has been reconstituted in both

body and soul as a part of the group. They seal the transformation with more vodka.

Even as many popular books, articles, and movies lauded the banya's curative powers or its centrality to Russian identity, the potential for corruption and vice in the banya were never entirely out of sight.[17] Business and political leaders met in the banya to hash out decisions before formalizing them in public. In the mid-1990s, a Russian businessman explained to an American reporter that investment banking was not worth the hard work, "When you could go have a banya session with your buddy at the Finance Ministry and they would put in $600 million."[18] Business, politics, and crime cross-fertilized. In 1994, a sniper murdered Otari Kvantrishvili as he was exiting a banya in the center of Moscow. Kvantrishvili was a prominent member of the "Sportsmen of Russia" political party, an administrator of a national sports foundation, brother of an underworld leader, and a renowned racketeer. Unlike in Soviet times, when unseemly events could be hidden from public view, the news was featured in the national press. The location of the murder, in front of a well-known banya in a prominent neighborhood in the capital, was cited as evidence of the disorder that was descending on Russia as a whole. It was accepted as obvious that criminal figures frequented banyas to relax, make deals, or establish trust with would-be partners. But a murder in front of one seemed brazenly to cross the line.[19]

The banya was also at the center of the first full-blown sex scandal of the post-Soviet era. In 1997 Yeltsin's Minister of Justice, Valentin Kovalev, was filmed in a banya carousing with three prostitutes. The newspaper *Top Secret* (*Sovershenno sekretno*) published blurry pictures of the encounter. The banya where the meeting took place was a notorious hangout for one of the most powerful criminal groups in Moscow. The scandal revealed that the highest-level government official in charge of the law was corrupt, meeting with prostitutes and connected with the underworld. The banya's association with salaciousness was alive and well, even as some claimed that the banya was not to blame. Sergei Stepashin, who replaced Kovalev as Minister of Justice, explained, "Well, I go to the banya and I will continue to go to the banya. What's important is why you go and with whom you go, not to make it the center of your life."[20] Films such as *Burnt By the Sun* had suggested the banya was a sacred, wholesome place; Kvantrishvili's murder and Kovalev's escapade made it clear that in post-Soviet Russia the banya was full of intrigue and danger as well.

By the late 1990s it was clear that the transition from a socialist economy to a market-based system had stalled out. The ruble collapsed in 1998 and most gains from the difficult years of "shock therapy" appeared to have been lost—or transferred directly from the accounts of citizens into the accounts of a very few, very wealthy oligarchs. With the economy in tatters and the prospects of Russian geopolitical power bleak, many dismissed the utility of emulating the West in politics, economics, or culture. Cynicism and skepticism appeared safer bets. The banya reflected the new mood well, only now cynicism shrouded the institution. Films and books began to portray the banya as a site of corruption and not just soulful rejuvenation.

Innocence, purity, and sincerity seemed out of date and perhaps even dangerous. In Galina Shcherbakova's 2001 novel *Molotov's Bed* (*Krovat' Molotova*), a granddaughter asks her grandmother (the narrator) why men were building a banya when they had baths in their homes. The question spurs the narrator to repeat the clichés about the banya that she had heard over the years: "I tell her the fairytale about the role of the banya in the life of the Russian people, who have always lived in the cold. Of how the banya cures and how it restores people to health, and my story is going over smoothly." She continues to explain "how overheated people jump in the snow, how they return to the heat and beat each other with *veniki*, pouring *kvas* on the burning stove." But the narrator senses that the fairytale motif is not quite right and an internal voice begins to question the lore. As she describes the idealized Russian banya to her granddaughter, she remembers that after the war her own grandmother had associated the banya with diseases and had forced her to rewash from head to toe at home after she had been in a banya. She recalls, but does not tell her granddaughter, that more than anything going to the banya had evoked a "feeling of shame, not personal shame, but some sort of otherworldly shame of nakedness and defenselessness." As she repeats the myth aloud and thinks about how it contrasts with her own memories, her granddaughter asks, "Are we going to go to this banya?" "No," the narrator responds, "It is not ours." "Thank God!" the granddaughter cries out. The narrator concludes with relief, "Something from my romantic tale splashed with *kvas* did not work out."[21] For some, the Russian banya's power to cure and to provide meaning contended with vivid memories of filth and disease, the fear of the vulnerability, and shame of communal nudity.

The political openness of the era allowed people to convey freely the negative aspects of the banya. It was in this era that memoirs about banyas in
the Gulag began to circulate widely and, for the first time, legally. The 1990s
involved coming to terms with the past and a new openness to challenging
simplified myths about that past. The fairytale banya was ripe for critique.
The banya was as multifaceted as Russia itself. The internationally acclaimed
movie *The Thief (Vor)*, which premiered in 1997, tells the story of a desperate
widow traveling with her six-year-old son, Sanya, after the war.[22] They meet
a handsome soldier, Tolya, who seduces the woman. He turns out to be a
thief and con man who uses Sanya in various schemes to cheat people out
of money even though the boy only slowly comes to realize the depths of
Tolya's depravity. At one point, Tolya takes Sanya to the men's side of a public
banya—a place where his mother cannot go and where Tolya can indoctrinate
the boy. Sanya is wide-eyed and ashamed as he sees naked men massaging
each other and strolling about. Tolya teaches him how to wash. When, out
of embarrassment, Sanya covers his genitals with his *venik*, Tolya tells him,
"Don't worry, squirt, if you're brave yours will grow too." He then tells the
boy a story in which the central message is that so long as you come out on
top in the end, there is no shame in anything. The scene ends with Tolya and
Sanya rushing out of the banya after other men discover that Tolya has been
cheating them at a game of cards in the dressing room. Tolya is a stand-in for
all of the deceitful men of the Stalin era, including Stalin himself. Like the
character in Vysotky's song, he too has a tattoo of Stalin on his chest. Only
unlike Vysotsky's character, Tolya never shows remorse. The Soviet, postwar
banya did not reestablish his purity or innocence or teach Sanya how to be
a Russian—it only further clarified that the world was a ruthless place. That
ruthlessness was not just a marker of the past; it was also part of the cultural
landscape of the late 1990s.

Even efforts to celebrate the banya suggested that its role in Russian society was deteriorating alongside conditions in the country. In the early
1990s the problems created by Soviet utilitarianism had been clear; by the
end of the decade the downside of the capitalist banya was coming into view.
Increasingly, banyas catered to the demands and desires of rich clients. Those
who went to the banya regularly to bathe were often priced out. In 1997, in
a decree that echoed policies of the 1920s, the city of Moscow ordered commercial banyas in the city to allow veterans, invalids, and families access at
reduced rates or for free.[23] Just as in the earlier era, compliance and enforce-
ment proved difficult.

In December 2000 the weekly news magazine *Itogi* celebrated the banya on its cover. But inside the issue six articles on various aspects of the banya suggested that the banya contained within it the contradictions that were plaguing Russia more generally. To be sure, they deemed the banya integral to a positive Russian identity. One article asserted that going to the banya was a healthy endeavor: "Our ancestors intuitively understood (based on the experience of many generations) the optimal technique for making [healthy] steam, which can be affirmed from the point of view of physics." Another article insisted that the steam in the banya did not just clean the body, "it cleaned out the pores of the soul as well." Readers learned that "from time immemorial the banya was an integral part of the Russian way of life" and that Soviet effort to turn banyas into "cleaning centers" instead of places of soulful relaxation had ultimately failed. In the late Soviet period famous actors, athletes, and other members of the cultural elite had bathed at Sanduny in a spirit of camaraderie.[24]

The *Itogi* articles suggested that the golden age of the banya was the late Soviet period, not the imperial period or the 1990s. The heyday of places like Sanduny was in the recent past: "The popularity of the banya notwithstanding, it has become clear that in the post-Soviet era the banyas that we are familiar with from childhood are slowly dying out." The cost of repairs and upkeep overburdened unsubsidized banyas, forcing them to focus on making money rather than creating an inclusive atmosphere. Instead of prioritizing the steam room, many new facilities advertised the fact that they had billiard rooms, cafes, offered pedicures and haircuts and other things that "had nothing to do with the banya we recall." The *Itogi* journalists lamented a new emphasis on individualism over the old egalitarian, communal approach. Many banyas had become places for wealthy New Russians and gangsters to gather, whether they had any intention of steaming in a *parilka* or not. Luxury, not spiritual or physical health, was the point. At some banyas, clients could buy "erotic massages" for exorbitant amounts of money. Officially, no sexual contact was allowed, but the women working as masseuses reported that "nobody leaves without having reached orgasm." As one young woman working at a banya happily explained, "When a man steams in a banya what does want? Beer and vodka. And when he has drunk, what does he ask? Where are the girls? And that's where we come in." Tips of $500 (US) were not out of the question.[25] Clearly the average Russian, making less than $100 a month at the time, could not possibly afford this experience. New banyas were for New Russians.

The *Itogi* journalists decried the corruption of a purer banya, one that was about cleaning the body, nurturing the soul, and creating a healthy atmosphere for friends and strangers to come together around a common interest deeply rooted in the Russian past. Whether such a banya had ever existed was less important than the fact that it appeared to be missing in contemporary Russia. The authors of the six *Itogi* articles were all men who seemed to presume that their memories and experiences summed up the meaning of the banya for everyone. They also appeared disappointed in the degradation of the banya, without any sense that the things they lamented—excessive luxury, the prioritization of leisure over health, and the appearance of only thinly veiled prostitution—were hardly new at all.

The banya had always been a place of perversity, sin, and shame. These themes had been latent in public discourse in the Soviet period. In the post-Soviet period they only appeared to come out of nowhere because it was possible to talk about them again openly. To the *Itogi* reporters, the degraded banya appeared indicative of the state of affairs in the country. But a more discerning look suggested that the banya's purity had always come with danger, the innocence always matched by corruption. The banya was at once a symbol of Russia's positive and negative attributes. It was hard to tell if things were palpably worse in 2000 than they had been in 1980 or if they only appeared so because the era brought with it new perspectives and new expectations for how things might be.

The acclaimed postmodernist Russian writer Vladimir Sorokin seemed determined to poke fun at the idea of the fairytale banya that had existed in the past or might yet still be possible in the future. To Sorokin, the banya was both cleansing and befouling, nurturing and corrupting, a place of bonding among equals and of power dynamics and gender segregation. This came through first in 1999 in Sorokin's phantasmagoric novel *Sky Blue Lard* (*Goluboe salo*).[26] The timelessness of the banya—and its popularity in all periods of Russian history—made it a convenient setting for talking about the past, present, and future of Russia all at once. If late-Soviet Russia was defined by the banality of waiting in line (the subject of Sorokin's breakout novel in 1983), post-Soviet Russia was defined by materiality, power, decadence, and a misplaced nostalgia for a pure past.

In one chapter of *Sky Blue Lard*, a young prince heads to his family banya, built specifically in "the Russian manner."[27] Under a full moon his assistant undresses him. The *banshchik* inquires whether he would like to steam "simply" or "with moaning." The prince opts for moaning and the reader is alerted to the fact that this is going to be an unusual banya. The *banshchik* heats up the fire and calls in a "not tall sixteen-year-old girl in a homespun skirt, with a beautiful square face, large brown eyes and thick flowing chestnut hair." She bows to the prince and, at the *banshchik*'s orders, undresses. Sorokin parades her nubile sexuality in front of the reader. She has "large, developed breasts with red blemishes around brown nipples that had not been sucked on by even one child." She lies down naked directly on top of the prince. The *banshchik* tosses more *kvas* onto the rocks to raise the temperature. He then takes a birch *venik* in one hand and a willow rod in the other and begins to beat the prince with the *venik* and the girl with the rod. She dutifully moans "I'm guilty, oh, I'm guilty." To the prince's ears, the repetition of rod-*venik*-moan, rod-*venik*-moan creates an "unworldly music." For a moment the scene melts into a soliloquy about the magic of the banya. The prince thinks, "God, my God, how good this is . . . Here in this incongruous banya, in the steam, isolated and locked away from the whole world, from the winter and the frozen trees, from the remote village and the well-marked roads, from the deeply sleeping men, from the dogs, from the snowy valley, from the distant people in distant cities, from relatives and strangers, from the sound of the frozen air and that round, cloudy moon hanging over the whole world—how wonderful it is for us, three warm and naked people doing something that inexplicably intoxicates and overwhelms us." Sorokin has juxtaposed debauchery and the idealized rural banya. The beating of a girl for a prince's pleasure mixes with physical and emotional purity. The two extremes of the banya are intimately connected.

The scene does not reach a synthesis with the rape of the girl or the sexual satisfaction of the prince. Instead, the *banshchik* suddenly interrupts the rhythm of the beating and moaning. He drops his tools and tosses a bucket full of ice-cold water on both the prince and the girl. The girl faints and the prince thinks, "It's probably possible that a person could die from this." The girl rolls over, slowly raises herself up, stops for a moment, and then "the prince felt the jet of her hot urine hit him in the lower back. The urine flowed over his body, mixed with the icy water, and dripped down." The girl leaves the steam room, her duty evidently fulfilled. The prince remains, pleased and entirely spent. The late 1990s was an era of wealth, pornography, and permissiveness in Russia. Sorokin's banya was not only about purity and cleansing of the soul. It was about aristocratic dominance and existential questioning. Myths and the promises of authenticity existed in tandem with violence, pain, and shame. These were not some modern addition—they too were authentic and indicative of the banya's history and meaning.

Seven years later, in 2006, Sorokin returned to the banya in his book *Day of the Oprichnik* (*Den' oprichnika*). The *oprichniki* had been Ivan the Terrible's Secret Police, who helped him violently rule Russia without needing to rely on the hereditary nobility. Sorokin's story takes place in a dystopic Russian future, which resembles a religiously infused mafia state where updated *oprichniki* do the bidding of their bosses. The story retells in the first-person one day in the life of an *oprichnik*. The ordinary day includes, among other things, the arrest and killing of a wayward nobleman and the gang rape of his wife, all done with humility and piety to God and to the boss. The *oprichniki* use archaic, religious language but also have futuristic mobile phones and cars. Russia's future involves devolution toward old Muscovy. Force and power determine fate and justice; the lines between government and criminality are entirely blurred.

The book ends with the *oprichniki* gathering at their boss's banya. The *banschiki* are either mute or deaf, making it a trustworthy place for the gang to report openly about its day's work. The boss divvies up rewards. In the slang of the book to be "naked" is to be exposed as weak and vulnerable. In the banya they are all literally naked. As with *Sky Blue Lard*, the tension and humor comes in the combination of the normal with the absurd. Some elements of the banya appear entirely traditional. There are *veniki, kvas* to heat the stones and create steam, and *banshchiki* to whisk the bathers. After the *oprichniki* steam, the *banshchiki* wash them down and massage them. "Great is the brotherhood of the banya," the narrator declares. "Everyone is equal here—the right and the left, the old and the young." The banya even induces open discussion: the *oprichniki* chat freely with one another.

So far, the scene would presumably be more or less recognizable to banya goers from any era of Russian history. But then things get strange. The *oprichniki* receive pills that they place under their tongues, "like for the Holy Communion." The banya has cleansed them and they are ready to enter communion with their leader and one another. The pills make the *oprichniki's* penises glow and become engorged. "The great strength of the oprichnik brotherhood lies here," the *oprichnik* narrator explains. They proceed to form a human chain in order of seniority with the boss in the lead. Each *oprichnik* inserts his penis in another's rectum and in turn receives one in his own. They moan and orgasm together. The narrator declares that the experience is "indescribable because it is so divine."

In most descriptions of the banya, the homoerotic potential of same-sex male bathing had been treated as unworthy of comment. It could be argued that hiring female prostitutes at the banya had been a way for men to assert their heterosexual impulses amidst an abundance of male bodies. A hundred years earlier in the novel Wings Kuzmin described same-sex attractions in the banya, causing an uproar, even though sex itself was only implied. In the *Day of the Oprichnik*, Sorokin is explicit about the sex, but mute about desire. The point is ritualistic male bonding involving drugs, dominance, and subordination. Amidst the absurdity, parody, and humor, Sorokin depicted the purifying and mischievous elements of the banya as intimately related. Not surprisingly, books that celebrate the banya rarely cite him.

The collapse of the USSR shifted the meaning of the banya for foreigners as well. In the 1990s and 2000s Russian culture was more thoroughly integrated into the West than Soviet culture had ever been. If they cared to, foreigners could easily watch *Burnt by the Sun* (which won the Academy Award) and *The Theif* (which was nominated for an Academy Award), read Sorokin, learn about Yeltsin's affinity for the banya, and read about murders and scandals in the banya. They also saw the banya in Western films and could even go to them in Western cities.

The Russian baths had been fairly innocuous in American and European cities during the Soviet period. In New York, Los Angeles, Chicago, London and elsewhere, banyas catered to Russian and Jewish émigrés who continued to enjoy steaming—what they sometimes called "the *schvitz*"—in diaspora. The collapse of the USSR arrived on the heels of the shuttering of many gay bathhouses as the HIV-AIDS epidemic spread in the 1980s. A decade later going to the banya surged again in popularity, partially because it was liberated in straight Americans' minds from an association with homosexuality. Articles in US newspapers lauded the recreational and health benefits of the Russian steam bath. By the mid-2000s post-Soviet banyas in upscale New York evoked luxury, style, and elegance, with an alluring hint of unsavory characters and illegal activities. The banyas of Brighton Beach and the East Village appeared to be kitsch reminders of Soviet austerity and exoticism.[28]

Going to the banya provided curious Westerners with a chance to gain insight into Russia and Russians. Countless popular accounts and some scholarly essays attested to the connection between Russia and the banya. When the mayor of Burlington, Vermont, Bernie Sanders, visited the Soviet Union in 1988, he joined his counterpart from the city of Iaroslavl' in the banya. Sophisticated observers focused on the banya as well. Literary scholar Nancy

Condee reasserted the significance of the banya for Russian women despite the preponderance of banya stories and sources written by and about men. The banya, she concluded, was a female space evocative of the motherland more generally: "Perhaps this intimacy of mother, motherland, and bath explains some of the public anger surrounding the modern day closures of bathhouses, as well as their sale and conversion into more lucrative downtown space. What is at stake is not merely profit or power, but the very material substance of Russia. It is the city's version of a painful question: Who will own Mother Russia?"[29] Journalist Bryon MacWilliams, who lived in Russia for much of the 1990s and 2000s and was a devotee of the Seleznevskie baths in Moscow, wrote a celebratory book about his experience of going to banyas across Russia. Banyas, he argued, could help outsiders break through their common misconceptions about Russians. His colleague and bathing partner, *New York Times* Moscow correspondent Steven Lee Meyers, also explained that going to the banya was a key for understanding the culture: "After five years in Russia it [the banya] means one thing to me: an act of purification and rejuvenation and, as an outsider in this vast, enigmatic country, the closest I've come to a true immersion in the particularities of Russian life."[30] Seemingly every few months in the 2000s, another foreign correspondent discovered the banya and wrote a story emphasizing the heat, the oddity of being nude in front of friends and strangers, and the degree to which the banya provided a clue to Russian national character. Many did not share Meyer's and MacWilliams's long-term experience with or deep appreciation for the institution, opting instead for more superficial descriptions. In a typical article, Margaret Coker of the *Atlanta Constitution* reported, quoting a Russian source, that "a foreigner hasn't glimpsed Russia's heart unless he strips bare, rushes into the fragrant, wood-paneled, steam-heated room, and sweats off the dirt, alcohol or unsettling weight pushing on his soul."[31]

Even foreigners who were unlikely to follow special publications on Russia came across the banya in popular culture. The book and film *Gorky Park* featured a scene in a Moscow banya in which a Russian police inspector, Arkady Renko, has a frank conversation with a chief prosecutor.[32] The prosecutor offers Renko a bribe, only to discover that the inspector had recorded the conversation. The banya was both a place of openness and deceit. In *Red Heat* (1988), Arnold Schwarzenegger plays a Moscow narcotics officer who gets in a brawl after being confronted by gangsters in a banya.[33] The film *Rounders* (1998) revolved around a conflict between a young card-shark (Matt Damon) and a Russian mobster (John Malkovich), with banya scenes suggesting the intimate and dangerous atmosphere of their New York City subculture.[34] In the first season of the HBO series *The Sopranos* (1999), one member of the mafia takes a friend to the Russian banya to try to determine if he's wearing a wire. Even to outsiders, the banya appeared to reveal all.[35] And in *Eastern Promises* (2007), a deadly brawl breaks out in a London bathhouse between a naked Russian killer (Viggo Mortensen) and two Georgian gangsters who have come to kill him. Foreigners could easily learn that bathing and the banya were intertwined with Russian identity both in Russia and abroad.[36]

Outside of the former USSR, the banya was associated with Russian and Jewish émigrés, political wheeling and dealing, and the underworld. Even before the collapse of the Soviet Union, Russian bathhouses became a hub for politicians, celebrities, and criminals alike. The Reverend Jesse Jackson famously frequented the Division Street Russian and Turkish Baths in Chicago, as did local mobsters.[37] Timothy Leary, Frank Sinatra, John F. Kennedy Jr., and John Belushi went to the Russian banya on 10th Street in the East Village of Manhattan.[38] But mostly the baths were associated with emigrants. Perhaps the most evocative image of the old-school Russian baths was Saul Bellow's description of the Division Street baths in Chicago in his Pulitzer Prize-winning novel *Humboldt's Gift*: "The patrons of the Russian Bath are cast in an antique form. They have swelling buttocks and fatty breasts as yellow as buttermilk. . . . Things are very elementary here. You feel that these people are almost conscious of obsolescence, of a line of evolution abandoned by nature and culture. So down in the super-heated subcellars all these Slavonic cavemen and wood demons with hanging laps of fat and legs of stone and lichen boil themselves and splash ice water on their heads by the bucket. . . There may be no village in the Carpathians where such practices still prevail." Bellow was wrong about the banya's obsolescence. It did not die out in the West. Instead, the antique static figures gave way to younger, hipper Americans.

After the collapse of the USSR, going to a Russian banya became a popular outing and not just for those with a connection to the former Soviet Union. In 2001, one bather in Chicago's Division Street Bathhouse described it as a "sanctuary." "Rich and poor come here from every ethnic background," he said, adding: "It's like a brotherhood. You close the door and leave the world behind."[39] In 2004 a Russian banya opened in Seattle, Washington. As one reporter noted, bathhouses had existed in the city before, but in the mid-1980s municipalities used their regulatory power to shut them down in an attempt to stamp out illicit gay sex. Now, the banya was back. "America may have won the Cold War, but the Russians have us beat with the hot bath," he concluded.[40] In 2016, the *New York Times* declared that a "bathhouse renaissance" was in full swing. The articled reported that baths "have been claimed by the denizens of the new New York, as *shvitzing* has joined shuffleboard, brewing beer and pickling as a pastime enjoyed by millennials as well as retirees." One banya-goer observed, "The hipsters come in with their Groupons, sporting their tattoos and their man buns."[41] Banyas were in style. In 2018 a CBS-New York segment declared that "old-school bathhouses" were "back in a big way."[42] In England, journalists were a bit more skeptical. The BBC pointed out in a report on a recently opened banya in London, "As leisure activities go, you would imagine that lying naked on a wooden table while two topless Russian men hit your back with bunches of oak leaves would only appeal to a very specialist group of enthusiasts." Yet the journalist soon discovered that only two years after opening, "almost half [the banya's] customers are non-Russians."[43]

To foreigners, the banya was often just another Russian export—like vodka or caviar—to be sampled and enjoyed. The banya, like Russia, was harsh and difficult, but worth it for anyone who could withstand the conditions. If the soul was open, it could be soothed. Going to the banya was a healthy and even enjoyable way of showing one's personal comfort with being around other naked bodies. Throughout much of history, the banya made Russians appear barbaric and uncivilized. By the twenty-first century, going to a banya— whether in Brighton Beach or Moscow—became a way for non-Russians to show their cosmopolitan engagement with a multicultural world.

———•—•———

Meanwhile, for Russians, the political, economic, and cultural turmoil of the 1990s gave way to a more austere age. The tougher, unsentimental banya grew stronger alongside the romanticized banya. The banya in Aleksei Balabanov's film *Brat-2* (which can be translated either as "brotherhood" or "Brother -2") was exemplary. The film (along with the original *Brat*) attained cult classic status in Russia and was immensely popular among the generation of Russians who came of age in the 1990s. In the films, Danila Bagrov is a veteran of the Chechen wars who finds himself enmeshed in the criminal worlds of St. Petersburg, Moscow, and Chicago. He is a just but ruthless killer and a patriot. Toward the beginning of *Brat-2*, Bagrov meets two of his war buddies, Ilya and Kostya, in a banya in Moscow. Kostya, who works as a security guard, tells his friends that his twin brother, a professional hockey player in Chicago, has run afoul of the Ukrainian mafia and also come under the control of a corrupt American businessman. The three discuss what they might do to help out Kostya's brother. As they talk over the situation, drink beer, and eat fish, three women, sometimes naked, sometimes covered with sheets, circle in and out of the conversation, vying for the men's attention. Kostya shoos them away—making it clear that they are talking about important things and that the women are not (yet) required. The men do not drink to excess, they do not womanize when there is business to attend to, and they do not go to the banya for sentimental reasons. After they have hashed out a plan, the men allow the women to join them at the table. The banya's importance is grounded in security and confidentiality. This is a space for men to have meaningful conversations and to make meaningful decisions. The *banschik* who brings them beer is an effeminate nonentity—he threatens neither their masculinity nor the confidentiality of their intimate conversations. The soul, which had been the focus of so much attention in the 1990s, was less relevant by 2000. These were men inspired by fraternal bonds in the present, not the past. Their banya was a place for unsentimental, hard-nosed veterans who had their emotions in check. The film presented the superiority of a present-day Russian world view over the corrupt and decadent West. The banya, like Russia, was not soft or vulnerable. *Brat-2* helped signal the end of the madcap and unpredictable first post-Soviet decade and the ascendance of sobriety and cynicism about outside solutions to problems. In the 2000s Russians would stick up for themselves, their country, and their own idea of what constituted civilized behavior.

Vladimir Putin, Yeltsin's handpicked successor, embodied and nurtured the new mood well. In many ways he was the antithesis of his political patron. Yeltsin was boisterous, improvisational, and out of control. Putin was cautious, calculating, and fastidious. Yeltsin drank to the point of drunkenness. Putin took pride in his physical control and toughness, as exemplified by his mastery of judo. Putin assumed power on the eve of the new millennium and ran for election in 2000. He waited out the results in a rural banya.[44] That much he had in common with Yeltsin. Yet Yeltsin's banya was a place to find solace and comfort, while Putin's was one of physical health and personal bravery.

In the 2000s, Putin propagated a story about a banya experience that helped to shape his personal and political trajectory.[45] In the 1990s, when Putin worked in the political apparatus of Mayor Anatoly Sobchak in St. Petersburg, he and his wife had built a dacha outside the city that included a banya. When Sobchak lost a bid for reelection in 1996, Putin was left to contemplate what appeared to be a bleak future in politics. He retreated to his dacha for a number of weeks to consider his next move. One day, he took a banya with friends as a "wake for my old job," as he later put it. After he jumped in a nearby lake to cool off, he noticed that the banya and house had caught on fire. He managed to save his family and valiantly re-entered the flames to rescue the small stash of money that constituted his life's savings. As he tells the story, this symbolic transition in his professional life was also accompanied by a miracle. Following Russian custom, he had removed the cross he wore around his neck before entering the banya. Though it was made of aluminum and had no material value, the cross was meaningful to him because it had been a gift from his mother. After the fire was doused, Putin asked firefighters to look for the cross. Somehow, amid the ashes they found it, completely undamaged. As with Yeltsin, the banya played a crucial role in a key moment in his life—and it also was laden with religious undertones. Putin emerged from the banya transformed, with little from his previous life except his cross. He was ready to start the next step in his professional and personal development.

Putin's banya was less a place to let his guard down than a place to heal, to rejuvenate oneself, and to size up others. In 2015, Putin confirmed that he continued to go to the banya. But if in the past the banya had been a place where foreigners had judged Russians, Putin saw it as a place where he could judge the strength and character of other people. When asked on national television whether he ever conversed with foreign leaders in the banya, Putin told a story about going to the banya with the German Chancellor Gerhard Schröder. When the banya building caught fire (just as it had at his dacha in 1996), Putin raced up to Schröder and said, "Gerhard, we need to get out of here immediately, we're burning." Schröder evidently responded, "Just wait until I finish my beer, then we can go." Putin shouted, "Are you crazy?" But Schröder finished his beer before escaping the flames. To Putin, this showed that Schröder was a "tough guy with a strong disposition." Putin concluded that he probably would not go with a foreigner to the banya again. But he clarified, "On the whole, I love the banya and go with pleasure."[46] The banya was important as a Russian tradition and a place where people's personalities could be revealed.

Putin, however, was relatively understated about the banya. His foil in this regard was less Yeltsin than the nationalist politician, Vladimir Zhirinovsky, who actively displayed his enthusiasm for the banya. Where Putin humbly told stories about going to the banya quietly with close friends and trusted colleagues, Zhirinovsky was flamboyant about his steaming. The banya also provided Zhirinovsky with the sort of theatrical atmosphere in which he loved to perform. As the *New York Times* reported, after the elections in 2008, Zhirinovsky gave a "virtuoso news conference at the Sanduny Baths in

Moscow . . . where he came for a Russian banya and a victory toast." Time and again, he lauded the banya as an emblem of Russia. In 2014 a YouTube channel devoted to Zhirinovsky posted a video of a trip he took to a banya. In it, the nationalist leader promoted the banya. He explained why he brought with him his own soap (a habit he developed during times when soap was hard to procure) and complained when the banya they were visiting turned out to be more of a "dry banya" or sauna. "Where's the Russian banya?" he demanded to know, before explaining to the young men in his entourage the superiority of the Russian banya and offering them a seemingly impromptu tutorial on how properly to bathe like a Russian.[47] In 2017 he complained about the lack of public banyas in the country—too many, he argued, had been shut down and replaced by saunas.[48] By that point, his was a common post-Soviet lament that held that the banya was in danger of becoming obsolete. The prevalence of saunas and health clubs threatened the vitality of banyas. The younger generation did not understand how to bathe properly. Russian identity and culture were under risk from the corrupting influences of modernization and foreign invasions, this time in the guise of a sauna.

Politics and politicians, however, did not monopolize how people thought of and used the banya in the 2000s any more than they had in earlier decades.

FIGURE 10.1 In 2008, as the *New York Times* reported, the nationalist politician Vladimir Zhirinovsky gave a "virtuoso news conference at the Sanduny Baths in Moscow on Feb. 25, where he came for a Russian banya and a victory toast." James Hill/Contact Press Images.

If anything, the banya of the twenty-first century was even more eclectic and full of contradictions than ever because it contained within it remnants of all the preceding eras. The banya continued to be about personal health and public hygiene. Putin's doctor emphasized to the media in 2013 that the president did not like taking medications. Instead, he healed himself in the "traditional Russian ways"—by drinking tea with honey and going to the banya.[49] He was not an outlier. Other medical experts continued to insist that going to the banya was healthy. One medical report recommended going to a wood-heated banya once a week to properly clean the body because the heat caused "waste and salts to evaporate through the pores," and "the *venik* would then wash the waste, salt, toxins, dead skin, and negative energy off of the body."[50] An article in the newspaper *Kommersant* confirmed that going to a banya was good for bodily health. In comparison with the sauna, the author concluded, the banya had its advantages and disadvantages. The banya "put more stress on the nervous system, as well as the cardiovascular and respiratory systems." For hardy people, though, the banya was more effective. The sauna, the article concluded with a hint of pride, was more "suitable for weaker people" and those only beginning to familiarize themselves with the benefits of steam baths.[51] An article in 2010 in the journal *Physiotherapy and Sports Medicine* carefully outlined when to go to the banya, for how long, and under what circumstances. The benefits of persistent use, the author claimed, were clear. If people used the banya "regularly and correctly, then [they] will soon feel more capable of hard work, become less tired, and will adjust to atmospheric changes better." If they went irregularly, the positive effects were diminished or lost entirely.[52] The author cited none of the old literature on the topic, but his conclusions clearly reflected ideas about the banya that had been discussed in the medical community as early as the second half of the eighteenth century and had likely been accepted, albeit in different terms, by members of the *narod* long before that. Communal, spiritual, and historical contexts aside, the banya remained for many a tool for physical improvement and health.

Given their purported importance to personal health, city governments continued to consider whether the banyas should be public goods or private enterprises. In 2000, the city of Pavlovo declared a state of emergency and raided one of its few extant banyas because it was charging rates that made it impossible for average people to bathe. From the point of view of some civic leaders, access to a banya was a basic human right.[53] In some places banyas clearly remained the primary means for many people to bathe. The Russian Union of Engineers reported in 2012 that across Russia 20 percent of urban housing still did not have hot water and 10 percent lacked indoor plumbing of any kind.[54] With an urban population of over 100 million people, this meant that between 10 and 20 million city-dwellers could not bathe at home. As in the Soviet period, Russians needed banyas to achieve a basic standard of cleanliness even as the banyas that served them had difficulty staying open. In the 2000s municipal banyas continued to shut down and were often replaced by expensive spas offering luxuries at high prices. Some cities had no banyas at all.[55] Even in major cities, a lack of public banyas was an acute problem.[56] A survey conducted in St. Petersburg found that two-thirds of those who went to the banya did so out of sanitary necessity rather than for recreational reasons; their homes lacked bathing facilities. One sixty-six-year-old's testimony would not have been out of place twenty, forty, or sixty years earlier: "I wash only in the banya because thirty people live in my apartment, all of whom need to wash, shave, clean their clothes. You can't even turn on the bath water before someone is banging on the door to get you out." He complained that the inexpensive Stalin-era banya in his neighborhood had recently closed down. His only option to access a banya he could afford was to travel by bus across town. Those banyas that were reasonably priced and provided basic services had lines even in the summer months, another person without bathing facilities at home complained.[57] In 2011 the city of Moscow, meanwhile, ceded the building and maintenance of banyas entirely to private investors, which ensured that the price of a ticket would be beyond the means of most people. Officially, the 1997 ruling that allowed pensioners, families, and veterans to bathe once a week for free or at reduced prices remained on the books. It was just difficult to find a banya that actually adhered to the rules.[58] The banya's importance as an institution of basic hygiene had not entirely receded, but its ability to serve that function turned out to be no better in a market economy than it had in a command economy.

For the majority of the population with indoor plumbing at home, the banya was no longer necessary for hygiene. Although the number of spaces to gather outside of work and home such as cafes, bars, and restaurants had grown since the end of the USSR, the banya retained its allure. Friends continued to meet in the banya regularly. Business deals continued to be struck there. To avoid formal channels, the president's administration sometimes used meetings in the banya to convey its wishes. One intelligence officer noted, "At an operational level, we never dealt with them [the president's adminstration] nor did we get any instructions from them. That was something negotiated high above our heads, in the *banya* over drinks."[59] Decisions that were made outside of the public eye and based on personal relations were dubbed the "banya factor."[60] The importance of these meetings for political decision-making was not lost on those on the outside. As the State Duma member Irina Khakamada observed, "Women politicians will really appear when the issues of power are no longer decided [by men] in the banya over vodka, beer, and girls."[61] The social bonding among men that proved crucial to decision making excluded women from the banya except as objects of sexual desire.

In post-Soviet Russia women, of course, could go to their own banyas for their own reasons. But the asymmetry of published information about male and female baths continued. Condee has grappled with the discrepancy between myriad sources on male banyas and the paucity of sources on the female banyas. "Nowhere do we find extensive verbal descriptions of the 'other norm,' so to speak: the women's side of the tile wall," she wrote, adding, "The reasons [women go to them] are as varied as (and essentially no different from) those often cited by her male counterpart."[62] The basic process was similar too—women steamed, used *veniki*, and relaxed afterward. But, as Condee understood, the meanings associated with the banya for women had significant differences. To take one clear example, men retained much more power than women in public life, rendering certain features of the male banya inaccessible. Women could not make major political or business decisions in the banya and they rarely seemed to use the space as a way of displaying their own sexuality vis-à-vis men. In fact, the appeal of the women's banya remained the fact that women could go about their personal tasks without the presence of men. If women and even the idea of women lingered in male banyas, in female banyas the male was blessedly absent. Sasha Rudensky's photographs of the early 2000s captured this spirit. Women in a Moscow banya go about their routines of cleaning the body and soul before applying their make-up and returning to the outside, male-dominated world. If Bulla's photographs in the early nineteenth century hinted at same-sex attraction, Rudensky's photographs suggested the pleasure women took in relaxing in an all-female environment that seemed to displace the topic of sex altogether.

When one woman recalled her weekly visits to the banya with her mother in her youth in the USSR, cleanliness was not the central focus. "Rather, the aim was purification and restoration of spiritual balance, accomplished through sharing and camaraderie," she wrote. "We went to the bathhouse in order to experience, with other naked women and children, a different kind of cleanliness."[63] That spirit remained a selling point in the 2000s. A typical women's banya in Moscow advertised its services by explaining, "Going to the banya with your girlfriends is both pleasant and useful. Not only can you wash and steam, you can also wash away the presence of men, exchange beauty secrets, and discuss fashion trends. Women's banyas are good because you can rejuvenate your soul by talking with friends without worrying about your appearance."[64] Banyas offered women the chance to escape from the male-dominated world and to return to it purified and self-assured.

Yet public commentary on the woman's banya continued to be dominated by male representations. A remake of the 1972 film *The Dawns Are Quiet Here*, about the heroics of a women's division in the Second World War, aired on Russian national television in 2016.[65] The director Renat Davlet'iarov retained the crucial banya scene and, even more than in the original, appears to have shot it to appeal to men's sexual fantasies about the female banya. In the original, the emphasis was on the banya, the buckets, and the *veniki*. Although the women were naked and marveled at one another's beauty, frontal nudity was minimal and the camera never lingered on anyone in particular for long. Maternal purity, not female sexuality, had been the point. In the remake, the camera takes in the actresses' naked beauty much more slowly and much less coyly than in the original. Women's banyas, in the male imagination, remained a place of sexual potential. The chance to look in on women bathing was presented as titillating. In Davlet'iarov's 2013 film *One Day (Odnazhdi)*, a group of sixteen-year-old boys pay money to be able to peek in on the women's section of the banya.[66] They remove a tile from the wall to allow themselves a vantage point. Tanya, a seventeen-year-old girl who is the object of one of the boy's desires, senses what they are up to. Before she teasingly exposes their peephole, she offers them a good look at her naked body, playfully, slowly washing herself in their line of sight. The message seemed to be that it was perfectly natural for boys to be boys and for the women's banya to exist in part to fulfill their curiosity. The fascination with seeing naked women in the banya had captivated foreign observers since at least the sixteenth century. In the eighteenth century the Russian state had passed laws to erect physical barriers between men and women's baths. Yet the taboo against looking only seemed to increase the pleasure that might arise from being able to do so. For centuries, the literature on the banya neglected the women's banya in comparison with the men's banya. But as an object of male imagination and visualization, the women's banya never disappeared.

In contemporary Russia, as everywhere, some men were less interested in catching a glimpse of naked women than they were in coming into contact with other men. Yet as was the case with women's banyas, few books, news articles, memoirs, or films elucidated the culture of gay banyas in Russia. Unlike women's banyas, gay banyas did not appear to be a common feature of the public male imagination. There has been no contemporary literary equivalent to Kuzmin or philosophical counterpart to Rozanov. Books and articles celebrating the banya rarely even reference the history of same-sex encounters that took place and continue to take place there. The political environment, particularly after a 2013 law that stigmatized LGBT identities and made it illegal to distribute "propaganda on nontraditional sexual relations" to minors, further discouraged open discussion of the banyas' role in the queer community. But unlike in other epochs of Russian history, gay banyas could be advertised explicitly, just not to minors. One website advertising banyas in Moscow reported that even though "a gay pride parade was not yet permissible" in Russia, many Russians found the idea of nontraditional sexual orientation familiar and natural. Gay and lesbian clubs, bars, saunas, and banyas had opened in Moscow. "Of course we will not pretend that such places did not exist before," the website's section on gay banyas reported, "but few people knew about them and finding them was impossible, because they were so discreet. Today, for the most part, there is no need for conspiracy." The website then listed and evaluated the banyas catering to "nontraditional sexual orientations" in the city.[67] Another website declared that openly "gay

FIGURE 10.2 The interior of the women's bath was the subject of speculation and fantasy for male film directors and writers. But for women their appeal was the opportunity to meet with friends and other women in a public space without the presence of men. Sasha Rudensky, the Vorontsovskaia banya, Moscow, 2001. Courtesy of Sasha Rudensky/ Esto.

saunas have become excellent places for comfortable relaxation, without the need for secrecy or the fear of oblique glances."[68]

As a physical space, the banya was neutral and available to everyone. As an experience, every banya for every person at every moment was unique. But as an idea propagated in public discourse, the banya was dominated—though not entirely—by the imaginations of straight males.

———

The most famous ultra-masculine male who brought attention to the banya was Putin. The fact that he told two different stories about confronting a fire in the banya might at first seem odd. But judging by newspaper reports, his experience may not have been that unusual. In one otherwise unremarkable two-day period in the spring of 2018, Russian news sources reported on banya fires in Alakurtti, Arkhangelsk, Cherepovets, Emanzhelinsk, Kalevala, Kuzbass, Magnitogorsk, Miass, Orenburg, Siniavino, Vacha, Velikii Novgorod, Vologda, Volskii, and Zelenograd. The fires were in cities and in the countryside, in small wood huts, and in communal banyas.[69] The threat of conflagration had been a part of the banya's history since at least the time of Princess Olga's conflict with the Derevlians. Fires were a harsh reminder of the potentially dangerous physicality of the banya. The articles attest to more than just the danger of the banya, however. They also suggest how banyas continued to proliferate across Russia.

Not every banya was going up in flames, of course. Nor were all banyas impure and corrupt. Banyas in Russia continued to be sacred to some and utilitarian to others. They remained elite and egalitarian, accessible to all and segregated by gender, outfitted to enhance conversation and tailored to sex, a place of mourning and rebirth, sin and salvation, inseparable from the Russian soil and spread widely throughout the world.

In the post-Soviet period the banya—perhaps more than any other Russian tradition—was well positioned to survive and thrive. To nationalists it was quintessentially Russian. For the so-called New Russians the banya served as a club to make business deals, meet with political insiders, and solidify relationships through conversation, drinking, and sex with prostitutes. To those left behind by the new economy, the banya was a place to feel whole and a place to discuss with friends the corruption that appeared pervasive among those who were getting ahead. Some women went to find a place without men; some men went to find a place without women. Others went to have sex with men or with women. Those nostalgic for the Soviet Union could take solace in the fact that the banya had been a Soviet priority. Those who were nostalgic for a purer Russian past could note that some villagers still performed marriage rites in banyas. Those unconcerned with the past could see the banya as a way of starting over. Banyas were still the primary means of maintaining personal hygiene in many villages, towns, and cities where some homes lacked running water. Friends continued to appreciate the banya as a place to discuss private matters. The banya's rich and varied past created an access point to every stage of Russia's history: the banya predated Peter and Westernization; it evoked imperial luxury and decadence; it typified both communal dreams of universal cleanliness and the erosion of socialist values in the 1960s and 1970s; it remained a place for oligarchs and workers alike. When so much that once seemed solid melted into air, the steam of the banya remained in place.

Epilogue

NAKED, I ENTER A *parilka* thinking about Volodya's claim that the banya is timeless. It's crowded, dark, and quiet except for the murmur of voices and the occasional thwacking sound of a *venik* hitting a bather's back. The heat nearly knocks me over. I take a deep breath. I try to recognize people in the shapes I see through the dense humidity.

On the bottom tier, foreigners cluster in dismay. Chappe D'Auteroche is aghast as Adam Olearius warns him not to climb any higher up the benches for fear that the heat will prove fatal. Mark Twain laughs as António Sanches attempts to convince him that if done properly, the banya will cure his exhaustion, headaches, and digestive disorders. Napoleon trembles in fear as Isadora Duncan steps past him staring at Casanova, who averts his eyes. A newspaper correspondent scribbling notes on a wet pad of paper looks up to see the Apostle Andrew cross himself. The False Dmitrii asks the others to make room for him. President Kekkonen politely obliges.

On a platform a few steps up the air is even hotter. God tosses some straw and a man appears. He is a sorcerer, who chants as Bely watches wide-eyed, mesmerized and terrified. Dostoevsky lies on a bench, face down. Stinking Lizaveta beats him with a fervor bordering on violence. Chekhov sits close by with his head in his hands, while Rozanov talks intensely to Kuzmin. They beckon to Alexander, the *banshchik*. He names a price and they agree to it. Watching this, the Grand Duke Konstantin wishes his shame could melt away. A medical student notes the temperature and asks if he might be able to measure Bulla's pulse. The photographer agrees. In the corner, women gather with buckets of hot water and rags, waiting for a peasant woman to give birth. Serebriakova nods her head, getting pleasure from the scene. Princess Volkonskaia does not. She is disgusted.

Catherine, though technically a foreigner, has no qualms about being here. She gesticulates broadly and talks loudly with Stalin about the benefits of a good steam, as Putin and Yeltsin take turns with the *venik*. Rasputin, who has removed his cross, slithers up to them, almost unnoticed, strokes his beard and recites a prayer. He insists on giving Zhirinovsky a curative massage and wonders whether he might someday join the brotherhood of the *oprichniki*.

Terkin stands tall, signaling to a fellow soldier to toss more water on the rocks. As they do so, they ignore the Division Commander Kotov, whose wife and daughter have apparently decided it's best not to bathe with him after all. Shukshin thinks they are all full of shit and heads into the washroom. His bucket is missing, and though he can't be sure who has swiped it, he thinks he notices Zoshchenko grinning over by the water taps. His amusement is short lived. Bulgakov announces that there is no water, hot or cold. A bureaucrat looks up, shrugs, and takes his turn at chess. In a corner a *banshchik* is applying glass jars to a bather's back, while another man sharpens scissors. Okunev wonders if he has enough money to have his nails clipped.

The changing room is crowded too. A bride listens to her attendants' stories, hoping that they will give her wisdom in marriage. It's New Year's Eve and Peter Sebeikin kisses Peter Poluorlov as Zhenia and his pals glance over at a brigade of young female soldiers who have let their hair down. Businessmen and up-and-coming party hacks eye them too, while quietly making a deal with Shalamov and some other *zeks* to burn down the place. Princess Olga adds her support to the plan. Vysotskii strums his guitar, singing urgently, as the baby lets loose her first cries.

The sound jostles me. I see Sergei and Volodia and remember what time it is and where I am. I feel relaxed and alive, washed clean enough to imagine that the banya has no beginning and, so long as there is Russia, that the banya will have no end.

Acknowledgments

GOING TO THE banya is a communal activity and so too is writing a book about the banya. With friends and colleagues next to me every step of the way, I entered into this project in stages, making my way up the hottest level—the writing—slowly and with some fear that I would not survive. Now that I am finished, I feel the scholarly equivalent of resting in the changing room, not entirely convinced that undertaking this activity was healthy but elated just the same. For all of those who accompanied me throughout the process, I feel deep appreciation and the rare camaraderie that comes from having experienced something together. I thank, first, the many people who introduced me to the finer points of going to the banya, including Sergei Cherepennikov, Viktor Cherepennikov, Marc Kasher, Sergei Mikhaelov, Evgeny Mikhaelov, Sasha Radostev, Vladimir Tsyganov, and Sasha Vorontsov.

The farfetched idea of turning the banya from a respite into a topic for scholarly inquiry began in 2002 with a conversation with Reginald Zelnik at the Kensington Pub. A few years later, Syracuse University and a short-term grant from the Kennan Institute funded the initial research that convinced me it was time to get serious about something than had always been fun. Support from Brown University's Humanities Research Fund, the History Department, and the Cogut Center for the Humanities made it possible to continue to think about the banya, even as the burdens of post-tenure administrative responsibilities kicked in. More substantial funding from the National Council of Eastern European and Eurasian Research allowed me to conduct the bulk of the research in libraries and archives in Moscow and St. Petersburg. A Burkhardt Fellowship from the American Council of Learned Societies sent me to the Center for Advanced Studies in the Biological Sciences in Palo Alto, where I stared at the hills, thought, and began to write the book.

A Fernand Braudel Fellowship (in combination with sabbatical funding from Brown) sent me to the European University Institute in Florence, Italy, where I stared at the hills, thought, and finished writing the book.

At various stages in the process Stephen Bittner, Deborah Cohen, Robert Edelman, Donald Filtzer, Sam Fleischacker, Jorge Flores, Ilana Gershon, Abbott Gleason, Samantha Kahn Herrick, Nancy Jacobs, Igor Kurukin, Norman Kutcher, Iris Litt, Maud Mandel, Bryon MacWilliams, Louise McReynolds, Marcy Norton, Daniel Orlovsky, Olga Petri, Amy Randall, Joel Revill, Joan Richards, Paul Sabin, Robert Self, Martin Sherwin, Olga Shevchenko, Yuri Slezkine, Richard Stites, Mark Swislocki, Uladzin Valodzin, Simine Vazire, Alexei Yurchak, Vladislav Zubok, and countless other people provided feedback on chapters, wrote letters of support, sent me citations, or offered points of guidance at crucial moments. Initial ideas were worked out in two articles: " 'Real Men Go to the Bania': Postwar Soviet Masculinities and the Bathhouse," *Kritika: Explorations in Russian and Eurasian History* 11, no. 1 (Winter 2012): 47–76 and "Public Health and Bathing in Late Imperial Russia: A Statistical Analysis," *Russian Review* (January 2013): 66–93 (cowritten with Konstantin Kashin).

Early presentations at Duke University and at the University of Toronto shaped the scope of the project. Later presentations at the UC Berkeley *kruzhok*, at Stanford, and at the European University Institute refined my ideas. In the middle, a presentation to the Modern European History Workshop at Brown kept me going.

Christopher Carr, Anastasiia Dmitrieva, Konstantin Kashin, Kseniya Konovalova, Fiona McBride, Joy Neumeyer, Olga Petri, and Josh Tobias assisted with research at various stages in the process. Christina Sokolaeva, Igor Chapkovskii, Ben Tyler, and Sasha Rudensky graciously assisted with images. Librarians and Archivists at the Brown Libraries, Beinecke Library at Yale University, the Central State Archive of Films, Photographs and Sound Recordings of St. Petersburg (TsGAKFFD SPb), the Ethnography Museum Library in St. Petersburg, the Historical Library in Moscow, the Hoover Institution Archive and Library, the Hygiene Museum Library in St. Petersburg, the Kennan Institute Library, the New York Public Library, the Lenin Library in Moscow, the Library of Congress, the National Library of Medicine, the National Library of Russia in St. Petersburgh, the Russian State Archive for Social-Political History (RGASPI), the Russian State Film and Photograph Archive in Krasnogorsk (RGKAFD), the Slavonic Library in Helsinki, the Stanford Library, the State Archive of the Russian Federation (GARF), the Sterling Memorial Library at Yale University, the

Syracuse University Library, and the Widener Library at Harvard University all endeavored to make my research easier and guided me toward materials that I would have been unlikely to discover without them.

Harold Cook, Bathsheba Demuth, Susan Ferber, Anne Gorsuch, and Willard Sunderland read a first draft and graciously got together on a cold winter day in Providence (with no promise of a banya to lighten their load) to work out ways that I might reorganize the material and strengthen my arguments. At that point—and at every point along the way—Susan provided sound guidance and encouragement. Yuri Slezkine also read that draft and offered key feedback at that crucial stage. David Engerman and Stephen Bittner stepped in whenever I needed to bounce an idea off of someone or whenever I despaired that the torture of writing was not worth the effort. David also valiantly read the penultimate draft and offered timely feedback when he had other more pressing concerns. For twenty-five years David and I have been sharing our work with one another; he's a famously smart reader and an even better friend.

I would not have written this book—or even gotten to the halfway point—without the almost weekly prodding, counseling, editing, productive criticisms, and timely encouragement of Michael Vorenberg. Every section of this book (except for this one) benefitted from his insight and wisdom. In return, I forgive him for not visiting the banya when he was in Russia.

To all my fellow bathers, real and metaphorical, I thank you and hope you travel onward with a light steam.

There is no apt metaphor for family. To my parents, brothers, and extended family—thank you for your patience and support and for resisting the temptation to ask me how the writing was going. To Zachary and Nadia—now that the book is done, I look forward to having more time to listen to the stories you want to tell and more time for your baths. To Amy—everything.

Note on Translation

IN THE MAIN body of the book, for clarity and readability, I follow conventional English-language renderings of Russian names, words, and places. For instance, I use "Dostoevsky," not "Dostoevskii," "banya" and "banyas," not "bania" and "bani," "Moscow" and "St. Petersrburg," not "Moskva" and "Sankt Peterburg." In the notes, I've used the Library of Congress system for transliterating Russian words. Unless otherwise noted, the translations are my own.

Notes

ABBREVIATIONS

ARAN   Arkhiv Rossiiskoi Akademii Nauk, The Archive of the Russian
Academy of Sciences

GARF   Gosudarstvennyi Arkhiv Rossiiskoi Federatsii, The State Archive
of the Russian Federation

PSZ   Polnoe Sobranie Zakonov Rossiiskoi Imperii, The Complete
Collecition of Laws of the Russian Empire

RGAKFD   Rossiiskii Gosudarstvennyi Arkhiv Kinofotodokumentov, The
Russian State Film and Photograph Archive.

RGASPI   Rossiiskii Gosudarstvennyi Arkhiv Sotsial'no-Politichsekoi
Istorii, The Russian State Archive of Socio-Political History

RGIA   Rossiiskii Gosudarstvennyi Istoricheskii Arkhiv, The Russian
State Historical Archive

TsGAKFFD SPb   Tsentral'nyi Gosudarstvennyi Arkhiv Kinofotofonodokumentov
Sankt-Peterburga, Central State Archive of Documentary Films,
Photographs, and Sound Recordings of St. Peterburg

ZhKKh   Zhurnal Kommunal'noe Khoziastvo, The Journal of Municipal
Services.

INTRODUCTION

1. For the banya in the arctic, Helen A. Shenitz, "The Vestiges of Old Russia in Alaska,"
The Russian Review 14, no. 1 (Jan. 1955), 57; for the banya in Antarctica, Charles
Swithinbank, "A Year with the Russians in Antarctica," *Geographical Journal* 132, no.
4 (December 1966), 469; for a makeshift banya on a Soviet submarine, V. Dorin,
"Na 'Otlichno'," *Pravda*, December 13, 1936, p. 4; for whaling ships, Bathsheba
Demuth, *The Floating Coast: An Environmental History of the Bering Strait*
(New York: Norton, 2019), 282.

2. The scholarly literature on bathing and hygiene is vast. For concerns with purity, see Mary Douglas, *Purity and Danger* (London: Routledge and Keegan Paul, 1966); on the Roman baths, Garrett G. Fagan, *Bathing in Public in the Roman World* (Ann Arbor: University of Michigan Press, 1999). For the bathhouses of Anatolia, see Nina Ergin, ed., *Bathing Culture of Anatolian Civilizations: Architecture, History, and Imagination* (Leuven: Peeters, 2011). For a comparison of various steam baths, see Mikkel Aaland, *Sweat: the Illustrated History and Description of the Finnish Sauna, Russian Bania, Islamic Hammam, Japanese Mushi-buro, Mexican Temescal, and American Indian & Eskimo Sweat Lodge* (Santa Barbara, CA: Capra Press, 1978).

3. António Nunes Ribeiro Sanches, *O parnykh Rossiiskikh baniakh, poeliku spospeshestvuiut one ukrepleniiu, sokhraneniiu i vozstanovleniiu zdraviia* (St. Petersburg: Pri imperatorskom sukhoputnom shliakhetnom kadetskom korpus, 1779).

4. Vladimir Il'ich Lenin, *Collected Works* (Moscow: Progress Publishers, 1956), 228. Report of the All-Russia Central Executive Committee and the Council of Peoples Commissars to the Seventh All-Russia Congress of Soviets, December 5, 1919.

5. V. V. Rozanov, *Literaturnye ocherki* (1902), 224–226.

6. A. I. Zabelin, *O kupan'iakh, vannakh, i baniakh kak sredstvakh sokhraniia zdorov'ia* (1856), 62. Cited in I. A. Bogdanov, *Tri veka Peterburgskoi bani* (St. Petersburg: Iskusstvo-SPb, 2000).

7. R. Oldenburg, *The Great Good Place: Cafés, Coffee Shops, Bookstores, Bars, Hair Salons, and Other Hangouts at the Heart of a Community* (New York: Marlowe, 1997), 20–33.

8. Jeff Weintraub and Krishan Kumar, eds., *Public and Private in Thought and Practice: Perspectives on a Grand Dichotomy* (Chicago: University of Chicago Press, 1997); For more on Russian and Soviet conceptions of place and space, see Svetlana Boym, *Common Places: Mythologies of Everyday Life in Russia* (Cambridge, MA: Harvard University Press, 1994); Jürgen Habermas, *The Structural Transformation of the Public Sphere: an Inquiry into a Category of Bourgeois Society* (Cambridge, MA: The MIT Press, 1989). Lewis H. Siegelbaum, ed., *Borders of Socialism: Private Spheres of Soviet Russia* (New York: Palgrave Macmillan, 2006); David Crowley and Susan Emily Reid, *Socialist Spaces: Sites of Everyday Life in the Eastern Bloc* (Oxford: Berg, 2002).

9. Dipesh Chakrabarty, *Provincializing Europe: Postcolonial Though and Historical Difference* (Princeton, NJ: Princeton University Press, 2000), chapter 7, "*Adda*: A History of Sociality." In ways similar to what Chakrabarty has argued about the *adda* in the city of Calcutta, the banya helps reveal how Russians attempted to, in Marshall Berman's words, "get a grip on the modern world and make themselves feel at home in it." Marshall Berman, *All That Is Solid Melts Into Air: The Experience of Modernity* (New York: Simon and Schuster, 1982).

10. See, for instance, Anatolii Zakharovich Rubinov, *Sanduny: kniga o Moskovskikh baniakh* (Moscow: Moskovskii rabochii, 1990); *Istoriia bani* (Moscow: Novoe literaturnoe obozrenie, 2006); S. M. Orlova, *Vse o baniakh* (Moscow: BAO Press, 1998); Bogdanov, *Tri veka Peterburgskoi bani*; A. Galitskii, *Shchedryi zhar: ocherki o Russkoi bane i ee blizkikh i dal'nykh rodichakh* (Moscow: Fizkul'tura i sport, 1974); Aleksey Nikolayevich Tolstoy, Anton Pavlovich Chekhov, and Ivan Alekseevich Bunin, *Russkaia eroticheskaia proza* (Moscow: Al'ta-print, 2004); V. N. Riabov, *Kak ustroit' sel'skuiu baniu* (Moscow: Medgiz, 1954).

11. For example, Steven Lee Myers, "Sunday at the Banya," *Departures*, October, 2007: 274–282.; Christi Phillips, "A Russian Thrashing," *Globe and Mail*, June 2, 2002; Bryon MacWilliams, *With Light Steam: A Personal Journey Through the Russian Baths* (DeKalb: Northern Illinois University Press, 2014).

12. For the most egregious example, see, Daniel Rancour-Laferriere, *The Slave Soul of Russia: Moral Masochism and the Cult of Suffering* (New York: New York University Press, 1995).

13. W. F. Ryan, *The Bathhouse at Midnight: an Historical Survey of Magic and Divination in Russia* (University Park: Pennsylvania State University Press, 1999); A. G. Cross, "The Russian Banya in the Descriptions of Foreign Travellers and in the Depictions of Foreign and Russian Artists," *Oxford Slavonic Papers* XXIV, 34–59. (1991). Dan Healey, *Homosexual Desire in Revolutionary Russia: the Regulation of Sexual and Gender Dissent* (Chicago: University of Chicago Press, 2001). Nancy Condee, "The Second Fantasy Mother, or All Baths Are Women's Baths," in *Russia, Women, Culture*, ed. Helena Goscilo and Beth Holmgren, 3–30 (Bloomington: Indiana University Press, 1994). Olga Petri, "At the Bathhouse: Municipal Reform and the Bathing Commons in Late Imperial St. Petersburg," *Journal of Historical Geography* 51, Supplement C (2016), 40–51; V. A. Lipinskaia, *Bania i pech' v russkoi narodnoi traditsii*, (Moscow: Intrada, 2004).

14. V. A. Giliarovskii, *Moskva i Moskvichi* (Moscow: Moskovskii rabochii, 1968), 228.

15. The universality of the importance of the clean/unclean binary makes the banya part of a broader, global history of bathing as well. See Cynthia Kosso and Anne Scott, eds., *The Nature and Function of Water, Baths, Bathing, and Hygiene from Antiquity Through the Renaissance* (Leiden: Brill, 2009). My emphasis, though, is on the banya as a peculiarly Russian institution, not its relationship to other, similar, institutions elsewhere.

CHAPTER I

1. Robert B. Strassler, *The Landmark Herodotus: The Histories* (New York: Random House, 2009), 311.

2. François Hartog, *The Mirror of Herodotus: The Representation of the Other in the Writing of History* (Berkeley: University of California Press, 1988); S. I.

Rudenko, *Frozen Tombs of Siberia; the Pazyryk Burials of Iron Age Horsemen* (Berkeley: University of California Press, 1970), 284–285.

3. Anatolii Petrovich Novosel'tsev, *Drevnerusskoe gosudarstvo i ego mezhdunarodnoe znachenie* (Moscow: Nauka, 1965), 388–389. He quotes Ibn Rusta's encyclopedia of geographic knowledge titled "Kitab Al Alak An Nafisa."

4. F. Yegül, *Bathing in the Roman World* (Cambridge: Cambridge University Press, 2009).

5. Juha Pentikäinen, "Baths," in *Encyclopedia of Religion*, ed. Lindsay Jones, 800–803 (Detroit: Macmillan Reference USA, 2005).

6. E. D. Zilivinskaia, "Bani Zolotoi Ordy," in *Praktika i teoriia arkheologichsekikh issledovanii*, ed. A. S. Smirnov, 174–225 (In-t Arkheologii RAN 2001).

7. Nestor, Samuel H. Cross, and Olgerd P. Sherbowitz-Wetzor, *The Russian Primary Chronicle: Laurentian Text* (Cambridge, MA: Mediaeval Academy of America, 1953), 54.

8. Ibid., 53–54.

9. Richard Hellie, *The Economy and Material Culture of Russia, 1600–1725* (Chicago: University of Chicago Press, 1999), 399, 540.

10. V. I. Dal', *Tolkovyi slovar' v chetyrekh tomakh* (Moscow: Russkii iazyk, 1989).

11. Andrei Siniavskii, *Ivan-Durak: ocherk Russkoi narodnoi very* (Moscow: Agraf, 2001), 61; A. D. Siniavskii, J. Turnbull, and N. Formozov, *Ivan the Fool: Russian Folk Belief, A Cultural History* (Moscow: Glas, 2007), 114.

12. Ryan, *The Bathhouse at Midnight*, 50. I. U. Lotman and B. A. Uspenskii, *The Semiotics of Russian Culture* (Ann Arbor: Dept. of Slavic Languages and Literatures, University of Michigan, 1984).

13. Ryan, *The Bathhouse at Midnight*, 51.

14. Nestor et al., *The Russian Primary Chronicle*, 151. Modified translation using "banya" for "bathhouse" based on D. S. Likhachev's translation of the chronicle from Old East Slavonic into Russian: D. S. Likhachev, *Povest' vremennykh let* (St. Petersburg: Nauka, 2007).

15. For a critique of the "dual faith" (*dvoeverie*) interpretation of early Russian religion, see Stella Rock, *Popular Religion in Russia: "Double Belief" and the Making of an Academic Myth* (London: Taylor & Francis, 2007).

16. Nestor et al., *The Russian Primary Chronicle*, 79–80.

17. Ibid., 170.

18. Charles J. Halperin, *Russia and the Golden Horde: The Mongol Impact on Medieval Russian History* (Bloomington: Indiana University Press, 1987), 104–119.

19. Zilivinskaia, "Bani Zolotoi Ordy," 174–225.

20. M. B. Bulgakov, *Organizatsiia melkikh otkupov v Rossii pervoi poloviny XVII stoletiia* (Tiumeni: Tiumenskii gos. universitet, 1997), 49–53.

21. PSZ vol. 3, pp. 116–117, law no. 1420.

22. Ryan, *The Bathhouse at Midnight*, 52.

23. Grigorii Kotoshikhin, *O Rossii v tsarstvovanie Alekseia Mikhailovicha*, Izd. 4. ed. (The Hague: Paris, Mouton, 1969); Ryan, *The Bathhouse at Midnight*, 176.

24. *The "Domostroi": Rules for Russian Households in the Time of Ivan the Terrible*, ed. Carolyn Pouncy, 225–227 (Ithaca, NY: Cornell University Press, 1994).

25. Ibid., 232, 36.

26. Kotoshikhin, *O Rossii v tsarstvovanie Alekseia Mikhailovicha*.

27. Linda J. Ivanits, *Russian Folk Belief* (Armonk, NY: M. E. Sharpe, 1989), 58–60; N. A. Krinichnaia, *Synove bani: mifologicheskie rasskazy i poveriia o dukhe-"khoziaine" bani* (Petrozavodsk: Izd-vo Petrozavodskogo universiteta, 1995).

28. Ryan, *The Bathhouse at Midnight*, 230; N. I. Tolstoi and T. A. Agapkina, *Slavianskie drevnosti: etnologicheskii slovar' v piati tomakh* (Moscow: Mezhdunarodnye otnosheniia, 1995), 138–140.

29. Ryan, *The Bathhouse at Midnight*, 37, 51; Ivanits, *Russian Folk Belief*, 59–60. While written evidence for much of this folklore was first recorded only in the nineteenth century, Ryan concluded that these ideas were prevalent in Muscovy as well.

30. *The "Domostroi,"* 119.

31. Ryan, *The Bathhouse at Midnight*, 237. This comports with Chester S. L. Dunning, *Russia's First Civil War: The Time of Troubles and the Founding of the Romanov Dynasty* (University Park: Pennsylvania State University Press, 2010), 237. Adam Olearius and Samuel H. Baron, *The Travels of Olearius in Seventeenth-Century Russia* (Redwood City, CA: Stanford University Press, 1967), 168–169, 61. Olearius mentions Dmitrii's failure to go to the bath as a sign of his foreignness. Karamzin also notes Dmitrii's inability to withstand the banya as a sign of his foreignness. See Karamzin, *Istoriia gosudarstva Rossiiskogo v dvenadstati tomakh*, tom 11, glava 4.

32. Ryan, *The Bathhouse at Midnight*, 50–51, 99–100, 71, 99, 230.

33. Ibid., 52.

34. Georges Birrell Jean Vigarello, *Concepts of Cleanliness: Changing Attitudes in France Since the Middle Ages* (Cambridge: Cambridge University Press, 1988).

35. Eve Levin, *Sex and Society in the World of the Orthodox Slavs, 900–1700* (Ithaca, NY: Cornell University Press, 1989), 40.

36. Ryan, *The Bathhouse at Midnight*, 53.

37. Jack Edward. Kollmann, "The Moscow Stoglav (Hundred Chapters) Church Council of 1551" (Ph.D. diss., University of Michigan, 1978), 559.

38. Levin, *Sex and Society in the World of the Orthodox Slavs, 900–1700*, 115–116.

39. Ibid., 270.

40. Ibid., 169, 208.

41. Ibid., 252, 171.

42. D. H. Kaiser and G. Marker, *Reinterpreting Russian History: Readings, 860–1860's* (New York: Oxford University Press, 1994), 195–196.

43. Nancy Shields Kollmann, *Crime and Punishment in Early Modern Russia* (Cambridge: Cambridge University Press, 2012), 90; Hellie, *The Economy and Material Culture of Russia, 1600–1725*, 399.

44. Vigarello, *Concepts of Cleanliness*, 14.

45. Katherine Ashenburg, *The Dirt on Clean: An Unsanitized History* (New York: North Point Press, 2007), 101, 65.

46. Vigarello, *Concepts of Cleanliness*. Changing of linens was not altogether new. See Carole Rawcliffe, *Urban Bodies: Communal Health in Late Medieval English Towns and Cities* (Woodbridge: The Boydell Press, 2013), 51 and 103.

47. Vigarello, *Concepts of Cleanliness*, 60.

48. Giles Fletcher, Jerome Horsey, and Edward Augustus Bond, *Russia at the Close of the Sixteenth Century: Comprising the Treatise "Of the Russe Common Wealth" by Giles Fletcher, and The travels of Sir Jerome Horsey, Knt* (London: Printed for the Hakluyt Society, 1856), 147. This is a reprint of the earlier treatise. I've slightly modified the prose for clarity.

49. Olearius and Baron, *The Travels of Olearius in Seventeenth-Century Russia*, 142–143.

50. Ibid., 161.

51. Ibid.

52. Ibid., 163.

53. Cross, "The Russian Banya."

54. Earl of Carlisle, Guy Faithorne William Miege, and engraver, *A Relation of Three Embassies from His Sacred Majestie Charles II to the Great Duke of Muscovie, the King of Sweden, and the King of Denmark* (London: Printed for John Starkey, 1669), 53–54.

55. Jacques Margeret, *The Russian Empire and Grand Duchy of Muscovy: A 17th Century French Account*, trans. Chester S. I. Dunning (Pittsbugh: University of Pittsburgh Press, 1983), 34.

56. Jodocus Crull, *The Antient and Present State of Muscovy*, 2 vols. (London: Printed for A. Roper and A. Bosvile, 1698), 151–152.

57. Ibid.

58. Friedrich Christian Weber, *The Present State of Russia*, (New York: Da Capo Press, 1968), 31–32.

59. *Iaroslavskie gubernskie vedomosti*, 1861, no. 35.

60. *The Muscovite Law Code (Ulozhenie) of 1649*, ed. Richard Hellie (Irvine, CA: C. Schlacks Jr., 1988).

61. Bulgakov, *Organizatsiia melkikh otkupov v Rossii pervoi poloviny XVII stoletiia*, 51–53.

62. Ibid.

63. *The Muscovite Law Code (Ulozhenie) of 1649*, 145–146.

64. Hellie, *The Economy and Material Culture*, 541.

65. P. Miliukov, *Gosudarstvennoe khoziastvo Rossii vo pervoi chetverti XVII stoletii i reforma Petra Velikago* (St. Petersburg: tipografiia M.M. Stasiulevicha, 1905). One source from a much later period—the 1770s—suggested that "baths and licensed houses" accounted for 1.6 percent of the tsar's total revenues. Joseph Marshall, *Travels through Germany, Russia, and Poland in the Years 1769 and 1770* (New York: Arno Press, 1971), 124.

66. PSZ vol. 2, pp. 561–562, law no. 1044.

67. Bulgakov, *Organizatsiia melkikh otkupov v Rossii pervoi poloviny XVII stoletiia*, 49–53.

68. PSZ vol. 2, pp. 329–330, law no. 876; PSZ vol. 3, pp. 116–117, law no. 1420.

69. Hellie, *The Economy and Material Culture of Russia, 1600–1725*, 541.

70. PSZ vol. 4, pp. 231–232, law no. 1955.

71. PSZ vol. 4, pp. 230–231; law no. 1954.

72. PSZ vol. 4, pp. 230–231, law no. 1954

73. Weber, *The Present State of Russia*, 32.

74. PSZ vol. 4, pp. 230–232, law no. 1954 and law 1955.

75. PSZ vol. 10, pp. 681–683, law no. 7718.

76. PSZ vol 5, p. 718, law no. 3395.

77. PSZ vol. 6, p. 352, laws no. 3730 and no. 3728, no. 4047; vol. 7, p. 652, law no. 4888.

78. Bulgakov, *Organizatsiia melkikh otkupov v Rossii pervoi poloviny XVII stoletiia*, 50. PSZ vol. 4, p. 309, law no. 2058, p. 310 law no. 2060; PSZ vol. 7, p. 385, law no. 4616; PSZ vol. 7, p. 733, law no. 5006.

79. Andrei Ivanovich Bogdanov, *Istoricheskoe, geograficheskoe i topograficheskoe opisanie Sanktpeterburga, ot nachala zavedeniia ego, s 1703 po 1751 god*, (St. Petersburg, 1779), 156.

80. Foy de Cutshall J. A. Hughes Lindsey La Neuville, *A Curious and New Account of Muscovy in the Year 1689* (London: University of London, School of Slavonic and East European Studies, 1994), 57.

CHAPTER 2

1. Vigarello, *Concepts of Cleanliness*.

2. Larry Wolff, *Inventing Eastern Europe: The Map of Civilization on the Mind of the Enlightenment* (Redwood City, CA: Stanford University Press, 1994).

3. John T. Alexander, *Catherine the Great: Life and Legend* (New York: Oxford University Press, 1989); Isabel de Madariaga, *Catherine the Great* (New Haven, CT: Yale University Press, 1991).

4. John T. Alexander, "Catherine the Great and Public Health," *Journal of the History of Medicine and Allied Sciences* XXXVI, no. 2 (1981), 185–204.

5. It was published in French under the title: *Traité sur les bains de vapeur Russie considérés tant pour la conservation de la santé, comme pour la guérison de plusieurs maladie*. See D. Willemse, *António Nunes Ribeiro Sanches: Élève de Boerhaave—et Son Importance Pour la Russie* (Leiden: E. J.Brill, 1966).

6. See H. Woolf, *The Transits of Venus: A Study of Eighteenth-Century Science* (Princeton, NJ: Princeton University Press, 1959), 115–126.

7. Marcus C Levitt, "An Antidote to Nervous Juice: Catherine the Great's Debate with Chappe d'Auteroche over Russian Culture," *Eighteenth-Century Studies* 32, no. 1 (1998), 49–63.

8. Ibid., 50.

9. Wolff, *Inventing Eastern Europe*, 345.

10. Abbè Chappe d'Auteroche, *A Journey Into Siberia*. (New York: Arno Press, 1970), 51.

11. Ibid., 54.
12. Ibid.
13. Ibid., 55.
14. Ibid., 57.
15. Empress of Russia Catherine II, *The Antidote; Or an Enquiry into the Merits of a Book, Entitled A journey into Siberia, Made in MDCCLXI ... and published by the Abbe Chappe d'Auteroche, . . . By a Lover of Truth*. (London: S. Leacroft, 1772), 45–50.
16. Ibid.
17. PSZ vol. 11, p. 984, law no. 8842; PSZ vol 15, 499–500, law no. 11094.
18. PSZ vol. 21, 468, law no. 15379, point 71.
19. See Simon Sebag Montefiore, *Prince of Princes: The Life of Potemkin* (New York: Thomas Dunne Books, 2001), 102. Montefiore cites RGADA (Rossisskii gosudarstvennyi arkhiv drevnikh aktov) documents to support the claim that Catherine had frequent meetings (sometimes with men) in the banya. See also "Banya Russkikh tsarei," *Architectural Digest* (in Russian) no. 7 July 2005, pp. 127–133.
20. On this trend, see Virginia Smith, *Clean: A History of Personal Hygiene and Purity* (New York: Oxford University Press, 2007), 219–223. Kathleen Brown, *Foul Bodies: Cleanliness in Early America* (New Haven, CT: Yale University Press, 2009), 133–135.
21. Information on Sanches's biography is taken from: Palmira Fontes Da Costa and António Jesus, "António Ribeiro Sanches and the Circulation of Medical Knowledge in Eighteenth-Century Europe," *Archives Internationale D'Histoire des Sciences* 56, no. 156–157 (2006), 185–197; Jose Luis Doria, "António Ribeiro Sanches: Portuguese doctor in 18th century Europe," *Vesalius*, VII, 1, 27–35, 2001; and C. R. Boxer, "An Enlightened Portuguese," *History Today* (April 1970), 270–277.
22. Peter H. Niebyl, "Galen, Van Helmon, and Blood-Letting," in *Science, Medicine and Society in the Renaissance: Essays to honor Walter Pagel*, ed. Allen G. Debus, 13–23 (New York: Science History Publications, 1972); Thomas G. Benedek, "The Influence of Ulrich Von Hutten's Medical Descriptions and Metaphorical Use of Medicine," *Bulletin of the History of Medicine* 66, no. 3 (Fall 1992), 355–375..
23. Empress of Russia Catherine II, *Rossiiskaia istoriia: zapiski velikoi imperatritsy* (Moscow: EKSMO, 2008), 22; Catherine the Great, *The Memoirs of Catherine the Great* (New York: Random House, 2007), 11.
24. Willemse, *António Nunes Ribeiro Sanches*.
25. Boxer, "An Enlightened Portuguese."
26. PSZ vol. 17, law no. 12741, pp 991–992.
27. PSZ vol. 17, law no. 12785. The law beginning on page 1050 entitled "Short report on the choices from the best authorities with some physical notes on the raising of children from birth to their youth." The banya is addressed on pages 1061–1062.

28. Willemse, *António Nunes Ribeiro Sanches*, 22–24.

29. See the preface of the Russian edition Ribeiro Sanches, *O parnykh Rossiiskikh baniakh*.

30. This and all subsequent quotations from the Russian edition: ibid., IX-XI.

31. Ibid., 16–18.

32. Ibid., 25–40.

33. Ibid., 11–15, 28–31.

34. Ibid., 11–15.

35. Ibid., 35–36, 46.

36. Ibid.

37. Ibid., 11–15.

38. Ibid.

39. Ibid., XX.

40. Ibid., 45–50.

41. Ibid.

42. Ibid.

43. Ibid.

44. Ibid.

45. Ibid.

CHAPTER 3

1. On these points see V. V. Godlevskii, *Materialy dlia ucheniia Russkoi bane* (St. Petersburg, 1883); P. I. Strakhov, "O Russkikh prostonarodnykh parnykh baniakh," *Moskovskii vrachebnii zhurnal* (1856), 9–63.

2. A. A. Pliushar, *Entsiklopedicheskii leksikon* (St. Petersburg, 1839), 250–258. On the importance of Pliushar's encyclopedia, see Miranda Beaven, "Aleksandr Smirdin and Publishing in St. Petersburg, 1830–1840," *Canadian Slavonic Papers / Revue Canadienne des Slavistes* 27, no. 1 (1985), 15–30.

3. Pliushar, *Entsiklopedicheskii leksikon*, 250–254.

4. Ibid., 251–252.

5. Ibid., 254–256. Much of the logic of the encyclopedia entries was repeated—sometimes verbatim—in *Drug zdraviia* in 1835. See Professor Spaskii, "Kratkii ocherk vrachebnykh otnoshenii bani," *Drug zdraviia*, 1835, no. 44, 384–389.

6. Both the "indispensable" quotation and the "weak and effeminate age" are from William Tooke, *View of the Russian Empire, during the Reign of Catherine the Second and to the Close of the Eighteenth Century, in three volumes* (London, 1800), vol. II, 7–12.

7. For the split more generally, see Gary Marker, "The Westernization of the Elite, 1725–1800," in Abbott Gleason, ed., *A Companion to Russian History*, 180–195 (Chichester: Wiley-Blackwell, 2009), 180–195.

8. John Atkinson, *A Picturesque Representation of the Manners, Customs, and Amusements of the Russians* (London: Printed by W. Bulmer and Co., 1803); Rayford

Ramble, *Travelling Opinions and Sketches in Russia and Poland* (London: Macrone, 1836); Leitch Ritchie, *A Journey to St. Petersburg and Moscow through Courland and Livonia* (London: Longman, Rees, Orme, Brown, Green, and Longman, 1836).

9. Marquis de Custine, *Russia. Abridged from the French* (London, 1854), 135.

10. *Drug zdraviia*, 1835, no. 4, p. 26.

11. *Drug zdraviia*, 1835, no. 9, p. 66.

12. *Drug zdraviia*, 1836, no. 11, p. 83.

13. *Drug zdraviia*, 1838, no. 3, pp. 18–19.

14. *Drug zdraviia*, 1841, no. 8, pp. 57–60.

15. *Drug zdraviia* 1866, no. 13, p. 103.

16. Strakhov, "O Russkikh prostonarodnykh parnykh baniakh."

17. M. Von Tietz, *St. Petersburgh, Constantinople, and Napoli di Romania in 1833 and 1834* (London, 1836), 62–63; and J. G. Kohl, *St. Petersburg, Moscow, Kharkoff* (London, 1842), 207–208.

18. Charles Lambert, *Traitè sur l'hygiène et la mèdecine des nains russes et orientaux*, 2. Èd. (Paris, 1842).

19. "Hygiène en Russie," in *Journal des Connaissances Medico Chirurgicales*, 1849, issues 1–6, 56–60.

20. Tooke, *View of the Russian Empire*; Cross, "The Russian Banya."

21. John H. Appleby, "Lyall, Robert (1789–1831)," *Oxford Dictionary of National Biography* (New York: Oxford University Press, 2004); online edition, May 2006 http://www.oxforddnb.com/view/article/17236.

22. Robert Lyall, *The Character of the Russians and a Detailed History of Moscow* (London, 1823), 112–115.

23. George William Lefevre, *The Life of a Travelling Physician* (London, 1843).

24. Matthias Roth, *The Russian Bath: Published With a View to Recommend its Introduction into England for Hygienic as Well as Curative Purposes*, 2 ed. (London, 1855); Judith Brody, "Roth, Mathias (1818–1891)," *Oxford Dictionary of National Biography*, online edition, Oxford University Press, September 2004, http://www.oxforddnb.com/view/article/56050.

25. Lambert, *Traitè sur l'hygiène et la mèdecine des bains russes et orientaux*; Bogdanov, *Tri veka Peterburgskoi bani* .

26. Marilyn Thornton Williams, *Washing "The Great Unwashed": Public Baths in Urban America, 1840–1920* (Columbus: Ohio State University Press, 1991), 1–21.

27. Mark Twain, "The Dreadful Russian Bath," *Alta California*, April 5, 1867.

28. See, for instance, Lawrence Wright, *Clean and Decent: the Fascinating History of the Bathroom & the Water Closet* (New York: Viking Press, 1960); David Glassberg, "The Design of Reform: the Public Bath Movement in America," *American Studies* 20, no. 2 (1979), 5–21; Brian K. Ladd, "Public Baths and Civic Improvement in Nineteenth-Century Cities," *Journal of Urban History* 14, no. 3 (1988), 372–393.

29. S. Iu. Fialkovskii, "Materialy k voprosu o vliianii bani na zdorovyi i bol'noi glas' cheloveka," *Vrach*, no. 9 (1881), 1. S. Gruzdev and F. I. Vetoshnikov gave slightly different timelines, suggesting that some Russian work on the topic began in the 1840s. But even they admitted that foreigners had led the way. Sergei Gruzdev, "Mineral'nyi obmen pri Russkoi bane" (Imperatorskaia Voenno-Meditsinskaia Akademiia, 1890); F. I. Vetoshnikov, "K voprosu o vliianii Russkoi bani na usvoenie zhirov pishchi v zdorovykh liudei" (Imperatorskaia Voenno-Meditsinskaia Akademiia, 1894).

30. Godlevskii, *Materialy dlia ucheniia Russkoi bane.*

31. Aleksandr Pavlovich Bashutskii, *Panorama Sanktpeterburga* (St. Petersburg: Tip. vdovy Pliushara, 1834), 209.

32. Rubinov, *Sanduny*; I. I. Gol'din, *Sanduny: i bani i muzei Moskvy* (Moscow: Nekommercheskoe partnerstvo ob"edinenie KSOK, 2012). M. I. Afanasiev and Eulenburg Albert, *Real'naia entsiklopediia meditsinskikh nauk*, vol. I (St. Petersburg, 1891).

33. V. A. Lipinskaia, *Bania i pech' v Russkoi narodnoi traditsii* (Moscow: Intrada, 2004), 116–117.

34. PSZ vol. 18, p. 545, law no. 17147, 1843 and vol. 21, pp. 140-141, law no. 20244.

35. Vissarion Znamenskii, *O Russkikh baniakh v gigienicheskom otnoshenii* (St. Petersburg, 1861).

36. PSZ vol. 21, pp. 140-141, law no. 20244.

37. Laws in 1848 and as late as 1867, for instance, dealt with how to create financial incentives for building banyas and with fire prevention—not with health per se. See PSZ vol. 23, p. 501, law no. 22475 and vol. 42, pp. 434-437, law no. 44524.

38. I. I. Verevkin, " O Russkikh baniiakh," *Arkhiv' sudebnoi meditsiny* 4, section III, part II (1865); M. P. Viatkin and A. Z. Vakser, *Ocherki istorii Leningrada*, vol. 1 (Moscow: Izd-vo Akademii nauk SSSR, 1955), 616.

39. Ivan Vasil'evich Eremeev, *Gorod S.-Peterburg s tochki zrieniia meditsinskoi politsii* (St. Petersburg, 1897), 236.

40. Ibid.

41. Ibid., 437.

42. Ibid.

43. Petri, "At the Bathhouse.". For a present-day comparison, there were 360 Starbucks in New York City in 2017. The city had a population of approximately 8.5 million, meaning there was one Starbucks for every 23,600 people.

44. For the enchantment with rural Russia in particular, see Christopher David Ely, *This Meager Nature: Landscape and National Identity in Imperial Russia* (DeKalb: Northern Illinois University Press, 2002).

45. Sally Sheard, "Profit is a Dirty Word: The Development of Public Baths and Wash-houses in Britain 1847–1915," *Social History of Medicine* 13, no. 1 (2000), 63–86.

46. Stephen M. Norris, *A War of Images: Russian Popular Prints, Wartime Culture, and National Identity, 1812–1945* (DeKalb: Northern Illinois University Press, 2006). The image of Napoleon was not reproduced or analyzed in Norris's book but the interpretation is certainly in keeping with Norris's broader argument. Note: the banya also appears in a second *lubok* at this time. See Gol'din, *Sanduny: i bani i muzei Moskvy.*

47. A. S. Pushkin, *Ruslan i Liudmila* (Moscow: Direct Media, 2016), Pesn' chetvertaia.

48. Rubinov, *Istoriia bani*, 107.

49. See, for instance, I. A. Bich, *Ocherk istorii Russkoi bani i ee fiziologicheskoe i terapevticheskoe znachenie* (Grodna: Tipografiia gibernskago pravleniia, 1893).

50. Fyodor Dostoevsky, *Zapiski iz mertvogo doma* (Moscow: Khudozh. lit.-ra, 1965), chapter IX; Gary Rosenshield, "Isai Fomich Bumshtein: The Representation of the Jew in Dostoevsky's Major Fiction," *The Russian Review* 43, no. 3 (1984), 261–276.

51. Dostoevsky, *Zapiski iz mertvogo doma.*

52. *Prestuplenie i nakazanie.* (Chicago: Russian Language Specialties, 1965); this interpretation was first put forward in 1891 by V. V. Rozanov, *Dostoevsky and the Legend of the Grand Inquisitor*, trans. Spencer E. Roberts, 60–61 (Ithaca, NY: Cornell University Press, 1972).

53. Dostoevsky, *Brothers Karamazov*, Book Three, parts I, II and VI.

54. Julian W. Connolly, *Dostoevsky's The Brothers Karamazov* (New York: Bloomsbury Academic, 2013), 50–51.

CHAPTER 4

1. Eremeev, *Gorod S.-Peterburg*, 236–364

2. Nancy Mandelker Frieden, *Russian Physicians in an Era of Reform and Revolution, 1856–1905* (Princeton, NJ: Princeton University Press, 1981).

3. See, for example, Jeff Wiltse, *Contested Waters: A Social History of Swimming Pools in America* (Chapel Hill: University of North Carolina Press, 2007). In Russia, the popular bathing habits in both their urban and rural form more closely resembled the ideal bathing environment put forth by doctors.

4. Strakhov, "O Russkikh prostonarodnykh"; Vissarion Znamenskii, *O Russkikh baniakh v gigienicheskom otnoshenii* (St. Petersburg, 1861); Godlevskii, *Materialy dlia ucheniia Russkoi bane.* On the broader discourse at the time on Rus', see F. Hillis, *Children of Rus': Right-Bank Ukraine and the Invention of a Russian Nation* (Ithaca, NY: Cornell University Press, 2013).

5. They began to cite, for instance, the Slavophile historian Ivan Zabelin on the life of the tsars. Ivan Zabelin, *Domashnii byt Russkikh tsarei v XVI i XVII stoletiiakh*, 3 vols. (Moscow: Iazyki Russkoi kul'tury, 2000).

6. Zabelin, *O kupan'iakh, vannakh, i baniakh.* Cited in Bogdanov, *Tri veka Peterburgskoi*, 3.

7. I. I. Illiustrov, *Sbornik Rossiiskikh poslovits i pogovorok* (Kiev: S.V. Kul'zhenko, 1904).

8. "Chast' neoffitsial'naia: Peterburgskiia bani," *Vedomosti Sanktpeterburgskoi gorodskoi militsii*, May 27, 1871, pp. 1-2.

9. I. A. Bich, *Ocherk istorii Russkoi bani i ee fiziologicheskoe i terapevticheskoe znachenie* (1893), 12–13.

10. Godlevskii, *Materialy dlia ucheniia Russkoi bane*; V. I. Zuev, *Bani i vanny* (1898).

11. Nancy Tomes, "The Private Side of Public Health: Sanitary Science, Domestic Hygiene, and the Germ Theory, 1870–1900," *Bulletin of the History of Medicine* 64, no. 4 (Winter, 1990), 509–539.

12. On physicians in the era, see Nancy M. Frieden, *Russian Physicians in an Era of Reform and Revolution, 1856–1905* (Princeton, NJ: Princeton University Press, 1981); on the banya in particular see, for instance, Sergei Gruzdev, "Mineral'nyi obmen pri Russkoi bane" (Imperatorskaia Voenno-Meditsinskaia Akademiia, 1890); Aleksandr Fadeev, "Materialy k ucheniiu o Russkoi bane" (Imperatorskaia Voenno-Meditsinkaia Akademiia, 1890); F. I. Vetoshnikov, "K voprosu o vliianii Russkoi bani na usvoenie zhirov pishchi v zdorovykh liudei" (Imperatorskaia Voenno-Meditsinskaia Akademiia, 1894).

13. See, for example, Znamenskii, *O Russkikh baniakh v gigienicheskom otnoshenii*; S. Iu. Fialkovskii, "Materialy k voprosu o vliianii bani na zdorovyi i bol'noi glas' cheloveka," *Vrach*, no. 9 (1881), 137–143; Godlevskii, *Materialy dlia ucheniia Russkoi bane*; A. F. Mendes, *Bani v obshchedostupnom izlozhenii*, (St. Petersburg: S. Peterburgskaia elektropechtnia, 1902), 1-32; and "Vestnik sudebnoi meditsiny i obshchestvennoi gigieny," in *Vestnik obshchestvennoi gigieny i prakticheskoi meditsiny*, 1915, vol. 51 part 1, 713–714.

14. See N. a. Maliavko-Vysotkaia, *Pol'za iv red krest'ianskoi bani* (Pskov, 1887) and V. I. Dolzhenkov, "K voprosu ob ustroistve sel'skikh obshchestvennykh ban'," in *Trudy sed'mogo s"ezda zemskikh vrachei i predstvitelei Kurskoi gubernii, 28 maia—4 iiunia 1899* (Kursk, 1900), 229–244.

15. L. L. Geidenreikh, *K ozdorovleniiu goroda Vil'ny* (1897); N. A. Goldenberg, *Bani dlia voisk i dlia narodnykh mass v gigienichestkom, sanitoarnom, lechebnom i ekonomicheskom otnoshenii* (St. Petersburg, 1898).

16. G. Liubarskii, *Teoreticheskoe obosnovanie postroiki podvozhnoi voiskovoi bani sistemy Prof. V. F. Ivanova* (Kiev, 1916).

17. V. V. Rudin, *Deistvie bani protiv zarazy i voobshche na zdarov'e* (Tula, 1899).

18. *Bania, ee pol'za i vliianie na organizm cheloveka*, (St. Petersburg, 1905); Mendes, "Bani v obshchedostupnom izlozhenii," 1-32; Zuev, *Bani i vanny*, 54.

19. Geidenreikh, *K ozdorovleniiu goroda Vil'ny*; Dolzhenkov, "K voprosu ob ustroistve sel'skikh obshchestvennykh ban'"; Goldenberg, *Bani dlia voisk i dlia narodnykh*.

20. Zuev, *Bani i vanny*, 46.

21. "Kommunal'noe khoziaistvo: dvukhnedel'nyi zhurnal Moskovskogo kommunal'nogo khoziaistva" (Moscow: Moskovskoe kommunal'noe khoziaistvo); I. I. Verevkin, " O Russkikh baniiakh," *Arkhiv' sudebnoi meditsiny* 4, section III, part II (1865), 25–31.

22. K. V. Markov, *Voiskovye bani i prachechnye* (1900), 5-7.

23. F. A. Brokgauz and I. A. Efron, *Entsiklopedicheskii slovar', tom III "Banki-Berger"* (St. Petersburg: Semenovskaia tipo litografiia, 1891), 17–22. Much of the logic of the entry is closely echoed in M. I. Afanasíev and Eulenburg Albert, *Real'naia entsiklopediia meditsinskikh nauk*, vol. I (St. Petersburg, 1891).

24. Brokgauz and Efron, *Entsiklopedicheskii slovar', tom III "Banki-Berger,"* 17–22.

25. All temperatures given in Reaumur in the Encyclopedia.

26. Brokgauz and Efron, *Entsiklopedicheskii slovar', tom III "Banki-Berger,"* 17–22.

27. Ibid.

28. V. N. Tenishev, V. M. Grusman, D. A. Baranov, A.V. Konovalov, and I. I. Shangina, *Russkie krest'iane—zhizn', byt, nravy: materialy "Etnograficheskogo biuro" Kniazia V.N. Tenisheva* (St. Petersburg: Rossiiskii Etnograficheskii Muzei, 2004).

29. Ibid., vol. 1, pp. 103, 51, 249; vol. 2, pp. 22, 396; vol. 3, pp. 44–45. (Archive of the Ethnographic Museum, f. 7, op. 1.)

30. P. A. Gratsionov, *O narodnykh baniakh* (excerpted from *Russkii meditsinksii vestnik*) (St. Petersburg: M. I. Akinfieva i I. V. Leont'eva, 1901), 1–8.

31. Dolzhenkov, "K voprosu ob ustroistve sel'skikh obshchestvennykh ban," 229–244.

32. Meditsinskii departament, "Vestnik obshchestvennoi gigieny, sudebnoi i prakticheskoi meditsiny," (St. Petersburg: Izdavaemyi med. departament, 1889). Note: article is in the journal in 1915.

33. V. V. Rudin, *Deistvie bani protiv' zarazy podvizhnaia disinfektsionnaia kamera bania* (Rybinsk, 1893), 3–5.

34. V. Portugalov, *Voprosy obshchestvennoi gigieny* (St. Petersburg: Izd. red. zhurnala "Dielo," 1873), 92-93.

35. N. A. Maliavko-Vysotskaia, *Pol'za i vred krest'ianksoi bani* (Pskov, 1887), 1-5.

36. Tenishev et al., *Russkie krest'iane—zhizn', byt, nravy*, vol. 1, pp. 103, 51, 249; vol. 2, pp. 22, 396; vol. 3, pp. 44–45. Tenishev cites: Archive of the Ethnographic Museum, f. 7, op. 1.

37. Ibid., vol. 3, 258.

38. Ibid., 273, 88; Archive of the Ethnographic Museum, f. 7 op. 1, d. 1784, ll. 14–22 and 53–68.

39. *Viestnik obshchestvennoi gigieny i prakticheskoi meditsini*, 1915, vol. 51 part 1, 713–714. Maliavko-Vysotskaia, *Pol'za i vred krest'ianksoi bani*.

40. Dolzhenkov, "K voprosu ob ustroistve sel'skikh obshchestvennykh ban," 229–244.

41. Rudin, *Deistvie bani protiv' zarazy podvizhnaia disinfektsionnaia kamera bania*, 3–5.

42. Dolzhenkov, "K voprosu ob ustroistve sel'skikh obshchestvennykh ban."

43. Portugalov, *Voprosy obshchestvennoi gigieny*, 92-93.

44. Assuming a population of St. Petersburg of 220,000 in 1800; 385,000 in 1821; and 485,000 in 1849. See *Ocherki po istorii Leningrada 1955–1967*, vol. 1 (1955) *Period feodalizma (1703–1861)*, 374; 616–617.

45. Eremeev, *Gorod S.-Peterburg s tochki zrieniia meditsinskoi politsii*, 506–517.

46. Ibid.
47. "Chast neoffitsial'naia: Peterburgskiia bani," pp. 1-2. RGIA f. 256, op. 3, d. 215 and 357.
48. *Gorod S.-Peterburg s tochki zrieniia meditsinskoi politsii.*
49. Liubimov, "Peterburgskiia bani," *Peterburgskii kommissioner* 1866, p. 4.
50. "Chast neoffitsial'naia: Peterburgskiia bani," pp. 1-2.
51. Ibid.
52. Eremeev, *Gorod S.-Peterburg s tochki zrieniia meditsinskoi politsii*; "Mal'tsevskiia bani," *Peterburgskii listok*, August 19, 1876; V. G. Isachenko, I. U. Artem'eva, and Prokhvatilova S. A., *Zodchie Sankt-Peterburga: XIX-nachalo XX veka* (St. Petersburg: Lenizdat, 1998), 503–508.
53. "Novyia Bani," *Peterburgskii listok*, December 21, 1880, p.2.
54. Ibid.
55. Petri, "At the Bathhouse," 40-51.
56. Zuev, *Bani i vanny*, 80–91; Verevkin, " O Russkikh baniiakh."
57. Zuev, *Bani i vanny*, 80–91.
58. RGIA f. 569, op. 11, d. 426 "Delo o zakrytii ban.'"
59. Petri, "At the Bathhouse: Municipal Reform and the Bathing Commons in Late Imperial St. Petersburg." RGIA f. 569, op. 11, d. 426.
60. RGIA f. 569, op. 11, d. 426.
61. Geidenreikh, *K ozdorovleniiu goroda Vil'ny*, 9.
62. Eremeev, *Gorod S.-Peterburg s tochki zrieniia meditsinskoi politsii*, 240–241.
63. Ibid., 240–264. RGIA f. 210, op. 1, d. 484.
64. Eremeev, *Gorod S.-Peterburg s tochki zrieniia meditsinskoi politsii* , 262–264; 470–475; 512–517.
65. Ibid.
66. V. I. Chugin, "Zametka o Russkikh baniakh v sanitar'nom otnoshenii," *Vrach*, no. 35 (1880), 577–578 and 36 (1880), 585–587.
67. V. I. Porai-Koshits, *Obshchestvenno-gigienicheskie kupal'ni i bani v Kharkove* (1881), 2–4.
68. Chugin, "Zametka o Russkikh baniakh v sanitar'nom otnoshenii."
69. Dal', *Tolkovyi slovar' v chetyrekh tomakh.*
70. Chugin, "Zametka o Russkikh baniakh v sanitar'nom otnoshenii," no. 35, 577-578 and no. 36, 85-87.
71. Ibid.
72. Ibid.
73. Ibid.
74. Ibid.
75. *Viestnik obshestvennoi gigieny i prakticheskoi meditsinoi*, 1889, vol 4, book 2, 712–713.
76. N. A. Gratsianov, "Otchet' Nizhegorodskago gorodskago sanitarnago vracha N. A. Gratsianova za 1896 god," (1897), 56–57, 70.

77. Markov, *Voiskovye bani i prachechnye*, 1–17.
78. For more on the survey and the state of banyas in the era, see Konstantin Kashin and Ethan Pollock, "Public Health and Bathing in Late Imperial Russia: A Statistical Approach," *The Russian Review* 72, no. 1 (2013), 66–93.
79. Ivan Ivanovich Ianzhul, *Fabrichnyi byt Moskovskoi gubernii: otchet za 1882–1883 g* (St. Petersburg, 1884), 138–139.
80. P. A. Peskov, *Fabrichnyi byt Vladimirskoi gubernii* (St. Petersburg: tip. V. Kirshbauma, 1884), 114–115.
81. "Peterburgskiia bani," *Vedomosti Sankt-Peterburgskoi gorodskoi politsii*, 1871, no. 118, 1–2 and no. 119, 1–2.
82. Ianzhul, *Fabrichnyi byt Moskovskoi gubernii: otchet za 1882–1883 g*. and Peskov, *Fabrichnyi byt Vladimirskoi gubernii*.
83. RGIA f. 256, op. 26, d. 537 "Banya na zavodakh."
84. Rudin, *Deistvie bani protiv' zarazy podvizhnaia disinfektsionnaia kamera bania*, 3–5.
85. Stanislav Glinskii, *Komnatnaia bania sistemu Stanislava Glinskogo* (Warsaw, 1896).
86. RGIA f. 513, op. 3, d. 337; op. 27, d. 77; op. 28, d. 2106.
87. RGIA f. 210, op. 1, d. 484, l. 2.
88. Petri, "At the Bathhouse: Municipal Reform and the Bathing Commons in Late Imperial St. Petersburg," 25–31.
89. RGIA f. 210, op. 1, d 484.

CHAPTER 5

1. Giliarovskii, *Moskva i Moskvichi*; Kashin and Pollock, "Public Health and Bathing"; V. Gilyarovsky and B. Kiernan, *Moscow and Muscovites* (Montpelier, VT: Russian Information Services, 2013), 264-291.
2. Nikolai Makovetskii, "K voprosu vliianii Russkoi bani" (Voenno-Meditsinkaia Akademiia v 1887–1888 uchebnom godu, 1888).
3. Stephen Frank and Mark D. Steinberg, *Cultures in Flux: Lower-class Values, Practices, and Resistance in Late Imperial Russia* (Princeton, NJ: Princeton University Press, 1994).
4. Mark D. Steinberg, *Petersburg Fin de Siècle* (New Haven, CT: Yale University Press, 2011); Laurie Bernstein, *Sonia's Daughters: Prostitutes and their Regulation in Imperial Russia* (Berkeley: University of California Press, 1995); Joan Neuberger, *Hooliganism: Crime, Culture, and Power in St. Petersburg, 1900–1914* (Berkeley: University of California Press, 1993).
5. I. A. Bich, *Ocherk istorii Russkoi bani i ee fiziologicheskoe i terapevticheskoe znachenie* (1893).
6. Daniel Beer, *Renovating Russia: the Human Sciences and the Fate of Liberal Modernity, 1880–1930* (Ithaca, NY: Cornell University Press, 2008); Laura Engelstein, *The Keys to Happiness: Sex and the Search for Modernity in fin-de-siecle*

Russia (Ithaca, NY: Cornell University Press, 1992); Healey, *Homosexual Desire in Revolutionary Russia.*

7. P. V. Shumakher, *Stikhi i pesni* (Moscow: tip. A. V. Vasil'eva i ko, 1902). Poem title, "Svoboda, ravenstvo i bratsvo."

8. V. V. Rozanov, *Literaturnye ocherki* (1902), 224–226; Engelstein, *The Keys to Happiness*, 299-333.

9. V. V. Rozanov, *Dostoevsky and the Legend of the Grand Inquisitor*, trans. Spencer E. Roberts (1972), ix. Quotation of D. S. Mirsky in the translator's preface.

10. *Literaturnye ocherki*, 224–226.

11. Ibid.

12. Ibid.

13. For a description from the elite intelligentsia's perspective of the backward rural banya and the superstitions that surrounded it see the story "Bannyi Chert" in N. A. Teffi, *Ved'ma* (Berlin: Petropolis, 1930), 81–95.

14. V. G. Isachenko, I. U. Artem'eva, and S. A. Prokhvatilova, *Zodchie Sankt-Peterburga: XIX-nachalo XX veka* (St. Petersburg: Lenizdat, 1998), 503–508; Ivan Vasil'evich Eremeev, *Gorod S.-Peterburg s tochki zrieniia meditsinskoi politsii* (St. Petersburg 1897). *Moskovskii putevoditel'-spravochnik 1897 g.* (Moscow 1897).

15. Giliarovskii, *Moskva i Moskvichi*, 228.

16. A. P. Chekhov, *Sobranie sochinenii v vos'mi tomakh*, 8 vols., vol. 2 (2005), 370–376.

17. Ibid.

18. "Novye narodnie bani Voronina," *Vsemirnaia illiustratsiia*, 1871, no. 148, 279–282.

19. Ibid.

20. "Bania," *Fiskal* 1906.

21. See, for instance, "Naprasnaia trevoga: rasskaz fabrichnogo," *Pravda*, April 26, 1912, pp. 4–5.

22. "Man'chzhurskaia bania," *Ovod* 1, no. 1 (1906), 5. Louise McReynolds and David McDonald helped me identify some of the characters.

23. "V ban' pered banei," *Sprut*, April 26, 1906, 7.

24. I. S. Shmelev, *Leto gospodne: prazdniki, radosti, skorbi* (Parizh: YMCA Press, 1948), 391.

25. Eugenie Fraser, *The House by the Dvina: a Russian Childhood* (London: Corgi, 1986), 176.

26. Linda Nochlin, *Bathers, Bodies, Beauty: the Visceral Eye* (Cambridge, MA: Harvard University Press, 2006), 1–53.

27. Ibid.

28. John E. Bowlt, *The Silver Age, Russian Art of the Early Twentieth Century and the "World of Art" Group* (Newtonville, MA: Oriental Research Partners, 1979).

29. Lowell Evan Gillespie, "The image of the Russian woman in the art of Zinaida Serebriakova" (MA thesis, University of Notre Dame); L. Hilton Alison, "Zinaida Serebriakova," *Woman's Art Journal* 3, no. 2 (1982), 32-35.

30. Zinaida Evgenievna Serebriakova, *Zinaida Serebriakova: pis'ma, sovremenniki o khudozhnitse* (Moscow: Izobrazitel'noe iskusstvo, 1987), 229; Gillespie, "The Image of the Russian Woman in the Art of Zinaida Serebriakova."

31. I. U. N. Mineeva and A. V. Sergeev, *Fotografii na pamiati: fotografy Nevskogo prospekta, 1850–1950* (St. Petersburg: Slaviia, 2003).

32. Healey, *Homosexual Desire in Revolutionary Russia*; TsGAKFFD SPb.

33. Ibid. and TsGAKFFD SPb.

34. Evgenii Bershtein, "An Englishman in the Russian Bathhouse: Kuzmin's *Wings* and the Russian Tradition of Homoerotic Writing," in *The Many Facets of Mikhail Kuzmin: A Miscellany*, ed. Lad Panova and Sarah Pratt, 75–87 (Bloomington, IN: Slavica, 2011); John E. Malmstad, "Bathhouses, Hustlers, and a Sex Club: The Reception of Mikhail Kuzmin's Wings," *Journal of the History of Sexuality* 9, no. 1/2 (2000), 85–104; Healey, *Homosexual Desire in Revolutionary Russia*, 101-102.

35. Malmstad, "Bathhouses, Hustlers, and a Sex Club: The Reception of Mikhail Kuzmin's Wings."; M. A. Kuzmin, *Wings* (London: Hesperus, 2007).

36. Malmstad, "Bathhouses, Hustlers, and a Sex Club," 90–91.

37. Ibid., 99. (The association of the book and author with the banya grated on Kuzmin.)

38. Rozanov got the name of the *banshchik* wrong. In the story it was Fedor; in his review he referred to "Boris." Quoted in Bershtein, "An Englishman in the Russian Bathhouse."

39. M. A. Bogomolov, N. A. Kuzmin, and S. V. Shumikhin, *Dnevnik 1905–1907* (St. Petersburg: Izd-vo Ivana Limbakha, 2000), 55. See also Malmstad, "Bathhouses, Hustlers, and a Sex Club," 94.

40. Isadora Duncan, *My Life* (New York: Boni and Liveright, 1927); Louise E. Wright, "Touring Russia with Isadora: Maurice Magnus' Account," *Dance Chronicle New York* 23, no. 3 (2000), 233–261; Maurice Magnus, "Memoirs of Golden Russia," in *Norman Douglas Collection*, ed. Yale University (Beinecke Rare Books and MS Library, n.d.).

41. V. I. Zuev, *Bani i vanny* (1898); N. A. Gratsianov, "Otchet' Nizhegorodkskago gorodskogo sanitarnago vracha N. A. Gratsionova za 1897 god'," (1898); Eremeev, *Gorod S.-Peterburg s tochki zrieniia meditsinskoi politsii;* V. I. Chugin, "Zametka o Russkikh baniakh v sanitar'nom otnoshenii," *Vrach*, no. 35 (1880), 577–578 and 36 (1880), 585–587. See also Engelstein, *The Keys to* Happines, 165-211.

42. Healey, *Homosexual Desire in Revolutionary Russia*, 28; V. Merzheevskii, *Sudebnaia ginekologiia* (1878), 208–209.

43. Kuzmin and Shumikhin, *Dnevnik 1905–1907*, pp. 85–86. October 23, 1905. Translations from Malmstad.

44. Ibid.; Malmstad, "Bathhouses, Hustlers, and a Sex Club," 94–96.

45. Kuzmin and Shumikhin, *Dnevnik 1905–1907*, pp. 55, 85–86, 102, 45–46, 308, 415; *Dnevnik 1908–1915* (St. Petersburg: Izd-vo Ivana Limbakha, 2005), 287.

46. V. V. Rozanov and A. N. Nikoliukin, *Poslednie list'ia*(Moscow: Respublika, 2000), 177–179; Bershtein, "An Englishman in the Russian Bathhouse," 82.

47. Quoted in "An Englishman in the Russian Bathhouse," 82.

48. Ibid.; Engelstein, *The Keys to Happiness*, 310–333.

49. See Bershtein, "An Englishman in the Russian Bathhouse."

50. Andrey Bely, *The Silver Dove*, Translated by John Elsworth (Evanston, IL: Northwestern University Press, 2000), 90–92. For his explicit juxtaposition of spiritual Russia with the soulless West, see pages 224–228.

51. P. I. Telepnev, *Ubiistvo v Puzyrevskikh baniakh* (Saratov: Ishchenko i Ko., 1879).

52. Preshipandonulo, *Strashnaia drama v Moskovskikh baniakh* (1909). The verdict reflected modes of justice at the time, particularly in fiction. See Louise McReynolds, *Murder Most Russian: True Crime and Punishment in Late Imperial Russia* (Ithaca, NY: Cornell University Press, 2013).

53. Kenneth Lantz, *The Dostoevsky Encyclopedia* (Westport, CT: Greenwood Press, 2004), 417.

54. "N. N. Strakhov—L. N. Tolstomu, 28 Noiabria, 1883, g. Sankt Peterburg," in *L. N. Tolstoi—I. I. Strakhov: polnoe sobranie perepiski*, ed. A. A. Donskov, 652–654 (Ottawa: Ottawa University Press, 2003); I. I. Iasinskii, "Roman moei zhizni," in *Sredi velikikh. Literaturnyi vstrechi* (Moscow: Novoe literatrunoe obozrenie, 2001), 355–357.

55. Quoted May 18, 1904. See Healey, *Homosexual Desire in Revolutionary Russia*, 278. Konstantin Romanov, "Dnevniki 1903–1905," *Moskovskii komsomolets*, December 6, 1998.

56. This is likely a reference to Matthew 18:6. The King James version reads: "But whosoever shall offend one of these little ones which believe in me, it were better for him that a milestone were hanged about his neck and that he were drowned in the depth of the sea."

57. Online copy of his "devnik": http://az.gay.ru/articles/articles/romanov1.html.

58. Healey, *Homosexual Desire in Revolutionary Russia*; Merzheevskii, *Sudebnaia ginekologiia*, 207–209.

59. Banyas were also strongly associated with prostitution and heterosexual acts. For a pornographic account of men with women in the late imperial bathhouse, see the story attributed to Alexei N. Tolstoy republished in Tolstoy, Chekhov, and Bunin, *Russkaia eroticheskaia proza*.

60. N. A. Teffi and B. V. Averin, *Smeshnoe v pechal'nom: rasskazy, avantiurnyi roman, portrety sovremennikov* (Moscow: Sovetskii pisatel', 1992).

61. Douglas Smith, *Rasputin: Faith, Power, and the Twilight of the Romanovs* (New York: FSG, 2016), 338.

62. Orlando Figes and B. I. Kolonitskii, *Interpreting the Russian Revolution: the Language and Symbols of 1917* (New Haven, CT: Yale University Press, 1999), 12.

63. Edvard Radzinskii, *The Rasputin File* (New York: Nan A. Talese, 2000), 118.

64. Smith, *Rasputin*, 291.

65. Radzinskii, *The Rasputin File*, 117–118.

CHAPTER 6

1. V. V. Rozanov, "V sovete rabochikh i soldatskikh deputatov," in V. A. Chalmaev, *Pod sozvezdiem topora: Petrograd 1917 goda—znakomyi i neznakomyi*, 33-43 (Moscow: Sovetskaia Rossiia, 1991). Original appeared in *Novoe vremia*, April 9–13, 1917.

2. Karl Marx and Friedrich Engels, *The Communist Manifesto: With the Condition of the Working Class in England in 1844: Socialism, Utopian and Scientific* (New York: Pathfinder, 2008).

3. For more on how early Bolshevik policies promised to improve Soviet health and hygiene, see Tricia Starks, *The Body Soviet: Propaganda, Hygiene, and the Revolutionary State* (Madison: University of Wisconsin Press, 2008).

4. Christina Kiaer and Eric Naiman, *Everyday Life in Early Soviet Russia: Taking the Revolution Inside* (Bloomington: Indiana University Press, 2006), 20.

5. David Glassberg, "The Design of Reform: The Public Bath Movement in America," *American Studies* 20, no. 2 (1979), 5–21; Brian K Ladd, "Public Baths and Civic Improvement in Nineteenth-Century German Cities," *Journal of Urban History* 14, no. 3 (1988), 372–393.

6. Abbott Gleason, Peter Kenez, Richard Stites, eds., *Bolshevik Culture: Experiment and Order in the Russian Revolution* (Bloomington: Indiana University Press, 1985).

7. "Na fabrikakh i zavodakh," *Pravda*, May 6, 1912, p. 13; "Ekatorinkoslav: truboprokutyi zavod," *Pravda*, June 16, 1912, p. 14.

8. "Rabochee dvizhenie: stachki," *Pravda*, August 26, 1912, p. 14.

9. "Dvizhenie rabochikh i ekipazhnikov," *Pravda*, January 28, 1914, p. 3.

10. "Iz zhizni rabochego," *Pravda*, February, 22, 1914, p. 4.

11. At least three dozen articles in *Pravda* between 1912 and 1914 mentioned the problem of poor conditions in banyas and the challenges that workers had in accessing them.

12. Peter Gatrell, *Russia's First World War: a Social and Economic History* (New York: Routledge, 2016).

13. "Nalog na roskosh," *Pravda*, May 24, 1917, p. 9.

14. "Sredi banshchikov" *Pravda*, May 26, 1917, p. 7; "Sredi banshchikov," *Pravda*, May 29, 1917, p. 9; and "Sredi banshchikov," *Pravda*, June 2, 1917, p. 11.

15. "Ot profsoiuz banshchikov," *Pravda*, October 27, 1917, p. 16.

16. "Dar' sovetskomu pravitel'stvu," *Izvestiia*, December 16, 1917, p. 12.

17. "General'naia chistka," *Izvestiia*, March 27, 1920, p. 1; "Moskovskoe kommunal'noe khoziastvo za 4 goda revoliutsii," *Kommunal'noe khoziastvo*, 1921, no. 7, 39–40.

18. Posters from the collection of the Lenin Library. Zal otdela izoizdanii (IZO). One printed in 1920 and the other in 1922.

19. "Bani Krasno-Presnenskogo raiona," *Kommunal'noe khoziastvo*, 1923, no. 21, p. 16.

20. RGASPI, f. 588. op. 1 d. 3882, "Otnoshenie Stalina I. V. Ermanu o zakaze bani dlia soldat," July 11, 1918; f. RGASPI, f. 558, op. 1 d. 1440, l. 1 "Prikaz RVS Iugo-zapadnogo fronta armiam fronta ob otkrytii v Kurske gospitalei i ban," January 11, 1920.

21. Stephen Kotkin, *Stalin: Paradoxes of Power* (Prinecton, NJ: Princeton University Press, 2014), 327.

22. "Organizatsia ban'" *Izvestiia,* August 30, 1918, p. 8; "Bor'ba s tifom," *Izvestiia,* December 18, 1918, p. 6.

23. "Bor'ba s tifom," *Izvestiia,* April 6, 1919, p. 3.

24. "Dekret o sanitarno-propusknykh punktakh na voksalakh g. Moskvy," *Izvestiia,* May 20, 1920, p. 2.

25. "Narodnoe zdravokhranenie: prokhodnye bani kak meri protiv rasprostraneniia tifa," *Izvestiia,* February 5, 1919, p. 5.

26. "Revoliutsionnyi tribunal," *Pravda,* February 22, 1918, p. 2.

27. Bogdanov, *Tri veka Peterburgskoi bani,* 142.

28. "Moskovskoe kommunal'noe khoziastvo za 4 goda revoliutsii," *Kommunal'noe Khoziastvo,* 1921, no. 7, p. 39.

29. Ibid.

30. "Bor'ba s epidemiiami: nuzhni besplatnye bani," *Izvestiia,* February 27, 1919, p. 4.

31. N. A. Mironova, "Epidemiia sypnogo tifa v Iaroslavle v 1919 g.: 'Kak vy budete ekonomiku provodit', kogda 70 percent v sypniake?'," *Iaroslavskij pedagogicheskii vestnik* 59, no. 2 (2009), 245–248.

32. A. A. Il'iukhov, *Zhizn' v epokhu peremen: material'noe polozhenie gorodskikh zhitelei v gody revoliutsii i Grazhdanskoi Voiny* (Moscow: Rosspen, 2007), 158.

33. "Moskovskoe kommunal'noe khoziastvo za 4 goda revoliutsii," *Kommunal'noe khoziastvo,* 1921, no. 7, p. 40.

34. Translation by Yuri Slezkine in Sheila Fizpatrick and Yuri Slezkine, eds., *In the Shadow of Revolution: Life Stories of Russian Women from 1917 to the Second World War* (Princeton, NJ: Princeton University Press, 2000), 160.

35. N. P. Okunev, *Dnevnik Moskvicha: 1917–1924* (Paris: YMCA Press, 1990), 5, 219, 346–347.

36. Lenin, *Collected Works,* 228. Report of the All-Russia Central Executive Committee and the Council of Peoples Commissars to the Seventh All-Russia Congress of Soviets, December 5, 1919.

37. Il'iukhov, *Zhizn' v epokhu peremen: material'noe polozhenie gorodskikh zhitelei v gody revoliutsii i Grazhdanskoi Voiny,* 170–192.

38. "V zapasnoi armii," *Izvestiia,* May 1, 1920; "Ranenyi soldat revoliutsii," *Pravda,* May 27, 1920, p. 2.

39. The decree was signed by the Commissariats of Internal Affairs and Health, but Lenin and the Sovnarkom were central to the discussion. The decree of September 30, 1920 is reprinted in: A. D. Kriachkov, *Bani i kupal'ni* (Tomsk: Kubuch, 1932), 381–382.

40. *Bani i kupal'ni,* 381–382.

41. Ibid., 383–384.

42. "General'naia chistka," *Izvestiia,* March 27, 1920, p. 1; "Khronika," *Pravda,* March 31, 1920, p. 2.

43. Lenin, *Polnoe sobranie sochenenii*, vol. 40, 273.

44. V. I. Lenin, "Once Again on the Trade Unions," January 25, 1921, in *Collected Works*, vol. 32, p. 84.

45. "Na pomoshch' golodaiushchim," *Pravda*, August 21, 1921, p. 1.

46. Elizabeth A. Wood, *Performing Justice: Agitation Trials in Early Soviet Russia* (Ithaca, NY: Cornell University Press, 2005), 90–91. This insistence on bathing continued through the 1920s. On visiting the USSR in the fall of 1927 the American author Theodore Dreiser noted, "The peasant—rightly—is requested to take a bath in the 'banya' or steam bath house on his arrival" at the Central Guest House of the Peasants. Theodore Dreiser, Thomas P. Riggio, and James L. W. West, *Dreiser's Russian Diary* (Philadelphia: University of Pennsylvania Press, 1996), 77–78.

47. Okunev, *Dnevnik Moskvicha: 1917–1924*, p. 439.

48. "Moskovskoe kommunal'noe khoziastvo za 4 goda revoliutsii," *Kommunal'noe khoziastvo*, 1921, no. 7, p. 39.

49. "Predpriitiia obshchestvennoi gigieny," *Kommunal'noe khoziastvo*, 1921, no. 7, 4–5.

50. "Instruktsiia o sdache v arendu kommunal'nykh predpriiatii," *Kommunal'noe delo*, 1922, no. 1, 54–55.

51. Ibid.

52. Ibid.

53. "Obiavlenie," *Izvestiia*, October 7, 1922, p. 12 and October 20, 1922, p. 8.

54. "Glavnoe upravlenie kommunal'nogo khoziastvo, NKVD, RSFSR," GARF, f. R4041, op. 2, d. 56.

55. Ibid.

56. "Promyslovoe oblozhenie kommunal'nogo predpriiatii," *Kommunal'noe khoziastvo*, 1923, no. 11, pp. 7–8.

57. "K kontsentratsii Moskovkikh ban'," *Kommunal'noe khoziastvo*, 1923, no. 12, p. 16.

58. "Nedelia priznaniia Kransoi armii," *Pravda*, January 19, 1922, p. 2; "V raionnykh sovetakh Moskvy," *Pravda*, July 1, 1923, p. 5; "Nedelia studenchestva," *Izvestiia*, December 16, 1923, p. 3.

59. "Statistika kommunal'nogo khoziastvo: uchet kommunal'nykh predpriiatii," *Kommunal'noe delo*, 1923, no. 3–4, pp. 153–160.

60. "Kommunal'noe predpriiatiia v 1922 godu," *Kommunal'noe delo*, no. 7–8, pp. 94–98.

61. "Finansovoe polozhenie kommunal'nogo khoziastvo v 1925/1925 godu," *Kommunal'noe delo*, 1925, no. 19, pp. 5–9.

62. "Kommunal'noe predpriiatiia," *Kommunal'noe delo* 1926, no. 7 pp. 55–56; "Bani," *Kommunal'noe delo*, 1926 no. 21–22, p. 98.

63. "Kommissiia po bannomu delu," *Kommunal'noe delo*, 1926, no. 2, 61–62.

64. "Kommunal'noe predpriiatiia," *Kommunal'noe delo*, 1926, no. 7, pp. 55–56.

65. Okunev, *Dnevnik Moskvicha: 1917–1924*, p. 439.

66. "Inzhener-mekhanik," *Izvestiia*, March 22, 1927, p. 8; "Bannoe khoziastvo," *Izvestiia*, July 13, 1926, p. 4; "Zabastovka banshchikov v Chite," *Izvestiia*, September 12, 1926, p. 4; "Irkutskii gnoinik vskryt," *Pravda*, December 11, 1926, p. 5.

67. "Zadachi uluchsheniia byta rabochikh," *Pravda*, September 20, 1928, p. 3.

68. "Moskovksaia zhizn': smotr gorodskogo khoziaistva," *Izvestiia*, October 27, 1927, p. 4.

69. "Ne bania, a grabilovka, "*Kommunisticheskii trud*, 9 Marta 1921, p. 4 (I thank Tricia Starks for sending the citation my way).

70. Mikhail Zoshchenko, "Before Sunrise," ed. Gary Kern (Ann Arbor, MI: Ardis, 1974), 81–82 .

71. Zoshchenko, "Bania."

72. Ibid.

73. Ibid.

74. Zoshchenko, "Before Sunrise."

75. Ibid., 82–83.

76. M. Mishev (S. Bulgakov), "Bannye dela," *Gudok*, July 9, 1924.

77. Ibid.

78. "Ataka na bani," *Izvestiia*, November 2, 1924, p. 7; "Krazha," *Izvestiia*, August 15, 1925, p. 4.

79. "K voprosu o baniakh," *Kommunal'noe khoziastvo*, 1927, no. 13–14, p. 120.

80. "Proisshestviia: ubiistvo," *Izvestiia*, June 20, 1925, p. 5; "Khronika dnia," *Izvestiia*, April 25, 1926, p. 6; "Ubiistvo organizatora batrakov," *Izvestiia*, September 22, 1926, p. 4; "Sud," *Pravda*, September 12, 1925, p. 6. Note: these are just some of the stories in the national paper that addressed illegal activities in the banyas.

81. "Na bor'bu s progulami i nepriadkami na proizvodstve," *Pravda*, September 16, 1928, p. 6.

82. "Samogonnoe tsarstvo," *Izvestiia*, December 6, 1922, p. 3; "Vologodskie vpechatlenie," *Izvestiia*, February 27, 1923, p. 4; "Kak grisha sovpartporabotal," *Pravda*, March 16, 1927, p. 2; "Pozhar ot neostorozhnosti," *Pravda*, October 15, 1927, p. 8.

83. "Leningradskaia oblastnaia partkonferentsiia," *Pravda*, November 17, 1927, p. 2; "Kommunisti Krasnoi armii protiv disorganizatorov partii," *Pravda*, November 18, 1927, p. 3.

84. "Protiv razvrata v Sandunovskikh baniakh," *Pravda,* September 26, 1923, p. 6. Dan Healey, "Homosexual Existence and Existing Socialism: New Light on the Repression of Male Homosexuality in Stalin's Russia," *GLQ: A Journal of Lesbian and Gay Studies* 8, no. 3 (2002), 359.

85. "Protiv razvrata v Sandunovskikh baniakh," *Pravda*, September 26, 1923, p. 6.

86. "Sud na fabrike," *Pravda*, October 9, 1923, p. 5.

87. "Mrachnyi byt," *Izvestiia*, June 1, 1923, p. 7; "Sud," *Izvestiia*, September 26, 1923, p. 5.

88. "Bor'ba s prostitutsiei," *Pravda*, November 11, 1926, p. 3.

89. "Zaporozhskaia zhut'," *Izvestiia*, April 9, 1926, p. 4; "Sud: delo Balasheva," *Izvestiia*, November 24, 1926, p. 5.

90. "Bor'ba s prostitutsiei," *Pravda*, November 11, 1926, p. 3.

91. Sheila. Fitzpatrick, *The Russian Revolution* (Oxford: Oxford University Press, 2001), 148.

92. "Rabochie i religiia," *Pravda*, January 30, 1923, p. 5; "Zametki pomogli," *Pravda*, October 18, 1924, p. 6.

93. H. C. Wilson and E. R. Mitchell, *Vagabonding at Fifty: From Siberia to Turkestan* (London: Hutchinson, 1928), 184–186.

94. Julie A. Cassiday, "Flash Floods, Bedbugs and Saunas: Social Hygiene in Maiakovskii's Theatrical Satires of the 1920s," *Slavonic and East European Review* 76, no. 4 (1998), 643–657.

CHAPTER 7

1. For more on the famine and terrors of the 1930s, see Paul Hagenloh, *Stalin's Police: Public Order and Mass Repression in the USSR, 1926–1941* (Baltimore: Johns Hopkins University Press, 2009); V. V. Kondrashin, *Golod 1932–1933 godov: tragediia Rossiiskoi derevni* (Moscow: Rossiiskaia politicheskaia entsiklopediia, 2008); Terry Martin, "The Origins of Soviet Ethnic Cleansing," *Journal of Modern History* 70, no. 4 (1998), 813–861.

2. S. Fitzpatrick, *Everyday Stalinism: Ordinary Life in Extraordinary Times: Soviet Russia in the 1930s* (New York: Oxford University Press, 2000).

3. Kotkin, *Stalin: Paradoxes of Power.*

4. R. W. Davies and Stephen G. Wheatcroft, *The Years of Hunger: Soviet Agriculture, 1931–1933* (New York: Palgrave Macmillan, 2016), 429–431, table 49C.

5. Amy E. Randall, *The Soviet Dream World of Retail Trade and Consumption in the 1930s* (New York: Palgrave Macmillan, 2008); E. A. Osokina, *Our Daily Bread: Socialist Distribution and the Art of Survival in Stalin's Russia, 1927–1941* (Armonk, NY: M. E. Sharpe, 2001).

6. S. Fitzpatrick, *The Cultural Front: Power and Culture in Revolutionary Russia* (Ithaca, NY: Cornell University Press, 1992).

7. "Leninizm i problema kul'turnoi revoliuzii," *Izvestiia*, January 27, 1928, p. 4; "Ratsionalizuruem roznichnuiu torgovliu," *Pravda*, August 11, 1929, p. 2.

8. A. D. Kriachkov, *Bani i kupal'ni* (Tomsk: Kubuch, 1932).

9. "K perspektivnomu piatiletnemu planu Moskovskogo kommunal'nogo khoziastva," *Kommunal'noe khoziaistvo*, 1928, no. 1–2, p. 11.

10. "Odna iz ocherednykh kul'turnykh zadach kommunal'nogo stroitel'stva," *Kommunal'noe khoziaistvo*, 1930, no. 10, p. 85.

11. "Vnimanie vsex kochegarov," *Pravda*, January 16, 1930, p. 4; "Kul'torno-massovuiu rabotu," *Pravda*, February 20, 1932, p. 1; "Sovet schastlivykh," *Pravda*, December 1, 1934, p. 2; "Liubov k opriatnosti," *Pravda*, September 8, 1935, p. 3; "Kul'turno-bytovye uchrezhdeniia na sotsialisticheskaia polia" *Izvestiia*, December 23, 1930, p. 5.

12. "Zakon nashei zhizni," *Pravda*, June 16, 1936, p. 2.

13. Stalin, *New Conditions, New Tasks in Economic Construction, Speech Delivered at the Conference of Business Executives*, June 23, 1931.

14. "Kommunal'noe i zhilishchnoe khoziaistvo," *Pravda,* February 2, 1936, p. 3.

15. A search for "banya" and its related forms in Eastview Press's digital database of *Pravda* and *Izvestiia* resulted in over 2,000 hits for the years 1928–1939. The vast majority either praised the banyas that had been built as meeting the needs of the workers or pointed out that the failure to build banyas was a threat to the conditions of workers.

16. M. A. Svanidze wrote in his journal in 1934 that upon returning from Sochi Stalin looked forward to steaming in the banya with Kirov. See Iu. G. Murin, *Iosif Stalin v ob"iatiiakh sem'i (sbornik dokumentov)* (Moscow: Rodina, 1993), 158–159. See also Stephen Kotkin, *Waiting for Hitler, 1929-1941* (New York: Penguin, 2017), 1.

17. RGASPI f. 558, op. 11, d. 858, ll. 9–14, "Pis'mo Matiukhina ia Stalinu I.V." June 10, 1931.

18. GARF f. A314, op. 1, d. 5412 and 5419. See also *Kommunal'noe khoziastvo,* 1931 no. 9.

19. GARF f. A314 op. 1, d. 5230.

20. GARF f. A314, op. 1, d. 5413, ll. 28–35.

21. Ibid.

22. GARF f. A314, op. 1, d. 5414, ll. 35–52. For more on the challenges of forcing new habits and identities on urban residents in the 1930s, see David L. Hoffmann, *Peasant Metropolis: Social Identities in Moscow, 1929–1942* (Ithaca, NY: Cornell University Press, 1994).

23. GARF f. A314, op. 1 d. 5413, ll. 28–35.

24. There were approximately 240,000 collective farms in 1935 in the USSR.

25. Collection of Lenin Library.

26. Poster "For the Sanitary Maintenance of the Banya" (1932). Collection of the Lenin Library.

27. For more on the typical posters of the era, see Victoria Bonnell, *Iconography of Power: Soviet Political Posters Under Lenin and Stalin* (Berkeley: University of California Press, 1999).

28. "Uluchshenie material'nogo polozheniia i byta rabochikh," *Izvestiia,* July 16, 1930, p. 3. The actual percentage of the plan was fulfilled varied, but in this sector it seemed to range from 60 to 80 percent fulfillment. S. G. Wheatcroft, R. W. Davies, and R. Stone, *Materials for a Balance of the Soviet National Economy, 1928–1930* (Cambridge: Cambridge University Press, 1985), 276.

29. "Bolezni stroitel'stva v Mariiskoi oblasti," *Izvestiia* September 22, 1928, p. 2; "Gorodskoe stroitel'stvo," *Izvestiia,* September 14, 1933, p. 3; "Sobiraetsia li Uralzapadoles provodit' splav?" *Pravda,* March 21, 1932, p. 2.

30. "Upala," *Izvestiia* September 30, 1928, p. 4.

31. "Kuznetsroi sovershenno ne imeet lesomaterialov," *Izvestiia* April 16, 1930, p. 3; For more on the state's struggles to address the shortage of lumber, see Lynne Viola, "The Other Archipelago: Kulak Deportations to the North in 1930," *Slavic Review* 60, no. 4 (2001), 730-755.

32. "Organizatsionnye voprosy partiinoe i sovetskoe stroitel'stvo," *Izvestiia,* February 11, 1934, p. 4.

33. "Sotsialisticheskomu Donbassu, sotsialisticheskomu goroda," *Izvestiia* September 30, 1933, p. 4; "Cherepash'im shagom," *Pravda*, December 25, 1929, p. 3; "Pod blagorodnoi Vybeskoi," August 10, 1934, p. 4; "Gorod bez bani," *Pravda*, October 5, 1935, p. 4.

34. "Korotkie signaly: o bane, iasliakh, bol'nitse," *Pravda*, August 4, 1934, p. 4.

35. "Profsoiuznye okhovtirateli," *Pravda*, September 8, 1934, p. 4; "O bane i prachechnoi," *Pravda*, August 13, 1934, p. 3.

36. "Bestrizornye stany," *Pravda*, March 6, 1935, p. 3; "Chernigovskie provintsialy," *Pravda*, June 5, 1936, p. 3.

37. "Kstati o 'melochakh," *Pravda*, May 12, 1932, p. 2; "Rabochikh ostavali bez bani," *Pravda*, April 25, 1934, p. 3; "Politotdely sovkhozov v bor'be za vesenniisev," *Pravda*, May 6, 1934, p. 2; "K voprosu o mestnykh usloviiakh," *Pravda*, September 9, 1938, p. 5.

38. "Baniu raspilili na drova," *Pravda*, February 6, 1935, p. 6.

39. For example: "Balkhinskii soviet ignoruet nakazy izbiritelei," *Pravda*, March 6, 1935, p. 3; "Bania . . . bez vody," *Pravda*, December 2, 1933, p. 4.; "Bania s pristrastiem," *Pravda*, April 24, 1934, p. 3.

40. "Sudak v myle," *Pravda*, April 9, 1934, p. 3; "Besprizornoi dom kol'khoznika," May 15, 1934, p. 4.

41. "Rech' Tov. I. T. Goliakova," *Pravda*, February 16, 1938, p. 3.

42. See for instance, "Zasluzhennaia kritika Irkutskogo gorsoveta," *Pravda*, November 10, 1934, p. 4 and "Gorod s razvalennym khoziaistvom," *Pravda*, January 7, 1937, p. 4.

43. "Poteriannye nakazy i uteriannoe doverie," *Pravda*, November 1, 1934, p. 2.

44. For the polar station: "287-I den'" *Pravda*, June 1, 1935, p. 4; For the solar banya in Tashkent, see "Nauka i tekhnika," *Izvestiia*, April 5, 1934, p. 6; for the submarine, V. Dorin, "Na 'otlichno," *Pravda*, December 13, 1936, p. 4.

45. "Kommunal'noe i zhilishchinoe khoziaistvo," *Pravda*, February 2, 1936, p. 3.

46. Ibid.

47. "K vorprosy sostaveleniia piatiletnego plana," *Kommunal'noe khoziaistvo*, 1929, no. 13–14, p. 9–22.

48. "My mobilizovany," *Izvestiia* February 7, 1929, p. 2.

49. "O baniakh i prachechnykh," *Izvestiia* July 23, 1931, p. 4; "V bane," *Izvestiia* March 30, 1934, p. 5.

50. "Ne 'uezd' a sovetskii raionnyi gorod," *Pravda*, November 26, 1934, p. 2.

51. "Problema vodosnabzheniia Moskvy razreshena," *Pravda*, July 14, 1937, p. 4; "Nash pishut," *Pravda*, June 25, 1932, p. 2; "Khronika," *Pravda*, March 22, 1929, p. 4; "Proisshestviia," March 1, 1937, p. 6.

52. "Proisshestviia," *Pravda*, October 17, 1937, p. 6.

53. "Proisshestviia," *Pravda*, May 31, 1937, p. 6; "Proisshestviia," July, 1937, p. 6.

54. GARF f. A314, op. 1, d. 5417, ll. 1–4.

55. Ibid.

56. GARF f. A314, op. 1, d. 5230; f. 9226, op. 1, d. 179.

57. GARF f. A314, op. 1, d. 8009.

58. GARF f. 9226, op. 1, d. 148, ll. 10–11.

59. GARF f. 9226, op. 1, d. 179 ll. 2–35.

60. "Bani i prachechnye stolitsy," *Pravda*, September 13, 1938, p. 6.

61. For the place of humor in Stalinist society, see Fitzpatrick, *Everyday Stalinism*.

62. " 'V bane' (ukradeno u A. P. Chekhova)," *Krokodil*, 1928 (no. 18), p. 5.

63. "Sluchai na ulitse brat'ev grakkhov," *Krokodil*, 1934 (no. 17), p. 5.

64. "Daite zhe baniu," *Krokodil*, 1928 (no. 6), p. 11.

65. "Seans okonchen!" *Krokodil*, 1934 (no. 5), p. 9. Another *Krokodil* article (1935 (no. 28–29), p. 21) cited an official document that allowed a woman who was unable to rinse in the banya the right to rinse the next day for free. *Krokodil* suggested the banya hang a sign reading, "Those citizens covered with yesterday's soap suds are allowed to bypass the line for the banya."

66. "Magnitigorskaia banya," *Krokodil*, 1930 (no. 34), p. 9.

67. "Dorogoi Krokodil!" *Krokodil*, 1934 (no. 26), p. 14.

68. "V bane i predbannike," *Krokodil*, 1935 (no. 30–31), p. 11.

69. Zoshchenko, "Rasskaz o banyakh i ikh posetitliakh," in *Veselye rasskazy*, vol. 1, 666–670, published in *Krokodil*, 1935 (no. 11), p. 2.

70. "Dorogoi *Krokodil*," *Krokodil*, 1938 (no. 2), p. 15.

71. GARF f. 9226, op. 1 d. 168.

72. GARF f. A520, op. 1 d. 4.

73. On the significance of the Plenum, see, Hagenloh, *Stalin's Police*, 233. The minutes of the plenum were published in *Voprosy istorii* (1995), no. 11–12, pp. 2–27. Shvernik's speech is on pages 18–21.

74. "Plenym Mossoveta," *Pravda*, March 25, 1937, p. 6.

75. "Novye shkoly, bolnitsy, bani: sovetshchanie v Moskovkom sovete," *Pravda*, October 1, 1937, p. 4.

76. "Bani i prachechnye stolitsty (na plenume Mossoveta)," *Pravda*, September 13, 1938, p. 6.

77. All this info is from the Memorial site's "Zhertvy politicheskogo terrora v SSSR": http://lists.memo.ru/index19.htm

78. See http://www.rostov50.ru/1950_rotov.html.

79. GARF f. 9226, op. 1 d. 179, pp. 1–55.

80. GARF f. A314 op. 1 d. 401. And Vyacheslav Molotov, *The Third Five-Year Plan for the Development of the Soviet Economy* (Moscow: Foreign Languages Publishing House, 1939), 50–51.

81. ARAN f. 1705, op. 1, d. 166, ll. 14–26.

CHAPTER 8

1. Donald A. Filtzer, *The Hazards of Urban Life in Late Stalinist Russia: Health, Hygiene, and Living Standards, 1943–1953* (Cambridge: Cambridge University Press, 2010).

2. Rebecca Manley, *To the Tashkent Station: Evacuation and Survival in the Soviet Union at War* (Ithaca, NY: Cornell University Press, 2009).

3. GARF f. 314, op. 1 d. 5518, l. 1–8.

4. I. V. Amchislavskii, *Kak ustroit' obshchestvennuiu baniu v kolkhoze* (Moscow: Medgiz, 1942).

5. Alexis Peri, *The War Within: Diaries from the Siege of Leningrad* (Cambridge, MA: Harvard University Press, 2017), 154–161.

6. Ibid.

7. GARF f. A314, op. 1, d. 5518, 11–12, 20; GARF f. A314, op. 1 d. 564, ll. 6, 17.

8. GARF f. A314, op. 1, d. 5578, l. 15; GARF f. A314, op. 1 d. 5610, l. 1–3.

9. See, for instance, Vasilii Grossman, *A Writer at War*, edited and translated by Antony Beevor and Luba Vinogradova (New York: Pantheon, 2005), 46–47, 75, 169 and Catherine Merridale, *Ivan's War: Life and Death in the Red Army, 1939–1949* (New York: Metropolitan Books, 2006), 57 and 62.

10. Stalin, *Complete Works*, speech at the Red Army Parade, Red Square, Moscow, November 7, 1941

11. K. Hodgson, *Written with the Bayonet: Soviet Russian Poetry of World War Two* (Liverpool: Liverpool University Press, 1996), 84–86, 185–201.

12. For more on the importance of the Terkin poem for soldiers and civilians alike, See Evgenii Grigor'evich Plimak, "Poet Aleksandr Tvardovskii i verkhovnyi v gody velikoi otechestvennoi i posle nee," *Otechestvennaia istoriia*, no. 3 (2006), 24–32. James von Geldern, "Radio Moscow: The Voice from the Center," in *Culture and Entertainment in Wartime Russia*, ed. Richard Stites, 53–55 (Bloomington: Indiana University Press, 1995).

13. Plimak, "Poet Aleksandr Tvardovskii," 24–32.

14. The line comes from a December 31, 1971 letter from Solzhenitsyn to the Central Committee, quoted in Michael Scammell, *The Solzhenitsyn Files: Secret Soviet Documents Reveal One Man's Fight Against the Monolith* (Chicago: Edition q, 1995), 181.

15. A. Tvardovskii, *Ia v svoiu khodil ataku: dnevniki, pis'ma, 1941–1945* (Moscow: Vagrius, 2005), 349–350.

16. Ibid.

17. He likely did not know that he was following a precedent that suggested that Napoleon as well had been unable to take the heat of the Russian banya. See chapter 3.

18. Tvardovskii, *Ia v svoiu khodil ataku*, p. 350.

19. A. Tvardovskii and Alex Miller, *Vassili Tyorkin: A Book About a Soldier* (Moscow: Progress Publishers, 1975), 350–351.

20. Ibid. Miller's translation.

21. Ibid., 354–355. While this verse was published elsewhere, it was cut from the version published in *Krokodil* for reasons that remain unclear to me. See "V bane (glava iz poemy 'Vasilii Terkin')," *Krokodil*, June 30, 1945 (no. 22), p. 5.

22. On the complications of reading Terkin as a Russian or Soviet war hero, see Hodgson, *Written with the Bayonet*, 196–201.

23. E. I. Zubkova, *Russia After the War: Hopes, Illusions, and Disappointments, 1945–1957* (Armonk, NY: M. E. Sharpe, 1998).

24. For more on the culture of consumption and its relationship to state policies, see Crowley and Reid, *Pleasures in Socialism: Leisure and Luxury in the Eastern Bloc* (Evanston, IL: Northwestern University Press, 2010); Susan E. Reid, "Cold War in the Kitchen: Gender and the De-Stalinization of Consumer Taste in the Soviet Union under Khrushchev," *Slavic Review* 61, no. 2 (2002), 211–252; Susan E Reid, "Khrushchev Modern: Agency and Modernization in the Soviet home," *Cahiers Du Monde Russe* 47, no. 47/1–2 (2006), 227–268.

25. V. F. Zima, *Golod v SSSR 1946–1947 godov: proiskhozhdenie i posledstviia* (Lewiston: Edwin Mellem Press, 1999).

26. As of 1946, Commissariats were renamed Ministries.

27. For a detailed description of the conditions in banyas immediately after the war, see, Filtzer, *The Hazards of Urban Life in Late Stalinist Russia*, chapter 3.

28. GARF f. A314, op. 2, d. 433, l. 134.

29. Filtzer, *The Hazards of Urban Life in Late Stalinist Russia*, 132–141.

30. GARF f. A314, op. 2, d. 433, ll. 131–135.

31. GARF f. A314, op. 2, d. 3292, l. 46.

32. GARF f. A314, op. 2, d. 433, ll. 117–120.

33. GARF f. A314, op. 2, d. 433, ll. 131–135.

34. Ibid.

35. GARF f. A314, op. 2, d. 446, l. 1.

36. GARF f. A314, op. 2, d. 3292, ll. 71–74.

37. GARF f. A314, op. 2, d. 9623, ll. 1–3.

38. GARF f. A314, op. 2, d. 9623, ll. 8–11, 34–42; 78–79.

39. *Krokodil*, August 30, 1945, pp. 6–7; *Krokodil*, May 20, 1945, p. 6.

40. D. L. Babichenko, ed., *"Literatrunyi front": istoriia politicheskoi tsenzury, 1932-1946, sbornik dokumentov* (Moscow: Entsiklopedia rossiiskikh dereven', 1994), 206

41. *Krokodil*, July 10, 1952, p. 6

42. *Krokodil*, May 30, 1946, p. 9.

43. *Krokodil*, March 10, 1949, p. 5.

44. *Krokodil*, February 10, 1954, p. 15.

45. *Krokodil*, October 20, 1951, p. 13.

46. See Anne Applebaum, *Gulag: A History* (New York: Doubleday, 2003), 202–206.

47. Aleksandr Solzhenitsyn, *The Gulag Archipelago*, vol. 2, p. 389.

48. Varlam Shalamov, *Kolyma Tales*, translated by John Glad (New York: W. W. Norton, 1980), 39–45.

49. V. T. Shalamov, *Sobranie sochinenii v chetyrekh tomakh* T. 1. (Moscow: Khudozhestvennaia literatura, 1998), 506–513.

50. Lazar Kaganovich, Georgii Malenkov, and Viacheslav Molotov, *Molotov, Malenkov, Kaganovich, 1957: stenogramma iun'skogo plenuma TsK KPSS i drugie dokumenty* (Moscow: Mezhdunarodnyi fond demokratiia, 1998), 125-127.

51. *Russkii suvenir.* Dir. Grigorii Aleksandrov. Mosfil'm. 1960.

52. Andrei Voznesenksii, "Siberskie bani" *Literaturnaia gazeta*, April 16, 1960.

53. "Prazdnik dlia glaz i dushi," *Sovetskaia kul'tura*, February 10, 1966, p. 3.

54. James H. Bater, *The Soviet City: Ideal and Reality* (Beverly Hills, CA: Sage, 1980), chapter 4.

55. GARF f. A314, op. 3, d. 3211, ll. 1–10.

56. "Plan razvitiia zhilishchno-kommunal'nogo khoziaistva na 1956 god," *ZhKKh* 1956, no. 1, pp. 4–6.

57. GARF f. A314, op. 3, d. 3211, ll. 1–10.

58. Ibid.

59. "Plan razvitiia zhilishchno-kommunal'nogo khoziastva na 1956 god," *ZhKKh*, 1956, no. 1, pp. 4–6.

60. P. Shukin, "Kak my uluchshaim rabotu bani," *ZhKKh*, 1956, no. 4, p. 9

61. P. Perepelitsyn, "Puti razvitiia banno-prachechnogo khoziastva," *ZhKKh*, 1958, no. 3, pp. 26–27.

62. Ibid.

63. G. Klechanovskii, "Ulushit' kachestvo tipovykh proektov ban'," *ZhKKh*, 1958, no. 6:11–12.

64. Iu. Krutogorov, "S nelegkim parom," *ZhKKh*, 1963, no. 6:17–18.

65. N. Sharapatov, "Vot oni, puty vysheniia rentabil'nosti ban'," *ZhKKh*, 1966, no. 7, p. 6.

66. Viktor Borokhov, "Topitsia, topitsia ogorode bania," *Sovetskaia kul'tura*, March 23, 1973, no. 24, p. 5.

67. GARF f. 9226, op. 1, d. 2916, ll. 10–13.; GARF f. 9226, op. 1, d. 2937, ll. 69–71.

68. GARF f. 9226, op. 1, d. 2916, ll. 204–205; GARF f. 9226, op. 1, d. 2937, ll. 269–271.

69. GARF f. 9226, op. 1, d. 2937, ll. 174–175.

70. GARF f. 9226, op. 1, d. 2916, ll. 228–229; GARF f. 9226, op. 1, d. 2937, ll. 185–186.

71. *Krokodil*, January 10, 1965: Cover.

72. *Krokodil*, March 30, 1965, p. 6.

73. *Krokodil*, January 20, 1962, p. 4.

74. *Krokodil*, February, no. 5, 1973, p. 5.

75. *Krokodil*, October, no. 28, 1971, p. 5.

76. GARF f. A314, op. 6, d. 4, ll. 190–192.

77. Ibid.

78. GARF f. A314, op. 6, d. 22, ll. 1–2, 11–31.

79. Ibid.

80. S. Rybkina, "Banno-prachechnym predpriiatiiam: rabotat' po novomu," *ZhKKh*, 1972 no. 3, 7.

81. A. Starostin, *Bolshoi futbol* (Moscow: Molodaia Gvardiia, 1964), 132–133.

82. Oleg Belousov, *Eto moi gorod* (Minsk: Belorus', 2005), chapter 13.

83. Kathleen Parthé, *Russian Village Prose: The Radiant Past* (Princeton, NJ: Princeton University Press, 1992).

84. V. Rasputin, *Farewell to Matyora* (Evanston, IL: Northwestern University Press, 1979), pp. 11, 49, 210.

85. *Neskol'ko dnei iz zhizni I. I. Oblomova*. Dir. Nikita Mikhalkov. Mosfil'm. 1980.

86. Boris Yeltsin, *Against the Grain: An Autobiography* (New York: Summit Books, 1990), 32.

87. John Givens, *Prodigal Son: Vasilii Shukshin in Soviet Russian Culture* (Evanston, IL: Northwestern University Press, 2000).

88. Vasilii Shukshin, *Stories from a Siberian Village* (Evanston, IL: Northwestern University Press, 1996), translated by Laura Michael and John Givens, 134–138.

89. Ibid.

90. Ibid., 144–148.

91. V. M. Shukshin, *Monolog na lestnitse//Shukshin V. M. sobr. soch: v 8 t.* (Barnaul: Izdatel'skii Dom Barnaul, 2009), t. 8, 30. Quoted in Anna Razuvalov, *Pisateli "Derevenshchiki."*

92. Ibid., 139–140.

93. Boris Vasil'ev, *A zori zdes' tikhie* (Sverdlovsk: Khudozh. Lit-ra 1978).

94. Anna Krylova, *Soviet Women in Combat: A History of Violence on the Eastern Front* (Cambridge: Cambridge University Press, 2011).

95. *A zory zdes' tikhie*. Dir. Stanislav Rostotsky. Gorky Film Studio, 1972.

96. "Kinofakty": A zory zdes' tikhie, Moscow-24 TV, https://www.m24.ru/shows2/79/173555?utm_source=mm&utm_campaign=video&utm_medium=cpc.

97. Vasilii Shukshin, *Nash sovremennik* 4 (April, 1973), 104–105. *Kalina krasnaia*. Dir. Vasilii Shuksin. Mosfil'm, 1974. Bathhouses in the Soviet prison camps, described as dangerous and hellish places, would not necessarily have prepared a *zek* for the rituals and routines of bathhouses on the outside.

98. Translation by Robert Bird in Russell Bova ed., *Russia and Western Civilization* (Armonk, NY: M. E. Sharpe, 2003), 168–169.

99. In Alexei Yurchak's terms, the banya allowed a person to live "vnye." Alexei Yurchak, *Everything was Forever Until It Was No More: The Last Soviet Generation* (Princeton, NJ: Princeton University Press, 2006), 126–157.

100. "Ballada o bane," in Vysotskii, *Sobranie*, 284–285.

CHAPTER 9

1. Nikolai Aivaz'ian, "S legkim parom!" *Sovetskaia kul'tura*, September 26, 1985, p. 8.

2. V. Maslakov, *Finansy zhilishchnogo i kommunal'nogo khoziaistva* (Moscow: Gosfinizdat, 1960), 52.

3. In his novel *Moscow 2042* Vladimir Voinovich affirmed that at least in his vision of the communist future, public banyas would remain and the problems dogging them would too. Vladimir Voinovich and Richard Lourie, *Moscow 2042* (San Diego, CA: Harcourt Brace Jovanovich, 1990).

4. N. Sharapatov, "Vot oni, puti povysheniia rentabl'nosti bani," *ZhKKh*, 1966, no. 7, 6.

5. Willard S. Smith, "Housing in the Soviet Union—Big Plans, Little Action," in *Soviet Economic Prospects in the Seventies: A Compendium of Papers* (Washington: U.S. Government Print Office, 1973), 416–417.

6. Carol Nechemias, "The Impact of Soviet Housing Policy on Housing Conditions in Soviet Cities: The Uneven Push from Moscow," *Urban Studies*, 18, no. 1, (February 1981), 1–8.

7. V. N. Ladygin, "Uluchshit' stroitel'stvo gostinits, ban', i prachechnykh," *ZhKKh*, 1973, no. 6, pp. 7–8.

8. GARF f. A314, op. 6, d. 224, ll. 88–91.

9. A Rodionov, "Banya vse popravit," with "Nash kommentarii" by A. Kabanov, *Turist*, 1969, no. 5, 18, 31.

10. N.A. Kafarov and G. S Reshetnikov, "Banya . . . nuzhna li ona sevodnia?" *Zdorov'e*, April 1973 (no. 4), 25–26. Or see, "Polezno li parit'sia v bane?," *Zdorov'e*, September 9, 1979, 16–17.

11. K. Kafarov, "Tselitel'nyi zhar sauny: uchenye otvetchaiut chitateliam," *Izvestiia*, December 25, 1974, p. 5.

12. Kafarov and Reshetnikov, "Banya . . . nuzhna li ona sevodnia?". Or see, "Polezno li parit'sia v bane?" *Zdorov'e*, September 9, 1979, pp. 16–17; V. V. Shestukhin, "Par kostei ne lomit?" *Zdorov'e*, September 9, 1977, 26–27.

13. V. V. Navrotskii, "Banya . . . i pestitsidy," *Zdorov'e*, September 9, 1990, 16.

14. Rodionov, "Banya vse popravit."

15. Chestukhin, "Par kostei ne lomit?"

16. M. V. Dopinskaia and T K. Matiunina, "Novyi tip bani—eto effektivno," *ZhKKh*, 1977, no. 6, p. 34.

17. A. S. Uralov, "Novye tendenstii v ispol'zovanii ban' i problem proektirovaniia," *ZhKKh*, 1973, no. 4, pp. 30–31.

18. N. Zalygalov, "Bol'she uslug posetiteliam ban'," *ZhKKh*, 1968 no. 3, p. 37.

19. K. Tenishev, "Banya—vodolechebnitsa—bassein," *ZhKKh*, 1969, no. 8, p. 30.

20. Uralov, "Novye tendenstii."

21. N. P. Mitrokhin, "Banya meniaet profil'," *ZhKkh*, 1976 no. 2, p. 22.

22. M. V. Dopinskaia and T K. Matiunina, "Navyi tip bani—eto effektivno," *ZhKKh*, 1977, no. 6, p. 34.

23. US Housing Census data suggest that by 1970 over 93 percent of homes had a bathtub or shower. See https://www.census.gov/hhes/www/housing/census/historic/plumbing.html.

24. Mitrokhin, "Banya meniaet profil'."

25. Hedrick Smith, *The Russians* (New York: Ballantine, 1976), 156–159.

26. In this sense the banya was like what the anthropologist Alexei Yurchak has identified as "deterriolized spaces" in late socialism. Yurchak, *Everything Was Forever*, 126–157; For other examples of how public (state-supported and easily accessible) spaces in the USSR could be used for private purposes, see the articles in Crowly and Reid, *Socialist Spaces* and in Siegelbaum, *Borders of Socialism*; Riazanov, "Ironiia sud'by," 301.

27. David MacFadyen, *The Sad Comedy of El'dar Riazanov: An Introduction to Russia's Most Popular Filmmaker* (Montreal: McGill-Queens University Press, 2003), 218–219. *Ironiia sud'by ili s legkim parom*. Dir. E. Riazanov. Programme One 1976.

28. On Russian banality and the intelligentsia's fight against *poshlost*, see Boym, *Commonplaces*, 41–73; Yurchak, *Everything Was Forever*, 36–37.

29. Ethan Pollock, ""Real Men Go to the Bania": Postwar Soviet Masculinities and the Bathhouse," *Kritika: Explorations in Russian and Eurasian History* 11, no. 1 (2010), 47–76.

30. *Staryi novyi god*. Dir. Oleg Efremov. Mosfil'm. 1980.

31. "Working class" is the term used in the film and the play.

32. The precise banya is unspecified in the play, but in the film the banya scenes were shot inside and outside Sanduny in Moscow.

33. Although it may be tempting to see the kiss as a suggestion of the porous line between the homosocial space and homosexuality, in the late Soviet context a kiss was an acceptable gesture of close friendship. See, for instance, the stamp depicting a peasant kissing a soldier on the lips, issued in 1968 to celebrate the 50th anniversary of the Soviet Red Army or the photograph of Leonid Brezhnev kissing Erich Honecker in 1979 at the celebration of 30th anniversary of the GDR.

34. Condee, "The Second Fantasy Mother."

35. *Ty—mne, ia—tebe*. Dir. Aleksandr Seryi. Mosfil'm. 1976.

36. He appears to be a model of what James Millar labeled Brezhnev's "Little Deal." He uses his position in a state run institution (the bathhouse) to obtain goods and services through friends and contacts as part of the "shadow" or "parallel" economy. See James R. Millar, "The Little Deal: Brezhnev's Contributions to Acquisitive Socialism," *Slavic Review*, IV (Winter 1985), 694–706. See also Alena Ledeneva, "Continuity and Change of Blat Practices in Soviet and Post-Soviet Russia," in Stephen Lovell, Alena V. Ledeneva, and Andrei Rogachevskii, *Bribery and Blat in Russia*, 183–205 (London: St. Martin's Press, 2000).

37. See Deborah A. Field, *Private Life and Communist Morality in Khrushchev's Russia* (New York: Peter Lang, 2007).

38. Nikolai Aivaz'ian, "S legkim parom!" *Sovetskaia kul'tura*, September 26, 1985, p. 8.

39. Kevin Moss, ed., *Out of the Blue: Russia's Hidden Gay Literature: An Anthology* (San Francisco: Gay Sunshine Press, 1997), 353. See Moss's introductory comments to Efim Yeliseev's story, "The Bench [Skameika]," translated by Anthony Vanchu.

40. Excerpt of transcript of an interview with an anonymous soldier conducted in 2015 by Vladimir Volodin (Uladzimir Valodzin). Provided to the author by Valodzin.

41. *Ch. P. raionnogo masshtaba.* Dir. Sergei Snezhkin. Lenfil'm. 1988.

42. S. Shcherbakova, "Takoi zhe, kak my," *Literaturnaia gazeta*, December 27, 1989, p. 8.

43. P. Gusev, "Neobkhodimoe proizshestvie," and A. Kiselev, "O pozitivnoi kritike," *Sovetskaia kul'tura*, June 8, 1989, p. 5.

44. E. Grafov, "S trudnym parom, ili ironiia sud'by," *Sovetskaia kul'tura*, May 22, 1979, no. 41, p. 3.

45. GARF f. A314, op. 6, d. 491, l. 211;

46. GARF f. A314, op. 6, d. 928, l. 18; GARF f. A314, op. 6, d. 931, ll. 157–163.

47. GARF f. A314, op. 6, d. 1301, l. 23, 109–110.

48. Ibid.

49. Anatolii Rubinov, "Operatsiia 'tuflia': konkretnoe issledovanie biurokratizma," *Literaturnaia gazeta*, August 10, 1988, p.10.

CHAPTER 10

1. Jack F. Matlock, *Autopsy on an Empire: The American Ambassador's Account of the Collapse of the Soviet Union* (New York: Random House, 1995), 579–583.

2. On the Belorussian banya, see Serhii Plokhy, *The Last Empire: The Final Days of the Soviet Union* (New York: Oneworld Publications, 2015). In between these two banyas, a third bit of communal bathing may have affected the outcome of events. Yeltsin was not arrested in part because his return from Kazakhstan on August 18 was delayed. Nazarbayev, who knew of Yeltsin's affinity for the banya, insisted they follow up the business side of their meeting with a trip to the countryside where they bathed. See Andrew Felkay, *Yeltsin's Russia and the West* (New York: Praeger, 2002), 53.

3. Yuri Slezkine, "The USSR as a Communal Apartment, or How a Socialist State Promoted Ethnic Particularism," *Slavic Review* 53, no. 2 (1994), 414–452.

4. Victoria Smolkin, *A Sacred Space Is Never Empty: A History of Soviet Atheism* (Princeton, NJ: Princeton University Press, 2018).

5. Murray Feshbach, "Russia's Population Meltdown," *Wilson Quarterly* 25, no. 1 (Winter, 2001), 15–21.

6. Gol'din, *Sanduny: i bani i muzei Moskvy*; Rubinov, *Sanduny: Kniga o Moskovskikh Baniakh.*

7. Allan Bérubé, "The History of Gay Bathhouses," *Journal of Homosexuality* 44, no. 3–4 (2003), 33–53.

8. Boris Nikolayevich Yeltsin and Catherine A. Fitzpatrick, *The Struggle for Russia*, 1st American ed. (New York: Belka Publications, 1994), 170–171; translation adjusted by me from the Russian original, Boris El'tsin, *Zapiski prezidenta* (Moscow: Rosspen, 2008), 170–171.

9. Condee, "The Second Fantasy Mother"; in Nadya Peterson, "Dirty Women: Cultural Connotations of Cleanliness in Soviet Russia," in *Russia—Women—Culture*, ed. Helena Goscilo and Beth Holmgren, 13.

10. A. V. Korzhakov, *Boris El'tsin: Ot rassveta do zakata* (Moscow: Interbuk, 1997).

11. Lev Sirin, "'Zaodno, byvalo, deboshirili', -- interv'iu pervogo posla RF v Finliandii," August 19, 2011: http://fontankafi.ru/articles/1759/.

12. "Spanking Good Time," *Independent,* July 14, 1997: https://www.independent.co.uk/news/world/spanking-good-time-in-sauna-1250659.html; Marina Kalashnikova, "Vizit president Finliandii," *Kommersant,* November 26, 1997,: https://www.kommersant.ru/doc/188446.

13. David Remnick, *Resurrection: The Struggle for a New Russia* (New York: Vintage Books, 1998), 50–51.

14. Dale Pesmen, *Russia and Soul: An Exploration* (Ithaca, NY: Cornell University Press, 2000), 111–112.

15. *Utomlennye solntsem.* Dir. Nikita Mikhalkov. Studiia TRITE and Camera One. 1994. For more on the film, see Susan Larsen, "National Identity, Cultural Authority, and the Post-Soviet Blockbuster: Nikita Mikhalkov and Aleksei Balabanov," *Slavic Review* 62, no. 3 (2003), 491–511; Denise J. Youngblood, "The Cosmopolitan and the Patriot: The Brothers Mikhalkov-Konchalovsky and Russian Cinema," *Historical Journal of Film, Radio and Television* 23, no. 1 (2003), 27–41.

16. *Osobennosti natsional'noi okhoty.* Dir. Aleksandr Rogozhkin. Lenfil'm. 1995.

17. Bogdanov, *Tri veka Peterburgskoi bani*; Rubinov, *Sanduny*; A. Galitskii, *Russkaia bania: ee blizkie i dal'nie rodichi* (Moscow: Akvarium, 1994).

18. David E. Hoffman, *The Oligarchs: Wealth And Power In The New Russia* (New York: Public Affairs, 2011), 252.

19. "Rassledovanie ubiistvo Otari Kvantrishvili," *Kommersant*, April 9, 1994. Gazeta Kommersant No. 64 (https: kommsersant.ru/daily/1220).

20. Quoted in *Zernistye mysli nashikh politikov.* Original source is *Itogi* 1997, no. 28.

21. Galina Shcherbakova, *Krovat' Molotova* (Moscow: Vagrius, 2001), 166–167.

22. *Vor.* Dir. Pavel Chukhrai. NTV-Profit. 1997.

23. "Rasporiazhenie mera ot 10.07.1997 N 551-PM O predostavlenii l'got po oplate usslug ban' otdel'nym kategoriiam grazhdan," http://zakon.7law.info/base70/part5/d70ru5502.htm.

24. All form *Itogi*, April 26, 2000.

25. Ibid.

26. For more on Sorokin's reception in Russia and the controversy surrounding him see: Eliot Borenstein, "Stripping the Nation Bare: Russian Pornography and the Insistence on Meaning," in *International Exposure: Perspectives on Modern European Pornography, 1800–2000*, ed. Lisa Z. Sigel, 232–254 (New Brunswick, NJ: Rutgers University Press, 2005).

27. Vladimir Sorokin, *Goluboe salo: roman* (Moscow: Ad Marginem, 1999), 102–107.

28. Annie Correal, "After 124 Years, the Russian and Turkish Baths are Still a Hot Spot," *New York Times*, January 29, 2016; Jennifer Bleyer, "Banya Fever," *New York Times*, May 22, 2005; Richard Solash, "Steam Heat—Reinventing the Banya in New York," *Radio Free Europe Radio Liberty* July 5, 2010. https://www.rferl.org/a/Reinventing_The_Banya_In_New_York/2091466.html.

29. Condee, "The Second Fantasy Mother," 21–22.

30. Myers, "Sunday at the Banya."

31. Margaret Coker, "Beating a Retreat at the 'Banya': Russian Spas Whip Clients for Their Own Good," *Atlanta Journal-Constitution*, February 4, 2001.

32. Martin Cruz Smith, *Gorky Park*, 1st ed. (New York: Random House, 1981). *Gorky Park*. Dir. Michael Apted. Orion Pictures 1983.

33. *Red Heat*. Dir. Walter Hill. Carolco Pictures. 1988.

34. *Rounders*. Dir. John Dahl. Miramax. 1998.

35. *The Sopranos*. Created by David Chase. HBO. 1999.

36. *Eastern Promises*. Dir. David Cronenberg, Kudos Film and Television. 2007.

37. John W. Fountain, "Broad-Shoulder Brotherhood, Forged in Steam," *New York Times*, February 21, 2001, p. a10.

38. Douglas Martin, "Steaming to Serenity at the Turkish Baths," *New York Times*, May 10, 1991.

39. Michael Sneed, "Sneed," *Chicago-Sun Times*, January 30, 2001, p. 4.

40. Dan Voelpel, "Seattle to Get Its First Public Russian Bath, Turkish Steam Room," Knight Ridder Tribune Business News, September 10, 2004. See also the *Vice* news story, June 20, 2012, https://www.vice.com/en_us/article/dp4x5k/amie-barrodale-and-clancy-martin-at-the-russian-bathhouse.

41. Annie Correal, "After 124 Years, The Russian and Turkish Baths Are Still a Hot Spot," January 29, 2016, *The New York Times*. https://www.nytimes.com/2016/01/31/nyregion/after-124-years-the-russian-and-turkish-baths-are-still-a-hot-spot.html.

42. Kristine Johnson, "'Not your Typical Spa:' Old-School Bathhouses Making A Comeback," *CBS New York*, April 19, 2018: http://newyork.cbslocal.com/2018/04/19/bathhouses-making-a-comeback/.

43. See http://www.bbc.com/news/business-31921778.

44. Andrew Higgins, "Why the Russian Police Tried to Take Public the Russian Bath," *Wall Street Journal*, April 24, 2000, p. 1.

45. For one report, see Steven Lee Myers, *The New Tsar* (New York: Knopf, 2015), 102–103.

46. "Putin rasskazal istoriiu o spasenii iz goriashchei bani s Shrederom," April 16, 2015: https://lenta.ru/news/2015/04/16/banya/.

47. "Zhirinovskii v bane 22 97 2014,": https://www.youtube.com/watch?v=xI4qTWqCl10.

48. "V. Zhirinovskii predlozhil vozrodit' v Moskve obshchestvennye bani i stolovye," April 4, 2017: http://www.mskagency.ru/materials/2653174.

49. Elena Mart'ianova, "Problema zdorov'ia prezidenta iavliaetsia kliuchevoi dlia Rossii," August, 05, 2013, *Kommersant*: https://www.kommersant.ru/doc/2248486.

50. E. G. Bryndin and I.E. Bryndina, "Kak pereiti na zdorovyi obraz zhizni," *Elektronnyi nauchno-obrazovatel'nyi vestnik zdorov'e i obrazovanie v XXI veke* tom. 16, 2014.

51. Konstantin Andrianov, "Bania vs. sauna: est' li raznitsa v tom, kak poddavat'?," *Kommersant*, November 5, 2009.

52. A. A. Biriukov, "Chto takoe bania i kak pravil'no ee pol'zovat'sia," *Lechebnaia fizkul'tura i sportivnaia meditsina*, 75, no. 3, 2010: 47–51.

53. Higgins, "When the Russian Police Tried to Take Public its Private Baths.".

54. *Ellen Barry*, "The Russia Left Behind: A Journey through a Heartland on the Slow Road to Ruin," *New York Times*, October 13, 2013, http://www.nytimes.com/newsgraphics/2013/10/13/russia/index.html.

55. Anton Nozdrin, "Pochemu zhitelei Lakinska nel'zia poslat' v baniu? Potomu chto ee tam net!" *Komsomol'skaia pravda*, May 11, 2018, https://www.vladimir.kp.ru/daily/26827/3867150/.

56. Anna Kachurovskaia, "Bannyi den' v Moskovkoi dume," *Kommersant*, March 30, 2001.

57. Denis Terent'ev, "Ne mytyi Peterburg," *Nevskoe vremia* July 30, 2008.

58. ". . . V Moskve est' besplatnye gorodskie bani?" *Ezhenedel'nik "Argumenty i faktky"* no. 9, February 29, 2012, http://www.aif.ru/dontknows/1233055.

59. Mark Galeotti, "Controlling Chaos: How Russia manages its political war in Europe," *European Council on Foreign Relations, Policy Brief*, September 1, 2017, http://www.ecfr.eu/publications/summary/controlling_chaos_how_russia_manages_its_political_war_in_europe.

60. Olga Filippova, "Thomas Gomart, Russian Civil-Military Relations: Putin's Legacy," *Journal of Power Institutions in Post-Soviet Societies* [Online] Issue 10 (2009), http://journals.openedition.org/pipss/3736.

61. Irina Khakamada, *Komsomol'skaia pravda*, March 5, 2002. Quoted in *Argumenty i fakty*, December 25, 2002, http://www.aif.ru/archive/1622754.

62. Condee, "The Second Fantasy Mother," 7–8.

63. Peterson, "Dirty Women," 177.

64. See "Den' krasoty v zhenskoi bane," http://www.banya-lefortovo.ru/bathhouse/see100.

65. *A zori zdes' tikhie*. Dir. Renat Davlet'iarov. Interfest. 2015.

66. *Odnazhdi*. Dir. Renat Davlet'iarov. Real Dakota. 2014.

67. "Gei sauny Moskvy," http://www.newdosug.ru/story/gay-sauna.html.

68. "Gei sauna– shikarnye sauny dlia men'shinstv," https://sauna.ru/news/info/gay-sauna.

69. These stories all came up from a search for the word "banya" (in Cyrillic) on news. Google.ru on May 28, 2018.

Index

- Traces banya as historical marker of Russia's position in Europe

—D Where there were Russians, there were banyas

—D Religious quality of war time